D0292055

Effective Evaluation

Improving the Usefulness
of Evaluation Results
Through Responsive and
Naturalistic Approaches

Egon G. Guba

Yvonna S. Lincoln

Effective Evaluation

 Jossey-Bass Publishers

San Francisco • Washington • London • 1982

EFFECTIVE EVALUATION
Improving the Usefulness of Evaluation Results
Through Responsive and Naturalistic Approaches
by Egon G. Guba and Yvonna S. Lincoln

Copyright © 1981 by: Jossey-Bass Inc., Publishers
433 California Street
San Francisco, California 94104
&
Jossey-Bass Limited
28 Banner Street
London EC1Y 8QE

Copyright under International, Pan American, and
Universal Copyright Conventions. All rights
reserved. No part of this book may be reproduced
in any form—except for brief quotation (not to
exceed 1,000 words) in a review or professional
work—without permission in writing from the publishers.

Library of Congress Cataloging in Publication Data

Guba, Egon G
     Effective evaluation.

     Bibliography: p. 383
     Includes indexes.
     1. Evaluation. 2. Evaluation—Methodology.
I. Lincoln, Yvonna S., joint author. II. Title.
AZ191.G8   001.4   80-8909
ISBN 0-87589-493-3

Manufactured in the United States of America

JACKET DESIGN BY WILLI BAUM

FIRST EDITION
First printing: April 1981
Second printing: January 1982

Code 8108

A joint publication in
The Jossey-Bass
Higher Education and
Social and Behavioral Science Series

Preface

The failure to use evaluation findings has almost assumed the proportions of a national scandal. Often such failure is laid to ignorance, laziness, or political sidestepping by responsible decision makers. We are more inclined to feel, however, that such failure simply illustrates the poverty of traditional evaluations, which are likely to fail precisely because they do not begin with the concerns and issues of their actual audiences and because they produce information that, while perhaps statistically significant, does not generate truly worthwhile knowledge. Given their general level of triviality, it is probably a good thing that evaluation results have *not* been more widely used.

This book offers a new model of evaluation that attempts to

overcome these problems: one that begins with real concerns and leads to useful knowledge. This model combines two currently emerging streams of thought, one relating to the field of evaluation specifically and the other to inquiry methodology more generally. Primitive concepts of evaluation that began to be formulated at the turn of the century and that at first were entirely measurement oriented were reshaped by Ralph W. Tyler during the 1930s and 1940s into the objectives-oriented approach that people typically think of when the term *evaluation* is used today. But Tyler's rationale proved seriously inadequate when it was applied to the evaluation of the national curricula in physics, biology, mathematics, and so on that were hastily put into production following the surprise of Sputnik in 1957. Various analyses of the shortcomings of Tyler's approach were launched by knowledgeable commentators, who called for new approaches that incorporated the values of project sites more closely, that organized evaluations around foci other than objectives, and that were more sensitive to the pluralistic nature of American society. Efforts to respond to these critiques have culminated, after many intermediate steps, in so-called *responsive* evaluation. This approach organizes evaluation activities so as to provide information that illuminates the claims, concerns, and issues raised by stakeholding audiences, that is, audiences involved with or affected by the "evaluand," as Michael Scriven has suggested calling an entity being evaluated. This book embraces the central themes of responsive evaluation as one of its major shaping forces.

Simultaneously, the methodology of inquiry in education and the social sciences has become involved in one of those paradigm shifts so well described by Kuhn in *The Structure of Scientific Revolutions* (1970). The scientific paradigm of inquiry had served the "hard" sciences well and had been embraced by early inquirers in the social sciences in the hope that it would function equally well for them. But it proved to have important shortcomings. The epistemological assumptions on which it was based (logical positivism and radical relativism), however appropriate to the hard sciences (a contention that is itself debatable), were not well met in the phenomenology of human behavior. Research results proved to be inconclusive, difficult to aggregate, and virtually impossible to relate to happenings in the real world. A competing paradigm, dedicated to the study of behavioral phenomena *in situ* and using methods drawn from ethnography, anthropology, and sociological field studies, began to gain in popularity. This is the so-called *naturalistic* approach.

Our intent, then, is to propose and describe a method of making evaluations that is based on the themes of responsive evaluation and that uses naturalistic methodologies in its application. Part One of this book is devoted to analyzing a variety of models of evaluation in order to provide the background and information necessary to an understanding of the responsive approach. Part Two delves into the nature of inquiry paradigms, contrasts the scientific and naturalistic paradigms, argues for the use of the latter whenever the study of human behavior is involved, and discusses the methodological issues inevitably associated with any proposed new paradigm.

In Chapter Six in Part Three we draw special attention to the advantages, as well as the problems, associated with the use of a human being as an assessment instrument and discuss ways in which that human instrument may be continuously improved. In Part Three we also devote a series of chapters to a discussion of the skills—the methods and methodologies—commonly associated with qualitative inquiry. While there is nothing intrinsic to the naturalistic paradigm to suggest that quantitative methods cannot be used with inquiries mounted within that paradigm, such methods are discussed at great length in many other sources and hardly need be treated again here. Most books in educational (or behavioral) research and evaluation do not, however, give adequate consideration to the qualitative methods that, more often than not, turn out to be the backbone of naturalistic research and evaluation. Accordingly, we provide some guidance as to how such techniques as interviewing, observation, analysis of documents and records, and unobtrusive measures may be used.

In Part Four we attempt an exposition of the actual steps by which naturalistic, responsive evaluation is carried out. The processes of contracting for an evaluation, establishing a bridgehead on site, developing productive contacts, avoiding overinvolvement and cooptation, and dealing with the human and political problems that inevitably arise are considered in Chapter Nine. Chapter Ten deals with the tasks of identifying audiences and eliciting the statements of claims, concerns, and issues from them that will become the focus for the information-collecting effort. Chapter Eleven describes how responsive information is gathered and discusses the kinds of information required, the sources of that information, and the means for obtaining it. The final chapter discusses the reporting process; it emphasizes the reporting requirements of different audiences and the continuous nature of reporting.

It is our belief that this book will provide useful information for a variety of readers. Practicing evaluators and students of evaluation will find in it useful guidelines and principles for the conduct of a very different and unconventional kind of evaluation. Members of the audiences for which evaluations are made, especially such stakeholders as funders, developers, and/or users of an evaluand, will discover more productive ways of relating to evaluation. We hope that, having read this book, they will identify better questions to raise with evaluators and better standards for judging the answers they receive. Finally, consumers of evaluation reports should be in a better position to understand and use what evaluators report to them.

It is our deepest hope, however, that this book will provide a modicum of legitimation to the many evaluators who have concluded that traditional evaluation methods are inadequate but have not felt powerful enough to throw off the yoke of the orthodoxy that now surrounds the evaluation process. Michael Scriven has suggested that the social science model is doomed—that is, what we have called the scientific model—but that "the establishment will rot away before they give way" in their point of view. If we cannot help to persuade the establishment of the inadequacy of that view, we can at least aspire to contribute to the enhancement of the rate of rot.

January 1981   Egon G. Guba
                                                      Bloomington, Indiana

                                                         Yvonna S. Lincoln
                                                        Lawrence, Kansas

Contents

xiii

Part Four: Implementing Naturalistic Responsive Evaluation

Tables and Figures

xvii

Figures

The Authors

Egon G. Guba is professor of education at Indiana University. He was awarded the A.B. degree in mathematics and physics from Valparaiso University (1947), the M.A. degree in statistics and measurement from the University of Kansas (1950), and the Ph.D. degree in quantitative inquiry from the University of Chicago (1952).

He has been a member of the faculties of the University of Chicago, University of Kansas City, Ohio State University, and, since 1966, Indiana University. At Ohio State he served for five years as director of the Bureau of Educational Research and Service, and at Indiana University for six years as associate dean for academic affairs of the School of Education.

Guba is widely known for his contributions to the theory of administrative staff relations (the Getzels-Guba nomothetic-idiographic model), to change process theory (the Clark-Guba model), and to the Context-Input-Process-Product model of evaluation as developed by Daniel Stufflebeam and others at Ohio State. He has contributed to the research literature in the areas of teacher effectiveness, instructional television, and the research and development role of schools, colleges, and departments of education.

His interest in naturalistic evaluation has produced two other works. In the summer of 1977 he served as a visiting scholar at the Center for the Study of Evaluation at the University of California, Los Angeles, which resulted in the publication of *Toward a Methodology of Naturalistic Inquiry in Educational Evaluation* (1978). During the summer of 1978 he again was a visiting scholar in conjunction with the Research on Evaluation Project of the Northwest Regional Educational Laboratory, Portland, Oregon, to study the relation of the methodologies of investigative journalism to those of educational evaluation. The result is "Investigative Journalism," a chapter in *Metaphors for Evaluation* (forthcoming).

Yvonna S. Lincoln is assistant professor of education at the University of Kansas. She was awarded the B.A. degree in history and sociology from Michigan State University (1967), the A.M. degree in medieval history from the University of Illinois-Urbana (1970), and the Ed.D. degree in higher education from Indiana University (1977).

Prior to joining the faculty at the University of Kansas in 1977, she served as research associate and Lilly Endowment administrative intern to the vice-president of the Bloomington campus of Indiana University, coordinator for Residential Life at Indiana University, and instructor in the Social Studies Division and counselor at Stephens College.

Lincoln has written articles on reward systems in higher education, on the role of professional schools in responding to pressures from practitioners in the field, and on knowledge production and utilization roles of special units in schools, colleges, and departments of education. At present, she is engaged in a funded study of expectancy theory as a predictor of college students' academic and social behaviors and their grade point averages. Her interest in naturalistic evaluation has resulted in several papers, especially on the concepts of merit and worth as context-free and context-bound determinants of value, on documentary analysis, and on other skills particularly useful to naturalistic inquirers. During the past two years, she has tested the naturalistic model in a variety of evaluation settings.

For Chris, Sue, Phil, and Clark

Effective Evaluation

Improving the Usefulness
of Evaluation Results
Through Responsive and
Naturalistic Approaches

Chapter 1

Comparing
Evaluation Models

===

Evaluation is not new; indeed, the emperor of China instituted proficiency requirements for his public officials, to be demonstrated in formal tests, as early as 2200 B.C. But evaluation as it is practiced today is less than a century old, and during that time it has evolved through a number of forms. Joseph M. Rice, often called the "father" of educational research, devised and used achievement tests during the last decade of the nineteenth century to support his contention that schooltime was inefficiently used. Alfred Binet was commissioned by France's minister of public instruction to devise a means for screening mentally handicapped children from regular classrooms; the test he published in 1904 has become the basis for all intelligence testing since. Two world wars greatly stimulated the testing movement and resulted in widely usable group tests of intelligence and other abilities. By 1945 Hildreth was able to list 5,294 mental tests and rating scales in her bibliography. Even a cursory familiarity with the instruments of this period, and of the philosophies and methodologies that undergirded them, validates the following characterizations:

First, evaluation and measurement were virtually interchangeable concepts. Indeed, the term *evaluation* was heard infrequently; and when it did occur, it was almost always in conjunction with measurement (which usually had top billing: measurement *and* evaluation).

Second, both measurement and evaluation were inextricably tied to the scientific paradigm of inquiry. The methods of science, of course, scored prodigious successes during the nineteenth and twentieth centuries. John Stuart Mill in 1843 urged that the scientific approach be adopted in the study of social phenomena; in particular, he attacked the use of philosophical and theological methods for such studies. The enormous impact of Darwin's *Origin of Species* lent weight to Mill's claim. By the time that Rice undertook his studies of school efficiency the paradigm was well established, and Rice sought to undergird his naturalistic observations of schools with hard measurement data. An early study by Starch and Elliott (1912) of teacher training utilized a comparative design. The momentous Eight Year Study, directed in its research aspects by Ralph Tyler, of whom more will be said in later sections, was based on pre-post experimentation with control groups. The methods of science were being widely utilized, and its legitimation was eagerly sought by the fledgling social sciences, including psychology and education.

Third, evaluation and measurement were focused on individual differences—and, as far as education was concerned, on a narrow range of differences relating to subject matter content. The rush to measure individual differences was precipitated by Darwin's work. Data collected in the centers established in England by Galton and in Germany by Wundt were studied with interest everywhere. It is thus not surprising that early tests focused on such differences also.

Fourth, evaluation and measurement had little relationship to school programs and curricula. Tests told something about individuals but nothing about the programs and curricula by which those persons were taught. It is not that tests were rejected as useful sources of such information; rather, it simply did not occur to testers that test results could provide it. Further, schools were not yet under the gun of accountability, and there was little reason for believing that the curriculum was not exactly what it should be.

Fifth, evaluation was oriented to standardized and objective measures that were norm referenced. It became apparent very soon that measures by themselves were relatively meaningless without some standard by which they could be interpreted. Since one point of comparison is the performance on the same test by other subjects, norms were invented. But if norms are to have meaning, all subjects must be tested under identical conditions, as objectively as possible, and in ways consistent with predetermined rules of administration. Establishing norms became a tricky business that called for adequate sampling and the maintenance of the most strict field controls. Thus the average score for the student's age and/or grade placement became the standard for evaluating him.*

Sixth, evaluation and measurement as conceived fit in well with the prevailing industrial metaphor that was guiding the schools. As measurement moved into its heyday during World War I and just after, another interesting phenomenon was beginning to dominate American culture—namely, scientific management. This was the period of time and motion studies, of "cheaper by the dozen," and of the Hawthorne studies. It is not surprising that school officials began to see the possibilities of applying these same concepts to school improvement. It is no accident that they began to refer to the top school official as the "superintendent," to the school building as the "plant," to the students as "raw material" to be "processed" by the "system," and so on. It was the spirit of the times, linked to the successes of science, to associationist psychology, to the industrial revolution, and to other aspects of the prevailing practical culture.

The Tyler Rationale

Into this context stepped Ralph W. Tyler. A faculty member of Ohio State University since 1929, he had achieved consider-

---

*The traditional use of the masculine pronoun has not yet been superseded by a convenient, generally accepted pronoun that means either *he* or *she*. Therefore the authors will continue to use *he*, while acknowledging the inherent inequity of this traditional preference.

able success in assisting other university professors to construct achievement examinations for their courses. In 1932 he was named research director for the Eight Year Study, which was intended to show that students trained under progressive high school curricula would work as well in colleges and universities as did their counterparts trained under conventional Carnegie-unit curricula.

Tyler's main contribution was to insist that curricula needed to be organized around certain objectives. Objectives were critical because they were the basis for planning, because they provided an explicit guide to teachers, and because they served as criteria for selection of materials, outlining of content, development of instructional procedures, and the preparation of tests and examinations. Most importantly from the point of view of evaluation, they served as the basis for the systematic and intelligent study of an educational program.

Tyler's formulation of the evaluation process is straightforwardly based on the concept of objectives. In his classic monograph, *Basic Principles of Curriculum and Instruction* (1950), he asserts: "The process of evaluation is essentially the process of determining to what extent the educational objectives are actually being realized. . . . However, since educational objectives are essentially changes in human beings, that is, the objectives aimed at are to produce certain desirable changes in the behavior patterns of the students, then *evaluation is the process for determining the degree to which these changes in behavior are actually taking place*" (p. 69; italics added).

The process of evaluation proposed by Tyler is essentially this:

1. Derive a pool of objective candidates by examining learner studies and contemporary life studies and by soliciting suggestions from content specialists.
2. Pass this pool of objective candidates through a series of three screens: philosophical, psychological, and experiential.
3. Cast the survivors of this screening process into a matrix whose rows stipulate the various areas of content involved and whose columns stipulate the behaviors of students expected in relation to those content areas. The individual cells of the matrix thus represent individual objectives.

4. Identify situations in which students can express the behaviors stipulated in the objectives.
5. Examine or develop instruments capable of testing each objective. These instruments need not be paper-and-pencil tests, but they must be capable of meeting conventional standards of objectivity, reliability, and validity.
6. Apply the instruments, usually in a before-and-after paradigm, so that changes in behavior that can be imputed to the curriculum may be measured.
7. Examine the results to determine areas of strength and weakness in the curriculum.
8. Develop and test hypotheses that seem to account for the observed pattern of strengths and weaknesses.
9. Make appropriate modifications in the curriculum and recycle the process.

Tyler's approach constituted a distinct advance over the pupil-centered, measurement-directed approaches that had been in common use. The rationale was systemic in nature, elegant, precise, and internally logical. Its elegance was based on its simplicity —the rationale was easy to understand and yet covered virtually all the evaluation contingencies that were recognized at the time of its statement. The model was very like the "systems" models of today, whose appeal also lies in their rationality and elegance.

Moreover, the rationale built upon the prevailing scientific tradition. The measurement approach had been so assiduously pursued because, among other reasons, it paralleled scientific inquiry (especially insofar as it yielded quantifiable results) and hence provided an aura of legitimation for the fledgling field of evaluation. But the rationale did differentiate the concepts of measurement and evaluation; Tyler made it clear that they were separate processes, with measurement being simply one of several possible tactics to be enlisted in support of evaluation.

Tyler's rationale represented a major step forward in that it focused on the refinement of curricula and programs as the central thrust for evaluation. Until this time evaluation had existed largely for the purpose of making judgments about individual students in relation to test norms and of labeling the students as overachievers, underachievers, or "normal" achievers. Tyler forged a new dynamic for evaluation, making it the mechanism for continuous curricular and instructional improvement. The scope of influence for evaluation was thereby greatly enlarged.

Further, the rationale was easy to understand and apply. The classroom teacher, for whom it was largely designed, had no difficulty with it—many teachers testified eagerly to its utility in revealing their previously hidden assumptions, in providing feedback, and in forcing them to think explicitly about what they were trying to do. The rationale assumed that teachers were fully functioning, competent, and autonomous professionals and provided a means whereby such professionals could check up on their own work.

Finally, the rationale had implicit within it some emergent and sophisticated concepts, including the ideas of feedback and recycling, foreshadowing the modern concept of formative evaluation, and it also drew distinctions between process and impact evaluation, as those terms have come to be defined. Unfortunately, the real possibilities inherent in these concepts were never fully appreciated or exploited by Tyler's followers.

But while Tyler's model did represent a major restructuring of the field, it nevertheless had certain disadvantages and limitations. First, the rationale led to no explicit judgment of worth or merit (more about these terms later). While Tyler was specifically concerned with what might now be called impact or payoff evaluation, the model did not provide explicit guidance on how evaluation data might be manipulated and interpreted for those purposes. Further, the model failed to provide a way to evaluate the objectives themselves. To be sure, possible objectives were to be passed through screens, but the model tells little about the screens. How are the screens to be fleshed out? What values shall be invoked? Whose values? Does the evaluator always accept stated objectives as a starting point, even when he feels that the objectives are somehow inappropriate?

Nor did the model provide standards—or ways of deriving standards—by which discrepancies between objectives and performance might be judged. How large must such a discrepancy be before a performance is judged to be inadequate? And what if the discrepancy is positive, as in the case of overachievement? Does such a discrepancy tell us anything? When does the evaluator accept the performance and when does he call for refinements and changes? The model helps even less with the problem of assessing the strengths and weaknesses of a curriculum through an analysis of noted discrepancies. The model suggests that such patterns be noted and that hypotheses then be formulated and tested. But of course it is unlikely that the evaluator would have collected data for testing such hypotheses beforehand—how could he, not knowing what they would be? And if they cannot be formulated ahead of time, is it not likely that the subjects from whom the evaluation data were collected would no longer be available for this follow-up work?

In practice, the Tyler model is convergent in its effects, particularly in creative situations such as curriculum development. Premature insistence on the *a priori* stipulation of objectives can lead to premature closure. Once objectives are formally stated and the evaluation process has begun, it becomes enormously difficult to break out from the original list, to delete useless objectives, and to add others that may have emerged.

Finally, the Tyler model focused attention on a pre-post design. Tyler's insistence that a behavior needed to be measured twice—before and after the "treatment" afforded by the curriculum—made the rationale a "natural" for the usual experimental design approach espoused in other behavioral science areas, for example, psychology. The desire of the emergent social and behavioral sciences to cast their inquiries into the orthodox and legitimated modes of the physical sciences was thus strongly reinforced.

Turmoil and Dissent

On October 4, 1957, the Russians launched Sputnik and changed the face of American education. Inadequate schooling was blamed for the fact that America was now Number 2—and at once the public determined to try harder. Translated into action, trying harder meant refurbishing the curricula of the schools. Millions of federal dollars were suddenly poured into the development of new courses. The National Science Foundation funded PSSC Physics, SMSG Mathematics, Project CHEM, and several biology sequences, while Project English and Project Social Studies were funded by the U.S. Office of Education. Of course, if such massive resources were to be expended, it was essential that the resulting products be evaluated.

It was not long, however, before the developers of these

new courses were complaining that evaluation was not serving them well. The problems they were articulating, along with some possible responses to these problems, were summarized by Cronbach (1963) in an article entitled "Course Improvement Through Evaluation." Cronbach made three major points. First, if evaluation were to be of maximum utility to the developers of new courses, it needed to focus on the decisions that those developers had to make during the time that development was occurring. This meant that evaluators, rather than asking about the objectives the developers had in mind and testing to see whether those objectives were being achieved, would instead ask: Who are the decision makers? What kinds of decisions do they make? What criteria do they bring to bear in making those decisions? It became clear that the organizer that had characterized evaluation to this point—objectives—was about to meet a serious challenge from another organizer, that is, decisions.

Second, Cronbach argued that evaluation needed to focus on the ways in which refinements and improvements could occur while the course was in process of development. As Cronbach put it, "Evaluation used to improve the course while it is still fluid contributes more to improvement of education than evaluation used to appraise a product already on the market" (in Worthen and Sanders, 1973, p. 48).

Finally, Cronbach asserted, if evaluation were to be of maximum utility to the developers of new courses, it had to be more concerned with course performance characteristics than with comparative studies. Cronbach was able to raise serious questions about the utility of comparative studies on technical, practical, and conceptual grounds, and he thereby began the methodological undermining that has come full circle at the present time.

Within several years of Cronbach's pronouncements, the federal government began to move even more heavily into educational research, development, and dissemination—a process that culminated in the Elementary and Secondary Education Act of 1965. It seemed so important to members of Congress that the impact of their new funding programs be assessed that they mandated evaluation for virtually every authorized activity. And so the evaluation community, hardly having made its adjustment to the turmoil induced by the national programs for improving course content, suddenly found itself inundated again. Needless to say, the profession was not up to it. A spate of new papers was soon to tell in what ways it was deficient.

The first of these papers was Scriven's (1967) on "The Methodology of Evaluation." In his introduction Scriven asserted: "Current conceptions of the evaluation of educational instruments (for example, new curricula, programmed texts, inductive methods, individual teachers) are still inadequate both philosophically and practically. This paper attempts to exhibit and reduce some of the deficiencies" (in Worthen and Sanders, 1973, p. 60). While not all of Scriven's ideas have had lasting impact, the paper as a whole deserves to be recognized as the single most important paper on evaluation written to date. Some of its contributions were drawing a distinction between formative evaluation and summative evaluation or between improving and judging the evaluand; distinguishing professional from amateur evaluation, with a call for the professional evaluator to take on himself the burden of rendering judgments; distinguishing evaluation from mere assessment of goal achievement—evaluation is concerned not only with whether goals are achieved but also with whether the goals are, in the first instance, worth achieving; distinguishing intrinsic or process evaluation from payoff or outcome evaluation; and contrasting the utility of comparative evaluations with that of noncomparative evaluation, arguing, in direct opposition to Cronbach, for the utility of comparative evaluations.

Scriven was not the only evaluator whose voice was raised in dissent. Eisner (1969) attacked the concept of objectives head on, arguing that statements of objectives are not value neutral but are based on certain implicit metaphors that guide thinking about the nature of education. According to him, there are three predominant metaphors: the industrial metaphor (already noted as having sprung from the era of scientific management), the behavioristic metaphor (stemming from behavioral psychology), and the biological metaphor (based on developmental theories in biology). The statement of objectives as proposed by Tyler rests heavily on the first two of these metaphors, but teachers, Eisner suggested, are influenced much more heavily by the third. Conventional objectives Eisner called instructional objectives while he termed those based on the biological metaphor expressive objectives.

When it comes to evaluation, Eisner argued, it is quite appropriate to evaluate instructional objectives by determining the congruence between the objective and student behavior; instructional objectives prescribe the behavior to be expected of all students. But expressive objectives cannot be dealt with in terms of a common standard; instead, evaluation of these objectives requires a "reflection upon what has been produced in order to reveal its uniqueness and significance" (1969, p. 16). No wonder, Eisner seemed to be saying, that there is a disjunction between evaluation and educational practice; what is needed is a fundamentally different approach to evaluation.

Guba (1969) pointed to certain "clinical signs" of evaluation's failure: that it was avoided whenever possible; that it produced anxiety in the persons exposed to it; that the field was characterized by immobilization rather than responsiveness to evaluation opportunities; that the very agencies that mandated evaluation were unable to provide reasonable and understandable guidelines for doing it; that evaluation consultants consistently provided misadvice to clients who sought their aid in designing or carrying out evaluations; and that evaluations consistently failed to provide useful information. Guba listed a series of basic lacks that he felt contributed to this failure: lack of an adequate definition of evaluation, lack of an adequate evaluation theory, lack of knowledge about decision processes, lack of criteria on which judgments might be based, lack of approaches differentiated by level of complexity of the evaluand, lack of mechanisms for organizing, processing, and reporting evaluative information, and lack of trained personnel.

Thus, Tyler's model, which had served so well for two decades, was shattered by Sputnik and the flurry of activities that followed in its wake. The model was simply inadequate to deal with the evaluation needs that accompanied these huge projects—perhaps because it was itself devised in conformity with a decentralized concept of curriculum making and teaching that had suddenly gone out of style in the cynicism of the time. The papers just mentioned are representative of the kind of writing that was going on during this period—writing that dissented sharply from the conventional ways of carrying out evaluations. The issues raised by these papers include the following:

- The underlying value structure of objectives was sharply called into question. Goals no less than performance were to be subject to judgment.
- The evaluator was urged to take up the role of judge. While many demurred, it was apparent that no one was better equipped for this role than the evaluator.
- The possibility of other organizers than objectives was projected. Once this possibility was raised, other alternatives readily occurred to evaluators.
- The need for more specific standards became clear, particularly in light of all the discussion about assessing the new goals and making judgments.
- New concepts emerged that gave the evaluator a new vocabulary and greater conceptual strength.
- The utility of comparative studies was called into question. While both sides on that issue had strong arguments, evaluators perforce had to wonder whether their favored procedural tactic was as sound as they had thought.
- A series of technical and conceptual impediments to further progress was identified, making possible concerted attacks that would help to eliminate or overcome the impediments.

That evaluators were not reluctant to rush in where angels feared to tread became immediately apparent. Beginning in 1967, a variety of new models were proposed that, it was believed, would be responsive to these now-identified needs and problems. More than forty have been sufficiently formalized to appear in the literature. Fortunately, these various models can be organized into schools on the basis of what they take as organizers. We are already familiar with objectives and decisions as possible organizers; added to these are effects and critical guideposts, as well as the concerns and issues that are the hallmark of responsive evaluation. In the remainder of this chapter we shall discuss prototypes of all but the responsive model, setting the stage for a closer look at that school in Chapter Two.

Countenance Model

Despite the many criticisms that had been leveled against objectives-oriented evaluation, many evaluators persisted in using

objectives as the organizers for new models and thus continued to
show the influence of Tyler. Chief among these models are the
Hammond cube (1973), the Provus discrepancy model (1971),
Popham's instructional objectives approach (1975), and Stake's
(1967) countenance model. The latter is probably the best known
and will therefore be used as an exemplar here.

The model proposed by Stake involves completing two
"data matrices": the so-called description matrix and judgment
matrix. Each matrix is divided into two columns: *intents* and *observations* comprise the description matrix, and *standards* and
judgments comprise the judgment matrix. Both matrices are divided into three rows, labeled from top to bottom *antecedents,
transactions,* and *outcomes.*

The first task of the evaluator is to determine entries for the
intents column at all three levels: antecedents, transactions, and
outcomes. Antecedents are conditions existing prior to the teaching and learning that may determine or relate to outcomes. They
may also be thought of in systems terminology as inputs. Transactions are the encounters that make up the teaching-learning
process (the process factors in systems terminology). Outcomes
are the resultants of instruction (the output factors in systems terminology). While Tyler prescribed objectives for outputs—the
terminal behaviors of students—Stake prescribes objectives for
contextual conditions and for teacher behavior as well. When the
three levels of intents have been spelled out and justified in terms
of some explicit rationale, the task of specifying intents is completed.

The next task of the evaluator is to collect data for the observations column of the description matrix. For each objective
specified in the intents column, data must be collected that will
show the extent to which that objective is met. At the level of
outcomes this process is tantamount to that proposed by Tyler;
but now, in addition, information is available that shows whether
antecedent conditions were fulfilled as specified and whether the
teaching-learning process was followed as prescribed. Thus, if the
desired outcomes are not achieved, there is some basis for proposing and testing hypotheses about causes for the failure by looking
at the antecedent and transaction data.

Discrepancies that arise at any of the three levels are referred to the standards listed in the first column of the judgment matrix. Standards are, according to Stake, "benchmarks of performance having widespread reference value" (in Worthen and Sanders, 1973, p. 120). Two kinds of standards may be used: absolute and relative. Absolute standards represent a set of ideal specifications as set by appropriate reference groups, for example, content experts. Since there can be many such groups, there can also be many different sets of ideal standards. Relative standards involve comparisons with competitors, that is, other curricula that are directed toward approximately the same objectives. There is a strong but imperfect analogy to testing: absolute standards are much like criterion-referenced tests, while relative standards are much like norm-referenced tests.

The final column of the judgment matrix, itself labeled "judgment," involves interpreting discrepancies between observed performance and standards. "Judging is assigning a weight, an importance, to each set of standards. . . . From relative judgment of a program, as well as from absolute judgment, we can obtain an overall or composite rating of merit" (in Worthen and Sanders, 1973, p. 122). Unfortunately, Stake does not provide any clues as to how weights can be determined or how weightings on individual standards can be combined to yield an overall or composite rating.

Like Tyler's rationale, the countenance model has certain advantages and disadvantages. Stake expanded the concept of objectives to include contextual factors, as well as objectives for teachers and other agents. He provided a basis, however incomplete, for the evaluation of the objectives by requiring a justification for them in terms of some explicit rationale. He included for the first time a focus on judgment as a major aspect of evaluation, defining the complete act of evaluation as involving both description and judgment (the two "countenances," as Stake puts it). He suggested means for deriving judgmental standards and distinguished between absolute and relative standards. He also provided an empirical basis for carrying out Tyler's recommendation that hypotheses be developed and tested to account for observed patterns of strengths and weaknesses.

Nonetheless, the countenance model also had its shortcomings. Stake left the means for deriving standards largely unspecified, providing little operational guidance to the evaluator on this important point. He did not come to grips with the question of how to manage competing values (whether in setting intents or in deriving standards). He continued the assumption that had been implicit in Tyler's rationale (and, indeed, that is implicit in all non-responsive evaluation models) that societal values converge. Consensus is deemed possible and value pluralism is ignored. Although he explicitly warned the evaluator not to overlook unintended effects, Stake failed to provide guidance on how to find and take account of them. He continued with an emphasis on formal evaluation, and this emphasis tied evaluation even more closely to the scientific paradigm and its attendant measurement processes. And finally, the twelve-cell design of the model was perhaps too complex; evaluation practitioners found it difficult to comprehend and operationalize.

Context-Input-Process-Product Model

While Stake and others continued to focus upon objectives as the major organizer for evaluation, still other evaluators began to take closer looks at other organizers. The first such organizer to be exploited seriously was the decision—no surprise in view of Cronbach's 1963 exhortation. Two models, Stufflebeam's Context-Input-Process-Product model (CIPP) and Alkin's Center for the Study of Evaluation model (CSE) are prototypic. We shall describe the CIPP model in some detail.

An evaluator taking decisions as the organizer for his activity does not require information about objectives but about what decisions are to be made, who is to make them, on what schedule, and using what criteria. Knowing, for example, that the director of purchasing would be making a decision about which of four competing lines of school buses to purchase, that he would base his decision on cost, safety, and maintenance factors, and that he would make his decision by January 1, the evaluator would collect information about each kind of bus, provide it to the decision maker before January 1, and conclude that he had serviced that decision well.

Stufflebeam's concern with decisions led him to an analysis of decision types. His intent was to generate a parsimonious taxonomy, each element of which could be serviced by a type of evaluation designed specifically for that purpose. His solution to the problem was to propose four decision types, generated by crossing an ends-means dimension with an intended-actual dimension: First, *intended ends* (goals or objectives) are determined through a series of planning decisions. These decisions are serviced by *context* evaluation, which continuously assesses needs, problems, and opportunities within the decision maker's domain. Second, *intended means* (processes or procedures) are determined through a series of structuring decisions. These decisions are serviced by *input* evaluation, which assesses alternative means for achieving the specified ends. Third, *actual means* are determined through a series of implementing decisions (following the plan or schedule outlined by the intended means). These decisions are serviced by *process* evaluation, which monitors and "debugs" the processes to keep them in as close conformity as possible with the intended means and which makes adjustments and refinements that seem to be called for by actual experience. Finally, *actual ends* lead to a series of recycling decisions (terminate, adjust, recycle as is). These decisions are serviced by *product* evaluation, which is concerned with comparing actual to intended ends but which also takes account of other, unintended effects.

Within this model, context evaluation is a continuing process, while input, process, and product evaluations are called into action whenever the context evaluation signals some need, problem, or opportunity requiring a response. Moreover, all four kinds of evaluation can be used in either a proactive or retrospective mode; that is, to service decisions still to be made or to provide accountability data for decisions made in the past.

There are, within this model, three separate components to evaluation: delineating, obtaining, and applying. Delineating involves face-to-face encounters with decision makers to whatever extent may be necessary to identify the information that will be needed. Obtaining, often called the technical part of evaluation, involves the physical collection and processing of information. Applying involves furnishing the collected and processed information to decision makers in ways that will render their decision making more rational.

Evaluation within the CIPP model is thus a process for delineating, obtaining, and applying descriptive and judgmental information concerning some object's merit as revealed by its goals, structure, process, and product. In addition, it is a process undertaken for some useful purpose such as decision making or accountability.

The CIPP model has its own configuration of advantages and disadvantages. On the positive side, it was the first to expand the list of available organizers for evaluation beyond objectives. Further, it responded to many of the new demands and requirements being imposed on evaluators and proved to be especially useful for programs or projects of large scope and multilevel organization. The model fit in well with the emergent interest in systems theory, and it was itself very rational and systemic in its approach. Finally, it was very well operationalized, and guidelines —even detailed work sheets—were available for virtually every application.

But the model also had serious faults. It made what are probably unwarranted assumptions about the rationality of decision makers, about the openness of the decision-making process (essentially political), and about the ease with which operational decision makers can be identified (in complex organizations or loosely coupled organizations decisions appear to "bubble up" rather than to be made explicitly at some particular time and place). CIPP took an essentially synoptic view of the decision process, while ignoring other models such as the political negotiations model or the human relations or "involvement" model. It failed to deal directly with the question of values and standards, although it emphasized the need to determine "merit." Finally, it proved to be difficult to operationalize; it was hard to mount and administer, as well as expensive to maintain.

Goal-Free Model

The suggestion from Scriven in 1972 that, far from relying on objectives to focus their work, evaluators ought to eschew them and to take every precaution they could to avoid discovering what the objectives were, was greeted everywhere by stunned disbelief. Calling for a substitute organizer, as Stufflebeam had done, was one thing, but to ignore objectives was something else indeed. "Surely you jest," seemed to be the sum total of the response from the evaluation community. But Scriven was not jesting, and his perseverance in making his point has had a dramatic effect upon the theory and practice of evaluation.

Scriven was one of a group of advisers employed by the Educational Testing Service to screen candidates for a "proven products list"—a list of innovations and developments that had been funded by the federal government and whose evaluations showed that they were worth warranting to schools in general. In reporting on this experience, Scriven (1974b) suggested that it appeared "natural" to this group to begin with the objectives for which each product had been designed, making recommendations for placement on the list as a function of whether or not those objectives had been achieved. But it soon became apparent that many of the products had very beneficial side effects that seemed to be at least as important as the initial objectives; indeed, there were cases in which the objectives were not achieved at all but for which the existence of useful side effects seemed to be a sufficient basis to recommend inclusion.

Scriven reports that at this juncture he became puzzled over the fact that intended and unintended effects should be so arbitrarily separated. Why distinguish them, he asked? "All that should be concerning us, surely, was determining exactly what effects this product had (or most likely had), and evaluating those, whether or not they were intended. . . . The rhetoric of intent was being used as a substitute for evidence of success" (1974b, p. 1). Moreover, Scriven noted, such phrases as "side effect" or "unintended effect" had the effect of obscuring what might be a crucial achievement or at least made one look less hard for evidence of it. In that sense, knowledge of goals might actually be a contaminating step. Hence, Scriven came to the conclusion that evaluation should be *goal free,* that is, that it should evaluate actual effects against a profile of demonstrated needs in education. Thus, Scriven's organizer became *effects* rather than goals or decisions.

To conduct a goal-free evaluation, then, the evaluator needs to generate two items of information: an assessment of actual effects and a profile of needs against which the importance or salience of these effects might be assessed. If a product had an effect that could be shown to be responsive to a need, that product was useful and should be positively evaluated.

At the operational level Scriven has not been very helpful in describing how goal-free evaluation should actually be carried out. He has made no definitive recommendations on how to generate a needs assessment, although some of his recent writing has begun to move in that direction (see, for example, Scriven and Roth, 1977). He has proposed a "pathway comparison model," which is described by Stufflebeam (1974b), that seems to relate to the assessment of effects.

Although in the main this model has remained at a conceptual level, it has had an effect on the evaluation community that goes well beyond its operational utility. It demonstrated that evaluation could occur even in the absence of information about objectives, and it thereby revolutionized thinking about evaluation and probably earned for Scriven the distinction of heir apparent to Tyler. It forced consideration of every possible effect—not only those intended—as the most adequate approach to the assessment of value. As a result all evaluators, regardless of their persuasion, began to pay more attention to so-called side effects.

But the model also had serious shortcomings. It failed to come to grips with the question of what effects to look at or even how to identify them. A metaphor frequently used by Scriven—that of the hunter "setting snares" where his experience told him animals would come—was clearly inadequate to provide guidance. Nor was the situation helped by reference to needs assessment, for the question of what needs to assess was unanswered. The model certainly placed a premium on evaluator competence; an incompetent hunter will scarcely know where to set snares. And despite Scriven's earlier insistence that evaluators should assume the burden of making judgments, the goal-free model did not take up the question of how judgmental standards are to be derived. Finally, Scriven undoubtedly overstated his case in an attempt to gain attention for it. Indeed, Scriven's own admission that goal-free evaluation is best used as an auxiliary, parallel activity (to goal-based evaluation) is evidence for this.

Connoisseurship Model

The connoisseurship model proposed by Eisner represents a departure from more conventional evaluation models in two respects. First, it is one of a number of judgmental models that utilize the human being as a measurement instrument. Data collection, analysis, processing, and interpretation take place within the mind of the judge and hence are not open to direct inspection. Whatever judgmental processes go on inside the judge's brain are based on the "critical guideposts" (the model's organizer) that he has internalized by virtue of his training and experience. Second, the connoisseurship model is derived by metaphoric analysis and uses the metaphor of the art critic for the generation of its basic concepts.

Eisner's formulation rests on the twin concepts of educational connoisseurship and educational criticism, terms clearly borrowed from the domain of art criticism. Educational practices, like works of art, are extremely complex. Connoisseurship is the "art of perception that makes the appreciation of such complexity possible" (Eisner, 1975, p. 1). The connoisseur, by virtue of his background, is able to "appreciate" the characteristics and qualities of phenomena that he encounters to a better degree than is a less sophisticated observer.

But, Eisner observes, "if connoisseurship is the art of appreciation, criticism is the art of disclosure. What the critic aims at is not only to discern that character and qualities constituting the object or event [but also to provide] a rendering in linguistic terms of what it is he or she has encountered so that others not possessing his level of connoisseurship can also enter into the work. . . . The function of criticism is educational. Its aim is to lift the veils that keep the eyes from seeing by providing the bridge needed by others to experience the qualities and relationships within some area of activity. . . . The critic must talk or write about what he has encountered; he must . . . provide a rendering of the qualities that constitute that work, its significance, and the quality of his experience when he interacts with it" (p. 1).

Obviously such an approach to evaluation represents a dramatic departure from the methodologies commonly exploited by evaluation practitioners. Hence, Eisner devotes considerable attention to the methodological issues that he suspects will be raised. How can one know whether or not to trust educational critics? How can one be sure "that what educational critics say about educational phenomena is not a figment of their imagination? How can we know what confidence we can place in the critic's description, interpretation, and evaluation of classroom life?" (p. 16).

With respect to the validity issue, Eisner suggests that there is no ultimate way to test whether one's perceptions are isomorphic to reality—to make such a test one would need to know what the reality is. It is, however, possible to look for instances of structural corroboration, demonstrated when separate pieces of evidence validate one another and when a coherent, persuasive whole emerges. One can also test whether the critic's language is "referentially adequate," that is, one can determine by persistent observation or through the analysis of specially prepared materials such as films and videotapes whether the referents of the critic's report in fact exist in the situation.

Eisner contends that two kinds of generalizations can occur. First, the critic himself can generalize his experience to make himself a more powerful critic as he gains experience. Second, the critic acquires "new forms of anticipation" that in turn require him to develop some generalized concept of typicality. It is probably of less import here to confirm or reject Eisner's proposals than to note the methodological revolution implied by the fact that he feels constrained to take up such questions.

The connoisseurship model can be credited with certain contributions. It is in effect a nonscientific supplement to traditional evaluation models, and it demonstrates that the scientific paradigm is not essential to the development of a powerful and useful evaluation approach. The connoisseurship model has the honor of being the first to break cleanly with that paradigm. Further, the model provides a fresh new perspective about how to make evaluations; it opens, as Eisner himself asserts, a "new window through which educational practice can be studied and described." It provides a better complement to the "biological metaphor" for education; and, according to Eisner (1969), this metaphor guides teachers' actions to a much greater extent than do the industrial and behavioristic metaphors.

But the connoisseurship model also has its deficits. It fails to provide operational guidelines for the evaluator who would follow it. It places too high a premium on the competence of the evaluator; the very term *connoisseur* implies a kind of elitism to which few evaluators would aspire. It carries an air of "artiness" that tends to repel potential adherents who were trained in more traditional ways. And finally, it proposes a methodology not subject to the usual criteria for methodological adequacy.

Summary

Educational evaluation, as we have seen, was fathered by the ubiquitous measurement movement that gained major momentum with World War I, although it had antecedents that went back almost another century. During this period evaluation had very few of the characteristics that have now come to be associated with it. It then focused on individual differences among students —differences that were determined largely through the application of standardized, norm-referenced tests. It was not seen as having special relevance for programs or curricula. It was bogged down within the scientific paradigm of inquiry, fitting well into the industrial and behavioristic metaphors that guided much of the thinking not only about schools but about many other aspects of American life as well.

The first blow—and a very major blow it was—that was struck against the prevailing view came from Tyler. While he continued to make use of the scientific paradigm, the comparative study, and the guidance of the industrial and behavioristic metaphors, he clearly broke with other traditions. Measurement and evaluation were finally separated, and the former became simply one tool in the service of the latter. The focus was shifted from a narrow range of individual differences that had virtually nothing to do with curriculum or instruction to a broader range of student behaviors that were directly tied to instructional objectives. Finally, while norm-referenced standardized instruments were still widely used, mere standardization was not enough to warrant the use of an instrument; its relationship to the objectives needed to be demonstrated. Curricular validity came into its own.

But the Tyler model was not, as it turned out, adequate to the challenges posed for evaluation by the projects for improving course content funded by the federal government following on Sputnik. Cronbach's paper calling for a shift from objectives to decisions as the organizer was quickly followed by other papers calling attention to the deficiencies of evaluation. Evaluators were urged to become judges and to make the underlying value structure of evaluation explicit. Other organizers emerged. The search for standards began, and new ideas and vocabulary that added conceptual strength to evaluation started to appear. And, finally, the need for new models was made explicit.

While no one of these models was responsive to all the objections that had been raised by the dissident writers, as a group they showed remarkable progress. Values and standards were becoming more and more explicit. Judgment was included in virtually everyone's definition of evaluation. Not only were new organizers emerging, but a new paradigm challenging the scientific method had also been proposed. Training, methodology, and theories had improved.

But other problems had emerged. It had become more and more evident that evaluation was a political phenomenon, but hardly anyone knew very much about the politics of evaluation or what the evaluator could do to guard against political influences, on the one hand, or to use them to his own best advantage, on the other. It was also becoming clear that there were human factors involved in evaluation; evaluation was almost universally dysfunctional to human performance, but no one knew how to assess the trade-offs between that effect and good evaluation information. Under what circumstances would the insights gained more than offset the dysfunctionality introduced? Further, epistemological and methodological questions still abounded; indeed, new ones were being introduced at a faster rate than the old ones could be disposed of. Finally, it was becoming more and more evident that life in a multivalued, pluralistic society was not well served by modes of evaluation that persisted in the belief that consensus was possible and that value congruence was a worthwhile aim. There was obviously room for a great deal of improvement.

Chapter 2

Emergence
of Responsive
Evaluation

Responsive evaluation is an emergent form of evaluation that takes as its organizer the *concerns and issues of stakeholding audiences.* In order to illustrate the principles of responsive evaluation, we shall first present a brief analysis of Stake's responsive evaluation, selecting this prototype because Stake was the first to use the term "responsive," because an earlier model proposed by Stake has already been described (the countenance model), and because this prototype is the one most closely allied to education. We shall then describe in some detail our own concept of responsive evaluation.

Stake's Responsive Model

Stake had established himself as a very influential figure in evaluation circles through his work on the countenance model.

Following this work, however, he slowly began to adopt a new kind of evaluation posture, one that he dubbed "responsive." In this, the evaluator is less concerned with the objectives of the evaluand than with its effects in relation to the interests of relevant publics, which Stake termed "stakeholding audiences." His first effort in this direction was the so-called T-CITY Institute for Talented Youth evaluation published in 1971; following upon the circulation of a fugitive paper and an American Educational Research Association (1974) presentation, he formalized his approach in *Evaluating the Arts in Education* (1975, chap. two).

Evaluation, Stake suggests, is becoming a national phenomenon, and arts-in-education programs are among those being evaluated. But "there are different ways to evaluate programs and no one way is the right way. I prefer to think of ways that evaluation can perform a service and be useful to specific persons. For an evaluation to be useful, the evaluator should know the interests and the language of his audiences. During an evaluation study, a substantial amount of time may well be spent in learning about the information needs of the persons for whom the evaluation is being done. The evaluator should have a good sense of whom he is working for *and their concerns*" (1975, p. 13, emphasis added).

But not all evaluation approaches are equally useful for such purposes, Stake notes: "To emphasize evaluation *issues* that are important for each particular program, I recommend the *responsive evaluation* approach. It is an approach that trades off some measurement precision in order to increase the usefulness of the findings to persons in and around the program. . . . An educational evaluation is *responsive evaluation* if it orients more directly to program activities than to program intents; responds to audience requirements for information; and if the different value perspectives present are referred to in reporting the success and failure of the program" (p. 14).

Evaluation, Stake suggests, can serve many different purposes; for example, to document events, to record student change, to aid in decision making, to seek out understanding, to facilitate remediation. *Which* purpose is served by a given evaluation should be determined by the "different purposes and information needs of different audiences" (p. 15). To choose the questions to which he will attend, the evaluator should first observe the program and only then determine what to look for. Lists of objectives or the availability of instruments should not be permitted to "draw his attention away from the things that concern the people involved" (pp. 15-16). The instrumental value of education should not be allowed to dominate the evaluation plans to the exclusion of intrinsic values. Statements of objectives, hypotheses, test batteries, teaching syllabi, and the like are to be treated as part of the instructional plan, not as the basis for the evaluation plan.

The proper organizer for an evaluation is thus the concerns and issues that are gathered in "conversations" with persons in and around the program; for example, taxpayers, program sponsors, program staff, students, parents, teachers, administrators, and others.

Stake (1975) suggests a number of steps for conducting a responsive evaluation. While these are serially listed, it is imperative to note that they need not be, and probably cannot be, carried out serially; instead, there is a continuing movement back and forth as the evaluation proceeds:

1. The evaluator talks with clients, program staff, and audiences—everyone in and around the program—to gain a sense of their posture with respect to the evaluand and the purposes of the evaluation.

2. As a result of these conversations, the evaluator places limits on the scope of the program. The limits are also set because of inputs from other sources such as the program proposal, documents emanating from program personnel, official records, and the like.

3. The evaluator makes personal observations of what goes on in the name of the program to get a direct sense of its operation. He thereby verifies its existence and can note deviations from his sense of the program as developed in the first two steps.

4. As a result of the preceding activities, the evaluator begins to discover, on the one hand, the purposes of the project, both stated and real, and, on the other hand, the concerns that various audiences may have with it and/or the evaluation.

5. As he becomes more involved with these preliminary data, the evaluator begins to conceptualize the issues and problems that the evaluation should address.

6. Once issues and problems have been identified, the eval-

uator is in a position to think about the design of the evaluation. Note that this step occurs well into the evaluation activity; the design could not have been developed earlier. For each purpose, issue, concern, or problem identified, the evaluator specifies the kinds of data and information that will be needed to deal with or respond to it.

7. Given these data needs, the evaluator selects whatever approaches are most useful for generating the data. The responsive evaluator will select whatever instruments are appropriate; most often, in Stake's judgment, the instruments will be *observers* or *judges,* that is, *human* instruments.

8. The evaluator now proceeds to carry out the data collection procedures that he has identified; that is, he moves into the empirical phase of the evaluation.

9. Once the data have been collected and processed, the evaluator shifts to an information-reporting mode. The information is organized into themes, and the evaluator prepares portrayals designed to communicate "in natural ways" and to provide as much direct personal experience as possible. Portrayals can thus take any form; the conventional research report qualifies as a form, to be sure, but much more effective are forms such as so-called thick descriptions, case studies, plays, videotapes, artifacts, and other "faithful representations."

10. Since the evaluator cannot report on every issue or problem, it is important that he winnow out those that will be reported. Moreover, not every audience will want or need to know about every issue or concern; the evaluator matches issues and concerns to audiences in deciding what form the report will take. There may be different reports for different audiences.

11. A final decision to be made by the evaluator has to do with the format to be used in reporting to each audience. The format is fitted to the audience as carefully as is the content. Reports may therefore take the form of written statements, discussion sessions, round-table discussions, newspaper articles, films, exhibits, or whatever may be deemed appropriate.

12. As a final step, the evaluator assembles formal reports, if there are to be any. Stake is not convinced that formal reports are either necessary or desirable in every case. Where they are mandated, the evaluator of course complies.

It is worth noting the synergistic interactions present in these several steps. Attempts to thematize, to portray, and to match issues to audiences may lead the evaluator to reformulations: a different way to define an issue, a different way of formulating information, a different way of reporting the results. There is no certain way to predict the final outcome of an evaluation until one has arrived at it; indeed, there is no "natural" end point but simply a place convenient (or required) for reporting. Given sufficient time and budget, the evaluator could recycle the entire effort; once the initial findings are in, the audiences' formulations and understandings of the concerns and issues will have altered sufficiently to reveal a new set, which could be investigated in turn. Responsive evaluation is truly a continuous and interactive process.

In his exposition, Stake (1975) distinguishes the responsive approach he advocates from more conventional approaches, which he calls "preordinate." Although his treatment of these differences is not systematic, it deserves detailed attention, for in Stake's flowing prose are hidden some epistemological and methodological distinctions of great importance. The more important of these differences are organized in Table 1.

Orientation. In his paper on the countenance model (1967), Stake differentiated formal from informal evaluation as follows: "Educational evaluation has its formal and informal sides. Informal evaluation is recognized by its dependence on casual observation, implicit goals, intuitive norms, and subjective judgment. . . . Formal evaluation of education is recognized by its dependence on checklists, structured visitation by peers, controlled comparisons, and standardized testing of students" (in Worthen and Sanders, 1973, p. 107).

Stake found fault, in 1967, with formal approaches to evaluation, but also many virtues. It is apparent that the countenance model was an effort to eliminate those faults. There can be no doubt that Stake was then arguing *for* a formal approach; indeed, his description of informal evaluation is somewhat pejorative— "casual" observation, "implicit" goals, "intuitive" norms, "subjective" judgment. But despite Stake's assertion that responsive evaluation builds on the countenance model, it is in fact a much more informal approach:

Table 1. Comparison of Preordinate and Responsive Evaluation Modes

Comparison Item	Type of Evaluation	
	Preordinate	Responsive
Orientation	Formal.	Informal.
Value perspective	Singular; consensual.	Pluralistic; possibility of conflict.
Basis for evaluation design (organizer)	Program intents, objectives, goals, hypotheses; evaluator preconceptions such as performance, mastery, ability, aptitude, measurable outcomes; the instrumental values of education.	Audience concerns and issues; program activities; reactions, motivations, or problems of persons in and around the evaluand.
Design completed when?	At beginning of evaluation.	Never—continuously evolving.
Evaluator role	Stimulator of subjects with a view to testing critical performance.	Stimulated by subjects and activities.
Methods	Objective; "taking readings," for example, testing.	Subjective, for example, observations and interviews; negotiations and interactions.
Communication	Formal; reports; typically one stage.	Informal; portrayals; often two stage.
Feedback	At discrete intervals; often only once, at end.	Informal; continuously evolving as needed by audiences.
Form of feedback	Written report, identifying variables and depicting the relationships among them; symbolic interpretation.	Narrative-type depiction, often oral (if that is what the audience prefers), modeling what the program is like, providing vicarious experience, "holistic" communication.
Paradigm	Experimental psychology.	Anthropology, journalism, poetry.

To do a responsive evaluation, the evaluator
conceives of a plan of observations and negotiations.
He arranges for various persons to observe the program, and with their help prepares brief narratives,
portrayals, product displays, graphs, etc. He finds out
what is of value to his audiences, and gathers expressions of worth from various individuals whose points
of view differ. Of course, he checks the quality of his
records: he gets program personnel to react to the accuracy of his portrayals; authority figures to react to
the importance of various findings; and audience
members to react to the relevance of his findings. He
does much of this informally—iterating and keeping a
record of action and reaction. He chooses media accessible to his audiences to increase the likelihood
and fidelity of communication. He might prepare a
final written report, he might not—depending on
what *he and his clients have agreed upon [Stake,
1975, p. 14].

Value Perspective. A major stimulant to the emergence of
responsive models of evaluation was the growing realization that
American culture was value pluralistic. Earlier models of evaluation had taken a singular value perspective and assumed that there
was general convergence on a consensual value system. Responsive
evaluation takes a pluralistic view and allows for the possibility
that there may be conflicts among different value positions. Different audiences have different information needs precisely because their different value structures lead them to see different
issues and concerns.

Basis for Evaluation Design (Organizer). Stake scores earlier
evaluation for having focused, in general, on program intents, objectives, or goals or on *a priori* hypotheses that were to be tested.
Too often the preconceptions of the evaluator himself were permitted to dictate the direction an evaluation would take—his concepts of such matters as performance, mastery, ability, or aptitude
ruled the design, as did the likelihood that outcomes could be
measured with available instruments. For the responsive evaluator,
however, the organizer was the concerns and issues of audiences
or, as Stake put it, the reactions, motivations, and problems of

persons "in and around" the evaluand. Program activities rather than program intents were the primary basis for organizing the evaluative effort.

Design Completed When? Preordinate evaluation starts with the assumption that in good evaluations every step of the way is laid out in advance and that the evaluation itself can be evaluated by noting whether or not there is conformity to the *a priori* design. When program intents, objectives, goals, or hypotheses are the basis for organizing the evaluation, such given-in-advance designs are of course possible; recall, for example, the discussion of the Tyler model in Chapter One. This model in effect *is* a design, needing only to be filled in with the particulars of the actual situation of application. But when audience concerns and issues, or program activities, are to be the organizing basis, it is impossible to provide a design in advance; the concerns and issues must first be determined, and the activities observed, before even rudimentary steps can be taken to mount the evaluation. Moreover, there is a continuing interaction among the prominent events of a responsive evaluation, so that even when a report is finally rendered, there is a feeling that an end has been reached not through lack of additional questions but simply because time and logistics dictate it. In short, preordinate designs are completed at the beginning of the evaluation; and, indeed, it is a major setback if they have to be changed in midstream. In contrast, responsive designs are continuously evolving and never complete; here it is a major setback if the evaluator does not actively work at continuous design change as a result of his ever-growing knowledge and insights.

Evaluator Role. In all preordinate evaluation the evaluator is supposed to be an objective, external agent who, in Tyler's prototype, screens someone else's objectives, identifies situations in which students can express the desired behavior, and develops instruments or who, in Scriven's prototype, sets game snares off the main trails. For Stake, the evaluator stimulates subjects with a view to testing critical performance. The evaluator is always the stimulator; persons related to the entity being evaluated (who are typically viewed as "subjects") are the respondents. But in responsive evaluation we find the evaluator taking a different role; it is he who is stimulated by the subjects and by program activities and who also makes the response—identifying concerns and issues, developing portrayals, and so on. The evaluator is drawn into the activity as a full partner, no longer objective and aloof but interactive. It is as though the physicist were suddenly to find himself among the particles he studies or the chemist to place himself in the test tube as part of the chemical experiment. Of course this shift in evaluator role raises a great many methodological issues, for example, the reliability of the evaluator's reports and the objectivity of his observations. These kinds of questions will be considered in detail in Chapters Four, Five, and Six; suffice it to say here that the responsive definition of the evaluator role is so fundamentally different from the preordinate definition as to require a different epistemological paradigm to accommodate it.

Methods. Following from this fundamentally different role is the difference in method which characterizes responsive evaluation. Preordinate evaluation follows the scientific paradigm; the prototype for data collection is the physicist's meter that, sensing a phenomenon, registers a reading directly proportional to it while not utilizing any of the energy itself. Thus preordinate evaluation aims to be "objective" and to "take readings" of phenomena with "instruments" whose validity and reliability are known and whose objectivity is patent (self-evident) in the form of the instrument, for example, standardized tests. In contrast responsive evaluation uses methods that are "subjective" and qualitative rather than quantitative, for example, observations and interviews. Moreover, the evaluator uses, as essential parts of his method, negotiation and interaction; for example, interacting with audiences to identify concerns and issues and negotiating portrayals of evaluation findings with them to ensure accuracy and communication.

Communication. Communication within preordinate evaluation is typically formal, consisting mainly of one-stage reports; that is, reports that are released to audiences without any prior negotiations with members of those audiences. The responsive evaluator is much more informal in his communication, which tends to consist of "portrayals." Moreover, communication is often two stage in that the portrayals have first been tested with a representative group of audience members. This test may challenge either the substance or the form of the portrayal, sending the evaluator back into the field for additional data and/or altering the nature of the portrayal so that it will communicate more effectively to that audience what the evaluator wants to communicate. The portrayal may, of course, be significantly changed as a result of this negotiation.

Feedback. For the preordinate evaluator, feedback and communication are virtually synonymous; feedback sometimes takes the form of written reports that are provided at discrete (and typically prearranged) intervals negotiated in advance (for example, quarterly reports and a final report). All too often, however, there is only one report—and that at the end of the evaluation when it is difficult indeed to alter it should there be any adverse reaction or criticism. (This is not to say that the evaluator would change his report simply because the criticism was adverse. He would, however, wish to investigate the allegations and respond to them.) For the responsive evaluator, feedback is a normal part of everyday activity. By virtue of his interactive, negotiating style he is continuously in contact with his audiences and providing them with cues about his activity, his insights, and his interpretations. And he can enter into dialogue whenever he perceives that these audiences need more from him than just hints. The final report, should there be one, will not come as a surprise to anyone, nor will its contents or form fail to have been thoroughly criticized before release.

Form of Feedback. For the preordinate evaluator, feedback is synonymous with communication, and the form of communication is the written report—a report that identifies variables and depicts the relationships among them, usually in quantitative ways. Interpretations are symbolic; that is, they are presented in the form of words, numbers, graphs, and so on. The responsive evaluator however, strives for "holistic" communication that provides at least vicarious, if not direct, experience of the entity being evaluated—it models what the program is like. Oral communication is used if that "fits" the audience, as are various forms of nonsymbolic communication: examples, artifacts, videotapes, skits, and the like. For the responsive evaluator, communication with his audiences is of the essence, for the most meaningful test of the validity of an evaluation is that it improves the audience's understanding of the evaluand.

Paradigm. The differences between preordinate and responsive evaluation are so fundamental that they can be said to follow completely different epistemological paradigms. This concept will be explicated in detail in Chapter Four, but it might be useful to mention here that preordinate evaluators find the approaches of experimental psychology (themselves modeled on the approaches of the so-called hard sciences) congenial, while responsive evaluators are more likely to look to anthropology, journalism, or even poetry for insight and metaphors.

An Expansion of Stake's Proposals

Stake's proposals regarding responsive evaluation have been elaborated in a number of extant models. Hamilton (1977) has characterized this emergent group as "pluralist" evaluation models, that is, as models that take account of the value positions of multiple audiences: "In practical terms, pluralist evaluation models (Parlett and Hamilton, 1972; Patton, 1975; Stake, 1967) can be characterized in the following manner. Compared with the classic models, they tend to be more extensive (not necessarily centered on numerical data), more naturalistic (based on program activity rather than program intent), and more adaptable (not constrained by experimental or preordinate designs). In turn they are likely to be sensitive to the different values of program participants, to endorse empirical methods which incorporate ethnographic fieldwork, to develop feedback materials which are couched in the natural language of the recipients, and to shift the locale of formal judgment from the evaluator to the participants" (p. 339).

It is our position that responsive evaluation as proposed by Stake and elaborated by others offers the most meaningful and useful approach to performing evaluations. There are, however, certain additions that it is necessary to make to this formulation. As we have noted, the organizer for responsive evaluation is the concerns and issues stemming from the several audiences that the evaluation will serve. The terms *concerns* and *issues* have been used loosely up to this point; more formal definitions are now in order.

A *concern* is any matter of interest or importance to one or more parties. It may be something that threatens them, something that they think will lead to an undesirable consequence, or something that they are anxious to substantiate in a positive sense (a claim requiring empirical verification). Examples of concerns would include the following:

- Lack of achievement of objectives of a course (a concern that might be expressed by a teacher or curriculum maker).
- Difficulty in applying the principles of new math to everyday tasks such as balancing checkbooks (a concern that might be expressed by a parent).
- Interest in showing that a new curriculum is superior to an existing one in dealing with problems introduced by the mainstreaming of youngsters (a concern that might be expressed by the program developer or someone adopting it).
- Fear that a new program will require one to spend more time doing homework (a concern that might be expressed by a student).
- Belief that a new teaching strategy will greatly increase the efficiency of teaching by providing for more time on task (a concern that might be expressed by a teacher or program developer).
- Fear that children will be weaned away from more traditional values by a new approach in school (a concern that might be expressed by a parent or clergyman).
- Belief that a curriculum is not in step with modern times (a concern that might be expressed by a university professor).
- Doubt that youngsters will enjoy being exposed to a new program and hence will be negatively motivated toward it (a concern that might be expressed by a teacher or administrator).

Thus, virtually any claim, doubt, fear, anticipated difficulty, and the like expressed by anyone with a legitimate basis for making such a representation could be entertained as a concern. Obviously concerns differ in their importance, in their credibility, in their relevance, and so on; but until they are investigated by the evaluator they cannot simply be dismissed. All are possible candidates for the evaluator's attention within the limits of available time and resources.

An *issue* is any statement, proposition, or focus that allows for the presentation of different points of view; any proposition about which reasonable persons may disagree; or any point of contention. Examples of issues are:

- Whether to cut the budget, even in the knowledge that cuts would represent a "conscious sacrifice of quality," in order to maintain a reasonable tax structure for the community.
- Whether to focus accountability on the individual teacher or on the system as a whole.
- Whether to use the schools in an effort to socialize the youth of the community to the existing value system.
- Whether to institute decision-making processes that are essentially centralized or decentralized.
- Whether to admit the public to policy determination or to reserve that privilege to professionals.
- Whether to support tenure over accountability, or vice-versa.
- Whether open or closed classrooms represent the best approach to elementary school teaching.
- Whether to mainstream handicapped youngsters or assign them to special classes.
- Whether to elect or appoint school boards to achieve the most intelligent and dedicated governance.

Again, virtually any proposition about which there is disagreement between legitimate audiences (or between subgroups of a single audience) is a candidate to be an issue, deserving of the evaluator's attention within the limitations of available time and resources.

On the one hand, an issue is a debatable proposition and hence involves a difference in point of view between two or more parties. The role of the evaluator is to develop information relevant to the two (or more) sides of the issue—information that may then be used to resolve or reduce the issue. A concern, on the other hand, may be felt by only a single individual; however, if that individual possesses special insight or has a special perspective (for example, the school superintendent), his concerns may have special importance. The role of the evaluator is to collect information that confirms or disconfirms the concern.

We define evaluation as a process for describing an evaluand and judging its merit and worth. Merit and worth, as we shall show in Chapter Three, are distinct aspects of value. Most evaluators now agree that the complete act of evaluation involves both description and judgment; that is, it involves attaching value. Description is important not only because it provides necessary information about the evaluand but also because it is essential in determining whether the results of an evaluation in a certain context might also be applicable in another context. This concept is more fully explored in Chapter Three and again in Chapter Five.

The guiding inquiry paradigm most appropriate to responsive evaluation is, we shall show in Chapters Four, Five, and Six, the naturalistic, phenomenological, or ethnographic paradigm. It will be seen that qualitative techniques are typically most appropriate to support this approach. There are times, however, when the issues and concerns voiced by audiences require information that is best generated by more conventional methods, especially quantitative methods. For example, the concern that a year's reading instruction produce a year's gain in reading ability is probably best addressed through a conventional pre-post design that uses some standard measure of reading ability as the dependent variable. In such cases the responsive evaluator will not shrink from the appropriate application, although in general he may feel that qualitative approaches are more applicable and flexible.

The major purpose of evaluation we define as responding to an audience's requirements for information, particularly in ways that take account of the several value perspectives of its members. We see four uses of evaluation: modification and/or improvement of the entity being evaluated; critique, certification, and warrant of the entity; fitting or adapting it to a local context; and certification and warrant for local retention, application, or use of the entity in its adapted form. For reasons that will become clear in Chapter Three, we shall refer to these four uses as formative merit evaluation, summative merit evaluation, formative worth evaluation, and summative worth evaluation, respectively.

We stress, with Stake, that the design of responsive evaluation is emergent (or unfolding or rolling or cascading—all terms in common use). A responsive design cannot be fully specified except in general terms because each step in the process is determined at least in part by what has emerged prior to that point. The necessity for this requirement will be fully explicated in Chapters Three and Four.

The procedures followed in carrying out responsive evaluation are typically qualitative in nature, although any procedures that will produce the information needed to respond to audience concerns and issues are admissible. The conceptual basis for the naturalistic qualitative procedures is given in Chapters Four, Five, and Six. Individual qualitative skill areas, such as interviewing and observation, are treated in Chapters Seven and Eight.

The information called for to do a responsive evaluation is various. First, audiences who have stakes in concerns or issues must be identified, a task not always easy since some audiences are unaware of the stake they hold or, if they are aware, may prefer to keep a low profile, as in the case of some minority groups. An extensive commitment of time and resources is then required to work with these audiences in clarifying their concerns and issues. Next, several classes of standards must be identified to make the several judgments necessary to determine merit and worth. Finally, both descriptive and judgmental data must be elicited—data that are responsive to the issues and concerns that have been raised and that are interpretable within the sets of identified standards. These processes are discussed in the last four chapters of the book.

The audiences for an evaluation are those persons entitled by virtue of holding a stake to propose concerns and issues and to receive a report responsive to them. These audiences must include the broadest possible array of persons interested in or affected by the evaluand, including audiences that are unaware of the stakes they hold. It is unethical for the evaluator to limit his reports to selected audiences while withholding them from others, or to fail to interact with any known audience in the search for concerns and issues.

There are numerous metaevaluation standards that might be used to determine the quality of a responsive evaluation. While we will not specifically take up this topic, we are committed to the standard methodological criteria appropriate to naturalistic inquiry (see Chapters Four and Five), to conventional technical criteria such as validity and reliability when these are appropriate, to criteria of relevance and timeliness for information, and to cost-impact criteria. We also share a commitment to Stake's ideal that the ultimate test of validity for an evaluation is an increase in the audience's understanding of the entity that was evaluated. A generally useful operational measure for this increase, we believe, is a reduction in the number and level of concerns held by the audiences and in the resolution of issues posed by them (although the reader should be aware that at times good evaluation may increase the number of issues or the level of concerns.)In addition, we commend to the reader the recently developed standards developed by the Joint Committee on Standards of Educational Evaluation (1980), which we believe offer excellent guidance on a variety of issues ranging from the technical to the ethical.

Summary

From our perspective responsive evaluation is the most generally useful of the several evaluation models that have emerged so far. First of all, responsive evaluation produces information that audiences want and need. Responsive evaluation does not undertake to answer questions of merely theoretical interest; rather, it takes its cues from those matters that local audiences find interesting or relevant. If evaluation results are rarely used, it is because those results are rarely relevant to local needs. This is not to say that an evaluator cannot, by virtue of his training and experience, sometimes see important questions that no local audience thinks to ask. If so, he surely has an obligation to introduce them. But in the final analysis audiences will use information that they themselves have suggested to be important. We believe that responsive evaluation comes closest to satisfying that requirement.

Second, responsive evaluation can be interpreted to include all other models. Evaluation models, as we have used that term, are differentiated on the basis of their organizers. The organizer of the responsive model is audience concerns and issues. If some audience wants to see information relating to the achievement of objectives, that is admissible within the responsive rubric. If another audience wishes to influence or service decisions, assess general effects, or elicit critical judgments, that too can be provided for within the responsive model. The responsive model can accommodate any other organizer, while other models can accommodate only the organizer on which they are based. The resulting flexibility gives the responsive model power beyond that of any of its competitors.

Chapter 3

Determining
Merit and Worth

We have already noted that the complete act of evaluation involves both describing and judging or valuing. Now the root of the term *evaluate* suggests that the function of evaluation is to place a value on the entity being evaluated—the evaluand. But there are two senses in which an entity may have value. On the one hand, it may have value of its own, implicit, inherent, independent of any possible applications. So, for example, "pure" science has value untainted by any considerations of meaning outside the sphere of science itself. It is enough that other scientists appreciate or admire the pure discovery or development for its own sake. We shall apply the term *merit* to this kind of intrinsic, context-free value.

On the other hand, an entity may have value within some context of use or application; thus, "applied" science is undertaken for the sake of solving some practical problem. The products of applied science are valued to the extent to which they provide such solutions, that is, have some utility in a practical context. While other scientists may denigrate them as having no theoretical significance and thus as not being meritorious, they may nevertheless have great value in an engineering or industrial setting. We shall apply the term *worth* to this kind of extrinsic or context-determined value. This use of the terms *merit* and *worth* is entirely arbitrary. They both mean value, but we have assigned certain distinctions to them for heuristic purposes. Scriven (1978) has made a similar distinction except that he uses the terms *merit* and *value* in the same sense that we use *merit* and *worth*. We agree with Scriven that there are two ways to evaluate (value); we prefer to avoid the redundancy and confusion that result when one of the subtypes is called by the same name as the more generic type.

The distinction made here between merit and worth is of course not entirely new to the field of evaluation. Scriven (1967) alludes to it by noting a difference between "intrinsic" and "pay-off" evaluation; and indeed, Tyler (1950) noted that while there were certain evaluative checkpoints built into the curriculum development process as he envisaged it—for example, subjecting proposed objectives to psychological, philosophical, and experiential screens—these internal checkpoints were not sufficient. He called for a more inclusive check "as to whether these plans for learning experiences actually function to guide the teacher in producing the sort of outcomes desired." We believe that we have addressed the issue in a more systematic way than Tyler and other earlier writers.

As an example of our distinction between merit and worth, consider gold, which might be judged for *merit* on its inherent beauty—it is attractive in itself and also has properties that permit it to be fashioned into objects of beauty, such as jewelry. It is judged for *worth,* however, in the mundane trading marts of London, Paris, and Frankfort, and daily fluctuations in its worth are worthy subjects for newspaper accounts worldwide. Or take the example of a professor who might be judged for *merit* on his scholarliness, that is, on his standing in the academic community and his contribution to his discipline. But he is judged for *worth* on such factors as whether he provides a good role model for students, whether he attracts outside grants to the university, and whether he teaches in a high-demand field.

A mathematical proof might be judged for *merit* on its parsimoniousness and its elegance. Given two proofs of the same proposition, one of five steps and one of seven, the shorter is preferred; a direct proof is considered more elegant than an indirect one. Boolean algebra, when first proposed, was greatly admired not for its utility (that came later) but for its logic and coherence —it was, in a word, an elegant formulation. That same proof, however, is judged for *worth* on its applicability in a practical context. The mathematics of complex (imaginary) numbers was considered a mere mental toy until it proved competent to solve the equations of alternating electrical circuits that had withstood conventional analysis.

In the same way, a language arts curriculum might be judged for *merit* on its simplicity, straightforward form, targeted scope, lack of convoluted writing, and degree of integration; that is, on the extent to which all its substantive and formal components are properly articulated or "fit." But it is judged for *worth* on such criteria as the extent to which it produces student learning, is appropriate to the ability level of the students with whom it will be used, is free from bias (especially bias toward the sex, ethnicity, or culture of the students exposed to it), and is teachable by the average teacher.

Merit and Worth as Pluralistic Phenomena

It is of interest to ask whether estimates of merit and worth, once determined, are fixed or whether they can shift as a result of circumstances.

In one sense, both merit and worth are variable. While merit is an estimate of intrinsic value and would therefore seem to be an immutable property of the entity whose merit is being assessed, it is clear that persons competent to judge merit may differ among themselves both in stating indicators of merit and in assessing the merit of any particular entity on those indicators. Just how does one tell whether scholarliness exists in *any* professor, for example, and then how does one assess a particular professor on the possession of those characteristics? Different judgments made in response to these questions, particularly when made at different times, may lead to substantially different judgments of merit.

Similarly, one may ask how one determines characteristics of worth and then assesses a particular entity on them. How does one tell whether a curriculum is appropriate to the learning ability of the youngsters exposed to it? How does one tell whether this particular language arts curriculum possesses worthwhile characteristics? Again, judgments about both indicators and the degree to which a particular curriculum conforms to those indicators are likely to vary depending on who makes the judgments.

From this analysis one might conclude that merit and worth are equally variable. In fact, they are not equally variable at all but vary in different degrees (worth being a great deal more variable than merit) and along different dimensions.

Variations in degree arise from the fact that judgments of merit are tied to intrinsic characteristics of the entity being evaluated and are therefore relatively stable, while judgments of worth depend upon the interaction of the entity with some context and thus vary as contexts vary. A professor, whatever his merit, has different worth, depending on whether that worth is being judged in the context of a university seeking a scholar, one seeking an entrepreneur, or one seeking someone competent to teach sections of beginning business law. The worth of gold, whatever its beauty, depends on what speculators are willing to pay for it on any given day. The worth of a mathematical proof, whatever its elegance, depends on the existence of a real problem (which might be another mathematical problem) which it can help to solve (Boolean algebra was relatively worthless, although extremely meritorious, until its relationship to verbal logic was exploited). And a language arts curriculum, however simple and well-integrated, is relatively worthless with a group of black youngsters if it was designed for use with an upper-middle-class white clientele.

Dimensions along which merit and worth may vary are time, degree of consensus, and boundary factors. Assessments of merit are made in terms of criteria that are relatively stable over time, while worth assessments are made in terms of criteria that may alter rapidly with changing social, economic, or other short-term conditions. Moreover, there is likely to be a relatively high degree of consensus about merit criteria, while worth criteria depend, among other things, on value sets likely to be very different both between and within social and organizational groupings. Finally, assessments of merit are likely to hold within diffuse geographic or spatial boundaries, while assessments of worth are much more geographically specific.

Consider the example of an internationally renowned professor of Russian history. What is taken to constitute merit for scholars in this field is likely to hold for long time periods—the criteria of merit in 1980 are probably not very dissimilar to those of, say, 1880; there is likely to be consensus among historians generally, and in particular among historians of Russia, about what those criteria are; and the same criteria are likely to hold over large geographic areas. But what is taken to constitute worth may change rapidly. If an institution decided for fiscal reasons to drop its programs in Russian history, a professor in that area would suddenly have little institutional utility. Again, different institutions might have different views on the value of Russian history programs; for example, a technological university might have less interest in such programs than one with a humanistic orientation. Or universities in different geographic areas might give very different priorities to programs in Russian history.

What is important to note in all these instances is that while merit remains more or less constant, at least in the sense that it is not unreasonable to expect that consensus about an entity's merit can be reached, worth can and does change dramatically: *change the context and you change the worth*. There are several immediate and crucial consequences of this fact:

First, the determination of worth requires an ad hoc evaluation at every site in which the entity being evaluated is contemplated for use. It is impossible to warrant an entity for use generally or once and for all. To be sure, it is possible to conduct an evaluation to determine the worth of an evaluand in a number of different situations and then to describe the entity's worth in each of those different contexts. But in that case, before worth in some particular context could be inferred, one would need to have a great deal of descriptive information (often called "thick description") about the settings in which the evaluations had taken place, as well as about the particular context, so that the degree of fit between that context and one of the evaluated contexts could be determined. Thus, local, specific evaluations to determine worth cannot be avoided, and this fact has enormous implications for dissemination strategies based on the assumption that innovations can be engineered, tested, warranted for general use, and disseminated to potential adopters. Each adoption situation must be assessed to determine whether the innovation fits the situation; the mere fact that it does fit some situations is no guarantee that it will fit another situation.

Second, one very important characteristic of local settings is the values held by the several audiences to whom an evaluation may be addressed. It has become patently clear over the past decade and a half that the United States is not a value consensual society but a value pluralistic one. Hamilton (1977) has stressed the fact that responsive models of evaluation have appeared in recent years partly in recognition of this country's pluralistic value structure. Worth must be assessed in relation to those differing values, as well as in relation to other contextual factors.

Third, the fact that pluralistic values exist leads to the inescapable conclusion that a particular entity being evaluated may be judged worthy by one group but virtually worthless by another group that holds different values. In general, it is unlikely that there will be a consensus on the worth of an entity. And if there can be different assessments *within* a particular setting because of the different value sets held by important local reference groups, it is even more likely that different assessments will be reached *between* sites. Thus, while there may be differences among groups in, say, Peoria, Illinois, those differences are likely to be smaller than the differences between groups in Peoria and groups in Birmingham, Alabama, because these two cities exist in rather different cultural settings. These different and perhaps even conflicting judgments of worth may all exist whatever the degree of merit of the evaluand; meritoriousness does not lead automatically to judgments of worthiness, although, as we shall see, merit and worth may be related.

Methodologically, the most important consequence of the preceding deductions is that evaluations of worth must be grounded in field studies of local contexts (see Glaser and Strauss, 1967, for a thorough explication of the term *grounding*). While an experienced evaluator may be able to generate *a priori* hypotheses about the value positions in a given setting, in most cases the evaluator will want, at the very least, to check his or her hypotheses, if not generate them *de novo,* by close study of and interaction with the context itself, especially with the people who inhabit it. And field studies call, in general, not for scientific approaches supported by quantitative methods, as in experimental psychology, but for naturalistic approaches supported by qualitative methods, as in anthropology. (This is not to argue that quantitative methods have no place. See, for example, Gibbs, 1979, for a cogent argument for the complementarity of quantitative and qualitative methods even within a naturalistic paradigm.)

Determining Merit and Worth

Merit, an intrinsic property of an entity being evaluated, is estimated in one of two ways: (1) by determining the degree to which it conforms to certain standards upon which a group of experts agrees, which might be called absolute merit evaluation; or (2) by comparing the evaluand to other entities within the same class, which might be called comparative or relative merit evaluation. For example, in determining the merit of a professor, we might canvass a group of professors about what they take to be meritorious characteristics; whatever emerged would then be used as a basis for testing the performance of actual professors. Or, in the case of a language arts curriculum, we might canvass a group of language arts educators, writers, editors, and so on to determine what the characteristics of a meritorious curriculum are. A proposed curriculum could then be tested for merit against these criteria. Both these instances are examples of absolute merit evaluation. But we might in many practical cases be more interested in comparative judgments. If there are three professors to be considered for merit increments this year but there is enough money for only one increment, we may not care what each professor's absolute standing is in terms of scholarliness but rather wish to focus on their relative scholarliness in order to be able to decide among them. Or, in the case of curricula, we may not care what the absolute degree of integration of a curriculum is but only whether it is more or less integrated than another curriculum currently in use.

Worth, an extrinsic property of the evaluand, is determined by comparing the entity's impact or outcomes to some set of external requirements; for example, the results of a needs assessment or a context evaluation. Here, the entity's benefits are assessed by reference to a set of criteria. These criteria are not drawn from a professional group or a group of experts but from the variety of local stakeholders groups that are related to or affected by the entity. So while merit criteria may be relatively stable, criteria of worth are highly variable and depend on *which* group in *which* context is being assessed. Thus, the minority faculty in an institution may insist that newly recruited faculty should provide good minority role models, while the vice-president for research and the vice-president for administration may be much more concerned about the ability of new faculty to attract outside grants. Or the NAACP in a local community may be much more concerned that a curriculum be free from cultural bias than are the teachers, who may instead focus on the curriculum's appropriateness to the learning levels of their students and on their own ability to teach the new curriculum.

There is of course no guarantee that any statement of criteria of worth made by a group represents its actual operating position. In a discussion of merit versus value (worth) as it relates to problems of faculty evaluation in a university, Scriven (1978) notes that four different kinds of value (worth) criteria emerge:

- Alleged or rhetorical values: the value system to which an institution publicly subscribes. For example, "teaching is very important at Berkeley—we never take personnel action without evidence about teaching" (p. 23).
- Actual or true values: the values that may be deduced from the institution's actual practices. "*Solid* evidence of *first-rate* research is required; only *weak* evidence of *minimal* teaching performance is required" (p. 23).
- Interests of the institution: the "set of factors the promotion of which would be actually valuable for—beneficial to the interests or welfare of—the institution (a really massive commitment to improving undergraduate education to the point of hiring (promoting, tenuring) for teaching talent, with research ignored, the use of a serious process of evaluation for teaching, and so on)" (p. 23).
- Ideal values: the normative value system that the institution *should* have. "There is the possibility that the morally, legally,

socially, and/or educationally *correct* set of (personnel) values for Berkeley *is* the research set" (p. 23).

We would argue that, in general, the evaluator should avoid being taken in by alleged or rhetorical values, should study practices to isolate the actual or true values, should determine insofar as he can what is in the interest of the institution or reference group that holds those values and convey that information to them, and, finally, should work out a normative set of values for the situation and compare the actual or true values to it. The latter step may not be possible in many situations because reference to "ideal" values immediately raises the question, "Ideal for whom, or in what sense?" Answering this question may well be beyond the scope of the typical evaluation.

Relationship of Merit and Worth

Merit considerations may figure in assessments of worth in three different ways.

First, merit and worth may be treated as synonymous. Scriven (1978) apparently believes this to be the case at Berkeley for personnel decisions; thus, both promotion and tenure at that institution seem to be dependent upon assessments of research and scholarly productivity. Many institutions make this definition by default when, in their faculty handbooks, they treat promotion and tenure decisions as equivalent and pose the same criteria (usually teaching, research, and service) for both. Merit and worth are also defined as equivalent by default in many dissemination programs for federally funded innovations, for it seems to be assumed that a meritorious innovation can be warranted for general use in the schools (recall, for example, the "proven products list" of the Office of Education or consider the Joint Dissemination Review Panel's (JDRP) more recent effort to certify innovations that have been evaluated positively).* In either case, the

*Note that the National Diffusion Network, also federally supported, encourages local school systems to look at JDRP approved innovations that appear to be responsive to some locally identified need and then make necessary adaptations (perhaps involving the developer to do so). This posture is more consistent with that advocated here—it is as though an otherwise meritorious innovation is made more worthy through specific adaptations.

attempt to equate worth with merit is a mistake; the distinction is worth preserving.

Second, merit and worth may be treated as independent. In a tenure case, for example, it might be argued that benefits derived from the presence of a certain faculty member (as a role model for a minority group, say) are so powerful that it does not matter what his merit is. In the earliest days of affirmative action, many universities took just this posture. Or a local school system, anxious to do something that would demonstrate its commitment to change, might well "jump on the bandwagon" regardless of the merit of the innovation in question. Obviously the long-range negative effects of such postures are serious; no institution or reference group can long take such a position and survive.

It is also possible to define merit as independent of worth. University faculty members may stretch their definition of a position in such a way that institutional benefits are overlooked for the sake of getting "a big-name scholar." Similarly, the worth of an innovation in a local setting may be downgraded simply because the proposed innovative curriculum has "gotten such good grades in national evaluations."

As Scriven (1978) suggests, standards of merit drive out standards of worth in some situations, while in other cases standards of worth drive out standards of merit. Neither situation is desirable.

Third, worth may be treated as dependent upon some minimal level of merit, among other things. Here, other considerations of worth are automatically irrelevant if the evaluand does not achieve the minimal level of merit specified. Thus, a professor who was not minimally meritorious (as demonstrated, say, by the fact that he had received promotions) would not be considered for tenure regardless of what other benefits might accrue to the institution by virtue of his presence. But minimal merit would not be enough; well-defined benefits would also have to be demonstrated to lead to a positive tenure decision. In the case of a curriculum, local adoption would not be made of a program that was not minimally meritorious, but adoption would also not occur unless other benefits could be demonstrated.

It is also the case that decisions about merit are not usually made without simultaneous consideration of worth. No university is likely to hire a professor simply on merit; some possibility that this professor could serve certain university purposes must also exist. And no one would undertake to develop a curriculum, no matter what its promise on merit, unless he had reason to believe that the curriculum would be useful in some setting.

The methodological problem for the evaluator in this more typical (and, we believe, more rational) real-world case is not to become confused about the separate components that go into "balanced" judgments simply because these components are related. While merit decisions reinforce decisions of worth, and vice versa, they are separate decisions, made on separate criteria, and require different methodological approaches.

Relation to Formative and Summative Evaluation

The relation of merit and worth to the concepts of formative and summative evaluation (Scriven, 1967) is complex. It is easy to be misled into believing that merit evaluations are formative and worth evaluations are summative. The aim of formative evaluation is refinement and improvement, which makes one think of the intrinsic aspects of entities being evaluated. The aim of summative evaluation is to determine impact or outcomes, which makes one think of contexts in which such impacts or outcomes may be noted. But in fact the dimensions of merit/worth and of formative/summative are orthogonal; evaluations of merit can be either formative or summative just as can evaluations of worth.

Consider, by way of illustration, the case of an innovative program or curriculum that is to be developed by a national team and is then to be considered for adoption in a local setting—a quite common situation. Evaluations that seek to establish the merit of such an innovative program or curriculum might properly be termed developmental evaluations; that is, evaluations occurring during the process of development that seek to improve or refine the evaluand to its optimal state as an instance of its kind. Evaluations that seek to establish the worth of such an entity may be thought of as adoptive evaluations; that is, evaluations occurring after a completed entity formatively evaluated for merit is available. These evaluations relate to the use of the evaluand in some concrete situation. Both developmental and adoptive evaluations may be carried out for either summative or formative purposes; four types are determined by crossing the merit/worth and formative/summative dimensions. We can identify and analyze these four types (see Table 2) in terms of their purposes, their audiences, and the sources from which judgmental standards are drawn:

Table 2. Relationship of Merit/Worth to the Formative/Summative Distinction: A Curriculum Example

| Type of Evaluation | Evaluation seeks to establish | |
	Merit (Developmental Evaluation)	Worth (Adoptive Evaluation)
Formative	Intent: modify and improve design. Audience: entity development team. Source of Standards: panel of substantive experts.	Intent: fit entity to local context. Audience: local adaptation team. Source of Standards: assessment of local context and values.
Summative	Intent: critique, certify, and warrant entity. Audience: professional peers; potential adopters. Source of Standards: panel of substantive experts.	Intent: certify and warrant entity for local use. Audience: local decision makers. Source of Standards: local needs assessment.

The purpose of formative developmental (or merit) evaluations is to modify and improve the design of an innovative program or curriculum while it is still under development. The audience for such an evaluation might be the members of a developmental team, since they are the agents who can act on the evaluation information to make whatever changes are indicated. The sources of standards might be panels of professional peers or other expert groups, who have reason to be well acquainted with the characteristics of meritorious innovations of that type. While such groups will not agree on every detail, they are competent to specify what shall be taken into account in determining merit. Standards are elicited from these sources by methods such as interviews or task-force deliberations and, if properly grounded, through use of questionnaires or Delphi technique.

The purpose of summative developmental (or merit) evaluations is to critique a completed entity in terms of professional or expert standards so as to be able to certify and warrant merit. The primary audience for this evaluation is the group of potential adopters who need to be reassured about merit before they can reasonably consider the worth of the innovative program or curriculum in their own contexts. The source of standards continues to be panels of professional experts, from whom standards are elicited by the same means as in the case of formative merit evaluations.

The purpose of formative adoptive (or worth) evaluations is to fit or adapt the program or curriculum to a local context or situation. As we have noted, there will always be local contextual differences, and no innovation could hope to fit all contexts. What is required is a local assessment of context and values so that the fit of the innovation can be determined. Refinements, adjustments, and other adaptations will be called for to optimize the fit; a local adaptation team analogous to the original development team will be required. This local adaptation team is the proper audience for formative adoptive evaluation information, and the local assessment of context and values (which might be construed as a needs assessment) becomes the source for standards. Standards are elicited using normal methods for needs assessment.

The purpose of summative adoptive (or worth) evaluation is to certify or warrant the adapted program or curriculum for permanent local use. The audience for this evaluation is that group of local decision makers (probably some from each of the audiences) who will make or shape the final decision about whether to adopt the innovation. This group will vary widely in composition and clarity from place to place, depending upon how decisions happen to be made in each locale. The source of standards for this evaluation is a local needs assessment, for unless the innovative program or curriculum meets local needs there can be no justification for adopting it. Again, normal needs assessment methods are employed.

This example focuses on the adoption of an innovative program or curriculum, but the distinctions that are illustrated by it apply whenever merit and worth are at issue. In the case of a university professor, as a further example, one can imagine a formative merit evaluation in which the professor is himself the audience, the purpose is to provide feedback that will help him to improve in the sense of becoming more meritorious, and the standards are the professional standards of his own peer group. Many universities now provide for annual reviews, sometimes in connection with awarding salary increments, that serve this function. The summative merit review occurs when the professor is formally considered for promotion in rank. Summative worth reviews are made when the professor is considered for tenure, and formative worth reviews can also be regularly scheduled (although they usually are *not*) to provide the professor feedback with respect to the university's criteria of worth (for example, role modeling, entrepreneurship, or carrying a fair teaching load). Similar examples could be provided in virtually every evaluation situation.

The distinction between merit and worth is not only conceptually intriguing but operationally heuristic. It has particular implications, we believe, for evaluation methodology. We have seen that the practice of responsive evaluation in and of itself requires extensive field contact with stakeholding audiences; that fact alone is sufficient to cause evaluators seriously interested in being responsive to seek some other methodology than the conventional (and, we believe, sterile) experimental, pre-post control-group approach. But the distinctions between worth and merit make it plain that evaluations of worth, at least, require extensive immersion in the context of the evaluand, for the values, standards, and conditions under which worth is determined can be found only there.

Fortunately an appropriate methodology exists, one rooted solidly in naturalistic epistemology and drawing its major tactics from among qualitative techniques. It is the purpose of the next three chapters to explicate this methodology.

Chapter 4

Advantages
of Naturalistic
Methods

How does one get at truth? This basic question has engaged epistemologists for many centuries, but it remains unresolved. A variety of competitors has emerged to claim the distinction of being *the* method; these competitors have often been termed *paradigms* (models, prototypes). Thus we may note:

- A logical paradigm, relying on analysis as a fundamental technique, which views truth as demonstrable; that is, truth is whatever can be demonstrated to be consistent with the basic axioms and definitions of the system, as a geometry theorem is "proved" by showing it to follow logically from other proved theorems and, ultimately, from the basic axioms and definitions. Mathematics is a typical instance.

Table 3. Some Paradigms for Getting at Truth

Paradigm	Exemplars	Fundamental Techniques	View of Truth (Truth is . . .)
Logical	Mathematics, philosophy, computer science, language, linguistics, literary science, accounting.	Analysis	Demonstrable
Scientific	Physics, chemistry, geology, botany, biology, zoology, physiology.	Experimentation	Confirmable
Naturalistic	Ethnography, history, political science, counseling, social work.	Field study	Ineluctable
Judgmental	Judging art forms (painting, music, literature, film); substances (wine, cheese, tobacco); performances (diving, gymnastics, dance); or objects (architecture, horticulture).	Sensing (seeing, feeling, tasting)	Recognizable
Adversarial	Law, congressional hearings, investigative journalism.	Cross-examination; triangulation	Emergent (on balance)
Modus operandi	Medical diagnosis, forensic pathology, troubleshooting checklist.	Sequential test	Trackable
Demographic	Economics, demography, geography.	Indicators	Macroscopically determinable

- A scientific paradigm, relying on experimentation as a fundamental technique, which views truth as confirmable; that is, truth is an hypothesis that has been confirmed by an actual experiment. The hypotheses are derived by deduction from an *a priori* theory; when enough hypotheses deriving from a particular theory have been verified, the theory itself is believed to have validity. Physics is a typical instance.
- A naturalistic paradigm, relying on field study as a fundamental technique, which views truth as ineluctable, that is, as ultimately inescapable. Sufficient immersion in and experience with a phenomenological field yields inevitable conclusions about what is important, dynamic, and pervasive in that field. Ethnography is a typical instance.
- A judgmental paradigm, relying on sensing as a fundamental technique, which views truth as recognizable; that is, as patent to persons of appropriate background and competence. The judging of wine or of an athletic performance is a typical instance.
- An adversarial paradigm, relying on cross-examination and triangulation as fundamental techniques, which views truth as emergent, that is, as resulting from an appropriate balancing of the cases made by a protagonist and an antagonist. The hearing of a trial before a jury is a typical instance.
- A *modus operandi* paradigm, relying on sequential tests as a fundamental technique, which views truth as trackable, that is, as determinable by tracking the "characteristic causal chain" of an event. Forensic pathology and television troubleshooting are typical instances.
- A demographic paradigm, relying on indicators as a fundamental technique, which views truth as macroscopically determinable, that is, as determinable through the study of indicators that transcend the more or less random behavior of individual persons, agencies, or institutions. Economics is a typical instance.

Which of these paradigms provides the best guidance for the conduct of an inquiry or evaluation? There is of course no definitive answer to that question, but two paradigms have emerged as the most widely used: the scientific and the naturalistic. The former has been the traditional method of the "hard" sciences and the life sciences; it has been widely adopted and emulated in the social-behavioral sciences as well. It is so commonly believed to be "the" method that it has acquired a patina of orthodoxy. The latter is an emergent paradigm that has begun seriously to challenge that orthodoxy. It is our position that the naturalistic paradigm is the more useful for all social-behavioral inquiry and certainly for responsive naturalistic evaluation. In any case, the choice between paradigms in any inquiry or evaluation ought to be made on the basis of the best fit between the assumptions and postures of a paradigm and the phenomenon being studied or evaluated.

Basic Assumptions of the Paradigms

It is a matter of some difficulty to tease out the assumptions underlying any conceptualization, and epistemological paradigms represent a particularly difficult case. Epistemologists regularly analyze one another's work, but the definitive analysis of the assumptions underlying *any* inquiry paradigm remains to be made. Accordingly the following discussion touches only a few critical high spots. It is clearly simplistic and inadequate, and its imputations are disputable. But given these *caveats,* it is still instructive to examine a few of the more salient assumptions made by proponents of each school.

Assumptions About Reality. The scientific inquirer sees the world as a series of real entities and steady processes, all of which are fragmentable into series of independent subsystems. The fragments are often called "variables"; these variables, and particularly their relationships, form the focus for disciplined inquiry. In any inquiry, certain variables and their relationships are of particular interest; the relationships can be expressed (as hypotheses) in functional form, for example, $y = f(x)$, in which x is the independent variable (the variable to be manipulated) and y is the dependent variable (the variable on which the effect of the manipulation of x is to be determined). Of course there are many other variables that can mask or simulate the independent or dependent variables, and the *confounding* effects of these other variables must be eliminated or controlled. Scientific inquiry discovers variables and describes their relationships, primarily for purposes of prediction and control. Thus, scientific inquirers tend to view the

Table 4. Basic Assumptions of the Scientific and Naturalistic Paradigms

	Paradigm	
Assumptions about	*Scientific*	*Naturalistic*
Reality	Singular, convergent fragmentable.	Multiple, divergent, inter-related.
Inquirer/subject relationship	Independent.	Inter-related.
Nature of truth statements	Generalizations—nomothetic statements—focus on similarities.	Working hypotheses—idiographic statements—focus on differences.

phenomena with which they deal as existing in and discoverable in the real world and as fragmentable into discrete or independent subsystems that can be dealt with a few variables at a time, so that the inquirer can converge upon the truth (without quotation marks).

Naturalistic inquirers make virtually the opposite assumptions. They focus upon the multiple realities that, like the layers of an onion, nest within or complement one another. Each layer provides a different perspective of reality, and none can be considered more "true" than any other. Phenomena do not converge into a single form, a single "truth," but diverge into many forms, multiple "truths." Moreover, the layers cannot be described or understood in terms of separate independent and dependent variables; rather, they are intricately interrelated to form a pattern of "truth." It is these patterns that must be searched out, less for the sake of prediction and control than for the sake of *verstehen* or understanding. The naturalistic inquirer tends to view the phenomena with which he deals as more likely to diverge than to converge as they are more fully explored.

Assumptions About the Inquirer-Subject Relationship. The scientific paradigm assumes that the inquirer will have no effect on the phenomenon being studied and, equally important, that the phenomenon will have no effect on the inquirer. This assumption is somewhat more problematic than the scientific assumption about reality because investigators are human beings subject to all the usual human foibles and biases. Hence, while assumptions about reality are more or less taken for granted, assumptions about subject-object dualism must be established. The investigator must take steps to ensure that the assumption is satisfied. Nevertheless, the general belief is that given reasonable precautions—for example, laboratory controls or adequate safeguards against the reactivity of subject to inquirer (see Campbell and Stanley, 1963; Webb and others, 1966)—it is possible for the inquirer to keep a suitable "distance" between himself and the phenomenon.

The naturalistic paradigm, conversely, assumes that all phenomena are characterized by interactivity. While certain "safeguards" may reduce that interactivity to its minimum, a large amount nevertheless remains. It is fruitless to pretend that it is not there; a more intelligent approach requires understanding the possible influence of interactivity and taking it into account. This stance does not merely involve a trade-off of less "objective" data for the sake of more understanding. *No* data can be objective in that sense. What is important is to determine the perceptions of the "data collector" (very often a human investigator) and the effect of those perceptions on the developing information.

Assumptions About the Nature of "Truth" Statements. The aim of science is often asserted to be the production of generalizations—statements of "enduring truth value" that are essentially unchanged from context to context. The scientific inquirer, who assumes the singular nature of reality and takes his data to be essentially uninfluenced by any interaction between inquirer and phenomenon, believes that the production of generalizations is entirely feasible. The focus of scientific inquiry tends to be on similarities among exemplars of the phenomenon, since it is their common properties that lend themselves to generalization. Scientific inquiry thus leads to the development of a nomothetic knowledge base, that is, one focusing on the development of general laws.

The naturalistic inquirer, given his view of multiple realities and the complex interactions that take place between an inquirer and the "objects" of an inquiry, tends to eschew generalizations in favor of "thick descriptions" (Geertz, 1973) and "working hypotheses" (Cronbach, 1975). Differences rather than similarities characterize different contexts; if one derives descriptions or interpretations of one situation and wishes to know the extent to which they hold in a second situation, it is necessary to have a great deal of information about both (that is, thick descriptions of each) to determine whether a sufficient basis for transfer exists. The focus of naturalistic inquiry is, moreover, as often on differences as on similarities; indeed, subtle differences are sometimes felt to be more important than gross similarities. Naturalistic inquiry thus leads to the development of an idiographic knowledge base, that is, one focusing on the understanding of particular events (cases). (See Marceil, 1977, for a recent discussion of the differences between nomothetic and idiographic disciplines.)

Which of these sets of assumptions—the scientific or the naturalistic—best fits the phenomenology that is encountered in social-behavioral inquiry, of which evaluation is a subtype? Let us consider the assumptions one at a time:

Views of Reality. For the physicist or chemist, the scientific view of reality is very appropriate indeed. It would be absurd to deny the self-evident reality of physical objects and forces, and the reactions of chemicals in test tubes speak for themselves. The basic terms of physics—force, mass, time, velocity, and so on—well demonstrate the utility of dividing the world into variables, and there seems to be little doubt that inquiry can converge upon these variables and their relationships in a meaningful way. But for the social-behavioral inquirer, the naturalistic assumptions about reality seem to offer a better "fit." Virtually all the phenomena with which the social-behavioral inquirer deals exist in the minds of people—what they take to be problems, their perceptions of one another and of the meaning of their environments, the extent to which they value anything, and so on. To suggest that there is some "real" thing on which social-behavioral inquiry could converge and that could be described in terms of a few salient variables, themselves noninteractive with the inquirer, seems quite simplistic. Social reality is, experientially, not singular, convergent, or fragmentable.

Subject-Object Dualism. That there is no interaction between investigator and investigated object is a reasonable assumption in virtually all areas of physical science. Chemicals react in a test tube regardless of who put them there or why, and in precisely the same manner that they would interact in the natural world. There are no known instances in which force does *not* equal mass times acceleration. But the assumption becomes suspect even in the physical sciences when the investigation deals with subatomic particles; the Heisenberg uncertainty principle warns that the act of measuring disturbs the entity measured, causing a different action than would have occurred without the measurement. But for many practical purposes such reactive phenomena in the physical world can be ignored because their influence is so slight, just as one can ignore the effect of the curvature of the earth in estimating the mileage from Los Angeles to Miami.

But whatever the actual state of affairs may be as far as the physical world is concerned, it is impossible to believe that investigations that involve people can occur without some kind of interaction taking place. Of course, the reactivity of subjects to an investigator is a well-known phenomenon. Elaborate subterfuges are sometimes used to keep the subject from knowing that he is involved in an inquiry just so that reactivity will not occur. Unobtrusive measures, described by Webb and others (1966) as particularly useful in overcoming reactivity, are now widely used by investigators.

Less recognized but equally influential is the reactivity of the investigator to the subjects and/or the inquiry situation. When the investigator is himself the data collection instrument, as in an interview or observational situation, the possible effects are obvious, ranging from fatigue to selective perception occasioned by biases or prejudices. So for example, females may be systematically scored as less aggressive than males simply because the investigator tends to view females as the "gentler" sex in conformity with the social stereotype. But even when the investigator interposes some more "objective" instrument between himself and the subjects, for example, a questionnaire, investigator-subject interactivity may occur. The questions asked are, after all, posed by the investigator in accordance with some perspective, and that perspective includes all the biases and prejudices that normally characterize him. Subjects may not interpret the items as the investigator intended, and the investigator, in turn, may misinterpret their responses. There is no guarantee that when information is collected from human subjects, by whatever method, that there will not be interaction between those subjects and the minds that determined what information to collect and how to collect it (Krathwohl, 1980).

Nor is all such subject-investigator interaction bad. One of the virtues of an open-ended interview, for example, is that the investigator need not return to ground zero at the beginning of each successive interview; he will have learned something from each that can be verified or perhaps even expanded in subsequent interviews. In this case the interaction can be characterized as a learning experience for the investigator, as a result of which successive stages of the inquiry become both more pointed and more sophisticated. Indeed, it is doubtful whether an investigator would want to lose all potential for interaction with his subjects, even if he could. To do so would be to trade away the potential for this successive learning.

Generalizability. While the concept of generalizability is appealing, it is proving to be a Holy Grail. Cronbach (1975) has suggested that generalizations decay over time and exhibit a half-life, very much like radioactive substances. He cites the following examples drawn from physical, biological, and behavioral sciences:

- The failure of DDT to control mosquitos as genetic transformations have made them resistant to that pesticide.
- The shifting of stars in their courses so as to render star maps obsolete.
- The shifting in the value of the gravitational constant, so that while s will continue to equal gt^2, the actual distances covered by falling bodies will differ.
- The suggestion by Ghiselli that the superiority of distributed over massed practice may not remain valid from one generation to another.
- Atkinson's proposition that a relation between personality variables describes only the "modal" personality at a particular time in history.
- Changes in the construct validity of the F scale.
- Bronfenbrenner's conclusion that class differences in parenting observed in the 1950s were just the reverse of those in 1930.

Cronbach makes the point that after a time *every* generalization is less science than it is history.

This line of reasoning should make us wary of generalizations in every field but especially in behavioral science areas. For what can a generalization be except an assertion that is context free? To be sure, generalizations can be hedged about with cautions and even with specific exclusions, but they are intended to be statements that have general meaning, free from situational constraints. $F = ma$, Newton's law that asserts that force equals mass times acceleration, is believed to be true everywhere, as is, presumably, the assertion that learning is subject to the recentness, frequency, and intensity of stimulation. It would be hard to find an exception to the physical law (although Cronbach's analysis would lead us to believe that, sooner or later, such exceptions will exist), but exceptions to the behavioral law abound. Surely one could not account for the lack of learning in many inner-city classrooms, for example, on the grounds that there was no recent, frequent, or intense stimulation to learn. *It is virtually impossible to imagine any human behavior that is not heavily mediated by the context in which it occurs.* One can easily conclude that generalizations that are intended to be context free will have little that is useful to say about human behavior.

It is not the intent of the authors to "demolish" the scientific paradigm as unworkable. What we have tried to say so far is that, first, there is no guaranteed path to ascertaining truth. There are instead a number of competing paradigms that describe different methods for determining "truth," and no one of these is, on its face, intrinsically superior to any other. There is no way to prove that one paradigm is superior to others.

Second, two paradigms for dealing with "truth" have emerged as major competitors. These are the scientific paradigm, based on a logical positivist epistemology, and the naturalistic paradigm, based on a phenomenological epistemology. These two paradigms differ on a number of basic assumptions, of which three have been singled out for attention here: the nature of reality, subject-object dualism, and the nature of truth statements. When an investigator begins the study of some problem (or area of problems, or discipline), he should determine as well as he can which set of assumptions best fits the phenomena to be studied.

Third, while the scientific assumptions have proved to be both valid and heuristic within the so-called "hard" sciences and the biological or life sciences, they can be seriously called into question with respect to the behavioral sciences. Thus, the behavioral scientist works with phenomena that exist largely in the minds of people or that are strongly mediated by what is in the minds of people, for example, their values. An assumption of multiple realities is simply more credible than that of a single reality. Moreover, it is impossible to believe, on the basis of experience, that an investigator can keep an objective distance when the objects of his investigation are people, and it might not be desirable to do so even if one could. Finally, it is difficult to imagine what a context-free generalization would be like with respect to human behaviors, which are so strongly contextually mediated.

On balance, then, the naturalistic paradigm is, with some exceptions, the method of choice when dealing with human behaviors, however much utility the scientific paradigm may have in other inquiry areas.

Derivative Postures of the Paradigms

The assumptions basic to the paradigms are barely visible in the day-to-day conduct of inquirers; rather, they reflect themselves in certain derivative elements. Moreover, each of these paradigms has acquired certain postures that cannot be deduced from the basic assumptions themselves or justified by reference to them. These postures have nevertheless become strongly associated with the paradigms.

In her insightful book *My Mother, My Self,* Nancy Friday (1978), in showing how characteristics of mothers are passed on to daughters, cites the following "classical example of mother-daughter role modeling":

> Peggy is cooking her first big meal for her parents since her marriage—a glorious Virginia ham. Standing up to carve, her new husband asks Peggy why she sliced off three or four inches from the shank end before baking. Peggy looks surprised. "Mother always does it that way."
>
> Everyone at the table looks at Peggy's mother. "That's how my mother did it too," she says, a bit puzzled. "Doesn't everyone?"
>
> Peggy phones her grandmother the next day, and asks why, in their family, has the shank end al-

ways been cut off before baking. "I've always done it that way," grandmother says, "because that is how my mother did it."

It happens that four generations of women are still alive in this family. A call is put in to great-grandmother, and the mystery is solved. Once when her daughter—Peggy's grandmother—was a little girl and learning to cook, they were baking a large ham. The family roasting pan was small, and so the shank end had been cut off to make it fit.

Four generations of women, each one ignoring present reality, each one conforming, unquestioningly, to a circumstance that was no longer relevant; each one certain in her mind "that's how you do it" because she had seen her mother do it that way. An amusing story, an illustration of how we incorporate those parts of mother we choose to imitate—like her skill in cooking—but right along with them we also take in less rational and unexamined parts all unaware [p. 430].

Similarly, inquiry procedures that students have learned from their academic mentors are used in an unexamined way. Serendipities become mandates; ways of proceeding whose rationale is buried in antiquity and whose circumstances no longer obtain are nevertheless believed to be "the way that one does things." An orthodoxy is born.

In this section we discuss certain characteristics of both scientific and naturalistic paradigms that are either secondarily derivative from the assumptions noted earlier or that have simply sprung up as accompaniments to these approaches. These characteristics are not essential to the paradigms but are nevertheless closely associated with them. A summary of these characteristics (here called "postures") is given in Table 5; we begin with more general or pervasive characteristics:

Preferred Techniques. Both quantitative and qualitative techniques can be used in support of either the scientific or naturalistic paradigms. It would surely be a gross error to equate quantitative methods with the scientific paradigm and qualitative methods with the naturalistic paradigm. Yet there is a strong relationship in that direction in practice; that is, naturalistic inquirers

Table 5. Derivative Postures of the Scientific and Naturalistic Paradigms

Postures about	Paradigm	
	Scientific	Naturalistic
General Characteristics		
Preferred techniques	Quantitative	Qualitative
Quality criterion	Rigor	Relevance
Source of theory	*A priori*	Grounded
Questions of causality	Can *x* cause *y*?	Does *x* cause *y* in a natural setting?
Knowledge types used	Propositional	Propositional and tacit
Stance	Reductionist	Expansionist
Purpose	Verification	Discovery
Methodological Characteristics		
Instrument	Paper-and-pencil or physical device	Inquirer (often)
Timing of the specification of data collection and analysis rules	Before inquiry	During and after inquiry
Design	Preordinate	Emergent
Style	Intervention	Selection
Setting	Laboratory	Nature
Treatment	Stable	Variable
Analytic units	Variables	Patterns
Contextual elements	Control	Invited interference

lean most heavily on qualitative methods, while scientific inquirers lean most heavily on quantitative methods. Perhaps it is the emphasis in the scientific paradigm on control and verification (and the opposite emphasis in the naturalistic paradigm) that accounts for this tendency: to verify something implies that there is something to be verified. If there is in fact something to be verified, it is likely that that entity can be expressed in the form of a specific hypothesis or question that lends itself to precise formulation. The more precisely a proposition can be formulated *a priori,* the easier it is to reduce it to a system of variables that lends itself to measurement and statistical manipulation. But when concepts or characteristics are yet to be discovered, it is not possible to state them precisely beforehand, and measurement is impossible, since an entity must be detected before its size can be assessed. Whatever the reason, there is a strong tendency for the naturalistic inquirer to lean most heavily on qualitative methods. These methods will therefore be the focus for the rest of this book. The reader should note, however, that we do not take an antiquantitative position; indeed, we urge the use of quantitative techniques whenever they seem appropriate to the inquiry being conducted.

Quality Criterion. In determining what constitutes "good" inquiry, the scientific inquirer relies almost exclusively on criteria of rigor, that is, on internal and external validity, reliability, and objectivity. As Bronfenbrenner (1977) has said of the state of research in developmental psychology: "To corrupt a contemporary metaphor, we risk being caught between a rock and a *soft* place. The rock is *rigor,* and the soft place is *relevance.* . . . The emphasis on rigor has led to experiments that are elegantly designed but often limited in scope. This limitation derives from the fact that many of these experiments involve situations that are unfamiliar, artificial, and short-lived and that call for unusual settings that are difficult to generalize to other settings. From this perspective, it can be said that much of contemporary developmental psychology is *the science of the strange behavior of children in strange situations with strange adults for the briefest possible periods of time*" (p. 513).

Gibbs (1979) states the problem more directly:

> The most popular reformist plea in contemporary psychological research is the call for ecologically oriented inquiry. . . . The general claim of the ecological reformers is that empirical psychologists have become so enamored of laboratory precision that they have lost their sense of the human problem, that generalization to the authentic significance of the person in the real environment has been sacrificed to the quest for certainty in our knowledge.
>
> Certainty and authenticity (or more narrowly, internal and external validity) represent traditional polar extremes of scientific inquiry. In the history of psychology, the more popular extreme has been the pursuit of certainty to the detriment of authenticity. Critics have bewailed the lopsided prevalence of method over meaning, . . . manipulation over understanding, . . . rigor over sensitivity to human subtlety, and narrow quantification over broad qualitative in-

quiry. Equally problematic at the other extreme are personalistic, . . . phenomenological, existential, and humanistic approaches, in which the purism of authenticity tends to undermine the objectivity and communicability of the inquiry. Consistent with personalistic approaches, some are skeptical of the very possibility of achieving a nomothetic science of human behavior [pp. 127-128].

There is nothing intrinsic to the scientific or naturalistic paradigms that forces scientific inquirers to eschew criteria of relevance or naturalistic inquirers to eschew criteria of rigor. We certainly do *not* want to minimize the importance of rigor; indeed, we devote much of Chapter Five to a discussion of how rigor can be achieved in naturalistic inquiry. But in the struggle between rigor and relevance in the field of evaluation, relevance has run a distant second.

Source of Theory. Much of social-behavioral inquiry has been directed to the verification of hypotheses generated from *a priori* theory. As Glaser and Strauss (1967) point out with respect to sociology, "Verification of theory is the keynote of current sociology. Some three decades ago, it was felt that we had plenty of theories but few confirmations of them—a position made very feasible by the greatly increased sophistication of quantitative methods. As this shift in emphasis took hold, the discovery of new theories became slighted and, at some universities, virtually neglected. Those who still wished to generate theory had to brook the negative, sometimes punitive, attitudes of their colleagues or professors" (p. 10).

But the point to be made here is much broader than simply a lament that the development of new theory has been somehow neglected. It is rather a question of how those theories are generated. Most theories in the social-behavioral sciences are logical and deductive in nature—on the pattern of theories in the physical sciences. A theory is somehow spun out and various deductions are made from it—deductions that can then be verified in the "real" world. As these deductions (hypotheses) are in fact verified, more and more credence can be placed in the theory; that is, the theory takes its validity from the number of the deductions derived from it that can be "proved" (not disconfirmed) in an actual test.

The testing of theory is important in any discipline. But

theory generated by logical deduction from *a priori* assumptions
can be verified, initially at least, only by serendipitous correspondence (isomorphism) with the real world, depending upon the
extent to which the theory's basic assumptions are in fact valid. A
more useful approach is to derive the theory not from *a priori*
reasoning but by grounding it in real-world data from the start.
The methods for "discovering" such grounded theory are the core
of the Glaser and Strauss (1967) book already cited; they devote
themselves to the "important enterprise of how the discovery of
theory from data—systematically obtained and analyzed in social
research—can be furthered. We believe that the discovery of theory
from data—which we call grounded theory—is a major task confronting sociology today, for, as we shall try to show, such a
theory fits empirical situations, and is understandable to sociologists and laymen alike. Most important, it works—provides us
with relevant predictions, explanations, interpretations, and applications" (p. 1).

We agree with Glaser and Strauss that grounded theories
meet two criteria—"fit" to empirical situations and meaningful
communication with both professionals and laymen—better than
do *a priori* theories, while also serving all the usual functions of
theory: prediction, explanation, and the like. While *a priori* theory
cannot be dismissed (Einstein's formulations were, after all, largely
based on what he liked to call "mental experiments"), grounded
theory offers a more solid and reliable base, particularly when
used in connection with responsive evaluation models that endeavor to deal with audiences in their own terms. Of course, even
grounded theories become *a priori* theories with each new inquiry
in which they are used.

Questions of Causality. Inquiry is often directed toward determining cause-effect relationships. Answers to cause-effect questions are important whether one is interested in prediction and
control, on the one hand, or *verstehen* on the other. But inquirers
using one or the other of the paradigms deal with questions of
causality in different ways. Scientific inquirers typically pose the
question in the form, Can x cause y?, and demonstrate in the laboratory that y can indeed be caused by x. But naturalistic inquirers
are less interested in what can be made to happen in a contrived
situation than in what *does* happen in a natural setting. Barker

(1965) has provided an interesting example of the differences in these approaches:

> Some years ago, when I was a student of Kurt Lewin, he and Tamara Dembo and I carried out some experiments on frustration. The findings of these experiments have been verified by others, and they have become a part of the literature of scientific psychology. The experiments provided basic information about the consequences for children of frustration, as defined in the experiments, and about the processes that produce these consequences. Time passed. In due course *I* had a student, and he undertook to study frustration. So far, so good. My student, Clifford L. Fawl, did not replicate the earlier study; he did not *contrive* frustration for his subjects; he pioneered, and extended the investigation from children *in vitro,* so to speak, to children *in situ.* He searched our specimen records of children's everyday behavior for instances of this allegedly important phenomenon without psychologists as operators. Here are the words of his report:
>
> > The results . . . were surprising in two respects. First, even with a liberal interpretation of frustration, fewer incidents were detected than we expected. . . . Second, . . . meaningful relationships could not be found between frustration . . . and consequent behavior such as . . . aggression . . . and other theoretically meaningful manifestations.
> >
> > In other words, frustration was rare in the children's days, and when it did occur it did not have the behavioral consequences observed in the laboratory. It appears that the earlier experiments simulated frustration very well as we defined it and prescribed it for our subjects (in accordance with our theories); but the experiments did not simulate frustration as life prescribes it for our children [p. 5].

Answers to the questions of whether *x* can cause *y* and whether *x* does cause *y* in a natural setting both have utility. Even "unnatural" events can have enormous significance for the development of theory—to know what is possible is sometimes just as important as to know what is likely or normal. Yet it does seem to be the case that current inquiry is heavily overloaded in the latter direction, especially so in dealing with the kinds of questions that normally confront evaluators, who are perforce dealing with the real world. Hence we place particular emphasis on real-world rather than laboratory questions.

Knowledge Types Used. Polanyi (1966) has drawn the distinction between propositional knowledge, that is, knowledge that can be stated in language form, and tacit knowledge, that is, intuitions, apprehensions, or feelings that cannot be stated in words but are somehow "known" by the subject. A useful analogy for understanding the distinctions between these two forms of knowledge can be found in the difference between the denotations and connotations of a word. A denotation is the particular meaning of a symbol, the explicit meaning of a word. A connotation is a suggestion or implication associated with a word beyond its literal sense.

Scientific inquiry limits itself exclusively to propositional knowledge. Indeed, it is the essence of that method to state propositions explicitly in the form of hypotheses that are then tested to determine their validity. Theories consist of collections of such hypotheses. In contrast, naturalistic inquiry permits and encourages connotative or tacit knowledge to come into play, for the sake of both contributing to the formation of grounded theory and improving communication back to information sources in their own terms.

There is a good deal of virtue in insisting on explicit, unambiguous statements. But such a tendency can be overdone, resulting in the dismissal of what is thought to be "merely subjective" information. It is our belief that scientific inquirers have tended to err in that direction. Accordingly, we shall adopt an opposite emphasis.

Stance. Scientific inquirers take a reductionist stance; that is, they reduce the inquiry to a relatively small focus by imposing constraints both on conditions antecedent to the inquiry (for the sake of control) and on outputs. Thus the scientific inquirer begins with preformulated questions or hypotheses and seeks only that information that will answer those questions or test those hypotheses.

Naturalistic inquirers, however, take an expansionist stance. They seek a perspective that will lead to the description and understanding of phenomena as wholes or at least in ways that reflect their complexity. They enter the field and build outward from wherever the point of entry happens to be. Each step in the inquiry is based on the sum of insights gleaned from previous steps. Thus, scientific inquirers take a structured, focused, singular stance, while naturalistic inquirers take an open, exploratory, and complex stance.

There is virtue in both positions. We have already noted, however, the overemphasis among scientific inquirers on the study of hypotheses derived from *a priori* theory, to the virtual exclusion of grounded theory. Grounded theory cannot be derived without the openness that characterizes naturalistic inquiry. It is our position that a swing toward an expansionist posture is long overdue.

Purpose. Scientific inquirers, on the one hand, view the purpose of inquiry to be the verification of hypotheses specified *a priori*. Naturalists, on the other hand, focus on the discovery of elements or insights not yet included in existing theories.

Persons who seek a compromise between scientific and naturalistic approaches—a kind of conceptual ecumenicism—often argue that naturalistic emphases are appropriate at an early stage of inquiry into an area; at that point, ideas are few and knowledge is weak. Coming face-to-face with the world on its own terms is an excellent way of getting new ideas. But then, when some ideas have been formulated and related, allowing the rudiments of a theory to emerge, it is appropriate to shift to the scientific paradigm so that the implications of that theory can be fully tested. Such a view relegates naturalistic inquiry to second-class status, useful only when the field is "sloppy" and when some "mucking around" can be tolerated. But one needs to shift back into the more rigorous, objective mode that characterizes "true" science as soon as possible. Such a position simply fails to comprehend the fundamental differences between the two modes.

We do not wish to argue against the scientifically-oriented inquirer deciding to use naturalistic modes when that will help to keep his inquiry in better touch with reality, that is, to ground it. Nor do we wish to argue against the naturalistic inquirer from time to time falling back on scientific methods in order to test some hypotheses that have emerged from firmly grounded theory. We take the posture, however, that the differences between these modes are sufficiently great that they cannot merely be relegated to different stages of the inquiry process. Accordingly, we shall resist that temptation, while noting that if more scientific inquirers used naturalistic means to ground their theories and if more naturalistic inquirers used scientific means to verify their hypotheses, probably both would gain.

Turning now to an examination of the more specifically methodological characteristics of scientific and naturalistic inquiry (the second part of Table 5), we may note the following additional differences in postures:

Instrument. The scientific inquirer, probably in the belief that he himself is an imperfect, nonobjective instrument, prefers to develop extensions of himself for purposes of collecting data. Thus he is likely to want to develop a paper-and-pencil test or questionnaire or to use a physical device, for example, a polygraph. But the naturalistic inquirer is much more likely to depend on himself as instrument, perhaps because it is frequently impossible to specify with precision just what is to be assessed.

There is certainly no *a priori* reason to reject a human being as an instrument; individuals can be trained to become highly reliable and objective observers, interviewers, and so on. In fact, human beings as instruments possess at least one virtue lacking in all others—judgment, along with the flexibility to be able to use it. Paper-and-pencil instruments or physical devices, nevertheless, also have their advantages: standardization, uniformity, and what might be called "aggregatability." The inquirer is well advised, as always, to assess the situation and make judgments accordingly. Our position is that humans as instruments have been dramatically underemployed and probably ought to be used more often.

Timing of the Specification of Data Collection and Analysis Rules. Scientific inquirers can specify all rules for data collection and analysis in advance of the inquiry. They know the hypotheses to be tested and can develop instruments appropriate to the variables involved. The instruments will yield measures of known properties so that it is possible to detail ahead of time what sorts of analysis will be carried out. It is widely believed that the ability to develop such specifications before the fact also increases the objectivity of the inquiry, since the inquirer cannot be tempted to alter his specifications to conform to emergent tendencies in the data, and thereby perhaps improve the chances that his judgment (as expressed in the hypotheses) will be borne out.

Naturalistic inquirers, by contrast, are not permitted the luxury of *a priori* formulation. Their data accrue in the "rawest" possible fashion and must be unitized and categorized after the fact. And so, it is claimed, the subjectivity of the process makes the resulting data suspect. But the naturalistic analytic process is no less guided by rules than is the scientific. Steps can be taken to be sure that rules are unambiguously stated and systematically and uniformly applied. And these naturalistic techniques have the advantage that they can build on emergent insights. If there is a loss in rigor, there is an enormous gain in flexibility.

Since there has been an overemphasis on so-called objective and standardized instrumentation, we think that the use of judgment in data collection and analysis should now be encouraged, so that the formulation of data collection and analysis rules during and after the physical collection of the data is appropriate and often desirable.

Design. In scientific inquiries designs must be constructed preordinately, that is, before the fact. Moreover, once a design has been implemented, it is important that it not be altered in any way, since such an alteration would confound the variables and thus make a meaningful interpretation of findings impossible.

Within the naturalistic paradigm a design can be specified only incompletely in advance. To specify it in detail would be to place constraints on the inquiry that are antithetical to the stance and purpose of the naturalist. The design emerges as the investigation proceeds; moreover, it is in constant flux as new information is gained and new insights are achieved.

Thus, preordinate, fixed designs are the hallmark of scientific investigations while emergent, variable designs are identified with the naturalistic mode. We believe that both approaches have merit but that the emphasis on rigid, inflexible designs has been overwhelming. We therefore focus on emergent designs, reserving preordinate designs for those instances in which very specific hypotheses are available.

Style. There are two distinct styles for testing hypotheses.

Within the scientific paradigm the style has been primarily one of intervention; that is, the independent and dependent variables are isolated and the context is arranged so that these variables and only these variables can account for whatever findings emerge. Such situations, often called experimental but probably better termed contrived, have advantages, such as rigor, but also disadvantages, such as loss of relevance.

In contrast, naturalists depend on selection. They sift through a variety of naturally occurring events until they find those in which nature has arranged the experiment without benefit of man's intervention. In many areas of science—for example, astronomy, geology, and geography, which are often called nonlaboratory sciences—selection is the only possible way to proceed. But scientists in these areas are nevertheless able to make substantial progress. The naturalist feels that noninterventionist approaches are, on balance, best; what they lack in rigor they more than make up for in relevance.

Again, we think that the interventionist style of investigation has been both vastly overrated and overused. Nature has contrived many "experiments" that can be exploited for inquiry purposes; all that is needed are patience and a willingness to search assiduously until appropriate instances are found. We are not opposed to intervention, but we do caution that interventions can sometimes result in more losses than gains for the unwary investigator. (Although many interventions are ethically unsound, natural experiments never are.)

Setting. Scientific inquirers lean toward the laboratory setting (for control, for managing an intervention, and so on), while naturalistic inquirers prefer to conduct their investigations in natural settings. The laboratory is the essence of a context-free environment, but for that reason it is unlikely that findings produced in it will have meaning in any setting other than another laboratory. We believe it would be useful for scientific inquirers to make their laboratories as "lifelike" as possible, while the naturalistic inquirer is well advised, we feel, to maintain as much control as possible over the natural situations in which he carries out an investigation.

Treatment. The concept of treatment is extremely important within the scientific paradigm. Very often evaluators conceptualize an entity being evaluated, for example, a new school curriculum, as a "treatment." Of course the treatment in any experiment must be stable and invariant; otherwise it is impossible to determine the effect associated with a given cause.

But the concept of treatment is foreign to naturalistic inquirers since it implies some manner of manipulation or intervention. If it should occur to these inquirers to consider some naturally occurring phenomenon as a "treatment," that is, as a likely cause for some observable effect, they would certainly not expect stability, for continuous change is virtually the essence of real situations. It is probably useful for naturalistic inquirers to stabilize as much as possible situations in which inquiries are going on. But restricting a situation to no change for the sake of keeping variables manageable seems equally absurd. We take the stance that more flexibility is needed than is exhibited in the typical scientific inquiry.

Analytic Units. The analytic unit of the scientific paradigm is the variable, and all relationships are expressed as between variables (or systems of variables). By contrast, the naturalistic paradigm takes such a view to be simplistic and instead emphasizes the complex patternings that are observed in nature. Useful metaphors to help in understanding this distinction are the tug-of-war and the spider web. In the tug-of-war, the single rope represents the only connection between the two "warring" factions; a stronger pull on one end overcomes the weaker pull on the other, and movement results. No question about the cause and effect relationship here. But consider the spider web. When a fly is caught in it, the entire web vibrates, and it is difficult indeed to know just how the impulse of the fly landing is transferred to the senses of the spider patiently waiting in the center of the web. Only through sensing the pattern of the web can one appreciate what is occurring.

While it is useful to analyze variables, too little attention has been paid to the more complex interrelationships that can only be described as patterns. And it is dubious whether conventional modes for analyzing data can catch these often kaleidoscopic patterns.

Contextual Elements. Scientific inquirers seek to control all extraneous elements that can distract them from the phenomena of central interest or confound the effects of those phenomena.

Naturalists are not only uninterested in control but actually welcome and invite interference, so that they can better understand real-world events and sense their patterns. The concept of "invited interference" is of great importance to the evaluator, who generally does not wish to know how the entity being evaluated works in the best of all possible worlds, but in the worst. Control, as we have now repeatedly implied, is overdone. Opening inquiry to the influence of unanticipated factors is probably useful as a way of stretching the mind and requiring expansions and refinements in existing theory.

Can the Scientific and Naturalistic Paradigms Be Integrated?

It is frequently argued that the difference between the scientific paradigm and naturalistic paradigm is more apparent than real and that a compromise position should be devised that takes advantage of their complementarity. For example, Dipboye and Flanagan (1979), in focusing on the trade-off between internal and external validity of these two approaches, conclude: "We believe that the content analysis in the present article accurately reflects several important characteristics of current laboratory and field research in industrial-organizational psychology. The results suggest that blanket statements concerning the inherent external validity of field research are not only inaccurate but serve to hinder the development of industrial and organizational psychology as a field of study. Rather than rejecting or accepting a study because of its setting, a careful examination of the organizations, people, and responses is needed to determine the possible limits on external validity. Rather than asking, Is this study externally valid?, a more appropriate question is, To what actors, settings, and behaviors may we generalize the findings of this study? Approached from the latter view, laboratory and field research may be viewed as complementary rather than conflicting strategies" (p. 149).

A critic of an earlier work of one of the present authors (Guba, 1978c), in which an analysis similar to that presented in this chapter was developed, indicated that a major disservice had been done to the profession thereby. To suggest that the two paradigms were in conflict in any essential way simply served, according to this critic, to open a schism between those members of the profession who happened to have a predilection for one way or the other. But is complementarity really possible? Can the schism be healed?

It is our opinion that this question must be answered both yes and no.

With respect to the postures often assumed by adherents of these two paradigms (see Table 5), complementarity is not only possible but desirable. There is no reason why both camps should not exploit both quantitative and qualitative techniques, should not be concerned with both relevance and rigor, should not be open to empirically grounded theory as well as to flashes of insight from conceptual leaders in the field, should not be interested in both verification and discovery, and so on. But we have argued that, for every item of Table 5, there has been an overemphasis in the direction of scientific predilections, and we have suggested that the pendulum not only be allowed but be impelled to swing in the other direction. The discussion by Dipboye and Flanagan (1979) of internal and external validity cited above deals with a Table 5 item, and we would concur with their conclusion that complementarity is possible on this dimension.

However, the basic assumptions discussed at the beginning of this chapter present a somewhat different countenance. Can one assume both singular reality and multiple realities at the same time? How can one believe in insularity between the investigator and the object of his investigation while also allowing for their mutual interaction? How can one work simultaneously toward the development of nomothetic and idiographic science?

Thus we conclude, however reluctantly, that with respect to the basic assumptions that differentiate scientific from naturalistic modes, hard choices must be made. Those choices should of course be made by determining how well the assumptions of each are met within the phenomenological field being investigated. It is our judgment that in the field of behavioral science, of which evaluation is surely a part, the naturalistic paradigm should be the paradigm of choice.

A Definition of Naturalistic Inquiry

The preceding pages have dealt at length with differences between the naturalistic and scientific paradigms, but have not offered a precise definition of what naturalistic inquiry *is*. There are of course many ways to define naturalistic inquiry. House (1976) offers a definition aimed directly at naturalistic evaluation: "I would label as 'naturalistic' evaluation that evaluation which attempts to arrive at naturalistic generalizations [sic] on the part of the audience; which is aimed at nontechnical audiences like teachers or the public at large; which uses ordinary language; which is based on informal everyday reasoning; and which makes extensive use of arguments which attempt to establish the structure of reality" (p. 37).

While this definition refers specifically to naturalistic evaluation, it also outlines many of the elements that characterize naturalistic inquiry more broadly conceived. However, the definition is hardly systematic or rigorous, and it does contain some allusions (for example, to generalizations) that are inconsistent with the epistemological position ascribed to naturalistic inquiry earlier in this chapter.

Wolf and Tymitz (1976-1977) suggest that naturalistic inquiry is an inquiry mode aimed at understanding "actualities, social realities, and human perceptions that exist untainted by the obtrusiveness of formal measurement or preconceived questions. It is a process geared to the uncovering of many idiosyncratic but nonetheless important stories told by real people, about real events, in real and natural ways. The more general the provocation, the more these stories will reflect what respondents view as salient issues, the meaningful evidence, and the appropriate inferences. . . . Naturalistic inquiry attempts to present 'slice-of-life' episodes documented through natural language and representing as closely as possible how people feel, what they know, and what their concerns, beliefs, perceptions, and understandings are" (p. 6).

This definition seems to focus on people as subjects for naturalistic inquiry and on interactions with people, probably through interviews, as the typical naturalistic data collection method. The emphasis on "slice-of-life" episodes suggests the informality of the approach as viewed by these authors.

The most useful source material for formulating a definition of naturalistic inquiry is found in the collection of papers edited by Willems and Raush (1969) under the title *Naturalistic Viewpoints in Psychological Research*. The volume presents ten papers ranging over fields as disparate as primate anthropology, third-grade classrooms, and ecological psychology. Of the various options described in this book the one that has the greatest utility for grasping the "essence" of naturalistic inquiry is the formulation proposed by Willems himself. This approach defines a "domain" of inquiry based on the extent to which the investigator places constraints upon two dimensions: antecedent conditions and outputs. Willems has developed a chart that displays these two dimensions orthogonally and permits labeling of various positions in the domain as "experimental," "naturalistic," and so on (Willems and Raush, 1969, p. 47). Figure 1 is an adaptation of his

Figure 1. Representation of the Domain of Inquiry

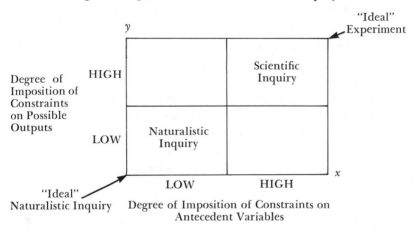

Source: Based on Willems and Raush, 1969, p. 47.

chart; for simplicity's sake, the two continua have been reduced to "low" and "high" segments.

The antecedent conditions, displayed along the x-axis of Figure 1, are of course all the factors (variables) that impinge upon the inquiry at its outset. From among their myriad number the investigator may choose to focus on (manipulate) certain specific ones, to control others, and to randomize still others. Every such decision that he makes acts as a constraint on the nature and scope of the inquiry; the further to the right that the inquirer moves, the more constraints are imposed. The outputs, arrayed along the yaxis of Figure 1, are all the factors (variables) to which the inquirer might attend once the inquiry is under way; from their number the inquirer may again make certain choices, focusing on some and electing to ignore others. Again each choice imposes constraints on the inquiry.

The extreme upper right-hand corner of Figure 1 represents the position of maximum constraints on both antecedent conditions and outputs and may be thought of as the epitome of scientific inquiry: the "ideal" experiment. The experimenter will focus on a few antecedent conditions to manipulate—these are commonly called independent variables—and will control or randomize all others. His outputs—commonly called the dependent variables —will also be carefully chosen in relation to the hypotheses to be tested, and all others will be ignored.

The extreme lower left-hand corner of Figure 1 represents the position of minimum (indeed, zero) constraints on both antecedent conditions and outputs and thus represents the "ideal" naturalistic inquiry. All antecedent factors are open to investigation, and all are allowed to play their "natural," that is, uncontrolled, role. All outputs are also eligible for study; none is barred on *a priori* grounds.

Theoretically, any inquiry could be plotted somewhere in this inquiry domain. Inquiries do, of course, occur in the lower right or upper left cell as well. As an instance of the former, consider Piaget's studies in which precise tasks (for example, conservation of volume) are presented under carefully controlled conditions, but the subjects (children) are allowed to say or do virtually anything in response. All their outputs are eligible for examination. As an example of inquiries in the upper left cell, consider the several modes of coding teacher behavior embodied in the Flanders interaction analysis scale. The scale can be used in any classroom, and no attempt need be made to impose conditions on the nature or size of the class, its subject matter, the nature of the teacher, and so on. No antecedent condition need be controlled. But only those teacher outputs that can be classified within the categories of the Flanders taxonomy can be recorded; any other outputs are ignored, including of course any pupil outputs, which are simply beyond the range of the recording instrument.

The concept of the domain of inquiry as displayed in Figure

1 is useful on several grounds. First, it suggests the possibility that all forms of inquiry can be understood within a single conceptual structure; the parsimony of this formulation is one of its strong points. Second, it suggests that "pure" forms of inquiry, that is, entirely scientific or entirely naturalistic, are rare; most inquiries combine these approaches in one way or another. Finally, this formulation will be useful in pinpointing certain methodological problems to be discussed in Chapter Five.

The definition of naturalistic inquiry implied by Figure 1 will be standard throughout the remainder of this book. All subsequent remarks and interpretations should be understood in these terms.

Relevance of the Naturalistic Paradigm
for Educational Evaluation

At the beginning of this chapter three basic assumptions that distinguish the scientific and naturalistic paradigms were described. It was stressed that there is no final way of "proving" that either one of these is always preferable; indeed, the investigator was asked to test the assumptions of each paradigm in terms of the phenomenology he was studying in order to make that determination. For example, there seems little doubt that the physicist (at least in all areas other than that of nuclear particles) should adopt the scientific paradigm: the physical world can be meaningfully divided into variables (so that concepts such as force, mass, acceleration, time, distance, and so on turn out to be highly useful); the physicist can manage a discrete distance between himself and the physical objects and entities he studies (levers work as well in the laboratory as in the real world, and chemicals do not know whether they are interacting in a test tube or a volcano); and generalizations do seem to hold up ($F = ma$, Newton's First Law, has never failed to predict correctly).

In the area of social-behavioral inquiry, however, the assumptions of the naturalistic paradigm have greater validity. Discrete variables and their relationships do not seem to be sufficient to deal with the complex interactions and patterns of human behavior. Investigators not only find their subjects reactive but are themselves changed by the quality of their interaction with subjects. Generalizations tend to have very short half-lives indeed (to revert to Cronbach's useful phrase).

Of course, there are areas of behavioral inquiry that are somewhat grey. A case in point is the developmental psychology of young children. There can be no doubt that their psychological development is intimately tied to their physical development, about which it has indeed proved possible to construct useful systems of variables, to maintain an adequate subject-object duality, and to generalize. Which paradigm is more useful here? It is likely that that question can be answered only in the specific terms of a particular inquiry; some questions can be better understood within a physiological framework and thus call for a scientific paradigm, but others are more properly understood as mental manifestations and therefore require a naturalistic paradigm. But these grey areas, troublesome as they may be, are not sufficiently frequent to undermine the high probability that the naturalistic paradigm will be found preferable in the large majority of behavioral inquiries and, most assuredly, in the large majority of educational evaluations.

But another point must be reviewed to understand why the naturalistic paradigm is so useful—a point that relates to the discussion in Chapter Three of the distinctions between worth and merit. Merit, it will be recalled, was defined as a context-free property or set of characteristics of the entity being evaluated—qualities that, in the opinion of knowledgeable experts, establish value for this kind of entity. Worth, in contrast, was defined as a context-related property or set of characteristics of the entity being evaluated. Worth is determined in relation to the values, demographic characteristics, motivational factors, and so on that inhere in the context or setting.

Merit might conceivably be determined through a scientific inquiry; since merit is context free, it is possible that statements of merit might take some generalized form. But it is certain that worth cannot be determined in that way. In order to determine values and motivational factors, if not demographic characteristics, the inquirer has to deal with persons in each context. Field studies are called for, and field studies cannot be carried out experimentally but only naturalistically.

Summary

In this chapter we have endeavored to describe the differences between two paradigms that have been widely used in behavioral inquiry. It was suggested that there are two subsets of differences: assumptions and postures. The assumptions are threefold, and they relate to views of reality (singular, convergent, and fragmentable versus multiple, divergent, and interrelated); the nature of the inquirer-subject relationships (independent versus interrelated), and the nature of truth statements (generalizations, nomothetic statements, and focus on similarities versus working hypotheses, idiographic statements, and focus on differences). It was suggested that compromises on these assumptions are not possible and that it is incumbent upon the inquirer to determine which set of assumptions best "fits" the phenomena he is studying and then to choose among paradigms accordingly.

Postures represent differences in usage among followers of the two paradigms—differences that are not intrinsic to the paradigms but represent "natural inclinations," such as preferences for quantitative or qualitative techniques or preferences for rigor or relevance. Compromises on postures are possible and should be sought assiduously, but the compromises must be worked out with respect to the particular inquiry problem—they are not simply "middle positions" or "golden means." Each of the postures summarized in Table 5 may be explored to determine in what ways complementarities can be devised to be most useful to the question at issue.

Naturalistic inquiry was then operationally defined as a function of the constraints placed upon antecedent conditions and outputs of the inquiry. The extreme of scientific inquiry, commonly called experimentation, severely constrains both antecedent conditions and output factors, while the extreme of naturalistic inquiry constrains neither. The distinction is portrayed in Figure 1. This formulation, it was asserted, is useful because it links all forms of inquiry within a single conceptual structure, because it suggests that pure forms of either scientific or naturalistic inquiry are rarely found, and because it helps clarify certain methodological problems to be discussed in Chapter Five.

Finally, the relevance of the naturalistic paradigm for educational evaluation was discussed. It was noted that the assumptions of that paradigm indeed fit the conditions of evaluation and that, more importantly, the distinctions between merit and worth drawn in Chapter Three make it imperative that worth, dependent on contextual factors, be determined through field studies, which are best served by naturalistic approaches.

Chapter 5

Naturalistic Solutions to Methodological Problems

When one of the authors spent a summer as a visiting scholar developing a monograph on naturalistic methods in educational evaluation, he was approached by a member of the faculty of the host institution with a request. "I understand," this faculty member said, "that *you* have been trained in quantitative methodology, and so are not likely to lose sight of the need for rigor in inquiry. But many persons, lacking that same kind of training, may take what you say as a license to do sloppy research. I would greatly appreciate it if you would somewhere make a strong statement warning persons *not* to attempt naturalistic inquiry until they possess adequate training in more rigorous methods and have been socialized to the need for rigor. Only then could one trust them to use naturalistic methods appropriately."

This statement reflects very well a bias held against naturalistic methodology because of its supposedly "inherent sloppiness." Naturalistic methods may be all right in an early stage of an investigation, but it is essential that the inquirer reestablish himself in the more rigorous conventional mode as soon as possible, because only this mode can yield trustworthy information.

On its face, this accusation seems to have merit. The definition of naturalistic inquiry proposed in Chapter Four prohibits constraints on either antecedent conditions or on outputs. But without constraints on antecedent conditions, how can the inquirer know what is important to his inquiry and what is not? And without constraints on outputs, how can the inquirer focus on those outputs that are relevant? And in any event, how can the inquiry fulfill the criteria of rigor—internal and external validity, reliability, and objectivity—that experience has shown to be so important in establishing the trustworthiness of information? We shall refer to these three classes of problems as problems of bounding, focusing, and rigor.

Bounding problems relate to the task of establishing the boundaries of an inquiry as a whole. In experimental inquiry, these boundaries are sharply constrained (controlled), so that there is no question what variables are to be studied, what questions are to be asked, or what hypotheses are to be tested. But in the case of naturalistic inquiry, antecedent conditions are not constrained in any way. Thus the boundary problem comes down to this: How is the inquirer to set limits to his inquiry? What are the rules for inclusion and exclusion? How can the inquirer know what is relevant and what is not relevant?

The argument will be made that, while the naturalistic inquirer does not impose *a priori* constraints, neither does he approach his task in a mindless fashion. In general, the naturalistic inquirer has some problem to investigate, and the parameters of that problem or evaluand serve to determine the inquiry limits. In the area of evaluation, moreover, the boundaries are set partly by the initial stipulations made by the evaluator's client or sponsor and partly through a recycling process common to all naturalistic inquiry. This process helps to identify the final boundaries.

Focusing problems arise because, if outputs are not defined before the inquiry begins, then those outputs that are noted must be collected, analyzed, categorized, and interpreted *after* the fact. This situation gives rise to two subclasses of problems, namely, the problems of convergence and divergence.

As for the problem of convergence, the naturalistic inquirer must somehow derive a set of units or categories within which he can classify and interpret observed outputs. A number of questions arise: What is the *nature* of a category? How can the inquirer identify a category when it emerges in an interaction with an information source (an informant, an observed subject, a document, and the like)? Again, what is the basis for *unitizing, categorizing,* and *prioritizing* information? What considerations enter into establishing categories? What guidelines exist for the process of classifying particular observations? How can the relative importance or salience of derived categories be established? Finally, what are the *criteria* for determining when a necessary and sufficient set of categories has been derived? That is, what are the criteria for determining when the categorizing process has gone far enough?

Once a naturalistic inquirer has a "fix" on the situation by virtue of having derived a set of categories, he is usually interested in fleshing out the categories with additional information. From the focal point of the category itself, the inquiry fans out or diverges to include as many data items and perspectives as are relevant. Again several questions emerge: What *strategies* exist that the naturalistic inquirer might employ to uncover relevant information? What is the basis for *inclusion* or *exclusion* of any particular datum? When should the collection of information *stop*?

Problems of rigor arise from the inquirer's need to persuade other inquirers or audiences of the authenticity of the information provided and the interpretations that are drawn from it. How can one tell whether the information and interpretations are correct? Whether the information has purely local significance or might have meaning in many situations? Whether it will be found consistently? Whether the interpretations are free from the particular biases of the inquirer? We will, in succeeding sections of

this chapter, deal with these various methodological questions at
length.

Establishing Boundaries

Naturalistic inquiries are not mounted in a vacuum; like all
other forms of inquiry, they emerge in response to perceived problems. This fact is of great importance, for it suggests a means by
which the investigator can limit the inquiry without imposing constraints that would force it into forms that are not naturalistic.

Despite the centrality of "problems" in all inquiry, the term
problem has itself gone undefined. Research texts devote long sections to procedural issues but treat the nature of problems very
cavalierly, often defining them simply as questions or objectives. A
proper understanding of this pervasive concept is the first step
toward integrated, directed, and meaningful inquiry, whether pursued by naturalistic or other means.

The definition of the term *problem* that we believe to be
most useful is the following:* A problem is a situation resulting
from the interaction of two or more factors (for example, givens,
conditions, desires, and the like) that yields: (1) a perplexing or
enigmatic state (a conceptual problem); (2) a conflict that renders
the choice from alternative courses of action moot (an action
problem); or (3) an undesirable consequence (a value problem).

It is convenient to think of problem statements as similar in
form to the logical syllogism; the two juxtaposed or interacting
factors are akin to the syllogistic propositions, while the conclusion states the problem. (For a fuller discussion, see Guba, 1978b.)

Formulation of problems into the syllogistic format is useful because this format suggests several strategies for boundary
designation. The inquirer can document the "facts" that are asserted in the juxtaposed propositions; the problem exists only to
the extent that the propositions are valid. He can look for the
causes of what is asserted in the propositions. He can look for

---

*The definition that follows and much of the accompanying discus-
sion is based on unpublished materials developed by one of the authors
(Guba) and by David L. Clark for use in inquiry courses taught by them at
Ohio State and Indiana universities.

mediating or ameliorating factors that might serve to contravene the propositions. Or he can determine the consequences that will occur if the propositions are permitted to go unchallenged.

These four possible classes of action—what might be called the verification or documentation mode, the causality mode, the contraventional mode, and the consequential mode—while not exhaustive, adequately make the case that the nature of the problem to be investigated provides a major means for setting boundaries. More importantly, the naturalistic investigator would, in this regard, act precisely and exactly as would his more experimentally minded counterpart; we can see no intrinsic difference between the two. The major difference between the two approaches is not in how the problems are bounded but in how they are identified in the first place. The scientific inquirer is likely to find his problem in the theory, the literature, or the conceptual structure of the field—an approach most naturalists would label as ungrounded. The naturalistic inquirer would prefer to have his problem emerge from observation, from experience, from data—in other words, by grounded means. But the discussion here is not about how problems emerge but about how they are bounded when they do emerge, and here we see no difference: boundary problems are the same for the scientific inquirer as for the naturalistic inquirer.

Any inquiry, including an evaluation, can be bounded through use of the problem statement as a limiting tool. But there are special circumstances that also markedly determine the boundaries of an evaluation. For example, the problem to be studied is not, initially at least, specified by the evaluator but by his client or sponsor. There seems to be no legitimate way to avoid this situation, nor indeed should it be avoided. The client is entitled to issue those "marching orders" that he believes are appropriate. But the evaluator need not be naive. He must recognize that the client may have many covert reasons for putting the charge in a particular way. He may, for example, select for evaluation only those program aspects that appear to be successful, cover up program failure by focusing on partisan testimonials, make evaluation gestures designed to promote a favorable public image, respond to government mandates that he does not take seriously but that must be complied with overtly, and the like. Sheer ignorance may also shape the client's directives.

The evaluator needs to be aware of these pitfalls and to guard against them. The time to negotiate these potential problems is at the beginning of the evaluation and not at the end. Chapter Nine provides some useful suggestions on how to proceed.

The naturalistic evaluator has another way out of the constraints that might otherwise be placed on him by the client's definition of the problem; that is, by use of the recycling process that he normally goes through. The naturalistic investigator begins with a discovery posture, but that posture may lead him to insights that he may then proceed to verify. The verification process in turn stimulates him to further discovery, and so on. Thus, if the client has either deliberately or inadvertently distorted the situation or given a charge that rests on covert motives, the naturalistic investigator is quite likely to uncover those facts and to be able to take them into account. He may, in fact, reflect back to the client the inconsistencies between the mandate given and the situation as it is found. The nature and extent of this reflection depend heavily on the politics of the situation and the quality of the relationship between evaluator and client. But there is no reason to believe that the naturalistic evaluator will simply become the dupe of the client, as long as he follows the normal strategies of naturalistic inquiry.

Another special circumstance surrounding evaluations is they are in general identified as such, and this creates certain kinds of relationships between the evaluator and other parties. Boundaries are set *de facto*. A role is defined both for the evaluator and for all other persons with whom he comes in contact. Fairness becomes a crucial element, and certain legalities and sanctions are involved, for example, the right to privacy. Indeed, the evaluator cannot take for granted that all parties will be open and cooperative; the evaluator may have to assume an investigative posture that takes account of the fact that subjects experience anxiety when being evaluated, wish to put their best foot forward, and have characteristics or have engaged in actions that, while perhaps not immoral or illegal, are nevertheless best kept from the attention of the evaluator. (See Guba, forthcoming; Douglas, 1976.)

The entity being evaluated is also known to everyone. Subjects are likely to take a jaundiced view of questions that, in their opinion, range beyond the legitimate area of inquiry. Of course, the evaluator cannot take for granted that the subject's definition of legitimate bounds is appropriate. But the normal procedures and tactics of naturalistic inquiry make it unlikely that a naturalistic evaluator will permit himself to be inappropriately boxed in or that he will fail to uncover relevant information, barring a massive cover-up conspiracy on the part of respondents.

Can evaluation be concerned with all three of the problem types just defined—conceptual, action, and value—or is there some "natural affinity" between evaluation and one of these types? At first glance, one is tempted to suggest that conceptual problems belong in the arena of research, action problems in the arena of policy studies, and value problems in the arena of evaluation. After all, the purpose of evaluation is to determine the value— merit or worth—of some entity, and that formulation seems to confine evaluation to value problems. Such a formulation is valid; evaluators will more often be concerned with value problems than with any others.

But it would be a mistake to suppose that conceptual or action problems never fall into the evaluator's realm. The evaluator may be called upon to help resolve some conceptual dilemma, particularly when engaged in formative evaluation activities that are intended to help with refinement or improvement. Barriers to improvement may involve elements that are logically, conceptually, or theoretically inconsistent; the developer or agent of change may look to the evaluator for help in resolving these dilemmas.

Similarly, the evaluator may be asked to assist with action problems. Indeed, if one accepts a definition of evaluation that makes it the handmaiden of a decision-making process, the link is clear. But even without accepting that definition, it is patent that evaluation can help resolve choices among action alternatives. And one need only point to the close affinity that is developing between evaluation and policy studies to note the synergism between these areas. (The title of the American Educational Research Association's new journal is *Educational Evaluation and Policy Analysis,* for example.)

Finding a Focus

Focusing problems emerge from the analysis, categorization, and interpretation of outputs occurring in the natural situation.

Two subcategories can be identified: problems of *convergence* and problems of *divergence*.

Problems of Convergence. Problems of convergence arise because the naturalistic evaluator must derive units or categories within which he will classify and interpret observed outputs. In fact, two different category systems are required because naturalistic evaluation is a two-step process: identification of the concerns and issues of the audiences involved and collection of information bearing upon those identified concerns and issues. Each step poses its own convergence problems.

Let us consider briefly the second of these steps. Each concern or issue will require the collection of certain information. For example, if parents voice the concern that the new math program to which their children are being exposed is not providing them the skills needed to balance a checkbook, that allegation has to be tested by collecting information about how well children *can* balance checkbooks. Insofar as the particular concern or issue calls for information most easily collected by conventional methodologies, as might be true of the "checkbook" example, there is no focusing problem. Insofar as the particular concern or issue calls for information best collected by naturalistic means (as might be the case, say, if parents suggest that their children not only lack arithmetic skills but are also developing a negative attitude toward computation in general), the focusing problem becomes one of organizing interview, observational, or other naturalistic data. This problem will be thoroughly discussed in subsequent chapters.

The first of the steps noted above, that is, the identification of the concerns and issues of audiences, takes a special form. In Chapter Two, a *concern* was defined as any matter of interest or importance to one or more parties about which they feel threatened, that they think will lead to an undesirable consequence, or that they want to substantiate in a positive sense. An *issue* was defined as any statement, proposition, or focus that allows for the presentation of different points of view; any proposition about which reasonable persons may disagree, or any point of contention. In thinking about how concerns and issues might be identified and processed, the naturalistic evaluator should consider categorizing processes, prioritizing processes, and tests for completeness of a set of categories.

1. Categorizing processes. The task of converting field notes and observations about issues and concerns into systematic categories is a difficult one. No infallible procedures exist for performing it. Since this process is highly intuitive, it is often viewed as "merely" subjective and hence not likely to lead to results worthy of serious consideration. There are, however, several useful categorizing steps that the naturalistic evaluator can take.

A first step is to look for recurring regularities in sources. Do the same kinds of observations or comments recur at different times, from different informants or documents, and in somewhat different contexts? These regularities form the basis for an initial sorting of information into categories that will ultimately be labeled as concerns and issues.

In this process it is likely that a considerable number of individual data items will be placed into an "other" or "miscellaneous" group because they do not seem to fit into a specific category. In some cases these data items can be safely ignored as subjective, idiosyncratic observations of no real substance. In other cases, however, they may represent incisive observations or judgments made by persons uniquely competent to make them. Often the evaluator will not be able to tell, at first, whether a given observation is of the former or the latter variety. He ought to take everything seriously until evidence accrues to the contrary; the importance or salience of an information item certainly cannot be judged simply by its frequency of occurrence.

Once a preliminary set of categories has been developed, certain systematic checks should be made. The utility of a category set is a function of the internal homogeneity among items classified in any particular category and of the external heterogeneity among categories. If a given category is to be defensible as encompassing a single concept, all the items within it ought to "look alike." Are they logically related? Do formulations of a particular issue or concern from different perspectives (for example, those of a protagonist and those of an antagonist) appear congruent? Do examples and counterexamples "dovetail" in a meaningful way? Similarly, differences among categories ought to be bold and clear. The existence of a large amount of unassignable or overlapping data is good evidence that some basic fault exists in the category system.

The development of an adequate category system cannot be accomplished in one step. Early accumulations of data give rise to a preliminary set of categories that can be tested, refined, and extended in later iterations in the field. The category system is thus a dynamic entity, constantly changing and improving. But there are several *caveats* that the naturalistic evaluator should keep in mind during this process.

Thus, the naturalistic evaluator cannot hope to devise as exhaustive a set of categories as he might like. Concerns and issues are probably endless; and, even after prioritizing them, the evaluator will not be able to convert all his observations into an easily manageable set (short of using a residual category). Nor is it likely that the naturalistic evaluator will be able to devise a scalar set in which categories are ordered in terms of magnitude or some other identifiable dimension. He will need to be satisfied with discrete categories that have no ordinality.

The naturalistic evaluator can and should, however, strive for categories that are unidimensional, that is, have internal homogeneity. It should be remembered that, as a next step after categories are initially defined, the evaluator will go back to the field to flesh out the categories. This task will be enormously complicated if care has not been exercised in establishing the categories in the first place.

Finally, the evaluator should aim for an appropriate level of discourse for the categories on which he does settle. Selection of too broad a level may cause the evaluator to overlook significant concerns and issues because they are "buried" in a larger category, while selection of too narrow a level may focus attention on detail to the exclusion of the larger picture.

2. Prioritizing processes. It is likely that the number of categories that the naturalistic evaluator derives in any given situation will be too large to be manageable, especially in the next stage of the evaluation, in which the categories are to be fleshed out. Further, resources will typically not permit the second-stage exploration of more than a limited set. What should guide the evaluator in prioritizing the categories that do emerge so that only those most worthy of further exploration will be identified? Hard-and-fast rules cannot be set down, but the evaluator should keep certain considerations in mind. For instance, while the number of

respondents who mention a particular issue or concern is not a sufficient criterion for assigning priority, that index can nevertheless be useful in the sense that concerns and issues more frequently identified have more salience in the situation and may therefore be more weighty with one or more audiences. Surely one would not wish to eliminate a concern or issue that received frequent mention.

Certain items will be accorded more credibility by the various audiences—some items will strike them as highly realistic and others as more or less incredible. Since the audiences are probably more in touch with the reality of the situation than is the evaluator, their estimates of credibility should be highly determinative of what is retained. Of course, the possibility that the audiences may have something to hide from the evaluator should be kept in mind.

Some concerns and issues may stand out by virtue of their uniqueness: they are noticeable simply because they are so different from other items. While they may be the product of highly idiosyncratic perspectives, unique items probably ought to receive higher priority than others simply because they add interesting detail and proportion to the evaluator's perspective.

Other concerns and issues ought to be retained because they have the property of opening up areas of inquiry not otherwise recognized or because they provide a unique leverage on an otherwise common problem. There are always some ways of formulating problems that are more productive than others, even when the root problem is the same. Thus, some concerns and issues have special value in providing points of entry for the evaluator and/or in facilitating the inquiry.

Evaluators will inevitably find that some concerns and issues, whatever their inherent interest, are simply not susceptible to inquiry. The methodology may not be available; there may not have been enough time for their effects to become noticeable; political factors may militate against exposing them to public view; resources may simply be inadequate. Rejection of a concern or issue on feasibility grounds may at times be painful because of other characteristics that would seem to make that concern or issue a fruitful one to pursue, but rejection may nevertheless be necessary.

Even though certain concerns or issues may not be intrinsically interesting, they may nevertheless be important to pursue because of the special interest taken in them by a powerful audience, such as project administrators, funders, or legislators.

Materiality may be the most important criterion in an evaluation. Concerns and issues that have an obvious and important bearing on the evaluand should be included, even though some audiences may prefer *not* to have those concerns and issues aired. Materiality obviously cannot be the sole basis for setting priorities; to assert that it is would be to remain blind to the fiscal, social, and political realities that surround every evaluation. Nevertheless, materiality must serve as the basis for the initial cut, as it were, with the other criteria being utilized to make adjustments and refinements in the prioritization process.

3. Determining the completeness of a set of categories. How can a naturalistic evaluator determine whether or not the categories that have been articulated constitute a necessary and sufficient set? We have already alluded to the fact that there should be a minimum of unassignable data items, as well as relative freedom from ambiguity of classification. But there are other considerations.

The set should have internal and external plausibility. Viewed internally, the individual categories should appear to be consistent; viewed externally, the set of categories should seem to set forth a whole picture. Often an incomplete set will suggest other categories for which no data yet exist. Such categories have not emerged inductively from the data collected up to that point but seem to be required by the logic of the subset of categories that does emerge. The naturalistic evaluator would regard this situation as a stimulus to look for data that would corroborate the existence of the suggested categories.

The set should be reasonably inclusive of the data that exist. Inclusiveness is partly indicated by the relative absence of unassignable cases, but can be further tested by referring to the problem that the inquirer is investigating or to the mandate given to the evaluator by his client or sponsor. If the set of categories does not appear to be sufficient, on logical grounds, to cover the various facets of the problem or mandate, the set is probably incomplete.

The set should be reproducible by another competent judge.

This injunction, however, should not be taken to mean that the set must be duplicated from the raw data by a second inquirer who has no contact with the first. We have already noted that there are multiple levels of reality, and different investigators may choose to "peel the onion" of reality to different levels, depending upon the purposes, interests, experience, and expertise that they bring to the task. Two independent observers could thus not be expected to devise the same set of categories. The second judge ought to be able, however, to verify that, first, the set of categories makes sense in view of the data from which they emerged, and, second, that the data have been appropriately assigned within the category system.

This process is similar to the fiscal audit common in business. The fiscal auditor performs two functions: he attests that the system of accounting is appropriate and that the bottom line is correct. In similar fashion, the evaluation auditor ought to be able to attest that the category system was derived by generally acceptable procedures and that the data have been properly fitted into it.

The set should be credible to the persons who provided the information that the set is presumed to assimilate. This property of credibility might also be termed "contextual appropriateness." Such credibility is far and away the most important criterion, particularly in view of the fact that what the category set purports to summarize are issues and concerns in the minds of people. Who is in a better position to judge whether the categories appropriately reflect their issues and concerns than the people themselves? More will be said of such credibility checks—often called "member checks" by sociologists—when problems of rigor are discussed later.

Problems of Divergence. When the naturalistic evaluator has identified a preliminary set of categories, he will wish to flesh them out by collecting information that will describe the issues and concerns in some detail, by providing perspectives for viewing them, and by developing sufficient evidence to permit judgments to be made about them. How shall the evaluator go about that task? What are some strategies that can be employed in searching for the needed information? How can the evaluator determine whether to include or exclude any particular datum? How can he tell when to stop collecting information?

1. Strategies. The typical situation confronting the naturalistic evaluator is shown in Figure 2. A focal area, that is, an issue

Figure 2. Representation of Divergence Strategies: Extending, Bridging, and Surfacing

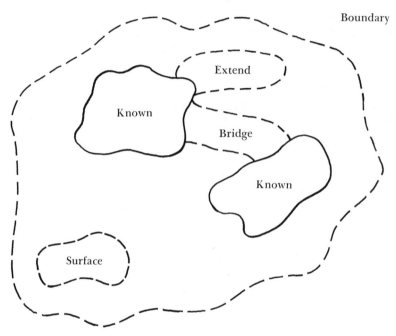

or concern, has been identified, but its boundary, depicted as a
broken line, is not well known. Within that area, certain information has already been accumulated, and that information is the
basis for establishing the category. This available information is
represented by the two areas marked "known." The task of the
evaluator is to fill in the remaining area (the problem of fixing the
boundary will be discussed later). There are three major strategies
that he can pursue.

In the first of these—extending—the inquirer begins with
known items of information and builds on them. He uses these
items as bases for other questions or as guides in his examination
of documents and records. In effect, the evaluator inches his way
from the known to the unknown.

When using the second strategy—bridging—the inquirer begins with several known, but apparently disconnected, items of information. The term *disconnected* simply means that their relationships are not understood. That there are relationships is a premise of high probability because the items have been placed into the same category on their face. The evaluator now uses these two known points of reference for further inquiry in an effort to identify the connections and understand them.

As the inquirer becomes more and more familiar with the area, he is able to propose new information that ought to be found in the field and then to verify its existence. This process of surfacing is thus similar to the familiar process of hypothesis formation or to the process of suggesting new categories, once a subset of known categories has been identified, because the logic of the situation "demands" them.

Obviously, these processes are more a matter of art than of science. But they should not be rejected simply because they cannot be scientifically explicated. All science depends heavily on the "artistic" formulations of its practitioners. Depriving scientists of the right to use intuition would render scientific pursuit sterile. Scientific hypotheses are, after all, nothing more than the reconstructed logic of hunches, the logic-in-use.

2. Inclusion and exclusion criteria. The evaluator attempting to flesh out an area inevitably confronts decisions about which new items of information to include and which to exclude. What guidelines shall he use? Listed below are seven; the first three relate directly to the strategies just discussed, while the latter four are additional criteria that should prove useful.

- Include any information that is germane to the area and not excluded by boundary-setting rules.
- Include any information that relates or bridges several already existing information items.
- Include any information that identifies new elements or brings them to the surface.
- Add any information that reinforces existing information but reject it if the reinforcement is merely redundant.
- Add new information that tends to explain other information already known.

- Add any information that exemplifies either the nature of the category or important evidence within the category.
- Add any information that tends to refute or challenge already known information.

3. Closure. The final question about divergence that faces the naturalistic evaluator is when to stop collecting information; that is, how to determine when he has reached the outer boundary of Figure 2. There are several criteria useful in making this decision. When there are no new situations to observe, subjects to interview, processes to describe, or documents to analyze, for example, termination is patently indicated. But this occurrence is rare. Typically, there are more sources than can effectively be tapped, and it is always possible, and probably desirable, to recycle—for example, to move through successive waves of discovery and verification, to triangulate sources, and to pursue strategies of extending, bridging, and surfacing.

Again, when successive examination of sources (recurrent or novel) tends to yield redundancy without useful reinforcement or produces seriously diminishing returns, that is, produces small additional information in return for substantial additional effort, it is probably time to terminate. Saturation may occur without the emergence of a sense of integration or completeness because the number of accessible or willing informants is small, because of a conspiracy of silence on the part of respondents, or because some crucial elements have failed to surface even though logically required by the structure of the category system. But, except for the third of these conditions, there is little that the evaluator can do to reopen founts of information; the third case will test his wit and cleverness.

It is also probably time to stop when the area "feels" integrated, that is, when the inquirer senses regularity in the available information. But several cautions should be observed. Regularities may occur early, at a time when some crucial items of information have not yet emerged. Moreover, regularities exist at different levels. A simplistic interpretation of information may make that information appear highly regular, but the interpretation may be grossly in error at some other, more sophisticated level. Eisner's (1979) concept of connoisseurship is relevant here: some persons are more sophisticated than others. For these reasons it is probably best to invoke the criterion of regularity only in conjunction with one or more of the other criteria.

Obviously, it is possible to collect information that goes beyond what is needed. How can one tell that this has happened?

Barker and Wright (1955) have introduced the concept of "synomorphism" to describe the relation between the pattern of behavior being investigated and the milieu in which it is found. They speak of the milieu as being "circumjacent" to the behavior. If an inquiry is extended too far, it will be difficult to maintain a feeling of synomorphism between behavior and milieu, and the milieu will appear distant rather than circumjacent to the behavior; that is, the area of investigation will appear far removed from the issue or concern that prompted it. When this is felt in the data, it is a signal that the inquiry has been overextended.

None of these four criteria is absolute, nor is even a combination of the four an infallible signal for closure. Nevertheless, the naturalistic evaluator can get reasonable guidance for a termination decision by attending to them. Continued inquiry in the face of exhausted sources, information saturation, data regularities, and overextension is clearly not a wise course of action.

We see, then, that despite the absence of *a priori* stipulations of rules for outputs, it is possible for the naturalist to solve both the convergence and divergence problems and to find meaningful foci for his work. But is it not the case that his solutions are less meaningful and creditable than are those of the inquirer working from the scientific paradigm, in which *a priori* stipulations do exist?

Consider first the convergence problem. So far as we can see, the problem of deducing meaning from data is identical for the scientist and the naturalist. The main difference is one of the time at which the rules for data analysis are made. For the scientist, all the categories are defined before the fact, and these categories are typically based upon hypotheses logically derived from some *a priori* theory. Transformation rules are explicitly formulated in advance. These differences are claimed as advantages by the scientist, who believes that he thereby achieves a greater degree of objectivity. But we suggest that *a posteriori* specification has an enormous advantage of its own—it results in grounded theory, that is, theory emergent from, based on, and verified by real-world data. On the one hand, *a priori* hypotheses represent a guess about what is likely to be the case; if one guesses right, that's fine; but if one guesses wrong, the hypotheses are simply disconfirmed, and that's that. Grounded hypotheses, on the other hand, are intimately connected with the real world—they do not represent guesses but directions indicated by actual information.

The question of when a necessary and sufficient set of categories has been generated is not particularly difficult either. There are of course no definitive tests, but useful guidelines do exist. Obviously the categories ought to be internally homogeneous (with "look-alike" content) but externally heterogeneous. The category set as a whole ought to "feel" integrated—indeed, if the category set is incomplete, the search for integrability may well lead to the identification of missing categories. The set should be reasonably inclusive of the information that comes to light; that is, there should not be a large "miscellaneous" category of information "left over." The set should be certifiable by a competent judge as having been developed by reasonable procedures, with the available data appropriately arranged into categories. Finally, the set ought to have credibility with the persons who provided the raw information on which it is based—this additional step of running "member checks" ensures adequate grounding as well.

We see no reason why these steps cannot be taken with as much rule orientation, as systematically, and as objectively as any process of data management conducted by an experimentally oriented investigator. As far as rigor is concerned, it matters little whether the categories are defined before the fact or after, provided that the data are fitted into the derived categories under some rule of procedure that is applied systematically and objectively.

Let us turn then to the matter of divergence—the fleshing out of categories once they have been tentatively identified. It is likely that categories, especially at the beginning stages of an inquiry, will be incomplete. The presence of several items of information may suggest the existence of a category, or the likely existence of a category may be inferred when the category system as a whole feels "incomplete." But, in either event, more information is needed.

Obviously the new information will be obtained by recycling the data sources. Known items of information can serve as the basis for extending information. Implicit relationships among items of information assigned to the same category can be explored and made explicit. New items of information can be brought to the surface by using developing insights about the category to stimulate thinking by the investigator himself or by any of his human resources. These processes are repeated until sources are exhausted, redundancy of information indicates saturation has been reached, sensible regularities emerge in the data, or a feeling of overextension emerges; that is, until the investigator perceives that he has gone too far afield and that the new information is at best marginally relevant.

These guidelines are not absolute, nor is there any foolproof way to apply them. But there seems to be no compelling reason for asserting that the processes of fleshing out naturalistic categories are fundamentally any different from those followed by scientists when they confront incomplete information and take steps to remedy that deficiency.

Meeting Tests of Rigor

For naturalistic inquiry, as for scientific, meeting tests of rigor is a requisite for establishing trust in the outcomes of the inquiry. The question to be confronted is simple: "What arguments might the naturalistic inquirer use to persuade a methodologically sophisticated peer of the trustworthiness of the information provided and the interpretations drawn from it?"

In this section we shall attempt to develop and apply naturalistic analogues to the four major criteria of rigor that have systematically evolved with respect to scientific inquiry. It is our contention that the basic concerns reflected in the criteria commonly used by scientific inquirers also hold for naturalistic inquiry but require some reinterpretation in order to better fit the assumptions of the naturalistic paradigm. The basic concerns are these:

1. Truth Value: How can one establish confidence in the "truth" of the findings of a particular inquiry for the subjects with which—and the context within which—the inquiry was carried out?
2. Applicability: How can one determine the degree to which the

findings of a particular inquiry may have applicability in other contexts or with other subjects?

3. Consistency: How can one determine whether the findings of an inquiry would be consistently repeated if the inquiry were replicated with the same (or similar) subjects in the same (or a similar) context?

4. Neutrality: How can one establish the degree to which the findings of an inquiry are a function solely of the subjects and conditions of the inquiry and not of the biases, motives, interests, perspectives, and so on of the inquirer?

The four terms naming these concerns within the scientific paradigm are, of course, internal validity for truth value, external validity or generalizability for applicability, reliability for consistency, and objectivity for neutrality (see Table 6). We propose

Table 6. Scientific and Naturalistic Terms Appropriate
to Various Aspects of Rigor

Aspect	Scientific Term	Naturalistic Term
Truth value	Internal validity	Credibility
Applicability	External validity/ generalizability	Fittingness
Consistency	Reliability	Auditability
Neutrality	Objectivity	Confirmability

certain analogous terms as more appropriate to the naturalistic paradigm: credibility for truth value, fittingness for applicability, "auditability" for consistency, and confirmability for neutrality.

Before undertaking a discussion of these terms, however, we might note that there are many other criteria that the typical evaluation is expected to meet. What is dealt with here are criteria of scientific adequacy, not utilitarian criteria such as timeliness, scope, and relevance or prudential criteria such as cost effectiveness. These have been well discussed by other authors (see, for example, the Joint Committee on Standards for Educational Evaluation, 1980; Stufflebeam, 1974a; Worthen, 1977).

Truth Value. Within the scientific paradigm, truth value, typically called internal validity, depends on the degree of isomorphism between the study data and the phenomena to which they relate. There is one reality, and information is internally valid if it describes that reality and facilitates its control and manipulation. The naturalistic inquirer, however, deals with multiple realities; and in the area of behavioral studies, those realities exist in the minds of people. In establishing truth value, therefore, the naturalistic inquirer is most concerned with testing the credibility of his findings and interpretations with the various sources (audiences or groups) from which his data were drawn. There are two truth-value questions that need attention: (1) What can be done to produce findings that are most likely to be found credible by sources? (2) How can credibility be tested with the sources?

Improving the Probability of Credible Findings. There are a number of strategies for increasing the probability that findings will be found credible. One way is to erect safeguards against potentially invalidating factors. An analysis by Speizman (n.d.), based largely on materials included in a collection of essays edited by McCall and Simmons (1969), suggests that the following invalidating factors may be present in a naturalistic inquiry:

First, there may be distortions resulting from the researcher's presence at the research site. Such distortions include the induction of reactive responses in subjects and the failure to provide sufficient opportunity for the researcher's preconceptions to "be thoroughly challenged by the data he collects." Speizman suggests that close monitoring of responses and a prolonged engagement at the site are sufficient to overcome these effects.

Second, there may be distortions arising from the fieldworker's involvement with his subjects. Failure to establish a minimum level of rapport, on the one hand, or "going native," on the other, can militate against a successful field study. Speizman counsels against too much involvement and proposes that the fieldworker constantly check himself to make sure that "objectivity" is being maintained. Debriefing by other disinterested peers is also useful.

Third, there may be distortions arising from bias on the part of either fieldworker or subjects. Such distortions may arise from wrong first impressions formed by the fieldworker, slavish adherence to hypotheses worked out earlier, or role and status differentials. Subjects may introduce distortions for similar reasons or simply out of a desire to be as "helpful" as possible. Speizman implies that special efforts and sensitivity on the part of the investigator will help to offset such tendencies.

Finally, there may be distortions arising from the manner in which data-gathering techniques are employed. Speizman suggests that careful recoding of data, continual scrutiny of data for internal and external consistency, cross-checking of inferences with selected interview material, and continual assessment of subject credibility are sufficient to overcome most of these distortions.

While the tactics Speizman proposes cannot finally establish the truth value of study findings to an outside observer, keeping these pitfalls in mind during the course of a study will help to ensure the overall adequacy of the inquiry when it is put to the more definitive test of audience credibility.

Establishing a degree of structural corroboration is also a means of increasing credibility. As Eisner (1979) suggests, "Structural corroboration is a process of gathering data or information and using it to establish links that eventually create a whole that is supported by the bits of evidence that constitute it. Evidence is structurally corroborative when pieces of evidence validate each other, the story holds up, the pieces fit, it makes sense, the facts are consistent" (p. 215).

Similarly, House (1978b) points out that "validity is provided by cross-checking different data sources and by testing perceptions against those of participants. Issues and questions arise from the people and situations being studied rather than from the investigator's perceptions. Concepts and indicators 'derive from the subject's world of meaning and action.' In constructing explanations, the naturalist looks for convergence of his data sources and develops sequential, phaselike explanations that assume no event has single causes. Working backwards from an important event is a common procedure. Introspection is a common source of data" (p. 37).

There are two useful techniques for establishing structural corroboration. (Note that both techniques are used during the course of the inquiry and, indeed, help to shape later stages of the inquiry by building on earlier stages.) The first of these techniques is triangulation, which depends upon exposing a proposition (for example, the existence of an issue or concern; the validity of some alleged fact; the assertion of an informant) to possibly countervailing facts or assertions or verifying such propositions with data drawn from other sources or developed using different methodologies. Denzin (1971) observes: "Triangulation forces the observer to combine multiple data sources, research methods, and theoretical schemes in the inspection and analysis of behavioral specimens. It forces him to *situationally* check the validity of his causal propositions. . . . It forces him to *temporarily* specify the character of his hypothesis. . . . It directs the observer to compare the subject's theories of behavior with his emerging theoretical scheme. . . . The naturalist must have an intimate familiarity with all his data sources so he can judge which ones to discount, which ones to treat as negative cases, which ones to build into his representative cases" (p. 177).

Webb and others (1966) conclude that triangulation, though difficult, is very much worth doing, because it makes data and findings credible: "Once a proposition has been confirmed by two or more measurement processes, the uncertainty of its interpretation is greatly reduced. The most persuasive evidence comes through a triangulation of measurement processes. If a proposition can survive the onslaught of a series of imperfect measures, with all their relevant error, confidence should be placed in it" (p. 3).

The phrase "imperfect measures, with all their relevant error" is especially illuminating. Obviously, the naturalistic investigator cannot place very much confidence in single observations or deductions. Each will contain its modicum of error, perhaps sufficient to cause suspension of belief if no other evidence is available. But when various bits of evidence all tend in one direction, that direction assumes far greater credibility. As statistical means are more stable than single scores, so triangulated conclusions are more stable than any of the individual vantage points from which they were triangulated.

The other technique for establishing structural corroboration is cross-examination. Tymitz and Wolf (1977), in discussing cross-examination as a feature of the legal model of evaluation, propose the following specific objectives for it:

1. To establish the witness' frame of reference or bias so that the values and/or assumptions underlying his . . . testimony will be clear. This will enable

the panel [jury] to understand the testimony's context, its subtleties and nuances, and perhaps even to understand why the witness believes the way he does.

2. To point out the flaws, alternative consequences, or trade-offs for any recommendations the witness offers.

3. To clarify, extend, or modify facts, opinions, or beliefs expressed in direct examination.

4. To help the panel [jury] understand that plausible inferences exist other than the one(s) established by direct examination for any piece of evidence.

5. To seek justification for certain judgments [pp. 59-60].

If, in this statement of purposes, the terms *panel* and *witness* are replaced with *investigator* and *subject,* a description of the use of cross-examination for establishing structural corroboration emerges.

Another way to establish the adequacy of a "fact" or inference is through the use of repeated observations from a single perspective. In discussing the connoisseurship model of evaluation, Eisner (1975) notes: "When one deals with works of visual art and works of literature, there exists a certain stability in the material studied. But what do we do with things and events that change over time; classrooms, for instance? How can something as fluid as a classroom be critically described and how can such descriptions be tested for their referential adequacy? . . . The classroom being studied needs to be visited with sufficient persistency to enable the critic to locate its pervasive qualities; those qualities through which aspects of its life can be characterized. Classrooms or schools are not so fugitive that their pervasive qualities change on a daily basis. What is enduring in a classroom is more likely to be educationally significant than what is evanescent. These enduring or pervasive qualities can become objects of critical attention" (p. 18).

In another context, Eisner (1979) makes the point that "one of the reasons why it is important for someone functioning as an educational critic to have an extended contact with an educational situation is to be able to recognize events or characteristics that are atypical. One needs sufficient time in a situation to know which qualities characterize it and which do not" (p. 218).

Thus, credibility is to some extent a function of the amount of time and effort that the naturalistic inquirer invests in repeated and continuous observation. The investigator who engages in persistent observation and makes extended contacts not only will be able to differentiate typical from atypical situations or identify the enduring or pervasive qualities that characterize a situation but will also know when to give credence to the occasional aberrant or apparently idiosyncratic observation that nevertheless carries great insight and meaning.

As part of his treatment of referential adequacy, Eisner (1975) suggests that it may be possible to compare an evaluation report with certain specially prepared materials in ways that will allow an external observer to make his own judgment about the credibility of the report. In relation to classroom observations, he indicates that "the availability of videotape recordings and cinematography now make it possible to capture and hold episodes of classroom life that can be critically described. Such videotaped episodes can then be compared with the criticism created and its referential adequacy determined. In addition, playback features of videotape make it possible to scrutinize expression, tempo, explanation, and movement in ways that live situations will not permit. Disputes about the adequacy of criticism can be resolved, at least in principle, by reexamining particular segments of the tape. The technology now available lends itself exceedingly well to the work to be done" (pp. 18-19).

Eisner's proposal is not dissimilar to the call from Barker and others for data archives. Not only would such archives provide original study material, but they could also be used to make the kinds of comparisons Eisner suggests in his discussion of videotapes and films.

Special techniques particularly suited to this approach might be worked out. The materials that both Eisner and Barker describe are largely fortuitous; they are collected during the investigation itself and primarily as original data, not for purposes of cross-validation. There seems to be no reason, however, why sampling designs could not be set up that would furnish materials collected primarily for the referential adequacy function. In essence, they would be parallel materials against which the adequacy of the fuller, more complete study materials could be tested.

Testing Credibility with Sources. The techniques discussed above do not themselves establish credibility—at best they simply increase the probability that data and interpretations will be found credible. The determination of credibility can be accomplished only by taking data and interpretations to the sources from which they were drawn and asking directly whether they believe—find plausible—the results. This process of going to sources—often called making "member checks"—is the backbone of satisfying the truth-value criterion.

It would, however, be naive to believe that sources will accept data at face value and render credibility judgments about them openly and honestly. There are of course many reasons why a source group (or individual members of it) might reject—find noncredible—the data and interpretations that an evaluator presents, including at least these:

First, the source may not be familiar with the information presented. If the information is new to it, the source cannot be expected to accept it without question.

Second, the source may not understand the information presented. In part this may be a reportorial problem—the information may be presented in jargon with which the source is unfamiliar. In such cases the modes of portrayal suggested by Stake (see Chapter Two) may be of great help. But the source may simply not possess the sophistication to deal with the information, for example, elaborate statistical tests. It may be more useful to omit such information for that source than to demand a reaction which it is not competent to give.

Third, the source may see the information as biased. Disadvantaged parents may, for example, see the school administration as consistently taking positions inimical to their own and buttressing those positions with concocted information. Also, information coming from sources with which the given source has a potential conflict of interest may be suspect.

Fourth, the source may see the information as conflicting with essential values that it holds. Amish families are not likely to be swayed by logical or data-based arguments about the utility of teaching evolution when they hold religious values absolutely antagonistic to such a program. The inquirer needs to be aware of value differences among sources.

Fifth, the source may see the information as conflicting with its own self-interest. If the effect of the information is to reduce the source's power or fiscal position, it will be difficult indeed for the source to accept the information as credible. It is easier to deny its credibility than to overcome its effects, once it is legitimated. The evaluator needs to be sensitive to the economic and political posture of the source groups.

Sixth, the source may see the information as conflicting with its own self-image. Teachers who pride themselves on always acting in the best interests of students are not likely to believe that they have embraced a new curriculum mainly because it cuts down on their workload.

Last, the source may see the information as contrary to some institutional myth it cherishes. Faculty members in schools of education will not accept data showing that they have failed to place their education graduates, as long as they believe that, despite declining placement opportunities, school officials continue to beat a path to their door because of the obviously superior quality of the teachers *they* produce.

If this analysis is at all valid, it means that the evaluator will not have an easy time of it when he attempts to run credibility checks. Sources may raise conflicts, resist, deny, and threaten. Yet credibility checks are the only possibility of establishing the truth value of information obtained naturalistically. What do these facts suggest about the ways in which credibility should be tested?

The evaluator should repeatedly make member checks to avoid overloading sources with a great deal of negative information at any given time. For the formative evaluator this continuous checking will probably occur "naturally," since he will need to be in touch with his sources for reporting purposes on a daily basis. But even in summative evaluations, the evaluator should recycle his activities and audiences to provide opportunities for more or less continuous member checks.

Since members approached overtly for credibility checks may respond inappropriately, it is useful to keep the members ignorant of the fact that such checks are being made. If checking is done on a continuous basis, members are less likely to be aware of what is going on. Moreover, much of the checking can be done in the form of "hypothetical situations" to which members are asked to respond. Note that we are not advocating manipulation or deceit, but simply suggesting that evaluators take advantage of opportunities to elicit member checks whenever possible.

In some cases, the evaluator may wish to adopt an investigative posture when it is apparent that he is dealing with a hostile audience. In another context Guba (forthcoming) has suggested that there are certain parallels between investigative reporting and evaluation. One of the steps typically taken by investigative journalists is the so-called key interview, in which the reporter confronts the targets of the investigation to get their reactions to whatever the reporter has uncovered, to permit the targets to tell their side of the story, and perhaps to get additional information volunteered by the targets once they understand what the reporter already knows. Many of the techniques used by investigative reporters for that sort of "confrontation" are adaptable to the evaluation situation.

Different audiences bring different values, different perspectives, different constructions, and so on to the credibility test. The evaluator can take advantage of this situation by playing the audiences off against each other—not in a manipulative way, but in a way designed to highlight and clarify their differences. Individual audiences may challenge the credibility of data or interpretations when the evaluator alone presents them; when the audiences are brought together, however, the source of the conflict is made clear, and audience hostilities and disbeliefs are focused on their proper targets (not the evaluator).

Following the lead of Stake (1975), we suggest that credibility checks are most conveniently made in two stages—first, with a surrogate sample of representatives of the audiences, and, second, with the audiences themselves. Problems of credibility that arise with the surrogates can then be recognized and managed in the interaction with the audiences themselves.

Of course, it is possible that the evaluator may exercise all the cautions and use all the procedures suggested above without having his efforts culminate in a full corroboration of credibility. No one can reasonably expect a *full* corroboration in any event. But if the evaluator has undertaken the correct procedures, his data and interpretations will be at least minimally credible to the audiences that are in a position to judge them.

Threats to Internal Validity. We turn now to the question of whether the truth value of naturalistic inquiry can be established at the same level of confidence as can internal validity in the case of scientific inquiry. The classic treatment is that of Campbell and Stanley (1963), who pointed out the existence of a number of threats to internal validity:

- History—the specific events occurring between the first and second measurement in addition to the experimental treatment;
- Maturation—processes ongoing within the respondents that operate as a function of the passage of time per se;
- Testing—the effects of taking a test upon the scores of a second testing;
- Instrumentation—changes in the calibration of a measurement or changes in the observers or scorers used may produce changes in the obtained measurement;
- Statistical regression—an occurrence whenever groups have been selected on the basis of their extreme scores on some test;
- Differential selection—a result of biases among different comparison groups;
- Experimental mortality—the differential loss of respondents from the comparison groups; and
- Selection-maturation interaction—in certain designs this may be mistaken for the effect of the experimental variable.

Some of these threats are common to both scientific and naturalistic studies: differential selection and experimental mortality probably affect the outcomes of both in about the same way. At least one of the threats is more serious in naturalistic than in scientific studies, namely, instrumentation. Since as often as not the naturalistic inquirer is himself the instrument, changes resulting from fatigue, shifts in knowledge, and cooptation, as well as variations resulting from differences in training, skill, and experience among different "instruments," easily occur. But this loss in rigor is more than offset by the flexibility, insight, and ability to build on tacit knowledge that is the peculiar province of the human instrument.

Some of the threats do not apply to qualitative approaches at all, and insofar as naturalistic inquiries tend to lean on qualitative rather than quantitative means, the naturalistic paradigm seems to be ahead. We refer to history, statistical regression, and testing. The latter two are strictly quantitative problems that can therefore be completely avoided if the naturalist sticks to qualitative methods. And when he does not, he is no worse off than his scientific counterpart. For the scientist, the threat of history is that it cannot easily be converted into a statistical equivalent that can then be used to covary or otherwise control the dependent and independent variables. The naturalist, of course, avoids this problem because he is continuously making observations, noting historical impacts, and taking account of these impacts as the study progresses.

Finally, naturalistic approaches seem particularly useful to overcome two of these threats, maturation and selection—maturation interaction: the fact that the naturalist typically engages in long-term and continuing interactions with subjects makes these special kinds of changes easily detectable and apparent. We must conclude that if the eight Campbell and Stanley (1963) threats are indeed those about which naturalistic inquirers should be concerned, then naturalistic approaches come off at least as well as do scientific ones.

As a second line of argument relating to truth value, recall that experimental inquirers depend on overt controls to contain the effects of confounding variables that might otherwise tilt the results in an inappropriate direction. Decisions must be made about what those variables are and what is the best way to control them. In the process of such a manipulation the experimenter may—to use Brunswik's (1955) term—*tie* certain variables, that is, make it inevitable that they will be related in the experiment even though in the real world they may not be; or, conversely, he may *untie* other variables that are in fact related but that, in the experiment, are forced into an orthogonal relationship. To put it another way, the experimenter, by the way that he sets up the experiment, may destroy internal validity out of ignorance. We need hardly point out that this risk, at least, is one that the naturalistic investigator does *not* run.

Finally, we must point out that the naturalistic investigator is by no means helpless with respect to actions he can take to shore up internal validity. Thus, he can establish the degree of structural corroboration; he can use persistent and extended contacts; he can establish congruence with specially prepared referential adequacy materials; and he can establish the credibility of findings with relevant audiences.

On the question of internal validity, then, we conclude that naturalistic inquiry is no more open to threats than is scientific inquiry and may be less so.

Applicability. For many purposes the question of whether the findings of one evaluation might be applicable in some other setting is meaningless. The teacher evaluating the extent to which his class has mastered certain facts or ideas, the school system interested in determining which of several textbooks is most appropriate for its pupils, the developer trying to decide which of several presentational formats to use—all provide examples of particularistic interests from which generalizations are unlikely to be made. Indeed, in most formative evaluations and in some summative evaluations (those in which the interest of the evaluator is focused on a particular time or situation) questions of generalizability are irrelevant.

Nevertheless, there are many situations in which generalizability is an issue. Will the data for this year's class hold for next year's? Is an innovation evaluated in Keokuk, Iowa, likely to function equally well in Birmingham, Alabama? Are the needs of teachers dealing with high school nonreaders likely to be the same everywhere? What should the naturalistic evaluator do when asked to conduct an evaluation in which one of the purposes is to generate information that might be applied in multiple sites?

It is a truism that there can be no generalizability (even from the scientific point of view) unless there is first a reasonable level of internal validity. There is no point in asking whether meaningless information has any general applicability. In that sense, internal validity (or, from the naturalist's point of view, credibility) reinforces external validity (the ability to generalize). But there is also a sense in which internal validity can truncate or inhibit external validity. An overemphasis on *a priori* control of the factors or conditions that influence an inquiry—control instituted precisely in the interest of achieving high internal validity—

may seriously affect external validity, because then the findings can, at best, be said to be generalizable only to other, similarly controlled situations. Since such situations rarely exist in real life, generalizability can usually be questioned in the case of tightly controlled experiments.

A leading reason for the resurgence of naturalistic methodologies can be found in this circumstance. Naturalistic inquiry and naturalistic evaluation are exempt from this criticism because no attempt is made to institute *a priori* controls either on variables entering into the investigation or on output measures. There is full congruence between the situation being explored and the real world about which generalizations are to be made. Thus, the naturalistic investigator *is* free of one problem that perennially plagues the experimentalist: the lack of isomorphism between the laboratory and the real world.

Unfortunately, however, the problem is not that simple. Whether or not certain information is generalizable is a function not only of the degree to which the locale of the study is in fact a "slice of life" but also of whether that particular "slice of life" is representative of other "slices of life." Thus, investigators with naturalistic leanings tend to take somewhat different views of how generalizability should be treated.

Some investigators think that generalizability is a chimera and that it is impossible to generalize in the scientific sense at all. Different people with different backgrounds and purposes will see different things when they view a situation. The onion has many layers, and it is difficult for two people to agree about which layer is to be viewed. Replication is impossible because circumstances change so rapidly. Chinese mythology tells of the wanderer who asked a philosopher whether it is possible to cross the same river twice. The philosopher replied that it is not possible to cross the same river even once, since the river is flowing by and changing as the crossing is taking place. A person viewing the same situation at different times will be forced to different conclusions. Situational interactions are always so complex that any observation can have meaning only in the actual situation in which it occurred. Thus, if the term *generalization* is to have any meaning at all, it must be with reference to particular audiences. It is up to each audience to determine what, if anything, the information means and to determine for itself the information's applicability. The principal burden of synthesis always lies with the recipient of an evaluation report; it cannot lie with the evaluator.

Certainly each of these points has validity. But the position they represent is extreme—it appears to be less a genuine position than a reaction to an overemphasis placed on generalizability by conventional methodologists. As such, it does not amount to a credible methodological alternative.

Other investigators think that generalizability continues to be important and that efforts should be made to meet the normal scientific criteria that pertain to it. Denzin (1971), for example, indicates that "to the best of his ability the investigator must offer evidence on the degree to which his samples of behavior are representative of the class of joint acts he wishes to generalize to" (p. 175). However, he quickly notes that the population to which one wishes to generalize may be unknown; "as a consequence the naturalistic observer seldom can specify with precise detail the universe of interactive relationships to which he wishes to generalize" (p. 175). Of course, that observation also holds for most behavioral inquiries; it is certainly not unique to naturalistic inquiry. Denzin does suggest several approaches that can be taken, as a function of the investigator's *focus*: (1) the investigator locates himself in a "representative" situation and argues generalizability to all persons who pass through that situation; (2) the investigator argues that the findings hold for all persons in a particular time frame; (3) the investigator generalizes to a special population, such as prisoners or schoolchildren; or (4) the investigator generalizes to types of encounter or to the population of which the persons involved in the encounter are a "sample."

While these are useful approaches and perhaps should be utilized whenever opportunities present themselves, they nevertheless fall sufficiently short of the theoretical ideal to prevent the naturalistic investigator from definitively claiming generalizability. They are analogous to the use of matching groups as a substitute for random selection and assignment. Some gains undoubtedly occur, but the basic question—how good a sample of the population is being dealt with—remains essentially unanswerable.

Still other investigators think that generalizability is a fragile concept whose meaning is ambiguous and whose power is variable.

This third possible argument, which is essentially the one reviewed in Chapter Four, is based on the assertions of Cronbach (1975) that generalizations decay; that soon after they are made, generalizations are more likely to be history than science; and that instead of making generalization the ruling consideration in inquiry, evaluators should place emphasis on careful description and make efforts to "describe and interpret the effect anew in each locale, perhaps taking into account factors unique to that series of events" (p. 125). Generalizations in this context have the form of working hypotheses, not of conclusions.

Cronbach's advice seems particularly appropriate to naturalistic evaluators. Since their major concern is often not generalization anyway, a willingness to move away from the most rigorous criteria of generalizability seems a small loss. Moreover, the rigor of generalizability is at best suspect. If deferred generalization is a hallmark of a good inquiry model, the evaluator, whose activity often leads to decisions that have major consequences, ought to be more interested than most in deferring generalizations. An error on the evaluator's part is not simply a theoretical mistake but a possible disaster in the making.

What can be concluded from these varying points of view? The concept of generalizability is clearly undergoing revision, even within the scientific paradigm. The evaluator needs to understand that generalization, in the traditional sense, is not possible. Does that mean that the concept should be abandoned altogether?

Assuredly not. What we would counsel is that the idea of "generalizability" should be replaced by the idea of "fittingness." A generalization cannot be anything other than a context-free proposition. As we have tried to show, such context-free statements cannot be made when the inquiry is concerned with human behavior (for what human behavior is ever completely context free?), and they assuredly cannot be made with respect to evaluations of worth (as distinguished from merit), since the very idea of worth rests upon the relationship of an entity to its context. Given these distinctions, it seems useful to think not in terms of generalizations but in terms of working hypotheses that fit more or less well into a context other than the one in which they were derived.

Working hypotheses are propositions that arise from a particular investigation or evaluation. They seem to be well borne out within the local context that spawned them. But one does not assume that they would, for that reason, be well borne out in other contexts as well. Suppose that a certain educational innovation is evaluated (in the sense of worth) in Keokuk, Iowa, and the question arises whether that innovation would also produce its results in Birmingham, Alabama. *That* question can only be answered by examining the extent to which the context of Birmingham is similar to the context of Keokuk. Or, to put it another way, one needs to ask, "What is the degree of fittingness between the two contexts?" If the fit is good, one might then suppose that the Keokuk working hypotheses might also hold in Birmingham.

The assessment of fit, however, requires not only that one should know a great deal about Birmingham, *to* which the transfer is being contemplated, but also a great deal about Keokuk, *from* which the transfer is to occur. Generalizations in the scientific sense are bare-bones statements, stripped of all contextual references, and can be so exactly because they are assumed to be context free. But working hypotheses are very much context related and can be neither understood nor transferred without extensive knowledge of the originating context. We like the term *thick description*, which was coined by Gilbert Ryle and adapted to anthropology by Geertz (1973), as a way to talk about what is needed.

Thick description involves literal description of the entity being evaluated, the circumstances under which it is used, the characteristics of the people involved in it, the nature of the community in which it is located, and the like. Evaluators have always tended to provide such information as a routine part of reporting on evaluations. But thick description also involves interpreting the meaning of such demographic and descriptive data in terms of cultural norms and mores, community values, deep-seated attitudes and motives, and the like. To know, for example, that a biology curriculum failed in a community of certain size, with teachers of certain training, and so on is informative but not really compelling; if we also know that it was an Amish community whose sense of values was outraged by the content of the biology curriculum, we have a much better grasp of the reason for failure. And indeed, knowledge of the latter kind is essential if we are to transfer an innovation from one community to another. Only then can we assess the degree of "fittingness" that actually exists.

To recapitulate, evaluators ought not to think in terms of

generalizations that have some kind of enduring truth value. Rather they ought to think in terms of working hypotheses and of testing the degree of fit between the context in which the working hypotheses were generated and the context in which they are to be next applied. Fittingness, rather than generalization, is the naturalist's key concept.

But does the naturalistic paradigm provide as much assurance that good external validity or fittingness can be achieved as does the scientific? Whether we focus on the trade-off between internal and external validity or on the possibility of developing generalizations that are more rigorous than "working hypotheses," it would seem that both situations favor naturalistic methodology. We may choose to believe that generalizability has lost its utility as a concept and that what is needed are working hypotheses and thick descriptions. Will scientific methods or naturalistic methods serve us better in achieving those ends? Or we may choose to believe that generalizability is still a useful concept but that, to achieve it, an appropriate balance must be struck with internal validity. Will naturalistic methods or scientific methods better help us to strike that balance? We believe that the answer to both these questions is obvious.

Consistency. The issue of replicability is frequently invoked by critics of naturalistic inquiry. Willems (Willems and Raush, 1969) observes that "naturalistic research is often criticized on the grounds that it is not replicable, and it often seems to be assumed that behavior represents a class of such unstable and complicated phenomena that unless it is constrained by experimental controls, it is not amenable to scientific study" (p. 57).

Consistency, like applicability, is often not even an issue for the naturalistic inquirer. The implications of a multiple reality for generalizability have been touched on in several contexts; similar arguments can be made in the case of consistency. Moreover, the naturalistic inquirer may be more interested in differences than in similarities. The odd case may intrigue him more than the recurrent regularity. Finally, it can be argued that consistency, as an issue, need not be faced directly. Since it is impossible to have internal validity without reliability, a demonstration of internal validity amounts to a simultaneous demonstration of reliability. Hence, if the evaluator places emphasis on shoring up validity, reliability will follow.

Whatever the merits of such arguments, they do not answer the question that deserves an answer: What can be done to demonstrate replicability if a naturalistic inquirer chooses to do so?

Consistency of studies is an empirical matter. Evaluations especially, but often other naturalistic studies as well, are singular; they are commissioned and carried out to inform a decision, to respond to a criticism or concern, or to determine the effectiveness of a method. Thus, the likelihood that such a study would be replicated is small, and almost no instances can be cited in which replications have been undertaken. Without replication, however, what steps can be taken to demonstrate consistency? There seem to be three, and we will cite them all, but the first two seem to be less feasible on logistical and fiscal grounds than the third, which we believe to be the most useful and important.

1. Overlap methods. Imperfect inquiry techniques such as quasi-experimental designs can achieve enormous power when used in tandem, that is, in such a way that the imperfections of one are canceled or covered up by the strengths of a second, complementary technique (see Webb and others, 1966; Campbell and Stanley, 1963). While such nested use of techniques is ordinarily recommended for the sake of validity, it can also bolster the case for consistency. Comparable results from two or more different approaches (triangulation) strengthen the reliability claims of each of the individual approaches.

2. Stepwise replication. Replications can be built into the several stages or steps of any study. Probably the most straightforward means for doing so is to divide both the information sources (interview subjects, observational situations, documents, and so on) and the study team (if it consists of more than one person) into two random halves. Each team then undertakes an independent study.

A major problem with this approach is that naturalistic designs are emergent, not preordinate, so that it is not possible to keep the two teams separated for the period of the study. To obviate this serious problem, the two teams must communicate with each other at the conclusion of each step, and probably at the conclusion of each workday. At early stages in which the intent is to identify issues and concerns, the teams may, after a period of independent work, share the concerns and issues they have each unearthed to that point. The purpose of such sharing is partly to run the necessary consistency cross-checks and partly to set a common stage for the next step—verification of the concerns and issues that both teams have identified. In the consistency cross-check, it is up to each team to convince the other that issues and concerns identified by that team, but not by the other, are valid. This team cross-checking is somewhat similar to the auditing process to be described next. The consistency of a study would be well established if it could be shown that, at every crucial stage, the independent teams corroborated each other's work or could be persuaded that each other's work had adequacy.

3. The audit. The point has been made that one criterion for the necessity and sufficiency of a categorical set is its reproducibility by another competent judge. While it cannot be expected that sets of categories developed by two independent judges from the same basic data will coincide, it was argued that a second judge should be able to verify that the categories derived by the first judge make sense in view of the data pool from which the first judge worked and that the data have been appropriately arranged into the developed category system. The second judge audits the work of the first much as an examiner audits the work of an accountant in the business world.

Similarly, a naturalistic evaluation can be audited by a second investigator or team. The second team could not be expected to reproduce the study without knowing the decisions made by the original investigators at every step of the process. The team could, however, review each decision and the consequent actions, verifying that substantively and methodologically sound options were chosen. Such a review or audit would give substantial assurance of the consistency of any evaluation.

Several points should be noted by anyone proposing to implement this kind of audit. First, it is essential that documentation of the decision trail (that is, the audit trail) be adequately maintained. Unless care is taken to record the nature of each decision, the data upon which it was based, and the reasoning that entered into it, the second team will not have appropriate information on which to base its audit. An examiner cannot examine an accountant's work unless the account books are available.

Second, auditing is a process that must be carried out by personnel external to the evaluation team. Just as General Electric must turn to Price, Waterhouse if the audit of its books is to have any credibility with its stockholders, so evaluators must turn to external, independent, and disinterested parties if the evaluation audit is to have any credibility for its audiences.

Finally, the audit process is very likely to be attacked as an inadequate basis for the establishment of consistency because, it will be asserted, the audit team does *not* in fact replicate the study but simply attests that it was carried out in a competent manner. Detractors will argue that a real test would require completely independent replication—then and only then could consistency be asserted. But this argument is specious on two grounds. First, it is unreasonable to require a complete replication in view of the resources that would be required to meet that criterion; no one would suggest that a scientific experiment could be labeled "reliable" if and only if it were completely replicated by a second inquiry team. Second, and more importantly, the test proposed is not fair. The naturalistic inquirer approaches his problem in a very open-ended way and is free to take it up at any point as long as he stays within the bounds prescribed by the problem being investigated. Given the phenomenon of multiple realities, it would be remarkable indeed if two investigators proceeded in exactly the same way. Consistency could hardly ever be demonstrated under such circumstances. This situation is analogous to asking two theorists, knowledgeable about the research and concepts of a field, to propose a series of hypotheses that would be most promising for upcoming work. No one would expect the two theorists to come up with an identical list (although some overlaps would surely occur), nor would one dismiss their work simply because it was not "consistent." But one would hope that each theorist, when shown the work of the other, would be able to say, "Of course those are perfectly reasonable hypotheses, given what we know about the field and given my colleague's particular experience, perspective, and so on." It is *that* level of agreement and consistency that we are arguing for here.

We are quite convinced that consistency is a reasonable criterion for any inquiry. But we reject the concept of reliability as that term has come to be used in the scientific paradigm and propose instead the concept of "auditability" as more appropriate to the naturalistic approach. And to repeat, auditability requires simply that the work of one evaluator (or team) can be tested for consistency by a second evaluator or team, which, after examining the work of the first, can conclude, "Yes, given that perspective and those data, I would probably have reached the same conclusion."

It must be conceded that the consistency of a naturalistic study is more difficult to establish than that of a scientific study. Nevertheless, the methods available for establishing consistency in naturalistic studies, while perhaps not so elegant as their scientific counterparts, give to naturalistic studies at least the minimum level of consistency necessary for producing trustworthy data.

Neutrality. The issue of neutrality, commonly called "objectivity" within the scientific paradigm, is probably the most thorny one that can be raised with respect to naturalistic inquiry. For how can an inquiry be objective if it simply "emerges"; if it has no careful controls laid down *a priori*; if the observations to be made or the data to be recorded are not specified in advance; and if, on the admission of its practitioners, there exist multiple realities capable of being plumbed to different depths at different times by different investigators?

On close examination, the difficulty stems less from the innate characteristics of naturalistic inquiry than from the meaning that is ascribed to the term *objectivity*. Scriven (1972) has pointed to a "fundamental confusion" in the use of the term:

> The terms *objective* and *subjective* are always held to be contrasting, but they are widely used to refer to two quite different contrasts, which I shall refer to as the *quantitative* and *qualitative* senses. In the first of these contrasts, "subjective" refers to what concerns or occurs to the *individual* subject and his experiences, qualities, and dispositions, while "objective" refers to what a *number* of subjects or judges experience—in short, to phenomena in the public domain. The difference is simply the *number* of people to whom reference is made, hence the term *quantitative*. In the second of the two uses, there is a reference to the *quality* of the testimony or the report or the (putative) evidence, and so I call this the "qualitative" sense. Here, "subjective" means unreliable,

biased or probably biased, a matter of opinion, and "objective" means reliable, factual, confirmable or confirmed, and so forth. Now it would certainly be delightful if these two senses coincided, so that all reports of personal experience, for example, were less reliable than all reports of events witnessed by a large number of people. But as one thinks of the reliability of reports about felt pain or perceived size, on the one hand, and reports about the achievement of stage magicians and mentalists, on the other, one would not find this coincidence impressive [pp. 95-96].

Thus, Scriven suggests that what one individual experiences is not necessarily unreliable, biased, or a matter of opinion, just as what a number of individuals experience is not necessarily reliable, factual, and confirmable. Although it is often assumed that individual concerns or thoughts are biased and unconfirmable (at least in the sense of intersubjective agreement), this assumption is not necessarily true. Depending upon the qualities, training, and experience of the single observer, his reports may be more factual and confirmable than the reports of a group. To follow up Scriven's example, one would be more inclined to accept the reports of one magician standing in the wings during another magician's performance than the reports of a large audience, all of whose members were being systematically deluded.

Further, what an individual experiences can be equivalent to what a group experiences; but unreliable, biased, or opinionated reports cannot be the equivalent of reliable, factual, or confirmable reports. That is, in the quantitative sense, subjectivity and objectivity can be identical, but in the qualitative sense subjectivity and objectivity can never be identical; they are polar opposites.

In any inquiry, the objectivity of the data is of critical concern. The data should be factual and confirmable. There seems to be no intrinsic reason why the methods of a properly trained naturalistic inquirer should be a more doubtful source of such data than the methods of an investigator using a quantitative approach. After all, data gained from quantitative sources may also be biased. Consider, for example, the cultural bias said to inhere in many so-called objective tests. The issue is not the intrinsic objectivity (in the qualitative sense) of the methods used to generate information or the objectivity of the investigator, but the confirm-ability of the information once it is obtained. In that regard, the methods for establishing truth value discussed earlier seem appropriate: triangulation, cross-examination, persistent observation, member checks, and testing of congruence with referential adequacy materials.

But the concept of confirmability has another important virtue: it shifts the burden of proof from the investigator to the information itself. Very often objectivity is said to be a trait of the investigator, and, to be sure, there are many ways in which characteristics of the investigator can influence objectivity—unconscious biases and conscious prejudices, incompetence, gullibility, or even corruptibility. (For a discussion of various aspects of evaluator corruptibility, see Guba, 1975.) But to imagine that an evaluator, by an act of will or by virtue of clever methodology, can rid himself of subjectivity is the worst kind of fantasy. No human being can ever be objective in that sense. The requirement that information be confirmable rids the inquirer of this impossible constraint; it simply asks that the inquirer report his data in such a way that it can be confirmed from other sources if necessary. We may assume that an inquirer who is properly trained and experienced will have fewer problems with objectivity than will those with less training and experience. However, one cannot expect all, or even most, inquirers to fit this mold. Requiring that information be confirmable, rather than that the inquirer be certifiable, is at once more reasonable and more to the point.

Scientists have used two approaches to guarantee their neutrality. First, they have dissociated themselves from the phenomena under study by devising a variety of objective extensions of themselves. Physical instruments, tests, and other impersonal data probes are widely used, and when these methods are contrasted with those of the naturalist, who is often himself the instrument, some claim that there is no comparison between these two approaches so far as guarantees of neutrality are concerned. Second, scientists have insisted upon making judgments about what data to collect, what to regard as important, how to analyze data, and how to interpret them beforehand, under the apparent assumption that to make such decisions *a priori* renders it more difficult for the investigator's personal biases to intrude into the process. But neither of these approaches can be regarded as guarantees. The instruments selected and decisions about data will be influenced by the predilections of the investigator. The investigator will select (or build) instruments that conform to those predilections or to whatever he regards as important. Biases about respondents can be built into objective test items as easily as into interview questions. Sampling plans can be devised to be unrepresentative whatever one's paradigmatic preference may be. Values cannot be kept out of inquiry simply by making most of the procedural decisions before rather than during the inquiry. Further, by making those decisions early, the investigator loses the advantage of developing insights and of establishing adequate grounding for his hypotheses and questions.

On balance again we would have to assert that naturalistic methods are no worse than scientific in achieving neutrality and may at times be better. Whatever degree of apparent objectivity may be lost is more than compensated for by the continuously emerging insights that naturalistic methods produce.

Chapter 6

The Evaluator as Instrument

One of the most difficult concepts involved in naturalistic inquiry is that of the inquirer as instrument. He is at one and the same time instrument administrator, data collector, data analyst, and data interpreter. He is, in the methodological terminology of traditional educational research, both an independent variable and an interaction effect.

This chapter is based on certain fundamental premises that are at heart phenomenological rather than scientific. Naturalistic method relies heavily on the human being as instrument. The skills required for all the inquiry roles that can be packed into a human being are wholly different from those needed, say, by someone constructing an attitude measure or a personality profile. The scientifically oriented inquirer who wishes to differentiate personality on a scale for testing tendencies to schizophrenia attempts to create and perfect an instrument that is essentially free of human judgment. The phenomenologist, however, is not interested in dismissing human judgment but seeks to sharpen and refine the skills that go into the judgment process. The former sees a human being as an imperfect processer of information and seeks to remove that imperfection from the measuring process. The latter is not interested in measuring but seeks to make human beings as instruments more personally and environmentally sensitive and to "create" an instrument that reflects idiosyncrasies rather than norms. The world of the scientific inquirer is based on a construct that the naturalistic inquirer finds only minimally (if at all) useful—the "normal." The naturalistic inquirer is constantly searching for that which is unique, atypical, different, idiographic, individualistic. The scientific inquirer perceives himself as an objective manipulator of situations and variables who wants to understand generalizable principles. The naturalistic inquirer refuses to manipulate his environment, seeking rather to understand how the environment acts on itself, as well as how the inquirer causes it to behave in different ways.

Major Characteristics of the Instrument

The foregoing discussion suggests that there are some important characteristics of the inquirer as instrument that are not to be found in other forms of instruments (performance tests, paper-and-pencil tests, certain kinds of observational measures). That is most certainly the case. The characteristics that follow, however, should not be regarded as a sufficient set, yet they are a necessary one. We do not know at this time what would comprise a list that was also sufficient. We can, however, suggest some characteristics of human beings as instruments that differ markedly from, say, paper-and-pencil tests as instruments.

Responsiveness. The human being as instrument is responsive, both to the environment and to the persons who occupy and create that environment. While it is true that a person may respond to a paper-and-pencil test (for example, by becoming nervous or anxious, by having already become "test-wise," by being offended by the language or values embodied therein, and so forth), the test itself will never become responsive to the person. It just lies on the table, waiting for the person to mark categories, respond to questions, work problems, lie, whatever. This rarely happens when the information collector is a human being (except in highly specialized cases, for example, a covert nonparticipant observer watching an interrogation through a one-way mirror). The human being is both interpersonally and environmentally interactive, and he not only responds to cues—foreseen and unforeseen—but he also provides cues to others. Furthermore, he is aware of the cues that he gives off (if he is a competent inquirer and constantly examining his own style), and he seeks to become increasingly aware of the way in which his own cues are interacting with the context that he seeks to understand and represent.

He is responsive because he must first "sense" the dimensions of a context, then seek to make those dimensions explicit—even if the dimensions are only or largely tacit to the participants themselves. The scientific inquirer, as opposed to the naturalistic, seeks to control the environment in order to filter out those factors that confound the information collected. The naturalist, in contrast, wishes to control the environment as little as possible, so that he can discover what the dimensions of "interference" are. His responsiveness opens him to avenues of observation—and hence to additional data collection—that are not possible to a paper-and-pencil test administrator. Two examples come to mind immediately. During an interview, the subject may indicate by a variety of body language and gesturing clues or by certain phrasing (for example, "Now to tell you the truth . . .") that he is uncomfortable, anxious, threatened, or about to lie to the questioner. Or the playground observer may note that there are certain groups of children who consistently play together while other children are consistently omitted from selection to teams or to unstructured play, leading him to generate sociograms on the basis of inclusion and exclusion.

The notion of environmental or contextual interactiveness is antithetical to the scientist, who cannot maintain his posture without the assumption of researcher neutrality. The posture of the naturalistic inquirer, however, gives rise not to neutrality, but to a profound responsiveness and interactivity. The result for a responsive inquiry is frequently—and optimally—a situation in which respondents do not adopt the constructs of the inquirer but rather relate their histories, anecdotes, experiences, perspectives, retrospectives, introspections, hopes, fears, dreams, and beliefs in their own natural language, based on their own personal and cultural understandings. The naturalistic inquirer's responsiveness not only calls this uniqueness forth; it is exactly what he wishes to have.

Adaptability. The human as instrument is almost infinitely adaptable as a data-gathering device. An IQ test will indeed measure IQ, but it will never measure authoritarianism, theoretical orientation, aesthetic inclination, or tendency to schizophrenia. A human being utilizing himself as a data collection tool, however, can assess any number of things. For example, he can assess artistic orientation by noting the furnishings, wall hangings, art objects, and so on in a corporate businessman's suite; intellectual interest by making note of the number and types of books in bookcases, as well as the magazines and newspapers lying around in an interviewee's home or office; interpersonal family communication styles by observing interactions between family members while an interview is in progress or interrupted; willingness to be open, as evidenced by verbal evasions, body language, and eye movement; power relationships, by watching how persons attending a meeting arrange themselves around power figures; general educational attainment by making note of linguistic and grammatical usage, sophistication of expression, subtlety of nuance, expressive variation, or specialized terminology in subjects' everyday language; or ethnicity by observation of dress, dialect, idiomatic expression, cultural referents, and so on.

The foregoing examples represent several of the many forms of data collection—usually on a secondary, auxiliary, or perhaps even subconscious basis—to which the human instrument is adaptable. For instance, any one or several of these assessments may be made while the inquirer is doing an unstructured interview to determine how the residents of a community view a proposed set of zoning regulations. Thus a human instrument is not only multipurpose but is highly differentiated, since the collection of various kinds of data is going on virtually simultaneously.

But the multipurpose quality of a human as instrument is important in another way also. If he can collect direct evidence on several levels at once, he can also adapt his "mode" of collection to suit changing circumstances and contexts or variable information needs and requirements. This ability to adapt to differing contexts and different informational needs is a virtue that a paper-and-pencil test can never achieve.

Further, the human instrument may not know except in the

broadest sense what it is he is to investigate when he enters the context. It is only by his perceptivity, discrimination, and instinct that he is able to focus his style, method, and approach on that which does emerge as important. His characteristic adaptability frees him to explore the context until either he senses he has reached a topic of concern (a relevant issue) or until he is satisfied that the subjects can provide him with no new information. Traditional measurement has no such flexibility or adaptability. Indeed, its hallmark is its highly targeted nature.

Holistic Emphasis. The targeted, tight construction of most scientific approaches suggests yet another important characteristic of human beings as instruments; that is, they are holistic rather than segmented. Unlike paper-and-pencil tests or a variety of other measures that are limited in the number of constructs that they can test, the inquirer as instrument has at his testing disposal an infinite variety of constructs, both conscious and unconscious. He has no limit save his own imagination and creativity, and that of his respondent, who may also be called upon to generate reasons, excuses, constructs, hypotheses, or explanations. The world is all of a piece to the naturalistic inquirer; it is not sorted into a set of artificially delimited topics or content areas, as are traditional instruments. The human being sees few, if any, boundaries to the world of his subjects, except those seen by the subjects themselves. The world is woven of seamless cloth for the naturalistic inquirer; and though he may explore only one portion of the garment at a given time or see it through only one pair of eyes, it nevertheless has the quality of being "all of a piece." The world is viewed in holistic fashion, as a continuous context within which program participants view themselves and their lives as real, true, and having meaning.

That holistic emphasis not only gives the inquirer the context—the subjects' and respondents' "real world"—but it also lends mood, climate, tone, pace, texture, and feelings. The inquirer in a naturalistic model ignores those aspects of his inquiry at his and his audiences' peril.

Not only is the naturalistic inquirer concerned with the context in a holistic fashion, but that context is present at every turn. It assaults his conscious and unconscious self, it insinuates itself into the corners of his mind, it picks at him and disturbs his sleep like small unidentified sounds. Every aspect—sights, sounds, smells —of the lives of his subjects is of intense interest. Like the Western traveler on the Orient Express, new to the Eastern world, every value, every assumption, every "truth" that the naturalistic inquirer owns must be examined in the light of native laws, rules, values, traditions, beliefs, and customs. Indeed, the salient features of the emotional and affective landscape are visualized by the inquirer as absolutely essential elements of the inquiry effort. It would never, for instance, occur to the naturalistic inquirer that aspects of the context are "unreal," as naive student fieldworkers will sometimes report. Goffman (1961) writes that it "is my belief that any group of persons—prisoners, primitives, pilots, or patients —develop a life of their own that becomes meaningful, reasonable, and normal once you get close to it, and that a good way to learn about any of these worlds is to submit oneself in the company of the members to the daily round of petty contingencies to which they are subject" (pp. 9-10). It is the totality of this meaning, reasonableness, and normalcy in each context and setting that the naturalistic inquirer seeks to understand, to explain, and to describe.

To make sense of the whole, the inquirer must, like an anthropologist in an utterly foreign culture, immerse himself totally in the new environment and suspend his own value judgments, adopting, in Dexter's (1970) words, "what the interviewee regards as a conceivable and pertinent frame of reference, something which the interviewee shares" (p. 36).

This does not mean that the naturalistic inquirer should "go native." The dangers of that particular phenomenon to social science have been well documented. Rather, the inquirer must develop a contextual, holistic sense of the situation. Dexter points out that for certain kinds of inquiry "to be worthwhile, I have got to see it fit into a pattern, a framework" (p. 16). That framework consists not only of what the respondent is saying but also of his surrounding ethos and events, as well as other parties who might know something about the situation. It includes information gleaned from "being able to hang around or in some way observe" (p. 17), at both a conscious and subconscious level, comings and goings, secretarial interactions, and social interactions, along with the "code, norm, affect, rule, and so on, guiding the actors" (p.

19). It is possible and indeed desirable that the inquirer should become increasingly attuned to observing at several levels at once,
and it is this quality that affords him the best prospects of a holistic account of the project.

Knowledge Base Expansion. The knowledge base from
which the inquirer as instrument works is necessarily expanded
from that of more scientifically oriented methods. The domains of
both propositional and tacit knowledge function simultaneously
for the naturalistic inquirer, whether he is interviewing, engaging
in observation, or using any other field method. The information
collection process continues even when he is not consciously
aware of it. For example, it took Dexter (1970) many years to
realize that this process of unconscious collection was going on in
his work:

> This point is a difficult one to discuss by refer-
> ence to the literature because a great many, probably
> the majority, of scholars who ostensibly rely upon
> interviews or upon an informant as their chief source
> of data actually have a good deal of independent
> knowledge about the situation. . . . Also . . . in other
> writings about Congress, I sometimes appear to rely
> chiefly upon interviews, but in fact I was living in
> Washington at the time, spent much of my "free"
> time in a congressional office, saw a good deal of sev-
> eral congressional assistants and secretaries socially,
> worked on other matters with several persons actively
> engaged in relationships with Congress (lobbying and
> liaison), had read extensively about congressional his-
> tory and behavior, and had some relevant acquain-
> tance with local politics in several congressional dis-
> tricts. All these factors made my analysis of
> interviews somewhat credible. And, as I look back,
> interviews sometimes acquired meaning from the ob-
> servations which I often made while waiting in con-
> gressional offices . . . and in fact it is only now, in
> 1968, that I realize how much these other factors
> affected what I "heard" [p. 15].

In fact, the realms of "knowing" not only may be extended
to include propositional and tacit knowledge but may be targeted

by the level of awareness or the processing mechanism as illustrated in Table 7.

Table 7. Four Kinds of Knowing

Level of Awareness or Processing Component	Knowledge Products	
	Propositional	Tacit
Conscious	Hypotheses Statements Assertions	Insights Apprehensions
Unconscious	Linguistic symbols Dreams Languages	Hunches Impressions Feelings "Vibrations" (in response to nonverbal cues and unobtrusive indicators) Nonlinguistic dreams

Table 7 is, of course, incomplete. It may be inaccurate according to newer theories of how human beings come to "know" and to learn. But until we understand more about the functions of the brain, we shall simply go on "understanding" that we somehow "knew" something of which we were not consciously aware. Human beings capture, filter, and process literally thousands of bits of data every day; these are sifted, sorted, and patterned to make a complex but meaningful whole; they represent both tacit and propositional knowledge and are perceived as having continuity. To the extent that the human as inquirer does this sifting and patterning better than a machine or a piece of paper, the human is the better research instrument. It goes without saying that the extent to which the human inquirer is able to move from the tacit/conscious or the tacit/unconscious cells to the propositional/conscious cell marks him as more or less effective. The better the naturalistic inquirer, the more readily (though not necessarily the more quickly) he is able to make explicit those portions of the context that have become, for the participants, the latent dimensions.

Extending awareness of a situation beyond mere propositional knowledge to the realm of the felt, to the silent sympathies, to the unconscious wishes, and to the daily unexamined usages will lend depth and richness to our understanding of social and organizational settings. It is finally the inquirer alone who can provide this expansion of our awareness.

Processual Immediacy. Another quality of the human as instrument is what we have termed *processual immediacy.* This is the ability to process data immediately upon acquisition, reorder it, change the direction of the inquiry based upon it, generate hypotheses on the spot, and test them with the respondent or in the situation as they are created. Naturally, the researcher will often want to remove himself from the site before he begins intensive analysis of the data that have been collected. Nevertheless, the process of data collection itself will generate insights, new hypotheses, and themes—all of which need to be taken into account as the collection process itself is refined in the field. The survey questionnaire cannot be changed in midcollection; that is not logistically feasible, and reliability, validity, and aggregatability will be affected. But the inquirer using naturalistic methods actually acquires reliability and validity when he expands the inquiry to account for new information and understandings. Bogdan and Taylor (1975, pp. 79-80) call this process "data analysis," a fairly simple term that "refers to a process which entails an effort to formally identify themes and to construct hypotheses (ideas) as they are suggested by data and an attempt to demonstrate support for those themes and hypotheses." They comment that "in a sense, data analysis is an ongoing process in participant observation research." To the extent that qualitative inquiry permits this on-the-spot analysis (and the possibility of redirection of inquiry), it allows for more penetrating observation and demonstrable plausibility than does quantitative analysis.

Opportunities for Clarification and Summarization. The sensitive interviewer can tell immediately if previous statements were not clear or if they need amplification. The ability to extend and amplify meanings that may have been lost through other means of data gathering is unique to the human inquirer. Even open-ended questionnaires, once they are filled out, leave little room for clarification unless there is continuing contact with the respondent. And often, even later contact will reveal that meanings have changed and perceptions have altered. But a person talking can tell you precisely what his last remark meant, can share with you the affect that caused him to frame the comment in precisely that fashion, or can grant additional or background information that will expand the understanding of a particular event, feeling, perception, or situation. The opportunity to probe, to delve, to scrutinize, or to cross-examine is one that only the human inquirer has.

Summarization, too, is a powerful tool that should be exploited. It serves three principal purposes that cannot be ignored in naturalistic inquiry. First, it acts as a credibility check. It is a way of determining that the inquirer has heard correctly, that he has understood and can consequently recapitulate what the informant has said. It demonstrates the extent to which the evaluator has listened carefully and has avoided imposing values on the conversation that were not those of the speaker, as well as the extent to which he can faithfully and accurately reproduce the spirit and style of the person interviewed. The ability to summarize well is largely a function of the experience of the inquirer, but training and practice can produce a superb listener.

A second valuable outcome of summarization is to "get the informant on record." When information is summarized ("Now, if I have understood you correctly, the key points that you have made with me were . . . "), the person interviewed has the choice of either agreeing or disagreeing; if the latter is the case, the record can be set straight. But once the interview or conversation has been summarized, there is a commitment on the part of the informant to stand by the information that he has given.

A third function of summarization is to allow the interviewee or informant to point out key items that may have been missed. Especially when an inquirer is new to a site, what might be important to those on site may not be perceived as important by the inquirer. He has to be told that the information just received is crucial to understanding. When significant or key pieces of information are not picked up by the observer or interviewer, the subject will sometimes point this out. But only a careful summary at the end of an interview or conversation will cause the person being interviewed to realize that the interviewer has missed a critical point.

Opportunity to Explore Atypical or Idiosyncratic Responses. The human being as inquirer also has an opportunity to explore responses from individuals who have special expertise,

who have unique perceptions or roles, or who may provide atypical or idiosyncratic responses. These respondents' reactions, feelings, or inside information would most likely be lost on a standardized questionnaire or in the context of a highly structured
interview, even if it were possible to persuade such "elite" subjects
to participate in the first place. But because of circumstances,
position, authority, or some other social structuring, their perspectives on the matter under investigation are sufficiently singular to
enable them to provide information that could not be duplicated
under any other conditions than those of the "elite" interview.
The atypical, the especially powerful, the "elite" interviewee is the
person, in fact, for whom no meaningful questionnaire could be
developed. Dexter (1970) writes: "In the standardized interivew,
the typical survey, a deviation is ordinarily handled statistically;
but in an elite interview, an exception, a deviation, an unusual
interpretation may suggest a revision, a reinterpretation, an extension, a new approach" (p. 6). It is this exception, extension, or
reinterpretation that finally grants the human as instrument a
power beyond that of other kinds of instruments. The power to
extend the boundaries of an inquiry into realms not touched by
typical social science investigations is an enormous advantage.

The atypical or idiosyncratic response has no value in a standard inquiry, where the question and the problem are posed by
the inquirer and the inquirer seeks answers that fall within his own
presuppositions. Within the boundaries of standardized inquiry the
atypical or idiosyncratic response would be lost, masked, or
treated as a statistical deviation not worthy of further investigation. Human inquirers, however, not only are open to the atypical
response but encourage and seek it. The ability to encounter such
responses and to utilize them for increased understanding is possible, in fact, only with human, as opposed to paper-and-pencil,
instruments.

What Are Desirable Qualities for "Human Instruments"?

There is no definitive answer to this question, but rather a
cumulative body of wisdom suggested by those who have conducted naturalistic inquiry over the years. The question is: given
an "instrument" that is responsive, flexible, and adaptable, that

brings a holistic emphasis and processual immediacy to inquiry situations, and that builds on tacit knowledge and the like, what personal characteristics ought this "instrument" to have? We suggest that while there are temperaments that lend themselves to the requirements of naturalistic inquiry, almost anybody can be trained to be a better interviewer, a more careful observer, a more rigorous document analyst, a more sensitive attender to nonverbal cues, regardless of what his personality configuration happens to be.

The argument here is not that one cannot be both a scientific and a naturalistic inquirer. There are times when one method serves inquiry better than the other. And while we feel that the scientific paradigm has not served education well in past decades, because it proceeds from assumptions that are not particularly suited to human organizations and enterprises, we prefer to make another argument: if nothing else, acquiring the techniques of naturalistic inquiry adds immeasurably to the repertoire of inquiry skills available to any researcher or evaluator. But past and present students, especially in the various disciplines of education, have received little, if any, training in these techniques. Thus there has been little opportunity for students and practicing professionals to determine if the techniques are useful or add to the domain of inquiry, and even less opportunity to question the assumptions that underlie most traditional forms of inquiry. Most of those already engaged in educational evaluation and research, and most training to do so in the future, hardly know whether they are or might be "good at it" or not.

The story is recounted in educational circles that a superintendent was asked by a judge, "Tell me, sir, do you think that money could solve the problems of your district?" The superintendent responded, "I don't know, Your Honor, but I would certainly like to try it for a change!" In much the same vein, we do not know whether naturalistic inquirers are made or born, but we would certainly like to try making them for awhile, for we think that people can and do change. They can learn to become more tolerant, more patient, more empathetic, better listeners, and the like. To postulate that, in the process of becoming professionals, individuals should also acquire more of those characteristics that we call humane, open, honest, and developmental is not to demand something that is antithetical to advanced learning; rather, this is consonant with the objectives of all higher learning.

With that in mind, what are the characteristics that make for good human instruments and that training should try to bring out?

The characteristic most applicable in any naturalistic study or evaluation is empathy.

Gorden (1975) suggests that empathy is essential to the study of human behavior. Interviewing cannot take place without an empathetic relationship between interviewer and respondent, he asserts; while taking on an empathetic posture does have certain dangers, such as overempathizing or misempathizing, there is no point in lamenting that fact. "Empathy is a necessary element in human communication" (1975, p. 516).

Gorden argues, in fact, that the possibility of empathy between observer and respondent is one of the advantages that the social sciences have over the physical sciences. Moreover, empathy not only facilitates understanding but the achievement of understanding builds greater empathy. There is thus a "complementary relationship" between empathy as "a human characteristic and social science as a specialized, abstract, objective analysis of human behavior" (p. 517). Thus, empathy and objectivity need not be antithetical; they can in fact facilitate one another.

One of the silent hallmarks of outstanding anthropological and sociological studies to date has been the empathy with which they have presented major actors, performers, and informants. It is almost axiomatic that, as Denny (1978) has said, "Good guys get better data. No sense leaving your humanness at home" (p. 10). The extent to which inquirers are able to communicate warmth and empathy often marks them as good or not-so-good data collectors.

The more sensitive the data being collected, the more personal the stories being recounted, the more an empathetic listener is required. In analyzing what makes a good fieldworker or field interviewer, Denny (1978) adds several other dimensions: "First, there are no good interviewers who are not exceedingly bright. Second, there are no good interviewers who are not interesting people in their own right. Third, here comes the circularity, there are no good interviewers who do not love interviewing. Fourth, good interviewers are able to work for long stretches of time without fatigue; and finally every good interviewer I know has a clear sense of self" (p. 13).

But these are not the only characteristics of good field-workers. Implied in Denny's work, and dealt with rather directly in the work of Zigarmi and Zigarmi (1978), is the ability to deal with the psychological stresses of fieldwork: the loneliness, the isolation, the inability to talk with anyone else for perhaps long periods of time about one's work or findings, the necessity to use evenings and weekends to cope with voluminous field notes. Another aspect, according to Zigarmi and Zigarmi (1978), "relates to the ethnographer's need to be constantly examining his feelings and actions and the impact those actions might be having on people in the research setting or on data collection. Over time, constant introspection is stressful" (p. 16). Reinharz (1979), however, contends that social environments change less than researchers do: "The assumption that social environments are relatively unstable leads to research strategies that minimize the disruptive effects of the researcher. Conversely, one could assume, as did Henry (1967) after living in the homes of families with psychotic children, that personality structures and social environments are stable and resistant to change. Custom and organizational structure perpetuate behavior patterns, the alteration of which requires great effort and usually meets with resistance. In addition, to the extent that behavior patterns are unconsciously derived, they are not amenable to conscious change" (p. 160).

In fact, the recognition that the fieldworker is subject to change is one of the more important realizations of social inquiry. That change, Wax (1971) commented, will not come because of "the things . . . suffered, enjoyed or endured; . . . nor by the things (one) did. . . . What changed me irrevocably and beyond repair were the things I *learned*" (p. 363). The willingness to undergo that change, to have one's perceptions of another's world permanently and unequivocally altered, is, according to Wax, "unqualifiedly a good thing."

Wax (1971) lists another trait of the successful fieldworker: "The inclination to talk and listen to as many different people as he can is one of the essential traits of the really good fieldworker. Indeed, the scrupulous fieldworker makes a conscious effort and, if necessary, forces himself to talk to the people whom he dislikes, mistrusts, or despises (or who dislike, mistrust, or despise him) and, in like manner, he listens to and tries to understand the things he does not want to hear" (pp. 272-273). No doubt the interviewee or informant with charm, with poise, with interest, with a willingness to talk freely, spontaneously, and informatively is the delight of the inquirer. Equally without doubt is that most persons with whom the inquirer talks will not be altogether without suspicion, hostility, or ungraciousness. But the inquirer who wants his work to be credible will talk with *all* persons who inform his inquiry, not just the charming and powerful. And he will do so not just because the canons of rigorous inquiry demand it, but because he is naturally inclined to seek out the weak as well as the powerful, the common as well as the extraordinary, and those who do not at first appear to be central to the social situation. Being uncertain where truth—or even a "good story"—might lie, he looks and listens everywhere. Curious about everyone, he is willing to listen to people and is aware that information can come from unexpected quarters.

To some extent, this approach has been well developed by Dexter (1970) in his treatment of elite and specialized interviewing, since he presupposes that interviewing skill rests upon:

1. stressing the interviewee's definition of the situation,
2. encouraging the interviewee to structure the account of the situation,
3. letting the interviewee introduce to a considerable extent (an extent which will of course vary from project to project and interviewer to interviewer) his notions of what he regards as relevant, instead of relying upon the investigator's notions of relevance [p. 5].

The emphasis upon pluralistic points of view and values is most pressing in educational environments, and indeed in all endeavors that might count as social action or social welfare programs. It is only by an inquirer's being willing to listen to many individuals and to many points of view that value-resonant social contexts can be fully, equitably, and honorably represented. The fieldworker who is willing to listen to and talk with anyone who will speak with him is very likely to end up with information that reliably depicts the social context in which he is working.

Tymitz and Wolf (1977), in their extensive manual of field-worker characteristics and responsibilities, give a somewhat lengthier and more formal list of necessary traits:

- People should not be placed as interviewers in situations where they will encounter pet peeves.
- People who are unafraid to enter into new situations but who can also be unobtrusive make good natural inquirers.
- Good listeners make good observers, as do people with a wide range of interests.
- People who are relatively unfamiliar or value free with respect to situations make good participant/observers because they don't feel compelled to interpret. Pick people with the most potential to "go in clean" whenever you can.
- Curious, inquisitive people are good candidates for natural inquiry [pp. 12-13].

In addition, Tymitz and Wolf (1977) also list "desirable skills and qualities of an interviewer" (interviewing being one of the necessary techniques in the naturalistic repertoire):

> Being able to structure . . . his role in a realistic, nonthreatening way; being able to observe a situation while being involved in it; being at ease but not overly casual, friendly but not too familiar and chatty, curious and investigative but not nosy or pushy; showing sincere interest in the interviewee and respect for his feelings and opinions, empathizing without becoming involved; showing curiosity and pleasure in listening without diverting attention to . . . himself or interjecting . . . his own feelings and opinions; staying neutral and uninvolved in feelings or issues; being self-confident but not opinionated, rigid, or moralistic; being self-aware, seeing . . . himself as others do in the situation and noticing how he is functioning.
> Being able to keep calm in charged situations, to take rebuffs without flaring back, to tolerate

changing moods and divergent opinions while keeping
reactions private; being able to keep personal projec-
tions at a minimum and yet retain insights; being tolerant of a variety of types of people and situations
and able to relate quickly to each situation or person
on [its or] his own terms; being quick to perceive the
details of a new situation, understand the relationships, grasp the terminology, and adjust one's stance
and tactics appropriately. This may mean being more
reserved and formal in one situation and more informal and open in another; being at ease in an unstructured, open-ended situation yet not allow the interview to become either a casual visit or a discussion of
irrelevant subjects; being able to shift roles easily as
the situation suggests, from active probing to passive,
by attentive listening; from eager, curious questioning
to reserved observing; being able to draw the respondent out without manipulating his or her response in
any way.

Having a keen sense of timing, encouraging responses, and keeping the interview moving but allowing spaces of silence for the respondent to think and
form his . . . response; knowing how fast to move
from superficial to more personal, sensitive subjects;
knowing how fast to move in a group situation; being
invested in the interview and the project but keeping
a sense of balance, objectivity, and perspective; having a sense of humor [pp. 39-40].

Needless to say, the person who fulfills all these qualifications not only could be a good inquirer but undoubtedly would
make a good president, a fine doctor, another Margaret Mead, or
could lead the United Nations to a peaceful resolution of world
conflict. Nevertheless, it is a fine list (Tymitz and Wolf astutely
note another twenty-two criteria that are "important relative to
dealing with the data") in the sense that it is a fairly complete
description of characteristics that one might work toward in training. That many of them also qualify as characteristics of socially
adept, cosmopolitan, urbane persons who are also warm and human and responsive is worth mentioning, because the point is
made again and again in the literature on social science research

methods that those who do fieldwork best are those whom we would have called a century ago "truly civilized persons." They are above all human beings who attend carefully to the social and behavioral signals of others and who find others intrinsically interesting. Many of these skills can be taught; others can be continuously cultivated and refined.

Can the Evaluator as Instrument Be Improved?

Makers of paper-and-pencil instruments may not intuitively see how the human instrument can be refashioned and refined. And yet they will readily admit that fine sopranos can, with good training, be transformed into breathtaking coloraturas; that persons who know relatively little about wine or painting or sculpture can, with practice, be turned into connoisseurs; and that other similar kinds of redirection, refashioning, and retraining can produce surprising results. We think that the same can happen with human beings as data collection instruments.

There are, we readily admit, some methodological issues with respect to instrument improvement. There are also considerations of what characteristics might make for a "reliable" instrument. There are characteristics—either personal or situational—that might act to prevent inquirers from finding and faithfully recreating real-world problems. And there are most assuredly some trade-offs and gains if one considers traditional instruments versus human instruments as data collection devices. Finally, there are questions of what one does if one does not "measure" and what ends might be served besides measurement.

Ways to Improve. There are many ways to "fix" paper-and-pencil tests that are not accurately measuring what they were designed to measure. If a test is found, for instance, to be culturally biased, then it is either rewritten in a more culture-free manner, or a parallel test is constructed that is "fairer" to the culturally disadvantaged child. If it is found that test takers are largely illiterate, then tests are constructed that do not require language arts skills (this was done, as some readers may recall, with the army aptitude training tests, when recruits were found to be nonreaders). Occasionally, tests may be reconstructed in a second language (bilingual transformation) to include nonnative English speakers. There are several options open to the test maker who finds that those in his testing group either cannot take the test at all or find themselves at a disadvantage when taking it.

The options open to the person who wishes to engage in naturalistic inquiry are less apparent on the surface. But they are similar to those of the test maker or test giver in many respects. If the social scientist (fieldworker, naturalistic inquirer, evaluator) finds that he "cannot speak the language," he needs a crash course in the language or the terminology of the site, which might range from a true language to jargon or slang. He can improve himself just as the test constructor improves an otherwise good test; he can "translate" himself into another language (or slang or terminology).

There are, however, two other proven ways of improving the instrument, as attested by the reports of anthropological and social science inquirers who have written on their own training and socialization, for example, Wax (1971) and Reinharz (1979). One way is to throw oneself into as many new situations and environments as possible, the purpose being to gain experience and exposure. The other way is to actually practice, in a clinical or training situation, with an expert qualitative inquirer; that is, to practice doing interviews, to practice observations of various sorts, to practice listening skills, to perform a series of document analyses, and the like under the guidance and critical eye of a trained naturalistic inquirer. Videotapes, recordings, analyses of "field notes" of interviews, and other forms of feedback are readily available to provide training in each of these skills areas (and, indeed, these techniques are now regularly used to train other types of clinicians, practitioners, and observers, including social welfare workers, counselors, and physicians who need training in taking medical histories). Each of these feedback techniques can be targeted to one or more fieldworker behaviors and used to hone skills in singly or multiply focused fashion. Instrument improvement is not a recondite science; it is being regularly utilized in the social service professions and can be easily extended to social science inquiry.

Characteristics of a "Reliable" Instrument. The "reliable" paper-and-pencil test is one that measures over and over again what it purports to measure. What a reliable instrument might be, however, when we talk about an inevitably imperfect human being is quite another question. But the good naturalistic inquirer might be one who is sensitive—open to a wide variety of stimuli and completely aware that the variety exists: who is a problem finder and a pattern creator; who is a reconstructor of realities; who is trustworthy, who can engage in bias-free observation, and who has patience, "systematic obsessiveness," and control enough to watch rather than intervene (Miles, 1978). To take one example, the document analyst who is competent could be expected to create taxonomies of issues or concerns that could be audited and verified by another competent document analyst looking at the same materials. Thus, a reliable human inquirer's work could be verified in much the same way that scientific laboratory work is verified: by multiple observation of the same phenomenon or by replication. Two reasonably competent observers of the same situation ought to observe the same general happenings; two similar interviewers (with the same level of expertise in the subject) ought to hear the same things in the same interview; and two document analysts ought to categorize the documents in about the same way.

Factors That Undermine Reliability. Those things that act to undermine reliable looking and listening in naturalistic inquiry are often precisely those things that confound communication in almost any human endeavor. They include filters and selective perceptions that cause human beings to "hear" certain things and not to hear others, to see or read into a person's actions something that is not there, or to fail to note what is clearly there. Human beings can also be guilty of misinterpretation—either because of lack of experience, lack of familiarity, or just failure to see the entire scene or hear the complete remark—and oversimplification, which can result from moving to closure too quickly and ascribing meanings to incidents and conversations that do not reflect their full intent. The inquirer can also be misled or duped by those who know something that they would prefer the inquirer not to find out. And, of course, the inquirer can also fail through plain incompetence.

In some instances, strategies can be mounted that sidestep some of the reliability difficulties. One approach is to use multiple observers and inquirers or evaluators on site, in split teams if possible. While it may be easy to dupe one inquirer, it is much harder to do it to two. The more time spent on site, the more unlikely it is that one will perceive selectively, will be guilty of misinterpretation or oversimplification, or will be systematically misled. It is less easy to make up for an incompetent member of a team, but that too can be done.

Of course, even the most competent observer or listener occasionally fails to hear, is temporarily led down the primrose path, or is guilty of bias. The best cure for biases is to try to become increasingly aware of our own biases and how they slant and shape what we hear, how they interfere with our reproduction of the speaker's reality, and how they transfigure truth into falsity. It is for this reason that we support, with Wax (1971), Reinharz (1979), and other writers, the injunction that each case study, evaluation report, or research report contain a section on researcher reactions and changes. Rarely does anyone report how he himself was changed by undertaking the study or what personal truths he found as a result of his interactions with a project or culture. Rather, we have settled for descriptions of the research itself and left the self-realization to another time and place. That is an unfortunate omission, since in the process of becoming aware of other value perspectives and cultures, we also become more aware of ourselves as persons, as professionals, and as scientists.

Trade-Offs in Human Instrumentation. We assume that, much of the time, evaluators have been performing quantitative analyses on phenomena that would be better studied using qualitative methods, that, in any event, qualitative observations must always precede quantitative transformations if the latter are to have proper grounding, and that there have been too few such qualitative observations in early stages of inquiry in the past. If that set of observations is correct, then the instrument of choice is the human being. Only the human instrument can produce descriptions of situations and cultures that provide the audience with an empathetic and vicarious experience of what it must have been like to be "on site."

A paper-and-pencil test, a set of test scores, or a technical report could never provide one-to-one correspondence with actual experiences and events on the site. Only human description, or other forms of reporting (storytelling, photography, film, and the like) that are geared to the oral or visual tradition, can convey the lives that are actually being lived on site. The losses in richness and clarity that result from technical reports are converted to gains with the comprehensive and sensitive description provided by qualitative methods.

But if evaluators do not measure, what then do they do? They do what anthropologists, social scientists, connoisseurs, critics, oral historians, novelists, essayists, and poets throughout the years have done. They empathize, describe, judge, compare, portray, evoke images, and create, for the reader or listener, the sense of having been there.

The role of description in the social sciences cannot be overvalued, since it provides the basis for grounded theory, that is, theory that is grounded in the "real world" of observable phenomena. Often, as Glaser and Strauss (1967) point out, the construction of grand theories has gone on without concomitant observation and description; the result of this process is that theory is found to have no meaningful correlation with real-world behavior and verifiable phenomena. To the extent that most educational programs—and indeed social action programs in general—fall under this rubric of human endeavor, they are hardly amenable to laboratory study. Yet we have typically applied the methods of the physical sciences to human enterprises, as though human variables might be controlled (and as though people populated laboratories instead of the messy real world). Thus, a social inquiry (including educational evaluation) that provides a fuller, richer, or more meaningful understanding of human enterprises ultimately increases the fund of knowledge about such organizational forms and enterprises.

The ends of judgment and comparison are also ill suited to test scores and other forms of "technical" information and are better informed by powerful and accurate description. Test scores and quantitative data alone do not tell us whether this program will work in that setting. To know whether it would be useful to try duplicating a successful program, we need to know something about the social and political context of the environment. What works in metropolitan Minneapolis will not necessarily play in Peoria. What works in the ghettos of New York may not necessarily fit—even in Spanish—in the *barrios* of San Antonio. The more extensive description we have of the political, social, and community contexts, the better the judgments that can be made about the "fittingness" of the program within another context. Similarly, the extent to which we know the total contexts of *two* sites, the better the comparisons that can be made about program success. Factors that militate against success in one community may enhance success in another.

Portrayal, a form of description with feeling tone, is another powerful end to be served by the evaluator using naturalistic methods. The extent to which a narrative not only portrays the context faithfully but causes vicarious experiencing to take place determines the relevance of the report. The blend of those elements of a community that cause its members to understand more clearly and to have their meanings extended and enhanced is a measure of its faithful reproduction of the realities of those who are a part of the context.

But portrayal should not only engender understanding in concerned audiences. It should also involve and move those who have never been to the site but who intuitively sense, through the report, that they could have been part of it. This sense of identity, of sharing, of exchanging mutual sympathies ought to be one outcome of portrayal or storytelling.

The ends that are served by inquiry into human organizations, milieus, and activities should not necessarily be those served by scientific inquiry into the physical world. To the extent that human inquirers can serve to illuminate our understanding of human behavior—rather than generate "laws" that noticeably fail to govern its behavior—and to extend, clarify, and enrich our appreciation of its forms and functions, they are appreciably the better instruments for inquiry.

Summary

This chapter has concerned itself with the potential of the human being as instrument. The potential of that instrument is imbedded in the ability of human beings to be observers, categorizers, and processors (on both propositional and tacit levels) of many forms of data: verbal, nonverbal, environmental, social, and contextual. Furthermore, the data-gathering activity that does occur is that which goes on as part of human interaction in every setting; that often forms a portion of the tacit social, interpersonal, and organizational environment of each person's life; and that has the potential of being systematically collected and analyzed as legitimate research and evaluation information.

The strength of such an instrument is its multidimensional quality. Human beings as instruments are most responsive to the very areas of social organization about which we know the least: the social, the value resonant, the cultural. The capability of human beings to comprehend and accurately reflect alternative value systems and to become resocialized to the values of others so that inquiry is grounded in real-world contexts is lost when traditional "measurement" takes place. Rather, what is needed are those qualities that are uniquely human. These include the capacity to be responsive, to be flexible, to see social organizations as holistic entities rather than as components, to rely on both propositional and tacit knowledge, and to search for that which is expert, which is atypical, idiosyncratic, unique, singular, or uncharacteristic of the mainstream.

There are, admittedly, methodological issues related to instrument improvement. We have preferred to sidestep the question of whether naturalistic inquirers are made or born. While there may be some whose temperaments are especially suited to such inquiry, in fact so few have received training in the requisite skills, and so few opportunities for formal training exist, that we have no idea whether or not there is a "naturalistic" type. But we do believe that many of the skills that are needed or required exist already in human beings as social organisms, and that those skills—observing, analyzing, categorizing, careful listening, and the like—can be sharpened and refined in anyone.

There are problems with the reliability of humans as instruments, but we believe that those problems can be overcome or compensated for in a variety of ways, including triangulation (multiple observations or analyses) and refinements in the instrument (increasing self-awareness, enlarged understanding of one's own value perspectives and how they act as selection filters on observations, and the like). The shortcomings of human beings as instruments are more than compensated for by the quality and richness of the data they can gather. Isomorphism, a one-to-one correspondence with reality as it is lived by those in the research site, is achieved only through thick description—generous, fertile, abundant, and above all accurate portrayal of the events, persons, and contexts that make up the whole of the inquiry site. Paper-and-pencil tests, test scores, and technical reports all have their place, but they cannot enter into the real lives of those that they so anonymously describe. Only human beings, depicting slices of their own lives in their own language, terms, and visions, can re-create reality.

Chapter 7

Interviewing, Observation, and Nonverbal Cue Interpretation

===========

There are three main kinds of human-to-human measures for collecting data in naturalistic evaluation: interviewing, observation, and nonverbal communication. This chapter will deal with each in turn.

Of all the means of exchanging information or gathering data known to man, perhaps the oldest and most respected is the conversation. Simple or complex, face-to-face exchanges between human beings have served for eons to convey messages, express sympathy, declare war, make truces, and preserve history. As an extension of that heritage, interviewing—the "conversation with a purpose" (Dexter, 1970, p. 136)—is perhaps the oldest and certainly one of the most respected of the tools that the inquirer can use.

The forms that an interview might take are many. It may be so highly structured that it is essentially an orally administered questionnaire, or it may concentrate on a single event or situation. It may take place in a group setting, or with a panel, or with more than one interviewer. It may be covert, and the subject may not know that he is being interviewed. Or it may be so loose and unstructured that the interviewer himself does not know what will emerge; his role becomes that of a prompter at an unfolding drama. The best known example of this last case would be interviewing for the purpose of collecting oral histories. Other kinds of interviewing, which might fit into one or more of the above categories or which might conceivably form categories of their own would include the "key" interview of the investigative journalist; here, the subject of the investigation is confronted with the results of the investigation and is allowed to give his interpretation of the evidence, provide additional information, or deny or confess. There is also the "circling and shuffling" interview of the journalist, in which a part of the story is known, but bits and pieces of information need to be added to complete some phase of the story—that is, the journalist makes the rounds with "tidbits" of information, which he uses to elicit a fuller picture; hence, he "circles" and "shuffles" between informants. Finally, there is the "informant" interview, where insiders to the social organization provide information that relates to the formulation of "latent values and latent assumptions" (Dexter, 1970, pp. 8-11).

At one time, field research meant a combination of two methods: participant observations and interviews (Becker and Geer, 1957; Trow, 1957; Cicourel, 1964). Now it is generally agreed that a variety of methods may be employed in field research. It is our belief, however, that interviewing—whatever form it might take, but particularly the unstructured interview—is the backbone of field and naturalistic research and evaluation.

When Is an Interview the Most Appropriate Tool?

According to Dexter (1970), "Interviewing is the preferred tactic of data collection when in fact it appears that it will get *better* data or *more* data or data *at less cost* than other tactics" (p. 11). The ability to tap into the experience of others in their own natural language, while utilizing their value and belief frameworks, is virtually impossible without face-to-face and verbal interaction with them. Getting better data, more data, and data at less cost often involves being on site. *How* one talks, to *whom* one talks, for *what purpose* one talks—all are important, and we will deal with each in turn. But interviewing in itself should be thought of as an almost indispensable tool in the tactics of the naturalistic inquirer.

Interviewing should not, however, be thought of as a single-faceted approach. Research that is based solely on interviews may be sabotaged or crippled. Dexter (1970) warns: "But no one should plan *or finance* an entire study in advance with the expectation of relying chiefly upon interviews for data *unless the interviewers have enough relevant background to be sure that they can make sense out of interview conversations or unless there is a reasonable hope of being able to hang around or in some way observe so as to learn what it is meaningful and significant to ask.* In fact, one should probably go one step further—such expectations may prove to be incorrect. . . . *Therefore, any planning for a study assuming a heavy reliance upon elite interviews should have a contingency plan—an escape hatch, an alternative—so that if the elite interviews prove basically uninformative some other technique can be substituted*" (p. 17).

Multiple operations research—the concept of which is embedded in the warning above—or triangulation of methods is the best means of ensuring that one will be able to make sense of data collected through interviews.

Although interviewing may be categorized in a number of ways, the major distinctions are between structured or "focused" interviews (Merton, Fiske, and Kendall, 1956) and unstructured, "elite," "specialized," or "exploratory" interviews (Dexter, 1970; Richardson, Dohrenwend, and Klein, 1965). We shall discuss the uses of structured interviews, but we shall emphasize the uses of unstructured interviews for the naturalistic evaluator. In the structured interview, the problem is defined by the researcher before the interview. The questions have been formulated ahead of time, and the respondent is expected to answer in terms of the interviewer's framework and definition of the problem. The unstructured or specialized interview varies considerably from this mode. In an unstructured interview, the format is nonstandardized, and the interviewer does not seek normative responses. Rather, the problem of interest is expected to arise from the respondent's reaction to the broad issue raised by the inquirer. As Dexter (1970, p. 3) defines this form of interviewing, it involves: stressing the interviewee's definition of the situation; encouraging the interviewee to structure the account of the situation; and letting the interviewee introduce to a considerable extent his notions of what he regards as relevant, instead of relying upon the investigator's notions of relevance. Thus, unlike a structured, focused, or standardized interview, the unstructured or "elite" interview is concerned with the unique, the idiosyncratic, and the wholly individual viewpoint. Dexter (1970) points out that "in the standardized interview, the typical survey, a deviation is ordinarily handled statistically; but in an elite interview, an exception, a deviation, an unusual interpretation may suggest a revision, a reinterpretation, an extension, a new approach" (p. 6).

The relation of this specialized or unstructured interview technique to naturalistic inquiry is quite direct. Naturalistic inquiry presupposes that communities, schools, and social settings of any variety, have pluralistic sets of values that may from time to time cause conflict in the management of social enterprises (including schooling, the provision of health services, and the management of municipal and state governments). In order to understand what those sets of values are and to understand at which points they are in conflict, it is necessary to ground inquiry and evaluation activities in the multiple perspectives that are held by group or community leaders and participants. The standardized or survey interview assumes value consensus (and handles variations in expected "norms" statistically) and therefore does not take account of multiple world views. But to get at manifold value systems the evaluator must let them arise from the context in whatever way the respondents express them. And it is the so-called elite interview that most readily allows such belief systems to emerge and allows the evaluator to record and systematize them in such a way that they can be arrayed against each other.

The "elite" interviewer desires to tap into the experience of others. He is "willing, and often eager, to let the interviewee teach him what the problem, the question, the situation, is—to the limits, of course, of the interviewer's ability to perceive relationships to his basic problems, whatever these may be" (Dexter, 1970, p. 6). Wolf (1979b) describes naturalistic evaluation as "aimed at a search for meaning" (p. 2). If that is the case, the distinction by Braybrooke and Lindblom (1963) between action and meaning is crucial to the argument for unstructured interviews. When the social norms that guide action are clear to all, the event is defined in terms of the action alone. But when the norms (rules, standards, principles, social codes, and so on) that guide the behavior or action are not clear, and when it is important to know those norms, the behavior dimension comes into play. And the only way to determine guiding rules for conduct when behavior is problematic is to ask participants what the rules are. Put another way, when reasons for behavior or action are manifest, there is no need to ask, but when behavior appears inexplicable, or when the inquirer finds that he does not understand the guiding rules for certain events or situations, then the behavioral principles are latent and must be sought by means other than simple observation.

This search for meaning is a search for multiple realities, truths, and perceptions. Those multiple realities are contained in the unique, the singular, the idiosyncratic, the deviant, the exceptional, the unusual, the divergent perceptions of individuals, as they live or lived the experience. The "elite" interview is thus an attempt to reach the nonnormative: the person who has a singular view because of his expertise, position, or insight; the respondent with special information; and/or the interviewee who is central to a situation or otherwise holds a unique position.

While other forms of interviewing have their place, the purposes of naturalistic inquiry are best served by nonstandardized interviews. The focus on multiple perspectives and multiple realities precludes heavy reliance on survey interviewing as a means of grounding an inquiry. We will also, from this point forward, follow Wolf (1979b) in describing the person being interviewed as the "respondent" rather than as the "subject" (except in cases where the interviewing is covert rather than overt and the person being interviewed does not realize what is occurring). As Wolf notes, the former implies mutuality, the latter control.

What Is Meant by Interviewing? Whatever else might be said about interviewing, it is, if done correctly, highly individualistic and does not involve a set of techniques. It is an exchange of information and impressions, carried on in a variety of styles (incorporating such elements as *pace*—whether leisurely or rapid-fire; *style*—whether cooperative or conflicting; *stage*—whether exploratory or verification-oriented; and *iteration*—whether it is a single instance, or the first of two or more interviews), depending on who is interviewing whom. Individuals will imprint upon their interviewing style a variety of personal characteristics and idiosyncrasies, so that, for instance, Dexter (1970) and Denny (1978) can both talk about "interviews I have done" and "great interviewers I have known" and elaborate upon vastly different ways of eliciting information from informants and respondents.

Experience suggests that the situation may to a large extent dictate what constitutes an "interview" at any given time. While it is important, for instance, to arrange time and place so that the respondent is relaxed, at ease, and the like, the actual face-to-face interaction will depend on a variety of factors, only some of which will be under the control of the interviewer. Experience in the field demonstrates that on some occasions, individual, one-on-one interviewing is very effective, that panel interviewing can sometimes elicit about as much information as it is possible to garner from a particular group, and that dual-interviewer modes may prove extraordinarily useful under some circumstances.

Whatever the style of the interviewer, the style of the interview to be carried out, or the nature of the inquiry (whether exploratory or descriptive, for example), an interview will "look like" a combination of the questioner's style, the questions to be addressed, and the flexibility that is brought to the interview, tailoring it to the respondent's own needs, interests, and expertise. While there are many guidelines for arranging successful interviews, that is, interviews that elicit rich and varied information on the topic of interest, there are no "cookbook" techniques or surefire recipes.

In our view, the characterization of an interview depends upon two main factors: (1) the extent to which one can, or cannot, form *a priori* questions to be asked; and (2) the extent to which one does or does not know, in advance, what one does not know (one can know what one does not know, and one can also fail to recognize what one does not know). A Venn diagram playing off these four contingencies against one another is given in Figure 3, which illustrates the eight different interview types based

Figure 3. Domains of Knowledge as They Relate to Types of Interviews

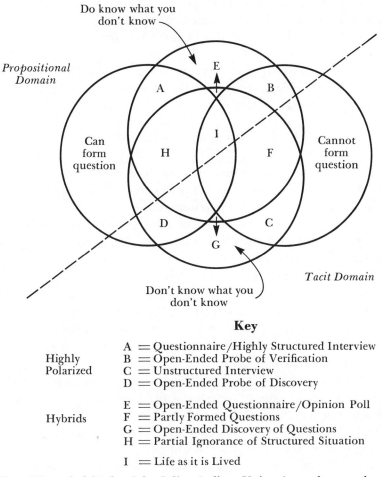

Key

	A = Questionnaire/Highly Structured Interview
Highly	B = Open-Ended Probe of Verification
Polarized	C = Unstructured Interview
	D = Open-Ended Probe of Discovery

	E = Open-Ended Questionnaire/Opinion Poll
Hybrids	F = Partly Formed Questions
	G = Open-Ended Discovery of Questions
	H = Partial Ignorance of Structured Situation

I = Life as it is Lived

Note: We are indebted to John Julian, Indiana University graduate student, who conceived this formulation in response to a class discussion of the domains of knowing and interviewing style and format.

upon these contingencies. The reader will be able to identify these eight types from the figure; for example, area "A" represents the common form of the highly structured interview, which closely resembles a questionnaire, while area "C" represents the unstructured interview.

The reader will note that a diagonal (dotted) line has been drawn through the diagram. Interview forms to the upper left of this line represent interviews that build primarily on propositional information, while interview forms to the lower right of the line rely heavily on tacit information as well. Note that the unstructured interview falls squarely into this latter domain.

Again we warn that a set of techniques or tricks will not guarantee a good interview. Practice, a clear understanding of self and of the problem, and a nonthreatening presentation of both will go a long way toward unlocking needed data.

Types of Interviews

Team and Panel Interviewing. The success of team interviewing seems to depend on what the context of the interview is, how skilled each of the interviewers is, how attentive each member is to the other's questions and to the responses that are elicited, and how sensitive each member is to the line of questioning being developed by the other.

As a training device, team interviewing is a superlative way to allow a novice interviewer to watch an expert interviewer work. One difficulty, however, is that the novice may begin to emulate the expert's style rather than to concentrate on developing listening skills—which are the foundation for good interviewing—and letting his own style emerge.

Dexter (1970) is rather "lukewarm" about team interviewing: "To some people, three is a crowd; others enjoy having several people around the table" (p. 110). One rule of thumb would be simply to ask the respondent ahead of time if he would mind having two interviewers or if he would prefer to talk to a single individual. Needless to say, the nature of the information being sought and/or the desire to guarantee anonymity and confidentiality would guide such an inquiry.

There is a reverse side to team interviewing that is occasionally useful. Here, there is one interviewer and a "panel" of interviewees—that is, a number of persons are interviewed at the same time. In a study several years ago on the demography of schools of education and their potential for knowledge production and utilization activities (see Clark and Guba, 1977), we decided that one of the groups that should be interviewed were graduate students who were presumably being trained to undertake research and development roles of their own upon completion of their degrees. It was initially hypothesized, however, that while these students might be able to tell us a good deal about the nature of their own individual training, they could nevertheless not be expected to know about schoolwide thrusts in knowledge production and utilization. We decided, therefore, to meet with small groups of students, who could not only give us accounts of their own research activities but could also trigger each other to mention kinds and types of activities of this sort in which they have been engaged over their careers as students, including work they had done for assistantships, funded projects, and the like. We found that these graduate students knew little about what kinds of activities were going on in departments other than their own but that they were able to give a variety of accounts of different types of training and apprenticeship experiences that cut across disciplinary lines. These accounts allowed us to make some judgments about the types of training that were going on in various departments (which, in turn, allowed us to make some judgments about scholarly productivity).

The danger in interviewing a number of people at one time is that either everyone may want to talk at once or certain members of the group being interviewed may defer to stronger or more vocal members. A second danger is that the group may become too large to allow for much give-and-take with the interviewer. Generally speaking, the larger the group, the more opportunity exists that one or two vocal members will dominate the others and that the interviewer will be unable to control for this because he cannot keep track of individuals' names. Our own experience has shown that having only three or four people in a group interview probably works best.

Covert Versus Overt Interviewing. The naturalistic inquirer and evaluator—particularly the evaluator—may wonder whether covert interviewing is appropriate to his inquiry. Covert interviewing takes place when respondents do not know they are being interviewed or when they do not know the true purpose of the interview. The old dictum in social science research is that those who are participants in a study should never in any way be deceived. Dexter (1970, p. 68) argues that they ought never "be harmed," which gives considerably broader latitude to the researcher. Much of the time, we would argue, the role of the evaluator precludes either deception or harm since covert interviewing is largely inappropriate to the public functions of the evaluator.

Both social scientists (Becker, 1970; Dalton, 1959) and investigative journalists (Hage and others, 1976; Guba, 1978a; Williams, 1978) argue the necessity of occasionally operating as a "veiled scrutineer," a "masquerading researcher," or undercover questioner in the interest of obtaining more "truth." There are very real questions of ethics in this enterprise, however, not the least of which is the question of the extent to which the covert researcher may violate the privacy of his subjects. An extension of this problem is, according to Dexter (1970), "that of creating ill will because of a feeling that trust has been abused, friendship betrayed" (p. 71).

The trade-offs must be weighed carefully. The literature is replete with examples of how researchers were led astray, misinformed, deliberately lied to, manipulated, or otherwise fed inaccurate or untruthful information. On balance, while we are aware that there are advantages and disadvantages to covert interviewing, we genuinely doubt that there are sufficient advantages to the educational evaluator or inquirer to cause this technique to be employed. For example, we have, elsewhere in the book (see Chapter Twelve), argued for a team approach to evaluation, simply because multiple observers with multiple inquiry methods make it extremely difficult to keep the truth or to keep—more appropriately—many truths under wraps for long. In short, the necessity for covert interviewing is largely negated with the application of other methods and the use of more than one evaluator.

Oral History Interviewing. Morrissey says of oral history interviewing: "let the interviewee talk. It's his show. Let him run with the ball. . . . He [will often] take off, usually chronologically; this might turn into a topical treatment, just running on haphazardly; I would sit and listen. There is a value to this because he's volunteering what's foremost in his recollections" (cited in Dexter, 1970, p. 111). Oral history interviewing, a special form of "elite" interviewing, focuses upon the recollections of those who have been participants in events of interest or perhaps even in major episodes of history. The interviewer interested in collecting information by this method should keep the following points in mind:

- Keep all questions, unless direct probes about unclear statements, as open-ended as possible.
- Since the reconstruction of events signifies the most important points to the respondent, delay filling in the gaps.
- Remember silence and its uses; often that uncomfortable wait produces a precise memory.
- Use documents to acquaint yourself with the event and to use as triggers for the interviewee's memory at more advanced stages of the interviewing.
- Build and utilize a web of informants and research contacts who might be able to furnish additional views of the event or era under investigation.
- Assume everything is important, at least at first; information can be sifted later.

Oral history interviews are quite different from other types. This particular form of conversation is the least structured of all forms of interviewing and the least readily organized. It also takes the most patience, and often the most gentle of probes. The historian or anthropologist who has sat patiently for hours while a backwoods raconteur unfolds his stories will understand exactly what this means. The novice interviewer who has had little practice with this form of interviewing, however, is often at a clear-cut advantage, particularly if relatively young. Among the easiest respondents to "interview," and often the most accessible, are one's own grandparents, aunts, uncles, or parents. An older neighbor with a "gift of gab" will also do nicely, as will a stranger on a park bench (with some history behind him). The sense of "unfolding" that Denny's (1978) work alludes to so beautifully is what needs to be achieved. A leisurely pace is best, and no interview deserving of the name "oral history" can be done in less than several hours. There are major, if subtle, differences between oral history interviewing and even nonstandardized forms, and the interviewer needs to be aware of the crucial considerations of timing, pace, structure (or lack of structure), and the probable necessity of repeated interviews. There may have to be exploratory interviews, interviews for "filling in," and interviews that take anecdotal, impressionistic form.

Structured and Unstructured Interviewing. We have alluded to the differences between these forms several times but will now attempt to define them more precisely. There are some fairly standard definitions, although a number of writers have elaborated those differences at greater length (Reik, 1949; Caplow, 1956-1957; Cannell and Kahn, 1968; Cicourel, 1964; Manning, 1967; Powdermaker, 1966; Gorden, 1975). For our purposes, however, a structured interview is one in which the investigator defines the problem and the questions. The investigator is looking for answers within the bounds set by his own presuppositions, hypotheses, and hunches. When an interview is tightly structured, it begins to approximate a questionnaire in appearance; indeed, the questionnaire might be thought of as a special form of structured interview that happens to be self-administered.

Structured interviews are likely to be used in situations in which representative samples of persons are asked identical questions about something that interests the investigator. All respondents are taken to be of equal importance. The object is usually to get representative or "typical" responses, and "a deviation is ordinarily handled statistically" (Dexter, 1970, p. 6). Examples of structured interviews would include a physician filling out a health history questionnaire for a new patient, a survey researcher collecting consumer preference data, a precinct worker collecting information on party preferences door-to-door, or a personnel officer interviewing a job applicant.

Questionnaires are less expensive than interviews, they are self-administering, they can be administered to many persons simultaneously, they can be mailed, they are logistically easier to manage than interviews, and they call for uniform responses (although items may often be subject to widely different interpretations). At the same time, they are impersonal and limit the respondent's response range significantly.

The interview, however, is more flexible than the questionnaire, allowing questions to be restated if they were not at first understood. Interviews are more personal than questionnaires, and they are a better exploratory tool. They are also better in sensitive areas (such as money, politics, and sex); they permit the interviewer to note the respondent's affective responses (that is, to make note of nonverbal cues or of how the respondent says what he says); they approximate real-life situations more closely than questionnaires; they don't require literacy on the part of the respondent; and they usually end with better sampling because there are fewer turndowns.

Many different types of interview protocols can be used. The simplest formats may be a series of questions that call for "yes" or "no" responses; various kinds of checklists may also be used. The next step up is in the form of a scale or continuum along which a respondent may place his response. Finally, the structured interview protocol may call for reasonably open-ended responses; the questions are all given beforehand, and they correspond to some grand design of the investigator. The cues should be well structured.

The formulation of good interview protocols is not simply a matter of making up a number of questions that appear to follow the broad outlines of the research. There are principles that guide this process, and they have been well reviewed in the methodological literature (Jahoda, Deutsch, and Cook, 1951a, 1951b; Festinger and Katz, 1953).

While it is true that any respondent might try to lead one down the primrose path, most persons will provide reasonably honest answers. An advantage of the structured interview is that it rarely probes deeply enough to cause a respondent to lie to the interviewer. Most of the topics on which large numbers of people are interviewed in this particular fashion are simply not that delicate.

The unstructured (intensive, "key," investigative, "elite," specialized, nonstandardized, or depth) interview is quite another matter. Unlike the structured interview, the unstructured or "elite" interview is much less abrupt, remote, and arbitrary than is the structured interview. It is used most often in situations where the investigator is looking for nonstandardized and/or singular information. As a result, it tends to stress the exception, the deviation, the unusual interpretation, the reinterpretation, the new approach, the expert's view, or the singular perspective. The unstructured interview has a very different rhythm from that of the structured interview, it tends to be very free flowing, and it is likely to move however the respondent causes it to move because of the cues that he provides. Respondents are usually selected because of their special characteristics; that is, they have special knowledge of, or familiarity with, the situation, they have information (or are likely to have) to which others are not privy, they have special status of some sort, or they are one of a kind (for example, the chief justice of the Supreme Court, the single survivor in a disaster, the only eyewitness to some special event, or the like). The "elite" interview is characterized chiefly by its fluid format. Questions may be phrased to fit the respondent's own unique characteristics or status, and the interviewer can choose to follow any and all leads that seem profitable. The exchange is likely to be spontaneous, to sound more like a real conversation than a question-and-answer interchange, and to deal with sensitive issues and problems. The interview is often lengthy and may be extended over several sessions. The end of the "conversation" is not reached when some initial or arbitrary set of questions has been asked, but rather when the respondent has "taught" the interviewer all that the interviewer needs to know, and when the interviewer senses that the point of diminishing returns has been reached.

The interviewer is likeliest to turn to "elite" or nonstandardized interviewing as a tool in any or all of the following circumstances:

• When he is dealing with elite subjects, that is, subjects who have special status or knowledge;
• When he is interested in pursuing some subject in depth;
• When he is operating in a discovery, rather than a verification, mode;
• When he is interested in the etiology of some condition;
• When he is interested in a direct interaction with a certain respondent;
• When he is interested in uncovering some motivation, intent, or explanation as held by the respondent (Cannell and Kahn, 1968; Dexter, 1970; Douglas, 1976); or
• When he is trying to ascribe meaning to some event, situation, or circumstance.

Some examples of the kind of interviewing that might be called unstructured include: tracing patterns of dope addiction, characterizing the life-styles of successful professionals (the reader is reminded of the Hennig and Jardim, 1976, study of women administrators); the debriefing of disaster victims; garnering the perceptions of deans of arts and sciences about a school of education; finding out why persons participate in nude beach behavior; discovering the different types of discipline problems that teachers face in their classrooms; discovering what the perceptions of Harvard classmates of Jack Kennedy were when he was a student with them; and many others.

Rarely, if ever, can one conduct a nonstandardized interview on the basis of goodwill alone. Often there must be a *quid pro quo,* a kind of trade, especially since—unlike the structured interview—there will be a large number of questions asked, some of a personal, intimate, or sensitive nature. In most cases, interviewees will not allow themselves to be interviewed at all unless it is made worth their while (although one of the cardinal rules of interviewing, research, and investigation is that an interviewee must never be paid in the sense that one pays for other services). Nevertheless, there are a number of trade-offs that can, in all honesty, be arranged.

First, it is important to the investigator's own understanding to remember that, in an "elite" or nonstandardized interview, the interviewee knows more about the topic than the investigator does. It thus does no harm, and often does much good, to allow the interviewee to function in the role of teacher. It is both quite honest and quite profitable for the interviewer to adopt the role of an eager learner—for that's what the nonstandardized interviewer is—pleased to be in the presence of a knowledgeable informant. Many famous and influential persons are delighted to be confronted with an understanding stranger to whom they can tell things they would not dare tell those they encounter on a daily basis.

The respondent may also want to influence some course of action. If the interviewer thinks that this is a possible result of the interview, then it is legitimate to tell the respondent that what he has to say "may help to change things that ought to be changed."

Finally, it is often gratifying to the interviewee just to have the quiet and thoughtful attention that a good interviewer can give.

A note here on "unsolicited testimony": In the course of a study, an investigator will often encounter persons whom he might not have initially considered interviewing or for whom an interview is inappropriate or not possible. Such sources, however, will sometimes supply valuable information that gives an extra dimension to the understanding of a context. The alert inquirer or evaluator should never pass up a chance to talk to people who volunteer information. We are speaking here of persons who, for example, corner the evaluator and "want to set the record straight"; of janitors or custodial help who might have intimate knowledge of the comings and goings of various project personnel and with whom one whiles away a few minutes in front of an elevator; and of the secretary with whom one must make pleasantries while waiting for the interviewee to be ready. While it goes without saying that such volunteered information cannot be accepted at face value any more than any other interview data, such "found" information can nevertheless lead to additional questions that might be raised, suggest relationships that the evaluator might not have known existed, and the like.

The point should not be lost that there are gatekeepers and observers that one ought to become accustomed to cultivating. They are gold mines of information, and unsolicited testimony can afford a handle on a situation that one cannot afford to ignore: that handle might save embarrassment, might allow questioning to be more subtle or delicate, or might grant the evaluator a social lever into the milieu. Douglas (1976), who has explored the conflictual, or investigative, model of social research rather thoroughly, suggests several "rules of thumb" for the "suspicious" researcher to follow:

1. Where there's smoke, there's fire; and
2. There's always far more immoral or shady stuff going on than meets the eye [p. 66].

While that might seem a little too strong for most evaluators and educational researchers, we would warn that research (and evaluation) cannot always be carried out in the cooperative mode and that one is well advised to run down every lead, until it can no longer be considered true or useful.

Our own preferences lie with the form of interviewing known as "elite" or unstructured, even though the other forms have their place and function. Like the forced-choice questionnaire to which Cicourel addresses himself (1964, p. 105), highly structured interviews provide little more than grids through which our understanding of social processes is passed, with concomitant distortions in both our own perceptions and the perceptions of those whom we interview. The search for contextual meanings, for situation-explicit and value-resonant grounding, may demand that more open and responsive methods be employed. The unstructured interview is the one most likely to cause those expressive intents to emerge.

Before we address the questions of how one arranges an interview and how one prepares for it, executes it, and analyzes the results, some mention of the use of informants seems appropriate. Dexter (1970) notes that an informant is "distinguished from an elite interviewee by two factors: participation and time. The informant is regarded to some, often to a considerable, extent as a subprofessional colleague or co-worker of the research investigator" (p. 7). Two divergent views on the utility and roles of informants are often expressed. Paul (1953) and others see key informants as "individuals who have not only proved themselves well informed and well connected, but have demonstrated a capacity to adopt the standpoint of the investigator . . . informing him of rumors and coming events, suggesting secondary informants, preparing the way, advising on tactics and tact, securing additional data on their own, and assisting the anthropologist in numerous other ways" (pp. 435-463). Scott (1966), however, takes the position that persons who are willing to assume the role of key informant are probably "marginal" to their cultural subgroup and unlikely to be truly representative of that subgroup. The literature on this point is mixed, although we tend to agree with Dexter (1970) that it probably depends in large measure on what *kind* of social or cultural subgroup is the referent, and whether the association with a researcher is likely to be construed as one more marginal activity for an already marginal social member, or whether such association might in fact confer prestige value.

Cicourel (1964) suggests that informants come in several types: the outsider (the truly marginal informant, who may nevertheless be a careful and astute observer of his society), the rookie, the natural, and the informant seeking some form of prestige. In addition, there is the naive informant (who does not realize the role that he is fulfilling), the frustrated informant, the *habitué* or "old hand," the needy person (whose social and affiliational needs are met by the researcher rather than by the social group), and the subordinate (who may see information brokering as an avenue to power).

Whatever the role of informants, rarely has a major anthropological study gotten far underway without having an informant appear. And although opinions on their usefulness and uses are mixed, there are many advantages to having such persons on a study. Among those advantages might be included help in acquiring a more complete picture of the norms, expectations, attitudes, and evaluations of a particular group; help in formulating the latent values and latent assumptions of the group under study; help in avoiding major social blunders that could alienate the group with which the researcher is working; help in describing events and situations to which the researcher is not privy (closed meetings, secret ceremonies, and the like); and help in pointing out events and behaviors that may have significance within the culture but that would have gone unnoticed for some time by the researcher (Cicourel, 1964; Scott, 1966; Douglas, 1976).

Techniques for Interviewing

An introduction to types of interviewing without some guidelines for arranging, planning, and conducting interviews, as well as for utilizing the results, would of course be incomplete. Extensive discussion of the intricacies of conducting various kinds of interviews is beyond the purview of this book; nevertheless, we do have some comments to make on how some of the best interviewing gets done and on how its results should later be analyzed.

Before setting forth these techniques, however, we want to remind the reader that field research is often lonely and painful (Wax, 1971; Zigarmi and Zigarmi, 1978; Denny, 1978). Douglas

(1976) characterized this classical field approach as the "Lone Ranger approach," in part because it was often carried out by a single researcher and in part because it demanded great "suffering" on the part of young researchers:

> This approach has demanded considerable strength and courage much of the time and almost always an ability to operate alone, with little or no support and inspiration from colleagues. . . . And it demanded that [the fieldworker] be a jack-of-all-interactional-skills, since he had to be all things to all people in his research setting. . . . The fact that so much really good field research was accomplished with this Lone Ranger approach is testimony to the skills, courage, audacity, integrity, and ability to accept suffering of so many young sociologists. . . . But, of course, these abilities and the willingness to suffer is especially short in supply, and this probably accounts for the fact that most field researchers only do one study, their doctoral dissertation, and then retire to the study to do theory and send forth unsuspecting graduate students to do battle. It is probably an even more important factor in the decision of so many graduate students and professionals to dedicate themselves to office interviews and, wherever possible, mail-order research. Putting a questionnaire in the mailbox may demand some faith in the postal department and the unseen subject, but it requires no suffering or courage of the academic. He can remain safely in his office and avoid all those vulgar conflicts [p. 192].

There is more than a grain of truth in Douglas' assessment of the strains experienced by the evaluator or inquirer setting about to ground his findings in the natural context. But we would argue that the utility of such inquiries more than compensates for their psychological costs. We are mindful, too, of Wax's (1971) confession that she "had not, in college or university, learned a blessed thing about how to study living, breathing, and thinking people" (p. 63).

Planning and Setting Up the Interview

Since unstructured interviewing is more complicated than structured interviewing, in the sense that it is not a matter of merely identifying a random or a representative sample from a predetermined population, we have elected to concentrate on the more formal and complex procedures, on the assumption that certain steps may be abbreviated, dispensed with, or handled in truncated form for more structured forms of data collection.

The first step in unstructured interviewing is deciding on whom to interview. Sometimes there will be only a few respondents who qualify, for example, the key subject and his most immediate collaborators in an investigation. At other times only the incumbents of selected roles will do, for example, the superintendent of schools, the chairman of the board, or the president of a certain company. At still other times, only persons with certain kinds of expertise or persons with access to certain desired information can be used. In general, the problem being investigated will dictate particular respondents—individuals, rather than classes of respondents—and those particular persons are the ones who must be involved. Occasionally, only certain persons to be interviewed can be identified initially. In those instances, initial respondents might be asked to identify others who are close to the event or situation or who might be knowledgeable about the area. This process is called "casting the nets."

Once one or more respondents have been identified, the inquirer needs to arrange to interview that person or persons. The Tymitz and Wolf guide (1977) is especially clear about this procedure, and they recommend a first step of establishing personal contact (p. 15). Their suggestion, and it seems to be a sound one, is to avoid delegating this responsibility to a secretary or other aide. While few experts comment on this directly, many who write about the art of interviewing seem to suggest that personal contact is both a necessary and a useful courtesy.

Dexter (1970) provides some interesting suggestions on how to make contact, as does Douglas (1976). Those suggestions include how to obtain introductions, tactful ways of circumventing overprotective secretaries, the necessity of persistent courtesy after initial refusals, how to explain to the respondent what the interview is about, the use of letters of introduction, and the use of personal friends, acquaintances, and other intermediaries to persuade a reluctant interviewee.

The third step in the initial planning and arrangement sequence is to thoroughly prepare for the interview. This means that the interviewer must practice introducing himself and practice giving a brief introduction to the inquiry that he is conducting (the briefer the better, and the less said—without misleading the respondent—the freer the interview will be). The interviewer must also do "homework" on the respondent—what are the respondent's interests, what kind of career has he followed, what are his hobbies, on what important task forces has he served, what does his community service record look like? Such questions will not only flesh out the person to be interviewed, they will also provide the interviewer with a means of breaking the ice should the start of the interview be stiff or awkward. The interviewer must also decide on his own role and appropriate dress, given the status of the interviewee and his likely surroundings, and he must decide on the recording tools to be used in the interview. (For most of this kind of interviewing, we recommend notepads and written notes; tape recorders can make one a victim of the "laters"—"later I will listen to these tapes, later I will analyze these data.") It goes without saying that the interviewer will also want to shape and reshape his questions, review the larger issues that are guiding the inquiry, and think of alternative ways of formulating questions based on possible responses. For the novice interviewer, writing out the questions that he intends to ask is often helpful (although taking them to the interview is not recommended). There are many good guides to formulating value-neutral questions, and the serious interviewer who does not know this literature is well advised to seek it out. Payne's little book on *The Art of Asking Questions* (1951) is both amusing and highly instructive.

As preparation for the interview, a letter should be sent to the respondent, confirming the time, date, and place of the interview. Some estimate of the time required for the interview ought to be included; a brief description of the project on which the interviewer is working may sometimes be appropriate. Tymitz and Wolf (1977) recommend a reconfirmation if there is a significant time lapse between arranging the interview and actually conduct-

ing it. This seems sensible, especially if the interviewer and interviewee were in different cities or locales when the interview was
originally set up. When an investigator is on the road, a telephone
call shortly before arrival will provide reconfirmation or will allow
the investigator to reschedule the interview should something have
gone awry with the original appointment.

Executing the Interview: On-Site Behavior. Setting up an
interview is one thing. Getting out with the desired information is
quite another. One of the determinants of behavior is, of course,
who is interviewing whom and for what purpose. As Dexter (1970,
p. 25) somewhat philosophically concludes, what is likely to work
in any given situation "depends." We think it is best to deal with
the "how-to" of interview execution in two parts: (1) situation-
specific behaviors, which are determined by social, contextual, and
strategic concerns, and (2) responsive behaviors, which are determined by the respondent's presentation of self and by his answers
to the questions the interviewer poses.

Courtesy demands that the interviewer be appropriately
dressed and a few minutes early for the interview. The determination of appropriate dress may not be easy, but clearly one dresses
to "fit the scene." Jeans are not appropriate for Capitol Hill, nor is
a three-piece suit likely to be the best on-site dress for interviewing
members of a motorcycle gang. The best look for any interviewer
is a serious, purposeful, professional, and understated look—child-
hood admonitions regarding neatness and cleanliness probably
hold as well as any. The respondent's first impression of the interviewer will be of his dress and demeanor; the outcome of the
interview may depend on that first impression, so the interviewer
owes it to himself to make the best impression possible.

Being on time will not only create a favorable impression, it
will allow the interviewer to gather his wits about him and to observe the context carefully. If the interviewer is going to be more
than one or two minutes late, he ought to phone the interviewee's
office so that the status of the interview—and the interviewee's
schedule—can be kept intact.

Dexter recommends (1970, p. 50), and we concur, that the
interviewer introduce himself, then reintroduce his project and
sponsorship immediately. A concise but careful explanation of the
interviewer's role, the nature of the project, and the project spon-

sorship ought to be rehearsed until it comes readily and succinctly. Wolf and Tymitz (1977) advise reminding the respondent of earlier contacts, telling him why he was chosen, and assuring him of as much confidentiality as possible.

Physical arrangements for the interview may vary; if at all possible, however, the interview ought to take place on a face-to-face basis. Surroundings should be comfortable, interviewer and respondent should be able to look each other in the eye, and there should be no observers or listeners. If possible, a private office is best. If the respondent does not have a private office, the interviewer might ask him to suggest a private place for their conversation. While privacy is not always strictly necessary, its benefits, both in ensuring confidentiality to the respondent and in creating an environment where he feels free to "let his hair down," are important to eliciting open responses.

The first questions may be posed by the respondent rather than the interviewer. Sometimes the questions will be directed toward the interviewer's professional preparation; occasionally they will be directed toward who the interviewer is as a person. Such questions, as most interviewers intuitively understand, actually address the question: Is this the sort of person I can be honest with? To what extent can I "open up" with him? Therefore, the interviewer should answer the respondent's questions as forthrightly as he can and should attempt, at the first comfortable moment, to direct the questioner to the cause for the initial contact and interview. Tymitz and Wolf (1977) give a number of rules for this stage of the interview process, and the prospective interviewer will find their guidelines extremely useful.

Our experience has been that unflagging courtesy and value-neutral behaviors are probably some of the most important strategies the interviewer can use. Value-neutral, but encouraging, cues allow the interviewee to be expansive without subtly influencing him to alter behavior or opinions in deference to the interviewer. Courtesy (or what Payne, 1951, calls the "care and treatment of respondents") will often salvage almost any kind of interview. While courtesy is important with any respondent, occasionally there will be respondents for whom the interviewer contracts an instant dislike. But courtesy that has become second nature, along with a practiced value-neutral stance, can aid and abet the obtaining of needed information from even the most unlovable of respondents.

With respect to the "rhythm" of the interview, some interviewers seem to enjoy a lively pace, while others collect large amounts of information while using what appears to be the most leisurely of paces. Dexter's (1970) reflections on that issue, while most assuredly reflecting his own personality and style as an interviewer, are nevertheless well taken: "It is my experience and impression . . . that many elite interviewees dislike a steady flow of questions. . . . They would prefer a discussion, or still more, perhaps, something which sounds like a discussion but is really a quasi-monologue stimulated by understanding comments. Often, at any rate, I try to handle the relationship as discussion—two reflective men trying to find out how things happen, but the less informed and experienced one (the interviewer) deferring to the wiser one and learning from him" (p. 56). That probably is exactly the right note to strike in unstructured interviewing.

The list of recommendations above will probably allow the interviewer to set and maintain the right tone, climate, and setting for maximum information sharing to take place. As tactics, they are as sound as any. But there is a good deal more to an interview than creating and maintaining the right environment. A reasonably unskilled interviewer can gain entrée and begin the process appropriately, only to find later that his notes contain very little of real value. What makes the difference?

More important than appropriate settings, more important than correct social and professional carriage, more important than any other tactic or strategy is the skill of *listening*. The best notes taken in the world will never achieve the same results as the listener who is able to immerse himself in his respondent's frame of reference; who is able to hear on most—if not all—of the levels on which his respondent is speaking; and who is able to empathize with his "teacher," even while a part of himself stands to one side and observes. The ability to "hear" accurately and clearly what another is saying, without overlays of values, attitudes, preconceptions, stereotypes, beliefs, or prejudices is perhaps the hardest "skill" for the inquirer to come by. But there are virtually no serious works on the art of talking to others that do not deal extensively with the ability to listen effectively (see Bingham and Moore, 1959; Dexter, 1970; Gorden, 1975; Douglas, 1976).

Part and parcel of the act of listening and truly hearing is the ability to frame questions; this requires training and practice, as well as an intuitive ear for the interesting or intriguing point. Gatz and Hoagland (1978) have explored some basic considerations for the framing and construction of questions for unstructured interviewing. The considerations cover five broad areas:

1. Is this question necessary? How will the response be used? Analyzed?
2. Does this question cover the topic? Are other additional questions necessary?
3. How will this question be interpreted? Does the interviewer need other facts concerning the matter before the answer will make sense? Does the interviewer need or want knowledge of the respondent's attitude (preferences, values, beliefs) on the matter? If so, ought one to probe the content, intensity, stability, or depth of those attitudes, values, feelings? What dimensions would be valuable to have?
4. Do the respondents have the information to answer the question? Has the interviewer allowed for differences? How reliable would the interviewer expect the responses to be?
5. How valid overall does the interviewer expect the answer to be? Is the question leading? Is it framed in value-neutral terms? Is it part of a response set? Is the response likely to be adequate? Will the respondent be willing to give the information? Under what circumstances? What assumptions are implicit in the question? What is taken for granted by the interviewer? What are possible frames of reference for the question?

In the unstructured interview, the responses most desired will often be elicited by open-ended questions. That kind of question is designed to permit a free response from the subject rather than one limited by stated alternatives or implied boundaries. The distinguishing characteristic of open-ended questions is that they raise an issue but do not provide or suggest any structure for the respondent's reply; the respondent is given the opportunity to answer in his own terms and to respond from or create his own frame of reference. Such questions are called for when the issue is complex, the relevant dimensions are not known, or the interest of the research lies in the description of a phenomenon, the exploration of a process, or the individual's formulation of an issue. It is especially useful for eliciting unanticipated responses and unique perspectives (Gatz and Hoagland, 1978).

The range of questions that may be asked are bounded by the nature of the inquiry, the personality of the interviewer, and the general responsiveness of the respondent. Nevertheless, there is a general typology of questions that may be ventured during such an interview. They include: (1) *hypothetical* or "what if?" questions; (2) questions that *pose the ideal* and ask the respondent to react to an hypothesized alternative past, present, or future; (3) *devil's advocate* questions, which challenge the respondent to consider an opposite frame of reference or explanation; (4) *interpretative* questions, which suggest possible interpretations to events for the consideration of the respondent; (5) questions that *suggest*; (6) *reason-why* questions, which address the respondent's explanations for an event or feeling; (7) *argument-type* questions, which attempt to provoke the respondent into revealing information or attitudes that the interviewer would not be able to obtain otherwise; (8) *source* questions, which attempt to uncover additional sources, the origin of information, or auxiliary data or documents; (9) *qualified yes-no* questions, which attempt to plumb the intensity of feeling or belief on an issue about which the respondent seems uncertain; and (10) *filter* questions, by which the respondent is asked to make additional sortings of the information he is providing.

The foregoing typology of questions may also be arrayed along a *direct or indirect* dimension; a *personal or impersonal* dimension; and a *retrospective, introspective, or prospective* dimension. We do not suggest that this list is exhaustive, nor do we suggest that every question be assigned to one or more of the categories mentioned. What we would suggest, however, is that consideration of the type of questions posed might have heuristic value for the analysis of those same questions, both prospectively—that is, before the interview—and retrospectively. Reflection on the responses received in any given interview alongside data collected in later ones might indicate where certain types of questions would have been more useful than others or where the interviewer missed opportunities to follow productive leads.

Another way of thinking of questions is to divide them into the categories of "peripheral" and "probing" questions. While peripheral is probably not the best word for making this distinction, it does suggest the idea of less depth than probe, which is the distinction for which we are striving. Probes, as opposed to questions that cause the respondent to educe an event or the like, should summon forth some associative and elaborative responses. Probes are questions designed to explore a given topic. Gorden (1975, p. 372), in his discussion of chronemics (an aspect of nonverbal communication having to do with time), lists the "silent probe" as one aspect of this form of communication, and it is clear that periods of silence, insofar as they prompt some social discomfort and/or some thoughtful reflection, are one form of probe. They indicate that the interviewer wants more information or that he is willing to wait until the respondent is satisfied with his own answer. Because the interviewer does not indicate what further elaboration he needs or wishes when using the silent probe, we would call it an undirected probe. Other forms of probes are what we would term directed or interviewer cued, since the interviewer suggests to the respondent the nature of the additional information he desires. These would include probes for:

1. *clarification*—when the interviewer needs more information on a previous response.
2. *critical awareness*—when the respondent is asked to justify, be critical of, reflect upon, evaluate, or give an example of something. The directive questions here would be "why?" and "in what ways?"
3. *amplification*—when the interviewer needs information on different aspects or dimensions of a question.
4. *refocus*—when the respondent is asked to relate, compare, or contrast his answer to another topic or idea, or when he is asked to think of alternative solutions or causal relationships.
5. information on the *intensity of the respondent's feelings*. The general movement of questions into this sector is from a "personalized question" to a "reason-why" question to an "intensity question."

This typology of questions and probes is directed toward the cooperative model of interviewing, but it can be used in conflict models also.

Question sequencing is yet another way to consider the art

of questioning. There are generally three ways of sequencing questions: the funnel sequence, the inverted funnel sequence, and the "quintamensional" plan. In the funnel sequence, the questions generally move from the more general to the more specific. Each succeeding question is related to the preceding one but has a narrower focus. When a comprehensive view of a respondent's experiences or feelings is desired, asking the most general question first may eliminate the need to ask a large number of specific questions. In addition, by asking an initial general question, the interviewer will not limit himself to a particular frame of reference. Such a question will prevent the interviewer from "conditioning" the respondent. The following illustrates a funnel sequence of questions:

Question 1: How do you think this country is getting along in its relations with other countries?
Question 2: How do you think we are doing in our relations with Russia?
Question 3: Do you think we ought to be dealing with Russia differently from the way we do now?
Question 4: If yes, what should we be doing differently?
Question 5: Some people say we should get tougher with Russia, and others think we are too tough as it is. How do you feel about it?

If the last question had been asked earlier, it might have conditioned the responses that followed it, since it implies a dichotomy that the respondent might have seen as artificial.

The inverted funnel begins with specific questions and proceeds to more general ones, with each new question having a wider scope than the last. The inverted funnel sequence is particularly helpful in motivating a reluctant respondent or in causing a shy one to become increasingly more comfortable or expansive. Occasionally, an interviewee feels inadequate, as though he may not know what the interviewer expects him to know, or he feels threatened when he is asked about a sensitive topic. Starting off with a discussion of concrete behavior or specific instances tends to get this kind of respondent involved and to make him feel more comfortable in answering general, personal, or affective questions. Here is an example of an inverted funnel sequence:

Question 1: Exactly what happened between Bill and John?
Question 2: Has this friction been an ongoing problem?
Question 3: How long has this been building up?
Question 4: Do they seem to have the same problems with other workers?

The quintamensional method of sequencing is a manner of focusing questions from the descriptive-awareness dimension to the affective, behavioral, feeling, or attitudinal dimension. The first question should be one that determines awareness: "Did you know about the altercation in the assembly shop last week between Bill and John?" The second question should be an open question on general feelings: "Did their disagreement seem to cause any further hard feelings on the part of other workers?" The third sequence of questions ought to focus on more specific parts of the issue: "Do you know exactly what the fight was all about? Can you describe how it started?" The fourth sequence ought to deal with "why" questions: "Has this trouble been brewing for some time? Is the quarrel between the two men fairly new? Do you know why it began in the first place?" Finally, the interviewer would begin to ask intensity questions, that is, those questions that probe the intensity of affect surrounding the event: "How do you as shop foreman feel that this will affect you and your working relationships? Do you feel that the sense of teamwork between the men has been interrupted? Are you concerned with union problems? Do you feel it affects your own leadership role with the men?" The sequence for this particular form of questioning is one of rolling or falling. If it is done correctly, the respondent "falls" from the more descriptive and less personal into the more affective, emotive, or personalistic (Gatz and Hoagland, 1978).

The structuring and sequencing of questions in interviews may be approached in numerous ways. The problem under investigation may dictate that questions of structure and sequence be handled in a nontraditional manner. The legislative interviews of Dexter (1970) were surely conducted in vastly different ways from the 100,000 or so interviews conducted over the years by Kinsey and his associates (Kinsey, Pomeroy, and Marton, 1948). Role playing often helps novice interviewers understand what form and shape the interview ought to take, and what degree of structure is appropriate for the desired results. Mastery of the wide realm of responsive behaviors in interviewing is difficult, but practice and experience can serve to hone the skills of any interviewer.

Post-Interview Tasks. There are several tasks that should be completed immediately after the interview. If there is time, the interview notes should be completed. Although every good interviewer ought to be taking better and better notes as he gains more skill and experience at interviewing, there will always be data that are not recorded at the moment the respondent offers them. Often several key words have to suffice, especially if the respondent is talking very rapidly. Thus, there will always be more extended notes on ideas, behaviors, and nonverbal cues that should be set down as soon as possible. Interviewers should try to schedule some time between interviews, not only so that they can arrive at the next interview on time, but so that they can flesh out the notes just taken. Otherwise, the field researcher will find himself doing double duty at the end of the day: filling in field notes and formulating preliminary analyses and hypotheses for the next day's interviews. When this happens, interviews begin to blend and merge, and, after some time, it may no longer be clear exactly who said what in reference to a particular topic.

Recording the interview data, both during and after the interview, can be done in any way that suits the interviewer, unless the interview has been a highly structured one with response sets predetermined. One noted fieldworker, in personal correspondence, recommends that exact quotations or word-for-word sentences be routinely enclosed in quotation marks in field notes to make them immediately identifiable and to distinguish them from the interviewer's summary notes. In addition, ideas that seem to be issues or concerns of major importance to the respondent should be numbered sequentially and related topics should be coded during the interview with their main-issue number and sequential letters (for example, 1a, 2a, 1b, 2b, and so forth). Finally, important observational data and nonverbal cues should be coded in the left margin with the notation "OC" for "observer's comments." These unobtrusive measures and nonverbal cues may add depth to the analysis or alert the investigator as to which issues and concerns are most sensitive to the respondent.

Upon return to home base, the interviewer should immediately send a letter of thanks to the respondent for his time and information. If there is a possibility that the interviewer may wish to interview the respondent again, he ought to make that possibility known to the respondent. Courtesy demands that each and every interviewee in inquiries other than survey interviews be personally thanked by the inquirer, preferably by letter.

Analysis and Integration of Field Notes

Once the interviewee is thanked and field notes are complete, the analysis, evaluation, and tabulation or integration of the interview data can begin. We will be interested principally here in the analysis and integration of field notes.

There are generally two stages of interview analysis. The first is the analysis of the single interview; this takes into account the respondent's personal context, the possibility of respondent bias, the credibility of what has been reported, and the interactional process between interviewer and respondent. The second is the analysis of the interview as part of a larger set of interview data, which will be integrated to form the total inquiry. In analyzing the first interview, the interviewer must render some judgment about its worth in terms of information gleaned (although it may be impossible to determine the actual worth of a single interview until the inquiry is over) and its contribution to additional leads in the inquiry. The personal context of the respondent has to be reconstructed (as nearly as possible) from the interview notes. Respondent bias has to be identified where possible (although, again, it may not be possible to ascertain where bias occurs until after a number of interviews have taken place with other respondents). The believability (credibility, plausibility, and consistency) of the data provided by the respondent has to be assigned some boundaries (in conjunction with what the interviewer knows about the respondent's personal context and possible biases). Finally, process data may be examined for the single interview (drawing heavily on those notes included in "observer's comments"). With respect to process, for instance, the interviewer may note shifts in conversation or transitions to new topics on the part of the respondent. He may want to trace the respondent's association of ideas; this may allow the interviewer to deduce what issues and concerns are related in the mind of the respondent and to conjecture how they are related. The interviewer may also want to examine length of responses; coverage or completeness of responses (whether the responses were informed or uninformed, what their range was, and what ideas or issues were omitted); inconsistencies, either with what the respondent has already said or with what the interviewer already knows to be true; ambiguities and peculiarities; and affective levels or changes in intensity and tone of feeling during the interview.

Gorden (1956) has suggested that notes be divided into three classes for analysis: observational notes, which result from watching and listening; theoretical notes, which represent self-conscious, controlled attempts to derive meaning from any one or several observation notes; and methodological notes, which are statements that reflect an operational act completed or planned, including timing, sequencing, stage setting, or maneuvering. Dexter (1970) has added to that the concept of transactions and admonishes the interviewer to be aware of the extent to which an interview is a "social relationship and the interviewer is a part of that relationship" (p. 140). The interactional nature of interviewing is rarely reported in the literature, and yet interviewer effects on the respondent must be sorted out, both while the interview is in progress—so that the impact of the interviewer as a stimulus may be modified as necessary—and after it is over—to determine to what extent the social interaction may have cued the respondent toward certain answers or positions. "The interviewer," Douglas (1976) asserts, "is both a part of the situation and *the instrument through which recording takes place, and therefore he should be, somehow or other, subject to report. In stressing this point, we are in fact modifying the universal validity or value of the subject-object dichotomy,* characteristic of common speech and of the Western tradition in epistemology" (p. 143, emphasis added). We would therefore argue for transactional notes to be added as a class of notes in the analysis.

Gorden (1956, pp. 160-164) also suggests that every set of notes, prior to final analysis, be summarized. The "packaging and repackaging" of notes—which are the "heart of final ideas"—help the researcher to remember, establish a stable chronicle of events, provide a vehicle for ordered creativity, give some account of the development of the inquiry, and are a constant source of inquiry renewal. From the summaries and resummaries come linkages, which become denser until all propositions fall into sets. The process of allowing the "linkages" to emerge from the interview notes and summaries is very similar to content analysis and to the process of identifying issues and concerns. The analysis of field notes is, in fact, a form of document analysis. In this case, the documents have been generated by the inquirer as a result of some transaction with an informed respondent.

The process of analyzing qualitative data, as we have often said before, is not only a science, it is also an art. Gorden (1956) suggests that the researcher's data have to be sifted into classes, which may then be refined or linked with other classes of events or phenomena. He offers three classes for an initial sort: common classes, which help to distinguish among varieties of things, persons, and events; special classes, which help to distinguish among things, persons, or events within their own environment; and theoretical classes, which are discovered by the researcher as observer and analyst and which allow him to build his own constructs. These constructs are particularly useful since they are grounded in the experience of the observer and are "demonstrably applicable and useful in the analysis" (p. 158). The sifting of people, events, and things in the environment continues until all the presumed data are verified by observation and fitted into classes. The final classes are what give the researcher "conceptual leverage" on the inquiry; they allow him to distance himself from the data and, at the same time, draw him closer to it in a new perspective. The process, in both analysis and in establishing reliability and validity, is similar to, and nearly congruent with, content analysis.

Determining Reliability and Validity of Interview Data

The problem of establishing validity and reliability in naturalistic inquiry is complicated by a series of issues that relate to social science as a whole. The concepts of credibility and auditability, as we have argued in Chapter Five, ought to be substituted for these scientific terms when carrying out an inquiry in a naturalistic mode. Cicourel (1974) suggests that overall validity and reliability can best be attained by ensuring the validity and reliability of each datum; this suggestion is not only logistically impossible but seems to beg the question. We suggest four methods for establishing credibility: host verification or "member checks," triangulation and corroboration, independent observer analysis, and "phenomenon recognition"—the recognition of a phenomenon as "real" by those who experience it.

Host verification or member checks involve checking the experiences the researcher has had against the experiences and understandings of members of the group. This may be accomplished either by using selected "facts" and involving several members of the group or by using the major propositions of the inquiry, along with all or nearly all the members. Triangulation and corroboration involve checking propositions either with other members, or, more often, with other methodological tools and measures. Independent observer analysis involves asking (and testing) whether another independent observer would have seen or heard the same things, events, or persons as the first observer did and whether, having done so, he would have made conceptual discoveries that empirically or logically validated the researcher's own conclusions. A final check, called phenomenon recognition, involves presenting the inquirer's "reality" to those who live it, and asking them whether it does, indeed, represent their common and shared experience.

The method to determine auditability has already been suggested: the outside audit (see Chapter Five). A competent outside auditor is employed to review the data collection and analysis procedures on the basis of documentation—an "audit trail"—developed during the inquiry itself. On the basis of that information, the auditor renders a two-fold judgment: that the procedures used are (1) appropriate, that is, within the realm of commonly accepted good practice, and (2) properly carried out. This separate judgment serves as an analogue to the "replicability" criterion, which scientific inquirers favor in dealing with questions of reliability.

Interviewing has many advantages with respect to data collection. Among its strengths is that there is less chance of misunderstanding between the inquirer and the respondent than in other approaches (and this is more true for unstructured interviewing than for structured, since unstructured forms elicit the respondent's own frame of reference). Questions can be tailored to fit the respondent's knowledge, degree of involvement, and status. The interviewer is likely to receive more accurate responses on sensitive issues, and the interview itself is likely to provide a more complete and in-depth picture than other forms of inquiry. The interview format is more flexible than other approaches to data gathering and provides wide latitude within which the respondent's responses can be explored and fruitful leads exploited. The technique provides for continuous assessment and evaluation of information by the inquirer, allowing him to redirect, probe, and summarize. Unstructured interviews in particular provide a picture of the event or thing in question in the respondent's own words and terms, his "natural language." Face-to-face encounters of the sort embodied in unstructured interviewing also allow for a maximum of rapport to be built between interviewer and respondent. Interviewing is virtually the only technique that provides access to "elites"—those with specialized knowledge of the situation—and it provides information much more quickly than observation.

Weaknesses in interviewing include its inefficiency and cost, although it does provide the richest information per unit of time invested. The materials are difficult or impossible to pretest (unless one is using a highly structured interview with predeveloped protocols). The results are unpredictable and may be nonaggregatable or nonequivalent over several interviews. Since only small samples can be handled by unstructured interviewing techniques, the generalizability of the results is moot. Such interviews are also difficult if not impossible to standardize (that is, to put into standard content or form), although this is to be expected since the respondents for unstructured interviewing are themselves often "unstandardized" and unique subjects. Nevertheless, interviews are difficult to replicate, since the data collection device is a human being, and the technique is also highly vulnerable to interviewer bias. The interviewer can influence the outcome of the interview enormously through the subtle cues he transmits. While the possibility exists that the interviewer can "train" the interviewee to be a good respondent by giving him cues, it is also possible to alienate the respondent by giving him the wrong kinds of cues, sometimes unconsciously. As a result, the maintenance of interviewer-respondent rapport is problematic, although the interviewer, by self-conscious examination of his own interpersonal style, can become aware of the cues that he is projecting and learn to modify them.

Observation

In her deft description of the pain and risk of anthropological observation, Wax (1971, p. 370) writes:

> The person who cannot abide feeling awkward or out of place, who feels crushed whenever he makes a mistake—embarrassing or otherwise—who is psychologically unable to endure being, and being treated like, a fool, not only for a day or week but for months on end, ought to think twice before he decides to become a participant observer. He might make a good interviewer or a good "detached" observer, but he does not have what it takes to appreciate the pains and joys of trying to involve himself with the people of another culture. An ideal participant observer is able to see himself as an educated and highly intelligent adult, and, simultaneously, as a ludicrous tenderfoot or *schlemiel* who knows less about what he is doing than a native child. He is able to accept the laughter and ridicule of his hosts as instructive, not because he is saintly in nature, but because making fun of improper or incorrect behavior is an ancient if painful method of pedagogy. He is also able to live with a sense of his own dangerousness, that is, the knowledge that any of the words or deeds which he considers natural or well intentioned may be interpreted by his hosts as hostile or insulting. Further, he is able, for weeks and months, to function like a sane and reasonable being in a situation which, for him, is largely without pattern or structure. He does not know whom he can trust, or whom he can trust about what, or, indeed, if he can trust anyone about anything at all. He may find, not once, but repeatedly, that he has been misled, cheated, exploited, or blackmailed, and that, in addition, "the community" knows all about this and is laughing at him. In

the last case, if he is really a sterling participant observer, he will be able to shake himself, laugh, and realize that slowly but surely he is learning how to stay out of trouble.

I have no advice on how to live graciously through the experience of being exploited, hoodwinked, shortchanged, blackmailed, robbed, or fooled, except by bearing in mind that every fieldworker could furnish examples which now sound hilarious but scarcely seemed funny at the time he experienced them. I myself have been fooled so many times that I cannot afford to even look at a stone, much less pick it up and throw it at my fellow anthropologists.

Wax's statement closely parallels the advice that Robert Park, a sociologist, purportedly gave to his students: "Go get the seats of your pants dirty in real research" (Williamson, Karp, and Dalphin, 1977, p. 198). Just what comprises observation, though, has been a subject of debate. The term *observation*, by which most social scientists mean participant observation, has come to be synonymous with field research (Williamson, Karp, and Dalphin, 1977, p. 199), fieldwork, or uncontrolled observation, participant and nonparticipant alike. Bogdan and Taylor (1975) define participant observation as involving "a period of intense social interaction between researcher and subject in the milieu of the latter. During this period data are unobtrusively and systematically gathered" (p. 5). We are not particularly enamored of this definition on several counts, however. First, the term *social interaction* seems to be too broad and not sufficiently focused on *inquiry*. Some social interactions are not focussed on inquiry (although Denny, 1978, and Wax, 1971, relate extensive social interaction with the community members of their study sites—baking bread for school sales and poker games with neighbors, for example). Second, we fail to see the need for requiring that the data be unobtrusively gathered. It appears to us that in many of the more classic instances (Whyte, 1943; Liebow, 1967; Wax, 1971) the subjects have known full well they were being studied. We prefer to define participant observation as a form of inquiry in which the inquirer —the observer—is playing *two* roles. First of all, of course, he is an observer; as such, he is responsible to persons outside the milieu being observed. But he is also a genuine participant; that is, he is a member of the group, and he has a stake in the group's activity and the outcomes of that activity. Of course, there is the case in which the observer adopts the role of participant as a cover for his *real* interest, that of observing, but it is impossible to even act the part (play the role) of a group member without becoming involved sooner or later. Indeed, this is the major trade-off between participant observation and other forms of data collection, and the one that causes concern on the part of more objectivist, scientific researchers, who feel that the observer in such a situation becomes co-opted and can no longer make appropriate observations. We shall speak to this objection shortly.

If participant observation occupies one end of the continuum of observation tactics, then nonparticipant observation, a method that requires the observer to play only the role of observer, is at the other end. As with participant observation, the subjects being observed may or may not be aware of the observer's role as observer.

Several examples of participant observation would be: a sociologist working in a social service agency to discover how referrals to such agencies are handled; an expert on organizational theory working within an industrial complex to determine typical patterns of communication; a graduate student working in a school to discover how definitions of proper teaching performance are arrived at by practitioners; a sociologist having himself committed to a mental hospital to determine how patients are handled; an investigator posing as a patient with a series of physicians to determine whether similar symptoms will give rise to different diagnoses as a function of the physicians' areas of specialization; or a graduate student serving as an administrative intern to collect data for his dissertation on the political behavior of school administrators.

Examples of nonparticipant observation would include: a psychologist standing on a school playground looking for instances of frustration in children; a teacher behind a one-way vision screen watching a school psychologist administer an IQ test to a retarded child; a teacher-educator sitting in a classroom and coding the teacher's interactive behaviors on a scale; a market researcher in a supermarket observing the way in which shoppers choose among competing brands of coffees; an experimenter noting the way in which two subjects asked to play a competitive game relate to one another; or a sociologist at a high school dance noting the patterns of interaction between students choosing and students being chosen as dance partners.

A Rationale for Observation

There are many good reasons for utilizing observational techniques; for example, these techniques build on direct experience. Douglas (1976) makes the point that in everyday life people use various tests of truth but that the most important of these tests is direct experience:*

> First, we use direct experience of things. "Seeing is believing." "Experience is the best teacher." People sum it up in many ways even in everyday abstractions. Most importantly, they use it all the time, commonly without saying anything about it. Direct experience seems to be the most pervasive, fundamental test of truth. All ... the everyday tests are used in conjunction, and they are chosen partly to fit the concrete situation people face, but direct personal experience is the most reliable to everyone. Someone who would continually take the word of other people about his own experience, even when their word contradicted his experience, would seem utterly insane. One of the most shocking experiences a person can have is deciding that his own direct experience of something was wrong. Paradoxes, magical mirrors, and the like are all intriguing to people precisely because they appear at first to contradict direct experience; but people almost always reassert direct experience in some way [p. 5].

*The other tests of truth are direct experience of other people, including independent tests, retests, or observations; abstract rules of logic or reason; and concrete, common-sense ideas about people, acts, events, and situations (Douglas, 1976, pp. 5-6).

Inquirers are of course often in the position of having to ask others about behaviors or events that they themselves did not witness. When possible, however, they prefer to observe the situation for themselves and are most convinced by their own direct experience of it.

Observational techniques also make it possible to record behavior and events as they occur. Selltiz and others (1959) point out that a major asset of observation is that it makes it "possible to record behavior as it occurs" (p. 201). The quality of simultaneity, the "I was there" quality, is enormously persuasive not only to the observer but also to others to whom the observer reports. The absence of a time lag between observation (or other data collection) and recording is a major guarantee of validity.

Moreover, observational techniques make it possible to build on both propositional and tacit knowledge. We have already noted that a major advantage in the inquirer's becoming his own instrument is his ability to use tacit as well as propositional understandings of a situation (see Chapter Six). Observation as a technique undoubtedly provides the broadest range of inputs that can be interpreted by the inquirer using his tacit knowledge base. In addition, as McCall and Simmons (1969) have noted, observational techniques are well adapted to "maximize discovery and description." This asset is of course particularly advantageous when no *a priori* theory exists to guide observation.

Further, when distance, memory lapses, or emotional reactions may cause significant alterations in the data that the inquirer is seeking, he may wish to observe events for himself as an added precaution against bias. Again, in most data collection, the active cooperation of the subject is required; for example, he has to fill in a questionnaire or respond to an interview. But observations can in many cases be carried out without such cooperation, and, indeed, even without the subject's knowledge that such observations are taking place.

Observation techniques also enhance the observer's ability to understand complex situations. When some behaviors are taken for granted or are "so much 'second nature' that they escape awareness and resist translation into words" (Selltiz and others, 1959, p. 202), or when meanings are problematic or the phenomena under investigation are not concrete and thus the more subject to moral or material-interest conflicts (Douglas, 1976, p. 25), the use of observational techniques may be the only way to understand the complexity of the situation or behavior.

Finally, observational techniques permit data collection in instances where other forms of communication are impossible. In inquiries in which the subject is either unable to speak—babies, for instance, or severely retarded children—or unwilling to speak— someone, for example, who distrusts the investigator and resists his inquiry efforts—observational methods allow at least some opportunity for study without the subject's active cooperation (Selltiz and others, 1959, pp. 202-203). Again, the ethical aspects of such observation should be fully considered.

The basic methodological arguments for observation, then, may be summarized as these: observation (particularly participant observation) maximizes the inquirer's ability to grasp motives, beliefs, concerns, interests, unconscious behaviors, customs, and the like; observation (particularly participant observation) allows the inquirer to see the world as his subjects see it, to live in their time frames, to capture the phenomenon in and on its own terms, and to grasp the culture in its own natural, ongoing environment; observation (particularly participant observation) provides the inquirer with access to the emotional reactions of the group introspectively—that is, in a real sense it permits the observer to use *himself* as a data source; and observation (particularly participant observation) allows the observer to build on tacit knowledge, both his own and that of members of the group.

The arguments against using observational techniques would include: observational techniques may lead to reactivity in the setting or on the part of members (House, 1978a, p. 18); the method leans heavily on personal interpretation; direct experience with or involvement in the situation necessarily leads one to experience a setting in a biased manner—the extreme form of which is "going native," as anthropologists like to say; direct involvement necessarily leads to self-deception on the part of the investigator; involvement will cause the investigator to take meanings for granted and thus make it impossible for him to observe or report on them.

There are, however, counterarguments to the objections raised above. Reinharz (1979) points out that reactivity may not be as important as is commonly believed—social environments are quite stable, and an inquirer's presence may seldom, if ever, produce the massive imbalances that researchers so carefully tiptoe to avoid. Douglas (1976) notes that the charge that observation relies too heavily on personal interpretation is based on the "absolute objectivist view" that the use of one's own direct experience is the principal sin for inquirers. Moreover, the inquirer can use a variety of means to determine whether his participation and/or observations are in fact causing him to distort experience. He may, for example, check the perceived reality against his prior expectations. If there are never any differences between the two, the inquirer has probably closed his mind to new and unexpected ideas. He can, again, check his initial ideas (abstracted from the setting) with his later ideas. His early ideas should from time to time be found wrong or misconceived. He can also check his early notes; they should *not* include much of what he later grasped as being crucial to the setting.

One way to overcome the predilection to see new situations in terms of old preconceptions is through a process that Douglas (1976) calls "immersion." He makes the case for field research as a valid tool on the basis of his belief that it is possible to leave behind—at least temporarily—preconceived notions of what the inquirer will find by becoming so deeply involved with the context that earlier prejudices are forgotten: "Rather than to relate the new experience to old ideas, according to our strategy the researcher tries to defocus, to stop thinking of his new experience in terms of prior categories and ideas. [The inquirer] flows with the experience—he lives it, does it" (p. 120).

Clearly, observation as we are considering it here is more than mere seeing. Each of us sees more things—and forgets more things—than we interactively observe in a given day. Many things escape our notice or are given short shrift in our mental processes because we become distracted or take meanings for granted, or because what we see does not seem to be important at the time. The kind of observation that we are talking about here refers to things that one notices and pays special attention to, things that one inspects, studies, remembers, and contemplates. All these shades of meaning will be important in observation. But it is necessary to listen as well as to look. If the inquirer is to understand and grasp social meanings, he will not only have to understand the context of events and behaviors, but he will also have to come to know their feeling tone. Without learning to listen to those he is observing, he will never learn to recognize humor, love, respect, fear, wonder, joy, sadness, scorn, or any of the shades of emotion that shape verbal communication.

McCall and Simmons (1969, p. 9) define three broad classes of field research (by which they mean participant observation and methods that are ancillary to observation):

> Type I: *Participant observation.* The fieldwork-er directly observes the setting but also participates in the sense that he has durable social relations in the setting. He may or may not play an active part in events, or he may interview participants in events which may be considered part of the process of observation.
>
> Type II: *Informant interviewing.* The field-worker elicits information from an "informant" who reports information about others or about events not witnessed by the fieldworker. Interviewing during the event itself is considered part of participant observation.
>
> Type III: *Enumerations and samples.* The field-worker conducts both surveys and direct, repeated, countable observations. Observation in this sense may entail minimal participation as compared with that in Type I.

The McCall-Simmons classes of fieldwork are useful because they describe types of activities in the inquiry setting itself.

The work of Gold (1958) explores observation from the perspective of roles that the participant observer may adopt (or that the nature of the setting may force on him). For Gold, "Every fieldwork role is at once a social interaction device for securing information for scientific purposes and a set of behaviors in which an observer's self is involved" (p. 218). In the role-taking and role-playing effort, success is measured in terms of how well "the demands of self-expression and self-integrity [are blended] with the demands of the role" (p. 218). The role-taking and role-playing dimension stretches from that of the complete participant, whose "true identity and purpose . . . are not known to those whom he observes" (p. 220), to that of the complete observer, who is totally removed "from social interaction with informants" (p. 222). Between those two extremes lie the roles of *participant as observer,* in which both the inquirer and his respondents (the observed) are aware that they are in a research or inquiry relationship, and the *observer as participant,* a role that is assumed apparently only "in studies involving one-visit interviews" (p. 221). Gold's formulations suggest dimensions of the *extent* to which the inquirer is known as inquirer to the respondents or subjects, the *degree of involvement* with the subjects, and the *extent to which a situation is durable* and interruptable or interrupted.

Our conception of the dimensions along which observations can be arrayed differs slightly from that of McCall and Simmons and that of Gold. Figure 4 illustrates what we consider to be three major dimensions, although others that are also important will be

Figure 4. A Typology of Subject/Observer Relationships

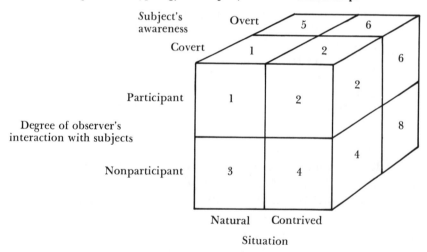

treated shortly. The first dimension may be described as the extent to which the observer is or is not a participant. We have used this dimension earlier to suggest the continuum of participant observation and nonparticipant observation, as Gold (1958) and Babchuk (1962) have also done. The second dimension is the extent to which the situation is natural or contrived. Barker (1965) refers to this dimension as a continuum along which the researcher operates either as a "transducer" (as an observer of natural phenomena) or as an "operative" (a contriver of phenomena that the researcher wishes to observe). One might ask: How "natural" is this setting? Is it a playground, a supermarket, a classroom, or other environment in which people actually live and work, or is it more "contrived"—for example a test administration, an experimental situation, a laboratory, or a "victim and shills" situation such as one finds on "Candid Camera"? Contrived situations are more prone to reactivity and therefore lose generalizability. We would note, in passing, that contriving the situation is tantamount to constraining the antecedent conditions, and that this is to move toward experimentalism and away from naturalistic inquiry (see Chapter Four). The third dimension is the extent to which the subjects are or are not aware of the observer's role as observer. Awareness can induce both reactivity and interactivity; both of these may therefore produce "uncertainty effects," that is, they may in part determine the phenomena being observed. It should be noted, however, that the observer's very presence in the field, if he can be seen or sensed, can be upsetting to the subjects, even if they are not aware of being observed.

From these three major dimensions, we can derive the eight-category typology shown in Figure 4. The figure depicts a cube of eight cells made up of combinations of two types of settings (natural and contrived), two levels of interaction between the observer and the observed (participant and nonparticipant), and two levels of subject awareness (overt and covert). The following is a list of examples to illustrate each cell:

Cell 1: A participant observer in the natural setting of a nude beach; others on the beach are not aware of his inquirer status.

Cell 2: The contrived setting of a laboratory in which the experimenter—a participant observer—presses a subject to provide greater and greater electric shocks to a "shill" who seems uncooperative. The subject, of course, believes it to be a real experiment.

Cell 3: Candid camera—a natural situation in which a nonpartici-

pant observer (usually hidden) photographs a subject's behavior without the subject's awareness.

Cell 4: A teacher viewing through a one-way vision screen the administration of an IQ test to a retarded child.

Cell 5: A student in a class, performing the role of class evaluator,
with the knowledge of the whole class that he is doing so.

Cell 6: Two students, aware of one another's intent, role playing
and observing one another.

Cell 7: A student moving through a university registration line
being stopped by an observer who needs to determine
whether the student's name appears on a checklist.

Cell 8: A learning experiment in a laboratory in which the subjects are quite aware that the experimenter is an observer.

These eight cells represent the major dimensions along which observations can differ (that is, natural versus contrived, participant
versus nonparticipant, and overt versus covert). There are, however, other dimensions along which observation situations may
also differ. And these should be taken into account within each of
the cells of the cube that we have just described.

First, there are factors relating to the investigator. Is the investigator engaged in problem-solving or problem-finding behavior? That is, is the inquiry directed toward discovery or verification? The former kind of inquiry is open to more inputs, is less
structured, and has an emergent design. The latter is relatively
more focused, is well-structured, and has a preordinate design. In
terms of the target of the inquiry, is the investigator interested in
observing overt behaviors or in making inferences about the traits,
attitudes, processes, and so on that underlie behavior? The former
requires little more than description; the latter requires judgmental
leaps that may be difficult to ground in empirical behavior. Further, is the inquirer a relatively passive onlooker or is he actively
involved? In the former case, he will not be likely to evoke reactive behavior; in the latter he may seriously influence the events
by his presence.

Second, there are factors relating to the subjects. Knowledge of purpose is of course not an issue if the subject is unaware
of the investigator. If he is aware, however, the observed behavior

may be unusual in a number of ways. For example, the subject may make strenuous efforts to *help* the inquirer achieve his purpose, and so may actually demonstrate unusual or even bizarre behavior (depending on what the subject perceives the purposes of the inquiry to be). Again, the subject's acceptance of the observer is dependent on awareness. The distinctions of Douglas (1976) between cooperative and conflictual models of research assume tremendous importance here. Acceptance of the observer leads to general cooperation, while nonacceptance may lead to various forms of conflict. It is important to note that even the subject who is "unaware" of the observer may nevertheless find the observer's presence unacceptable (by virtue of the fact that the observer is an "outsider" to the group).

Third, there are factors relating to the situation. Is the observation guided by an *a priori* structure or is it relatively unstructured? In the former case it is likely that a formal instrument exists on which the observation is systematically recorded. In the latter case, evidences of observations would more likely be notepads filled with immediate observations that would then be translated into longer and more complete field notes at the end of each day (including straightforward descriptions of observed behaviors, questions on the meanings of the behaviors generated by the observer, and the observer's own affective reactions to these behaviors). Clearly, again, there is a relation between degree of structure and output constraints. More structure implies less emphasis on naturalistic inquiry. It can also be asked if the observations will be made over an extended period of time (longitudinally) or at selected intervals or periods (cross sectionally). The former might be done when extended protocols or archives are to be assembled for later analysis. The latter are often used for reasons of logistics or economy.

Needless to say, the description of methods used in observational inquiry should include not only some reference to where data gathering fell on the "cube" but also some analysis of the factors relating to the investigator, subjects, and situations, since the circumstances of observations and data collections help explain how decisions are reached and what might be the limits and purposes of the inquiry.

Overt and Covert Observation: Are There Trade-Offs?

Besides the classical arguments for and against each type of observation, there are several especially cogent considerations for evaluators who are contemplating an inquiry or evaluation effort that might be considered "covert." Williamson, Karp, and Dalphin (1977, p. 107) consider settings to fall along a continuum, from the most public (supermarkets, bars, shopping centers) to the most private (private clubs, households, labor organizations, and the like). The inquirer's access to these settings may to some extent determine what role he will assume in attempting to observe and garner information. Maximum access could be expected in those areas where public access is a matter of course and where activities are not "secretive." Using Gold's classification system (1958), we can say that both the complete observer and the complete participant are in roles where their identity as researchers is unknown to the subjects. Participants as observers and observers as participants are considerably more open about their status as researchers.

Covert participation generally takes place in situations where the "actors consider the sharing of their knowledge potentially dangerous to themselves, or when the information is highly ego involved (lying buried under a protective layer of rationalization such that direct methods of information seeking could well elicit faulty data)" (Williamson, Karp, and Dalphin, 1977, p. 206). In addition to the problems of situational access that dictate the use of "disguised observation," there are other ethical problems that the observer faces, including, but most assuredly not limited to, questions of whether the "information sought is in any sense public" (p. 206); whether the inquirer is violating laws to obtain the information he seeks; and whether or not there are limits—legal and moral—to the rights of researchers to know certain things or to observe settings that are essentially private.

Participant observation, and indeed any observation, requires that the observer get onto the subject's home ground. The entire posture of covert observation implies that it is occasionally impossible to do this without using deceit or misrepresentation and that one therefore cannot study the subject's behavior with his cooperation and consent. As Douglas (1976, p. 43) points out, in the past field research has often assumed that disorganization and conflict are somehow deviant, extraordinary phenomena; that social values are shared by all members of a society; and that cooperation was the natural state of society. These assumptions in turn had implications for the methods used for inquiry. The assumption of homogeneity "was the unspoken rationale for the in-depth study of one (generally) small group by one investigator" (p. 45). These researchers did not worry about the big picture or representative findings. They assumed that they could rely on the cooperation of their subjects and "that they would act naturally while he was studying them. . . . The classical paradigm exudes the small-town, Protestant public morality of openness, friendliness, and do-gooderism" (pp. 46-47). And the researchers assumed that research could be done "from one perspective within the group and the report written from the one perspective of the host group. . . . Social reality was assumed in some way to be uniperspectival" (p. 46).

Douglas (1976) asserts, however, that these assumptions and their consequences have tended to be bad for field research, and he urges inquirers instead to adopt what he calls the conflict or investigative paradigm: "The investigative paradigm is based on the assumption that profound conflicts of interest, values, feelings, and actions pervade social life. It is taken for granted that many of the people one deals with, perhaps all people to some extent, have good reason to hide from others what they are doing and even lie to them. Instead of trusting people and expecting trust in return, one suspects others and expects others to suspect him. Conflict is the reality of life; suspicion is the guiding principle. . . .

"Our society is a mixture of the highly patterned and the highly unpatterned, the cooperative and the conflictual, the open and obvious and the secret and the obscure. Because of this, the methods of investigative social research rely upon a crucial combination of cooperative and investigative methods" (pp. 55-56).

One of the crucial assumptions of our own naturalistic model is that most programs, whether they are educational, mental health, social welfare, or criminal justice programs, operate in an environment characterized not by value consensus, but by value pluralism and, therefore, by conflicts in attitudes and beliefs. The implications for inquiry modes are self-evident. If it is true that value conflicts inhere in most social action programs, then the assumption of cooperation on the part of the subjects of the inquiry is probably unrealistic.

Nevertheless, there are even more serious ethical considerations that can confront the investigator. Since most programs that the evaluator investigates are public (and funded by public funds), does he have the option of assuming the role of a covert observer? We think not in the majority of cases (and indeed we cannot think of a single instance in which it might be appropriate for the inquirer to go "undercover" in the evaluation of a publicly funded program). The public character of the program, along with the public nature of whatever final report is delivered, almost certainly demands that the evaluator enter the site openly, with his intents and purposes clearly explained to all involved, and that no member of the team attempt "infiltration."

That is not to say that the evaluator should expect cooperation. Quite the opposite. If Douglas is correct, there will inevitably be reasons why people will not want an evaluator to know what is going on, and there will be many times when they will—consciously or unconsciously, overtly or covertly—subvert his attempts to understand and collect data on various programs and settings. So while the inquirer probably cannot justify "undercover" operations, he must assume that conflict, problematic meanings, and noncooperation will be a part of his milieu and take appropriate measures to compensate for lack of cooperation.

Observation and Recording of Data

As we noted earlier, one can hardly make observations unless one can get onto the subject's home ground. The steps for this process—gaining admission, building relationships, providing explanations, striking a bargain, establishing trust, and the like—are more fully discussed in Chapters Nine through Twelve. Our intention here is rather to explore ways in which evaluators and inquirers might record observations and to discuss a view of the process of observation that differs from classical sociological and anthropological models.

There are a number of ways in which information can be recorded. Most of these means can be used either in direct observation or in a first-cut analysis of observations that are in recorded form—for example, audiotapes, videotapes, or films. Indeed, the use of some form of electronic recording has a great deal to commend it: it can be analyzed at leisure (although the reader is again reminded of Denny's injunction [1978] that it is what one proposes to do "later" that can eventually overwhelm the analysis stage); it can be viewed or listened to repeatedly in case of doubt about interpretation; it forms a permanent record that can be re-analyzed by subsequent researchers; it provides bases for reliability and validity studies; and in some cases, it provides a legal base for proving that what the inquirer said happened did indeed happen. But those advantages must be balanced off against the negative factors of time, cost, and obtrusiveness, which more often than not argue against the use of such devices.

But even if we put these mechanical or electronic tools to one side, there are still numerous ways to collect records of observations. Some of these are listed below, although doubtless both new and experienced fieldworkers could give additional examples of how they have recorded observations in the field or of how they intend to do so in the future.

1. Running notes. Field notes are probably the most common way in which to collect nonparticipant observational data. The observer is relatively free to record almost anything he wants to record at any time. The notes may be straightforwardly anecdotal or may be organized into categories at the time they are taken. And of course the field notes may take the form of dictated comments.

2. Field experience log or diary. The major difference between the diary and field notes is that the former is written after the fact, for example, in the evening following the observations of the day. Of course, diaries can be constructed from field notes; this is a way of putting notes in more legible and organized form. (Indeed, it is our recommendation that both field notes and interviews be re-recorded, filled in, and possibly organized in different fashion after *every day* of interviewing or observing. Analysis begins after the first observation or interview, and reanalysis ought to be a continuous, iterative process, while the creation of categories by the inquirer is part and parcel of the dialectic with the data.)

3. Notes on thematic units. When the inquirer is interested

in particular behaviors—for example, how a writer goes about organizing himself to begin on a writing task—he may take detailed notes on any observed behaviors that fall into that thematic class. And, of course, running behavioral descriptions can also be broken into thematic units later.

4. Chronologs. These are sometimes called "hemerographs" if they cover a single day in the life of the subject. A good example of a fictional hemerograph is Solzhenitsyn's *One Day in the Life of Ivan Denisovich* (1963). These are literally running accounts of a subject's or group's behavior, often recorded in the form of "episodes." Missing numbers in the chronologs indicate missed episodes. So, for example, a chronolog of a preschool child at breakfast might look like this:

15. getting glass (7:12 A.M.)
18. looking for socks (7:14 A.M.)
20. seating himself again at breakfast table (7:19 A.M.)
21. commenting about breakfast chocolate (7:21 A.M.)
22. replying to mother's query about clean socks (7:22 A.M.)
24. begins eating breakfast (7:23 A.M.)

5. Context maps. These are maps, sketches, or diagrams of the context within which the observation takes place, for example, the classroom layout, the playground, the arrangement of office space, and the like. A context map is useful because it allows for shorthand entries in notes and facilitates reference to the position of a subject, the relative positions of several subjects, the content of the visual field of a subject, the visual field of an observer, and so on.

6. Taxonomies or category systems. These are usually used in relatively structured situations in which the taxonomic (or other) categories represent *a priori* hypotheses or questions. The number of instances, or exemplary instances, may be recorded in more or less open-ended fashion.

7. Schedules. Time layouts for locales or types of observations or for simple determination of recording intervals are called observation schedules. They indicate where the observer is to be, when he is to be there, how often he is to make a notation, and any other direction concerning the observation.

8. Sociometrics. These are relational diagrams developed by the observer about who talks to whom, who plays with whom, who complains about whom, who interacts in any way with whom. This may be developed in the form of simple notation first. For example, the observer may have a sheet labeled "Who plays with whom" on which, at some scheduled interval, he records who is playing with whom by simply noting groups and names (1—John, Mary, Bill; 2—Jim, Freddie, Joanne; and so forth). Later, he may develop the more familiar sociometric diagram (or "sociogram") from these notes. Overlays may show movement of groups over time.

9. Panels. It is often of interest to observe the same persons systematically over time—for example, once a week, every quarter, and the like—to determine changes in whatever is being observed. A panel of subjects may be designated whom the observer will re-observe according to an *a priori* schedule.

10. Debriefing questionnaires. These questionnaires are intended not for subjects but for observers, who may fill them out after an observation period. Especially useful if the observer is prevented from using any other form of recording device, the questionnaire will call his attention to salient factors about which he can then recall and record his observations. He, of course, is familiar with the questionnaire before he makes his observations. This particular form of field record is really a debriefing instrument for the observer.

11. Debriefing by another investigator. The observer may also be debriefed by another investigator.

12. Rating scales. In. structured situations the observation may be reduced to a number of scalable items on which the observer can record the amount and/or type of behavior observed. One such scale is the Flanders Interaction Analysis Scale.

13. Checklists. These can be thought of in two ways: (1) as listing things to look for and to check off as often as they are found, and (2) as guides to the observer's observations, similar to the schedules discussed above but dealing with content rather than with timing.

14. Concealed devices. The observer may leave behind a "bug," for example, a hidden videotape camera. This category may also include wiretaps. Such devices are useful because they

release the observer from being on the scene and because they provide long-term surveillance. Sometimes, such devices need not be
concealed; the subjects become accustomed to them and learn to
ignore them more easily than they do live observers. But conceal-
ment without the consent of the subjects raises serious legal and
ethical problems, and this particular form of field recording is not
likely to be one that educational inquirers and evaluators would
ever have cause to consider.

15. Steno-masks. Steno-masks—sometimes called "elephant
noses"—are comprised of dictating equipment connected to dictating masks. Attached to the body of the observer, these masks conceal the observer's comments and so maintain the privacy of field
notes. The advantage of using such equipment is that observed behavior may be recorded immediately, and final field notes (which
must be transcribed from tapes in the dictating equipment) are not
subject to memory lapses or later reinterpretation far from the
field.

While this list of methods used by observers in the past is
fairly complete, a fieldworker should always feel free, within the
boundaries of his inquiry, to generate other ways of recording the
information he feels that the study needs.

There are certainly as many alternative ways of viewing the
process of conducting field research. Our own set of steps, presented in Chapters Nine through Twelve, is by no means sacred,
even to us. Depending on the site and circumstances, some steps
may need extra attention, or may be skipped entirely. But
Douglas' (1976) account of the "general strategies of field research" provides a sufficiently different view of the process that a
summary of the major steps seems appropriate.

1. Initial stage: grasping the research setting.
   a. De-focussing or immersion, by which he means ". . . a semi-
      conscious, largely presymbolic perception of the overall
      nature, inter-relatedness, and truth of the setting" (Douglas,
      1976, p. 123).
   b. Running interaction-effectiveness tests (being able to pass,
      having a sense of what fits, being able to joke with members
      and the like).
   c. Understanding the situation, by which he means being able

to put it all together in "a conscious, symbolic, rational totality" (p. 124).

2. Secondary Stages: understanding and reporting on the research setting.
   a. Understanding in member terms (the basis for grounded theory).
   b. Testing for understanding, by maintenance of the integrity of the members' experience, by evoking the setting in an audience of outsiders, and by making sense to the members themselves.
   c. Member review (or member checks).
   d. Checking and testing (by which he means following new, emergent leads; triangulation and the like).
   e. Refocussing (refocussing on theory to draw out relationships between the observer's understandings and any previous theories).

Note that this particular set of terms does provide insight on the *processual* steps for understanding sites and social groups.

Drawbacks of Observation

There are some special limitations, constraints, and problems associated with observational techniques, especially participant observation. These appear to merit some special consideration here, since they have some influence on what inquiries will be undertaken, what observations will be made, and what analyses the data will finally undergo. These limitations and problems seem to fall into a number of subareas or special categories, relating to settings, logistics, method, and the investigator himself. Observational techniques (particularly participant observation), for example, cannot readily be adapted to large, complex settings. They may raise problems of secrecy, wound sensibilities, touch on taboo topics, or invade the privacy of individuals or groups. And observation, as a technique, is typically confined to the single setting, thus eliminating the possibility of comparisons and contrasts.

With respect to the logistics of studies involving observational techniques, there are three special constraints imposed by these techniques. First, the observer is limited to seeing only those

things permitted by his role (or sex), that is, by his place in the
group, his relationships to the members, and the like. Second,
since in participant observation the observer must participate as
well as observe, it often tends to be difficult to find enough time
away from the group to make extensive notes. Third, observation
typically generates huge amounts of raw data that pose formidable
analysis problems. Finding time to "interact" with the data is a
difficult task.

There are, additionally, problems with the methods employed in observation. There is a tendency for observation to be
unsystematic (the less structured and more open the inquiry, the
more unstructured and unsystematic will be the observation). And
because observation is such a melange of methods, there is a general absence of standard operating procedures and guidelines. In
fact, the unsystematic nature of most observation may be due to
the lack of standard operating procedures and guidelines.

Finally, there are problems associated with the observer,
who is, after all, the instrument for an observational study (the
more unstructured the study, again, the more reliance is placed on
human beings as instruments). First, it is difficult, although not
impossible, for the observer to guard against the intrusion of his
own biases, attitudes, prejudices, or assumptions. One way to neu-
tralize such biases and assumptions is to include them, insofar as
they become known to the observer, in the final report. To the
extent that the observer understands his own prejudices and value
conflicts and can offer them to his audiences for examination
alongside the study, audiences can make independent judgments
concerning the extent to which such biases shaped or shaded the
ultimate study. As Wax (1971) and Reinharz (1979) suggest, the
observer ought to report how he himself was changed by his study,
including to what extent he was ultimately able to reexamine his
old values and beliefs and own up to his own prejudices. There is
the problem of the sheer necessity for the observer to be selective
in data collection, that is, to exhibit selective perception and selective memory. Moreover, there may be "calibration shifts" over
time, and observers sometimes have a tendency to focus on what
may be called "exotic" data, since those are likely to generate the
most attention in the final report.

Whether the subjects are aware of the observer's role or not, his presence will in some way disturb the "natural" situation, although Reinharz (1979) warns the social scientist that social settings are more stable over time than we have generally given them credit for being; said another way, the inquirer is apt to cause less *permanent* disturbance than he has imagined. Findings from observational studies are impossible to replicate, since the observer's experience will be uniquely his own, shaped by both previous experiences and a highly individualistic interaction with members of the group. The observer should also be aware that involvement in any part of the situation may make him suspect in other parts because of power alignments within the group (Williamson, Karp, and Dalphin, 1977). The reader is referred to Wax's excellent description of the suspicions about her true role (initially) at Tule Lake (a Japanese internment camp in World War II) (1971, p. 61). Finally, there is the ongoing danger that the observer will gradually become a member of the group that he set out to study and will finally lose all objectivity. The extent to which this has actually happened in the past is uncertain, but the inexperienced fieldworker should probably plan to spend some time away from the setting to remind himself who and what he is and to reconsider his original role in moving onto the site.

Ethical Problems of Observing

There are a number of ethical problems associated with both participant and nonparticipant observation. These deserve some special mention here, since there are fewer ethical guidelines for observation than for other naturalistic methods such as interviewing and document analysis.

Most social scientists, whether educational evaluators, anthropologists, sociologists, or political scientists, are bound by ethical principles that require full, informed consent from their subjects. (Investigations based in universities or funded by federal dollars now strictly require "informed consent" forms for the protection of human subjects.) There are, moreover, laws regarding invasion of privacy. Nevertheless, the investigator may at times find himself in grey areas of interpretation, where the temptation will be to depart from strict informed consent procedures or strict adherence to the law. The observer may rationalize by saying that some deception is needed to uncover the truth or that prior knowledge by subjects that they are involved in an observational study will destroy their utility. So, in the name of pursuing truth, the observer will take steps that are, at the very least, ethically questionable. This is especially apt to happen in participant observation, where the subjects are less likely to be aware of their true role than they would be in nonparticipant observation. Caution thus becomes more urgent as the inquirer increasingly takes on a participant role.

The golden rule of observation is that the observer should examine what he is about to do from the perspective of the subject. Would the observer want to happen to himself what he is about to perpetrate on the subject? Would his own sense of moral outrage be awakened by an invasion of privacy, for instance? Would he himself be convinced of the need for "scientific study" of his personal life, habits, behaviors, and the like, especially if he had not been given the chance to raise questions or objections or to agree to take part in the study? Actually, the golden rule is inverse in this case, but it does no harm to the principle for the inquirer to try to place himself in the subject's shoes. Considerations of privacy and consent must, in the last analysis, be balanced off against the need to gain scientific knowledge. In any event, the choice between new (or better knowledge) and the protection of those at risk will never be an easy one.

The observer is bound, finally, to have explored alternatives in terms of protection of subjects and uncovering data and to have weighed them as carefully as possible. One cannot possibly justify use of a questionable practice when there are perfectly ethical alternatives available. And if the observer must do something of a borderline nature, it should be given the test of publicity; that is, the tactic should have public approval before the fact (see Bok, 1978).

Training for Observation

In training someone to do a one-time observational task, the investigator ought to be certain that he has thought of, and provided for, every conceivable contingency that might arise. Trainees should be made thoroughly familiar with the purposes and procedures of the observation. Generally, it is not feasible to employ very open-ended techniques in cases where observers are to be trained for one-time use only—the investment is too great for the return. When the trainees have become conceptually as familiar as possible with what they are to do, then the next logical step is to have them practice those procedures. Role playing may be done with two or more trainees or in real observational situations.

If it is a question of becoming a competent observer generally, only long-term professional training and experience will do. An apprenticeship on some project in which one uses observational techniques and works under the direct supervision of someone well experienced in the area is probably the best way to learn careful observation. But vicarious experience is also extremely useful; thus, the novice ought to familiarize himself with all the literature on observation—learning what problems other fieldworkers have faced and coming to know their misgivings, failures, self-doubts, fears, embarrassments, stresses, and hopes may help him to understand that he is neither the first nor the last to be faced with duress, chagrin, and isolation. On a bitterly cold night, in a bitterly cold room in South Dakota, one of the authors was reminded of what Wax (1971) had said of her experiences in the Tule internment camp: "[The room] contained four dingy and dilapidated articles of furniture . . . —and it was hotter than the hinges of Hades. Since there was no one around to ask where I might get a chair, I sat down on the hot mattress, took a deep breath, and cried. I was too far gone to be consciously aware that I was isolated or to wonder why I had left a beautiful and comfortable university town to stick myself in this oven of a concentration camp. Like some lost two-year-old I only knew that I was miserable. After a while, I found the room at the end of the barrack that contained two toilets and a couple of wash basins. I washed my face and told myself I would feel better the next day. I was wrong" (p. 68). Knowing that Wax had been miserable didn't make the heating system work any more efficiently, or make the room any less drafty, or warm cold feet. But it helped to remember that someone else had been just as miserable while doing fieldwork.

Another way to train oneself for observation is to set tasks related to looking, listening, and recording skills and to keep performing those tasks until the confidence that goes with solid performance is achieved.

Determining Reliability and Validity of Observational Data

Much of what was said in Chapter Five about the bounding and focusing of inquiries and determining the reliability and validity of qualitative data is applicable to the methods of participant and nonparticipant observation, so it will not be repeated here. But several checks will be reviewed, since they undergird all observational study; to the extent that those procedures are followed, the results of the inquiry may at least have some fit with reality. McCall (1969) calls attention to two "traditional" checks, the first of which is "to inquire whether the account seems plausible. Does it hold up internally and make any sense in light of one's broad understanding of human behavior?" (p. 130). To the extent that the observation is plausible and accountable in terms of human behavior, it has the likelihood of being a valid observation. Even if the observation does not seem plausible, it can serve an important purpose: it can be probed to discover whether it represents some unknown bias or some "possibly symptomatic distortion."

The second test, according to McCall (1969, p. 130), "is to assess the stability of the account to determine whether it is consistent with other accounts from the same source," or whether it is consistent with other accounts from other sources who may have been party to the event. A high degree of consistency (with either intramember or intermember checks) would indicate a high degree of "fittingness," overlap, isomorphism, or reliability. McCall suggests that "the two checks should be applied as a continuous, intrinsic procedure in . . . observation. Every item of information, whether derived from direct observation or from interviewing, should be continuously evaluated for its internal and external consistency. . . . The key to data quality control in . . . observation is, thus, the thorough use of multiple indicants of any particular fact and an insistence on a very high degree of consonance among these indicants, tracking down and accounting for any contrary indicants" (p. 130). Given the possibilities for contamination of data, continuous checking (through multiple methods of inquiry, triangulation, members checks, and the like) ought to be employed from virtually the first day on site. And again, *which* methods are chosen for either the initial inquiry or checking procedures is determined by "criteria of 'goodness' " measures, including "*informational adequacy,* meaning accuracy, precision and completeness of data, [and] *efficiency,* meaning cost per added input of information" (Zelditch, 1969, p. 9).

Why, then, would anyone want to use observation in a scientific study or an evaluation? Goode and Hatt (1952) provide a succinct answer to this question: "All scientific study depends ultimately on the observer. . . . Science begins with observation and must ultimately return to observation for its *final validation*" (pp. 119-120, emphasis added). Particularly for studying social groups, the methods of laboratories are not appropriate simply because they do not, and cannot, take account of complex human behaviors and interactions. In situations where motives, attitudes, beliefs, and values direct much, if not most of human activity, the most sophisticated instrumentation we possess is still the careful observer—the human being who can watch, see, listen (as Reik suggests, with "the third ear"), question, probe, and finally analyze and organize his direct experience.

Direct experience of a situation or event is, of course, problematic. Two independent observers, living in the same community and witnessing the same events and talking to the same persons, could easily write very different final reports, simply because they were different individuals whose own direct experience of the events and settings was shaped by different forces. But the *replicability* of any given experience is less important in understanding human behavior than is the *recognizability* of the description by those who lived the experience. Good description is the beginning of all good theory, and questions of social experience and human motivation should first be approached through a well-grounded body of descriptions—descriptions that exhibit fittingness and isomorphism with the realities lived by those in the setting. This cannot be accomplished without careful observation.

The novice fieldworker or observer will often question how he might manage his own feelings as an observer, and there is no easy answer to that problem. There are stresses to field research, and social scientists have begun to deal with those problems as part of the larger question of how they have been changed by conducting social inquiries (Wax, 1971; Johnson, 1975; Zigarmi and Zigarmi, 1978; Reinharz, 1979). Special feelings do occur and do influence what the observer feels and reports. As Johnson (1975) points out, the "passionate feelings" (p. 172) of researchers may play a very important part in the decision and motivation to engage in inquiry in the first place. In discussing the psychological stresses incurred in doing field research, Zigarmi and Zigarmi (1978) make the points that different inquirers will react to the same stress situation differently; that the strategies used to cope with stress sometimes lead to more stress; but that not all stress is negative, particularly if it leads the researchers to learn more about themselves and their ability to cope with stress. "These understandings," they contend, "are what make the experiencing of stress worthwhile and growthful" (p. 40). We agree.

Nonverbal Communication

Much of the political behavior that occurs outside the arena of government occurs between individuals, most of whom sense in only the vaguest way that interactions are satisfying or not satisfying or have brought them pleasure or discomfort. The political and physiological indicators that affect us most highly—and of which we are most unaware on any cognitive or propositional level—are the elements of nonverbal communication. This code of nonverbal, expressive, emotive, and social communication is far older than spoken language, and it serves a multitude of purposes that we are only beginning to fully understand. Scheflen (1972), in his fine work on body language, has commented on how observation of this form of communication has gradually become a science:

> Since the time of the Greek philosophers, Western man has idealized the rational mind and attributed nonrational events to tricks played by the gods, demonical possession, original sin, and, finally, instincts. There persists to this day the dichotomous view that language expresses thought and the body expresses emotion. No less an authority than Darwin . . . described this viewpoint.
>
> In the last thirty years or so another view of human behavior has developed. Efron, . . . Birdwhis-

tell (1952), and since then many others have described body movement as a traditional code which maintains and regulates human relationships without reference to language and conscious mental processes. ... In this newer tradition, language and thought are given an uncustomary role; they are believed to comment on, make judgments about, and conceal or rationalize actions that are already going on.

Thus, at present, there are in the behavioral sciences two schools of thought about bodily behavior. In the psychological school, "nonverbal" communication is considered to be the expression of emotions, as it has always been in Western thought. From the communicational point of view (held primarily by anthropologists and ethnologists), the behaviors of posture, touch, and movement are studied in relation to social processes like group cohesion and group regulation.

We will see ... that these views are not incompatible. The behaviors of human communication are both expressive and social or communicational [pp. xii-xiii].

That body language shapes our interactions ought to come as no surprise. The extent to which it shapes them, however, may come as a great surprise. As Wolfgang (1977) has pointed out, "our culture is so *word oriented* that we tend to forget that there are other important channels of expressive behavior that play an important role in human communication" (p. 147).

Although most nonverbal communication operates at the level of total unawareness, the careful observer of individual or group process may train himself to understand the messages that are being delivered, not only at the verbal and highly cognitive level but also at the nonverbal and cultural level. To the extent that such observations are accurate and serve to uncover depths and complexities in the verbal messages that are being delivered, they enhance understanding of the social, cultural, and interpersonal contexts being studied. The sensitive social inquirer ignores these nonverbal messages at his peril.

Nonverbal communication may be defined as the exchange of information through nonlinguistic signs. Nonverbal communication may be intentional or unintentional on the part of the sender of the communication, and either sender or receiver or both may be unconscious of the fact that some form of communication is occurring. Further, either or both may act on the information thus received.

Students of nonverbal communication sometimes speak of several branches of nonverbal behaviors. The first is *kinesics,* defined in the work of Birdwhistell (1970) as communication through body movement. Body motion, according to Birdwhistell, "is a learned form of communication, which is patterned within a culture and which can be broken down into an ordered system of isolable elements" (p. xi). The second is *proxemics,* or communication through spatial relationships, first defined by Hall (1966) as a reference to the individual (and cultural) usage of space in relation to other individuals and to objects in the environment. The third branch, called by Mehrabian (1972) *synchrony,* refers to communication involving the rhythmical relationship of sender and receiver. The fourth branch, *chronemics,* refers to the use of time (pacing, probing, pausing) to convey meaning in interpersonal relationships. The fifth branch of such communication is called *paralinguistics,* which refers to the extraverbal elements of speech that give added dimension to the meaning of verbal communication. These include "volume of the voice (loud or soft), quality of voice (tense, growly, breathy), accent (nuances of pronunciation), and inflectional patterns (intonation or pitch patterns)" (Gorden, 1975, p. 374), along with such other indicators as "tone of voice, pauses, hesitations, errors in speech, rate of speech" (Wolfgang, 1977, p. 147). The sixth branch, called *haptics* (Longstreet, 1978), refers to the communicative elements of touching: both the different qualities of touching and the variations in the connotative meanings of touch. Most of these terms, however, are more technical than needed for our purposes, and we shall use them sparingly.

But why should we even be interested in the various forms of nonverbal communication? We should first note that the inspection of nonverbal cues is not a technique that can be used by itself. Such inspection is not, for example, similar to an interview, an observation, or a content analysis. Rather, it is always and without exception used *in tandem* with some other technique, most often with interviews and observations. In fact, most good observers make use of nonverbal cues all the time, although they may do so in a very informal and unconscious way. Nonverbal cues, sent and received on some unconscious level, form a large part of the "art" that finally informs the taxonomizing and categorizing tasks that are an integral part of naturalistic inquiry. That is to say, the conscious and unconscious sifting of data collected in naturalistic inquiries is probably informed to a very high degree by the cultural and interpersonal cues that are sent, delivered, received, and "logged" by the inquirer—without his conscious awareness of the process. The degree of correlation between different observations of the same phenomenon, we hypothesize, is directly related to the observers' sensitivity in receiving and sending—and accurately decoding—the kinesic, proxemic, paralinguistic, and other cues that are integral to the context.

Such forms of communication are particularly useful for naturalistic inquirers because they fit with singular logic and elegance the investigative paradigm within which such inquirers often operate. They give inquirers cues about thoughts and feelings that may be quite different from the thoughts and feelings that are stated or exhibited openly. A sensitivity to nonverbal communication often permits an inquirer to infer what kind of relationship the subject or respondent has to the inquirer; what kind of relationship a subject has to one or more other subjects or informants; or what the subject's own feelings about himself are—feelings that would otherwise not be expressed, either because the subject would be unwilling to express them or because they exist at such an unconscious level that the subject is simply not aware of them. If one believes that the "truth will out," then nonverbal communication is probably the best indicator of truth. As Mehrabian (1972) says, "Inconsistent communication can be defined and measured in terms of the degree of discrepancy that is implied by different behaviors produced simultaneously by a speaker" (p. 23).

Examples of nonverbal communications are so numerous and so easy to come by that we are tempted to simply leave blank pages and let the reader fill them in for himself. Most authors on the subject, however, develop taxonomies within which they can then discuss exemplars of various kinds of nonverbal communication. Unfortunately, these taxonomies are arbitrary, and they offer little help in exploiting nonverbal communication in any context, including ours. Not only are the taxonomies not particularly fruitful for our purposes, but in fact scholars in the field do not agree on what the dimensions of nonverbal communication are. Nevertheless, we can point out certain instances of such forms of communication:

- Body movements—for example, leaning forward, avoiding eye contact, twisting one's hands, making gestures, and leg and foot movements;
- Gestures that close interpersonal distance—for example, bumping, touching, or stroking another person.
- Body-orientation—for example, turning toward or away from another person, the angle of incline of head or trunk, folding of arms or crossing of legs.
- Facial expressions, both voluntary and involuntary—for example, frowning, raising eyebrows, gritting teeth, smiling, and the like.
- Timing—for instance, smiling at the wrong point, keeping the interviewer waiting, cutting an interview short.
- Physiologic signs, including narrowing of eyes, perspiration, nervous tics, or clammy hands.
- Reaction pacing, such as interruptions, long pauses, and stumbling over the words of others.
- Implicit verbal indicators—for example, Freudian speech errors, vocal qualities of speech such as tone and pitch, and the use of sarcasm or irony.

The last category of examples, from the branch called paralinguistics, highlights the fact that speech itself contains aspects that contribute to our nonverbal understanding of messages. Thus, the form, as well as the content of speech, lends meaning to cultural understandings, and the "reading" of nonverbal communication may be done with the ears as well as with the eyes.

Since nonverbal behavior is rarely the subject of direct training, it is difficult to control and therefore difficult to falsify. It is revelatory (once a cultural context has been established) of interpersonal warmth, distance, coldness, emotive content, attitudes, and values. It may "replace, modify, clarify, and underscore speech [although] it is more limited in conveying logical, sophisticated, or creative ideas" (Wolfgang, 1977, p. 147). Like culture, "nonverbal behavior is elusive, normally out of awareness, difficult to erase or control, and has a potent influence in intercultural communication"; nonverbal behavior not only "transcends the written or spoken word" (Wolfgang, 1977, p. 146), but it is at one and the same time culturally determined and individually flexible. Thus, whole cultures and ethnic groups may be classified by means of the types of nonverbal behaviors they most commonly exhibit, for example: contact versus noncontact, monochronic versus polychronic, and/or high-context versus low-context cultures (Hall, 1976; Wolfgang, 1977). The position of Wolfgang, which we would support, is that individuals "communicate simultaneously on at least three levels in interpersonal situations: the *verbal, nonverbal,* and the *cultural* level which moderates and shapes the other two" (p. 147).

Categorization of Nonverbal Communication

There have been several kinds of categories generated for the various forms of nonverbal communication; two of the most useful are the descriptive and interpretative categories.

Descriptive Categories. There are generally recognized to be three such systems: one focuses on the sign being interpreted, one on the functions of the signs, and one on the distance of the signs from speech. Since each of these descriptive categories has several subsets, we will deal with each in turn.

Category systems that focus on the sign being interpreted would include four dimensions: (1) sign language, where gestures are deliberate replacements for words or other verbal cues; (2) action language, where movements occur but are not done with the express intent of communicating (in the case, for example, of the tired gardener who straightens her back after hoeing or the person deep in thought who unconsciously shakes his head, but to no one in particular); (3) object language, which refers to the display of material things such as clothing or other personal display, the placement of desks, the arrangement of items upon a coffee table; and (4) appearance language, which includes cues provided by appearance and which may be temporally fixed (for example, age, race, ethnicity), semifixed (hair style), or flashing (for example, a smile, raised eyebrows, or fleeting gestures).

Category systems that focus on the functions of the signs (proposed by Ekman and Friesen in Mehrabian, 1972, p. 3), that is, on the purposes that nonverbal communication may serve, include five functions: (1) the *emblem,* a nonverbal act that may be translated into words (for example, a handshake, a smile, shaking the fist, and the like); (2) the *illustrator,* which gives emphasis, for instance, pointing, "buttonholing," gesturing, stressing key words and the like (additionally, the illustrator may add punctuation to a statement made verbally by, for example, slamming his fist into the palm of his other hand to indicate determination); (3) the *affect display,* which indicates the affect of the sender (for instance, happiness, anger, surprise or astonishment, fear, disgust, sadness, interest, amusement); (4) *regulator functions,* which act to initiate or terminate speech or to pace its expected delivery—these signs say, "Keep talking," "Hurry up, I'm busy," "I don't understand," or "Slow down, I'm lost"; and (5) *adapter functions,* which act to satisfy bodily needs (for example, moving to a more comfortable position, uncrossing and recrossing the knees, scratching, and the like).

The final variety of descriptive taxonomies is a system that differentiates on the basis of distance from verbal speech (Mehrabian, 1972; Weitz, 1974): (1) actions as distinct from speech, which include such things as facial expressions, hand and arm gestures, postures, positions, and various movements of the body or the legs and feet; (2) paralinguistic or vocal phenomena, which include such things as fundamental frequency and intensity ranges, speech errors, pauses, speech rates, and speech duration (Mehrabian, 1972, p. 1); and (3) actual formal speech characteristics, which include any inconsistent combination of verbal and nonverbal behaviors, such as the use of sarcasm or irony.

Interpretative Categories. There are two systems that lie within the interpretative category. An older system is based on awareness levels (the extent to which either sender or receiver recognizes cues), while a somewhat newer analysis is presented by Mehrabian (1972).

The interpretative taxonomy of communication types as a

function of the sender's and receiver's awareness of the signal is displayed in Table 8. The four contingencies shown in the table

Table 8. Communication Types as a Function of
Sender-Receiver Awareness of Signal

	Receiver	
Sender	Aware	Unaware
Aware	Normal communication	Manipulation by sender
Unaware	Trained reception	Most nonverbal communication

are: (1) sender is aware, receiver is aware. This is the situation of normal communication, whether carried out by verbal means or by symbols such as sign language. (2) Sender is unaware, receiver is unaware. This is the normal situation for most nonverbal communication. The sender is unaware of transmitting a signal, and the receiver is also unaware, at least on any conscious level, although the receiver may respond to the signal nevertheless. (3) Sender is aware, but receiver is unaware. In this situation we have a sophisticated sender who knows how to transmit signals that will manipulate the receiver, that is, will produce responses in the receiver that the receiver does not realize he is being stimulated to produce. (4) Sender is unaware, but receiver is aware. In this situation, there is a sophisticated receiver who can interpret the unconsciously sent signal—he possesses the trained reception capability of a good naturalistic inquirer.

There is a second interpretative taxonomy based on the analytic dimensions proposed by Mehrabian (1972) that we rather like. This has three dimensions that, while undoubtedly forming continua, can conveniently be thought of as polar, that is, as having positive and negative termini. Each dimension has a name, a general descriptor for the dimension it represents, and a number of operational indicators.

The first dimension is that of immediacy, which represents the respondent's affective evaluation, cathexis (attitudinal attraction or repulsion), positive or negative reaction, and the like. Immediacy is measured along a dimension of proximity and distance, and its indicators include such physical ones as touching, eye contact, and position of the body and such verbal ones as pronoun forms, verb tenses, personal modifiers, and temporal closeness. The second dimension is that of status, or the respondent's evaluation of the relative status of himself and the inquirer (whether the respondent belongs to a higher or lower class and has more or less authority or power than the inquirer). Status is generally measured along a dimension of relaxation and tenseness, and it includes physical indicators such as asymmetrical or symmetrical position of the body 'ánd limbs, along with such verbal signals as ease of response to questions, smooth flow of the conversation, and negative or deferential use of titles and ceremony. The third dimension is that of responsiveness-importance or the respondent's evaluation of the salience of the interaction. It is measured along a dimension of activity and apathy, and indicators include frequent gestures, a rising voice, continuous nodding, or other signs that the respondent is deeply involved.

For our purposes, it is important to note that persons exhibiting dissonance between their spoken and nonverbal languages are likely to be less responsive and more status oriented than persons who do not exhibit such dissonance. Put the other way, low responsiveness, low immediacy, and high deferential behavior might well raise one's suspicions about the truthfulness of what one is being told, depending, of course, on the culture and ethnicity of the respondent.

Reconstructed Logic of Nonverbal Behavior. Since nonverbal communication may not be thought of as an independent method for inquiry, it possesses no reconstructed logic (the operational mode) in the usual sense. What the inquirer or evaluator needs to ask himself is, "Where does nonverbal communication fit into the reconstructed logic of the particular technique(s) with which it is used in tandem?" Two answers suggest themselves. First, the major use of nonverbal cues in connection with other forms of data collection is to test for dissonance between what the verbal language says and what the nonverbal language supports and rejects. If the nonverbal behaviors do not support the verbal assertions, then further inquiry is needed. Just as we have suggested that contradictions, gaps, or verbal slips in language and content need to be checked (by direct questions, recyclings of responses, and the like), so do contradictions that are suggested by verbal-nonverbal disparities. But nonverbal cues can at best lead only to hypotheses (or hunches) about discrepancies that might exist; it is not as though we could "catch" the person in a direct verbal contradiction that might be read back to him. In fact, there may be times when the contradiction suggested by the disparity between verbal and nonverbal behavior should not be checked on the spot or with that particular respondent. The respondent's nervousness, anxiety, fear, or other aversive reaction may signal the inquirer that he needs to verify discrepancies (or possible discrepancies) using another source or another measure in order to avoid seriously upsetting or frightening the respondent. Caution is needed on this point.

Second, there is the problem of recording what is noted under the heading of nonverbal communication. The typical observation form or interview protocol, for example, does not provide an easy means for such notations. They can, though, be conveniently noted in the margins or interpolated in the notes—in parentheses or with some other notation to indicate their nature. Our personal system includes marginal notes that are clearly noted "OC"—for "observer's comments"—to distinguish them from statements that capture the sense of what the respondent is saying and from direct quotations of the respondent. Thus, any given interview would have notations for direct statements, and observer comments, which are essentially comments on the continuing interaction, including nonverbal cues, of the respondent. In analysis, the observer's comments are treated like any other statements except that their highly inferential nature must be kept in mind. They are often, as suggested by the foregoing discussion, useful in formulating additional hypotheses that may be checked out on the spot or with other respondents.

Strengths and Weaknesses of Nonverbal Communication Cues. First and foremost, it is hardly ever necessary to think of nonverbal communication in terms of trade-offs with other methods. These data are always gathered as a supplement to other techniques. The question is not whether one gets more, better, or less expensive data by attending to nonverbal forms of communication. It is not what one gains by adding them but what one loses by ignoring them, for they are always there to be tapped. They constitute a bonanza for the knowledgeable inquirer. It is almost always convenient to pick them up, they are continuously available, and they act as an immediate cross-check on everything else that is observed or heard. Finally, the respondent is almost always unaware that he is providing such data; hence, they can be relied on as representing the "true" state of mind of the respondent—with some cautions.

There are possible problems. First of all, nonverbal language depends heavily on inference. No nonverbal behavior is self-inter-preting. Is a smile really a sign of approval and responsiveness or is it a sardonic grin? Is the respondent gritting his teeth because he is uncomfortable with the inquirer's questions or because his partial plate hurts? There are almost always alternative possibilities for what the inquirer observes, and often there are multiple interpreta-tions. This is not to suggest that nonverbal communication cues have mortal deficiencies but that reasonable caution and cross-checking before jumping to conclusions would be the best policy.

Nor are nonverbal observations as reliable as one would like. It is questionable whether different observers would credit a par-ticular nonverbal sign with the same meaning or even whether the same observer would assign the same meaning to the same sign at different times. And there are major cross-cultural patterns of non-verbal language that would cause those who observe cultural, lin-guistic, or ethnic groups different from their own to assign patently incorrect meanings to nonverbal communications. There are, between various ethnic and cultural groups, major and power-ful differences in the kinds of nonverbal cues that are sent and received. The evaluator or inquirer who is moving into an area where minority groups (cultural, racial, ethnic, or linguistic) are involved would do well to either suspend his initial impressions about group interactional nonverbal behavior or to prepare himself by some anthropological reading to understand what comprises the interaction rituals of that particular group.

The question might also arise, "How can I control my own feelings while I am trying to track another person's nonverbal cues?" The problem in this situation is how to keep one's feelings in sufficient tow in order not to *send* nonverbal signals that will undermine the ongoing inquiry. Most respondents will be rela-tively unsophisticated about nonverbal communication, and some will not be able to read the inquirer's signals (save for the most overt) even if he sends such signals. But some respondents will be sufficiently sophisticated to read nonverbal cues and some will read these whether they understand them at a conscious level or not. For that matter, a respondent may know more—either at a propositional or a tacit level—about nonverbal communication than the inquirer does. The inquirer who is good at reading such cues will probably, however, also predict what a knowledgeable respondent might make of his cues and can control them accordingly.

There are some who feel that overt and conscious control of one's behavior in the inquiry setting is "unnatural" or manipulative and that conscious effort to systematically record the nonverbal behavior of respondents constitutes an invasion of privacy. But we would simply repeat again that body movement and other nonverbal clues have shaped, defined, and described interpersonal relationships for millennia. Nonverbal cues are powerful indicators of cultural values and beliefs, and, furthermore, they are face-making and public behaviors. To ignore such cues is to miss many nonconscious but pervasive cultural norms and values. Our posture is that the description, use, and explication of nonverbal cues add immeasurably to the larger understanding of social contexts.

Chapter 8

Using Documents, Records, and Unobtrusive Measures

Just as sociology at some point became caught up in the exercise of creating *grand theorie* to the exclusion of grounded theory (Glaser and Strauss, 1967), so education and other social action research became enamored of creating fresh data: new tests, new questionnaires, new sets of interview protocols, and new interviews—all related to *a priori* concepts. In the process of generating such findings, however, researchers often overlooked or scorned other valuable materials because of their very availability or "routineness."

But the cost of research has skyrocketed in every area—personnel, travel, equipment, subjects, research assistants, computer technicians, and computer processing—and the enterprise of research has become costly, time consuming, and labor intensive. In the face of these rising costs, hard questions are being raised about the value of many kinds of research, especially when the results indicate "no significant differences," when the overall body of accumulated knowledge has not been well informed, or when the description provided has proven inadequate or misleading to other inquirers. Senator Proxmire's monthly Golden Fleece awards are but an amusing, if embarrassing, tip of the iceberg when the subject under consideration is waste in sponsored research and evaluation (especially federally funded efforts).

Some of this problem may surely be attributed to the fact that it has appeared more prestigious to social inquirers to generate "new" information than to resort to other activities that may be promising but hardly lend "star status" to careers. We refer to reanalysis of previously collected data; to metaanalysis of data (that is, cluster analysis, case-study aggregation analysis, or propositional analysis); to secondary analyses (including document analysis); and to unobtrusive measures.

Documents, records, and unobtrusive measures are usually readily available, and why educational inquirers would not want to use them is unclear. Records in particular are an enormously useful source, although documents such as evaluation reports, technical reports, and case studies can now be used in analyses that not only aggregate common information but lead to new insights into public policy and its formulation (Lucas, 1974a, 1974b; Lincoln, 1978). But educational inquirers appear to be bent on generating new data for every problem they attack, perhaps because they typically want to test hypotheses, and such tests seem to call for new instruments or special data collection arrangements. According to Denny (1978), however, "if the contributions of educational psychology and evaluative research to our understanding of teaching and learning could be translated into human stature, it would stand a little over four feet high" (p. 21).

Moreover, the consistent failure to utilize documents and records (at least in fair proportion to their existence and availability) accounts in part for the fact that educational inquiry inputs so often are not grounded. If experimental situations and findings had to make sense in terms of context, the results of inquiries would be more meaningful, and there would be less of the "dreary palaver we call research and evaluation literature" (Denny, 1978, p. 18).

This chapter will deal first with documents and records—

their acquisition, aggregation, and analysis. Though both are usually written records, a document is not the same thing as a record. Nevertheless, both are forms of communication based on verbal behavior. If "the work of the world, and its entertainment, is in no small measure mediated by verbal and other symbolic behavior," (Cartwright, 1953, p. 422), then making sense of the records of verbal behavior is a crucial part of the investigation of man and his social behavior.

Documents and Records

Neither the dictionary nor the methodological literature is of much assistance in making a distinction between documents and records. The dictionary, for example, defines a *document* as "an original or official printed or written paper furnishing information or used as proof of something else" and a *record* as "an official written account of proceedings" or "the known facts regarding someone." The overlap between these definitions is obvious; indeed, following the lead of the dictionary, one might well define a document as a record and a record as a document. The methodological literature confounds this problem even further by admitting as documents a variety of written materials that are produced only because an inquiry has been undertaken. Thus Holsti (1969) indicates that documents include "verbal data produced by subjects at the behest of the investigator, . . . the psychiatric interview, and various projective instruments such as the Thematic Apperception Test [and] responses to open-ended questions generated in survey research, . . . written messages derived from a simulation study, . . . or communication produced during group interaction." Bogdan and Taylor (1975) give similar definitions of records and documents. While it is true that written residues of these kinds can be analyzed by the methods to be described in this chapter, it is useful for analytic and pedagogic purposes to exclude them from consideration here. Hence, a *record* is defined here as any written statement prepared by an individual or an agency for the purpose of attesting to an event or providing an accounting, and a *document* as any written (or filmed) material other than a record that was not prepared specifically in response to some request from the investigator.

A list of examples of documents could go on for pages. But good examples of documents include: letters, memoires, autobiographies, diaries or journals, textbooks, wills, position papers, suicide notes, speeches, novels, newspaper articles and editorials, epitaphs, television and film scripts, memoranda, case studies, life histories, medical histories, political propaganda pamphlets, government publications, photographs, diplomatic communiques, and the like.

Documents can be sorted into various typologies. The most obvious category is the source of the document. Another very useful distinction is that between "primary" and "secondary" documents, the latter falling into the class of what would be called "hearsay" in a court of law. A secondary document is one that was not generated from firsthand experience of a particular situation or event but from other sources. Other useful dichotomies for sorting documents include those of "solicited" versus "unsolicited"; "comprehensive" versus "limited"; "edited" versus "complete" or "unedited"; and "anonymous" versus "signed" or "attributable" (Bogdan and Taylor, 1975, p. 96). To these we would also add another distinction, that between "spontaneous" (as in a diary) and "intentional" (as in a letter to an editor), although "spontaneous" may come close to being "unsolicited" and "unedited," and "intentional" may closely resemble "edited" and "signed."

The very number of these typologies makes the whole matter of documentary classification very complex. If we used the six dichotomies suggested above, we could arrive at 2^6 or 64 categories. Further, these 64 categories could each be further subdivided in terms of the apparent motivation of the writer. If, for example, it were decided to use a simple 5-category motivational system—explication, support, self-justification, moral duty, and self-aggrandizement—we could enlarge our taxonomy to 64 × 5 or 320 categories. Since the prospect of dealing with that number of possible cells boggles the mind, the bases for categorization are probably more usefully viewed as criteria for judging the utility of a document rather than for assigning it unequivocally to some cell of known properties within a taxonomy.

Records have typically not been utilized in educational research or evaluation, and indeed they have been ignored in many forms of social research, with the notable exceptions of demography and cliometrics. Examples of records include: airline manifests, audits and consultants' reports, birth records, business records, campaign contribution and expenditure records, records of tax-deductible gifts, chattel mortgage records, city directories, death records, expense account vouchers, financial information, government directories, gun registrations, income tax records, records and membership lists of private organizations, legal notices, marriage records, military records, professional, business, and trade directories, religious directories, school directories, state regulatory records, vehicle records, voting and registration records, welfare records, property tax records, county plat books, and court records. With computer technology revolutionizing record storage and retrieval, it can be reasonably expected that the kinds of records kept will grow exponentially over the next few years.

Unlike documents, which come into being for a variety of motivational purposes, records are generally compiled simply to "keep track" of events or transactions. They form an official statement that some event or transaction has occurred. While they may be altered or forged in some way, much of the time they are public, reasonably direct, and reasonably accurate (access to them may, however, be limited, since some records—such as bank records and income tax returns—are generally not available to those who are not authorized to review them).

Why Differentiate Between Documents and Records?

There are two major reasons why distinctions are made between documents and records. The first is that they represent different motivations or purposes on the part of the writer. Records, as has been noted, attest to an event or transaction and form an official chronicle that is part of a larger work, usually on the processes and proceedings of public affairs. Documents, however, may be personal (private) or public. If public, they serve to make others aware of a point of view, to persuade, to aggrandize, to explicate, or to justify. If personal, they may be a form of special pleading (for example, a letter) or of exhibitionism; they may arise from a desire for order or for relief from tension; they may give literary pleasure or provide some public service; they may spring from the desire for monetary gain (witness the Howard Hughes "autobiographies"); they may be assigned (for example, one may be instructed to create a memorandum that forms a "letter of understanding"); they may be written for scientific interest (for example, the observation logs of Thomas Jefferson and Benjamin Franklin); or they may serve as social reincorporation devices, as did the Nixon interviews with David Frost (Allport, 1942, pp. 68-75). Thus records and documents arise from different motivations and serve separate purposes.

A second and much more important reason to differentiate carefully between documents and records is that the modes of analysis appropriate to each are substantially different. In the case of records, appropriate analytic tools include aggregation-integration methods, trend analysis, and what we shall call "tracking." (The former two are essentially quantitative methods and hence will not be discussed here.) In the case of documents, appropriate analytic tools include content analysis and the case-survey aggregation method, both of which will be described.

Utility of Documents and Records

Some social scientists have never questioned the value of records and documents for inquiry. They have utilized them extensively to predict and explicate fertility patterns, population shifts, patterns of education, and needs and desires for housing, transportation, and consumer goods. Likewise, an investigative journalist learns early on that records and documents are invaluable resources for tracing transactions that may shed light on cases and relationships under scrutiny. But as Hage and others (1976) caution, "Investigative reporting is not often as exciting and glamorous as that of Woodward and Bernstein. More often it involves laborious checking of public records, finding documentation for the story" (p. 41). Williams (1978) likewise asserts that "the first and great commandment of investigative journalism is this: get the record" (p. 37).

If other types of inquiry have relied heavily on documents and records, why hasn't educational inquiry? Perhaps this failure is related to the earlier arguments for collection of fresh data. It may also be related to lack of training in the use of records and documents, to the relative ease with which most records and documents are acquired—does familiarity once again breed contempt?—or to a general lack of regard for the contexts in which educational decisions are made, programs are carried out, and policy is constructed. But, for several reasons, inquirers can no longer afford to ignore this resource.

First, documents and records are a stable, rich, and rewarding resource. Both tend to persist; that is, while they may be buried in files that are no longer used, they are often available for the asking. They provide a base from which any subsequent inquirers can work and thus lend stability to further inquiry.

Second, records, if not documents, constitute a legally unassailable base from which to defend oneself against allegations, misinterpretations, and libel. The best defense in a challenge to an evaluation report is for the evaluator to be able to show that he did in fact tell the truth, and the best evidence for truth is often the public record.

Third, both documents and records represent a "natural" source of information. Not only are they, in fact, an "in context" source of information—that is, they arise from the context and exist in it—but they consist of information about the context. Records show what happened in the context, and documents record a variety of other evidence about the environment and people's perceptions of it. They are thus repositories of well-grounded data on the events or situations under investigation.

Fourth, they are available on a low-cost or even free basis; their use often requires only an investment of time and energy on the investigator's part. Public records are readily available and for the most part are open to scrutiny. Although some documents exist in easily accessible corporate or project files, tracking down others might involve some ingenuity.

For the naturalistic inquirer, the obvious places should be searched first. Obvious sources of documents are old files, as well as individuals who were associated with the project or program in question. But often, files are stored and cannot be easily retrieved, and individuals have moved on to other sites, died, or retired. A next move would be to try to locate other individuals who may not have been as closely related to the project but who did have some connection with it. Such persons may, for example, have collected random documents from the project. Failing easily reachable sources, the document hunter moves in ways that resemble either the historian searching for written evidence (Altick, 1950) or the interviewer attempting to interview someone who does not wish to be seen or to talk (Dexter, 1970). If some source has a document or is thought to have some document that is particularly important, often persistent courtesy will prevail. Sources of documents or records can often be persuaded to part with them simply because it is finally easier to get rid of an inquirer by giving him what he wants than to keep saying no. Most possessors of documents do not allow access for four reasons: indifference, hostility, ignorance, and avarice (Altick, 1950, p. 116). Nearly all these reasons can be overcome by a final tactic; that is, an introduction through a friend of the document holder. Introduction by trusted familiars has long been used to make social connections. It is an equally worthwhile technique for those desiring interviews or seeking missing documents.

Fifth, documents and records both are nonreactive. Although there are times when access to primary persons is impossible in any event (the person has died, for example) and the only remaining way to study him or his connections is through documentary analysis, there are also other times when, although a person is available, documents still provide the most objective means for understanding some aspect of his behavior. Holsti (1969) writes: "Despite their very real merits for social research, even the best experiment or survey studies the subject and his responses in a highly artificial situation. Knowledge that one is being studied may, in some circumstances, materially alter those aspects of behavior under analysis. Especially when it is important to get repeated measures of the subjects' values, attitudes, and the like over a period of time, and if one has reason to believe that continued interaction between analyst and subject may affect the nature of the responses, then content analysis of the subject's statements may be a useful way to gather the required data. An important feature of content analysis is that it is a 'nonreactive' or 'unobtrusive' technique" (p. 16). Thus, when live interaction with a subject would likely alter his behavior or perspectives, document analysis (specifically, content analysis) becomes a useful way of gathering information.

Sixth, whether or not the inquirer finally decides to interact with his subjects, content analysis and other forms of document and record analysis enable supplementary and contextual data to be gathered; that is, such analysis may form an extension of a larger body of research, may be employed as an additional technique, or may comprise the primary form of research. In any event, it lends contextual richness and helps to ground an inquiry in the milieu of the writer. This grounding in real-world issues and day-to-day concerns is ultimately what the naturalistic inquirer is working toward.

Within the framework of historiography, that is, the art and science of writing history, the importance of context has been asserted continually. Clark's (1967) injunction to writers of history holds true: *"The most important principle of historical scholarship is the principle of importance of context.* When considering any historical evidence, an investigator must take account of the situation at the moment in time when the event it records happened and also at the moment when it was recorded" (p. 25). Even earlier than Clark, Gray and others (1964) warned document analysts to "beware of that worst of judicial sins—taking the evidence away from its context" (p. 58).

Within the framework of educational research and evaluation, document and record analysis serves an additional grounding function: it helps the inquirer to maintain interest in the context and helps to ensure that research is not removed from its social, historical, and political frame of reference.

Allport (1942), acting as devil's advocate, met some of the criticism against the use of personal documents in social science research. Some of those criticisms he found "to be well grounded, others to be irrelevant or trivial, and still others to be contingent upon the type of document employed and the use to which it is put" (p. 125).

The first of these criticisms is that documents and records provide unrepresentative samples. This is particularly true of personal documents, but it is also occasionally true in social action programs: often no one on the project keeps very good notes on processes, few memoranda are generated, and, even more often, the only writing that is done is in response to funders' requests for technical reports or other periodic statements about the progress of the program or project. If no documents exist, however, or if the documents are sparse and seem uninformative, this ought to tell the inquirer something about the context. The absence or paucity of documents relative to a project can be as commanding a statement as a careful content analysis if the overall situation or environment is what is to be described.

Records and documents are also said to lack objectivity. To this criticism, Allport answers: "Since personal documents are, and always will be, completely subjective, there is no way of convincing the bitter-end objectivist that he should employ them. [But] (1) extreme objectivism has disclosed its own weakness. The resurgence of phenomenology has brought back to favor the personal report. (2) The conflict is not so irreconcilable as it appears. Users of the personal document have learned many lessons from behaviorism and positivism" (p. 127).

To the list of criticisms may also be added concern about the validity of a document. More will be said about this later in the chapter, but Allport maintains that there are at least three tests that one can use in establishing nonquantitative validity measures: "the general honesty and *credibility* of the report . . . this is the *ad hominen* test. . . . The *plausibility* of the document in terms of our own past experiences, as they are relevant, can be considered [and] the test of internal consistency or *self-confrontation* has to be widely relied upon. A document that hangs together, that represents a structured configuration of human life and harbors no impossible contradictions has at least a *prima facie* validity" (p. 128).

There are also the problems of deliberate deception, self-deception (which Allport calls "unintentional self-justification"), and blindness to motives, which Allport ascribes to either the difficulty "for men to report adequately their own motives" or the "lapse of time that occurs between the completion of an act and its recording" (p. 132). Additionally, there are problems of over-simplification, wherein the writer "does not want unsolved riddles, visible gaps, unexplained conduct. His desire for completeness leads him to fill in unknown parts in a manner that fabricates a satisfying closure." But, Allport cautioned, "third-person documents likewise simplify, and . . . laboratory and field investigations do the same thing" (pp. 134-135). In that case, the document analyst need simply be prepared to understand that programs, projects, and persons are not as straightforward and coherent as they are likely to be pictured, either by those involved in them or by others. To some extent, this is responsive to the later pleas of Wax (1971) and Reinharz (1979) to note, along with descriptions of research, the changes that occurred on site and in the inquirer. Likewise, the effects of mood or errors of memory may impinge on the accuracy or completeness of the document. However, Allport (1947) steadfastly maintains that mnemonic errors are as significant as what the individual recalls and records because "the very fact that the subject structures and recalls his life in a certain manner is what we want to know" (p. 136).

The last two criticisms involve the implicit conceptualizations of documents and records (inherent in the writer's choice of theme and phrase) and the arbitrariness of these conceptualizations. Implicit conceptualizations—or the limitation of the author to data that he thinks are important—are in and of themselves useful, as Allport (1942) points out, and the arbitrariness of those same conceptualizations, especially "when the interpretation is given on the basis of manifestly meager data" (p. 139), is no worse than what psychologists and other social scientists already do to more "experimental facts." Allport concludes rather wryly that it is doubtful "that personal documents actually are any worse off at the hands of psychologists than are other forms of raw data" (p. 139). So it would seem that as long as one operates with a set of *caveats,* the use of documents (especially) and records (to a somewhat less extent) is legitimate, either as a primary or secondary technique. As ever, the guiding rule for choice of a method is which of the techniques available provides more data, better data, and data at lower cost than other methods. Further, a source that is replete with clues as to the nature of the context should never be ignored, whatever other inquiry methods one chooses.

Using Documents and Records

Although documents and records fall into a class of research evidences (verbal and primarily written), their acquisition, treatment, and analyses are very different. For that reason, we shall treat those topics in separate sections.

Documents, as noted previously, are distinct from records in several ways. Persons interested in using records are primarily interested in "tracking," that is, in following official recordings of transactions or events and perhaps in determining the frequency or serial quality of these events or transactions. Persons using documents, however, are often interested in a number of other items; they sometimes want to make inferences about the values, sentiments, intentions, beliefs, or ideologies of the sources or authors of the documents; they sometimes want to make inferences about group or societal (or personal) values; and they sometimes want to evaluate the effects of communications on the audiences that they reach (Williamson, Karp, and Dalphin, 1977, pp. 291-297). An investigator might also want to carry out document analysis because he has come into possession of a series of documents that contain valuable information about some inquiry problem of interest or because he has sought out such documents as part of an inquiry that he thinks might lend greater clarity to his understanding of the research setting.

What does it mean to do document analysis? There are two ways to respond to this question, depending on whether we are talking about the analysis of a single document or the analysis of multiple documents. Communication theorists have tended to analyze communications in terms of the following questions: "Who says what, to whom, how, and with what effect, and why?" (Holsti, 1969, p. 24). The key words are *who* (conceptualized as the *sender*); *why* (conceptualized as the *encoding process*); *how* (conceptualized as the *channel*); *what* (conceptualized as the *message,* which may address either *what* or *how*); *with what effect* (conceptualized as the *receiver's reaction* or, to use a more abstract term, the decoding process); and *to whom* (conceptualized as the *recipient*). Thus communication can be thought of as "composed of six basic elements: a *source* or sender, an *encoding process* that results in a *message,* a *channel* of transmission, a *detector* or recipient of the message, and a *decoding process*" (Holsti, 1969, p. 24).

One form of document analysis is concerned primarily with the "what" or "message" portion of the communication. Whether concerned with a single document or with multiple documents relating to the same event or written by the same person, analysis directed toward the *message* portion of communication is called "content analysis." For instance, a social scientist might be studying the last suicide note of a deceased person for clues to his attitudes or beliefs. Or he might be concerned with the letters, journals, *and* last note of a suicide. Or he might be interested in suicide notes as a class of evidence about despondent persons. In all three instances, the investigator would most likely use content analysis, at least in part, for his inquiry.

In other forms of inquiry, the investigator may be concerned with a collection of documents that will, in general, display neither the same format, organization, or content categories but will instead deal with different instances of the same or a like phenomenon. That is to say, the documents are case studies of similar events, programs, settings, situations, but they do not all concern themselves with the same phenomenon. Several good examples of this form of document analysis, which is called case-study aggregation analysis (Lucas, 1974a, 1974b), would be: evaluation reports from multiple sites of a locally adopted bilingual education program; policy statements from a series of mental health clinics regarding collection of payments from indigent clients; or case studies of citizen participation in electoral campaigns in various cities. Each of the foregoing sets of documents contains information that is probably common to all settings but that, until recently, could not be aggregated or integrated to provide a body of common understandings. The case-survey aggregation method, developed at the Rand Corporation, now allows such diverse, random, and often qualitatively uneven documents to be aggregated so that new understandings can be derived from old bodies of literature. We shall talk about both content analysis and the case-survey aggregation method in turn. First, however, some primary questions about the nature of documents themselves need to be entertained.

Presuming that one has come into possession of a document, how does one know that the document is what it purports to be? That is, what questions ought to be asked in order to determine that the document is as represented? Clark (1967) addressed the issue of "documents genuine and spurious" and suggested a series of questions that might establish the credibility of the document as the real document constructed by the writer:

• What is the history of the document?
• How did it come into my hands?

- What guarantee is there that it is what it pretends to be?
- Is the document complete, as originally constructed?
- Has it been tampered with or edited?
- If the document is genuine, under what circumstances and for what purposes was it produced?
- Who was/is the author?
- What was he trying to accomplish? For whom was the document intended?
- What were the maker's sources of information? Does the document represent an eyewitness account, a secondhand account, a reconstruction of an event long prior to the writing, an interpretation?
- What was or is the maker's bias?
- To what extent was the writer likely to want to tell the truth?
- Do other documents exist that might shed additional light on this same story, event, project, program, context? If so, are they available, accessible? Who holds them?

Some of these questions are directed toward historiographical and textual criticism. But a number of them are also particularly useful to ask when documents are not ascribed (as many project reports are not these days), when one comes into possession of some form of "copied" paper (a photographic reproduction that may have been edited or altered), or when documents are assembled from sources who do not wish their identity known.

As another caution, when multiple copies of the same document are available from different sources, one ought to acquire them all, especially if they are "sensitive." A bit of careful checking, while time consuming, can at least establish, if earlier and later drafts are available, what has been excised from a final draft. The excisions themselves may provide important clues for further inquiry. Clark (1967) also issues this warning: "Documents as documents, especially formal documents, sometimes have a semi-hypnotic effect on the minds of those who use them, and it is important to remember that all documents have been produced by fallible and potentially dishonest human beings, and that before they reach the scholar they may have passed through the hands of others who may also have had their failings, and were also potentially dishonest" (p. 62).

Methodology of Content Analysis

The meaning of "content analysis" is itself evolving. Berelson's (1952) definition, "content analysis is a research technique for the objective, systematic, and quantitative description of the manifest content of communication" (p. 18), relies on assumptions of counting, of translating the analysis into some form of numerical statement. Barcus (1959) uses the term *content analysis* "to mean the scientific analysis of communications messages. . . . The method is broadly speaking the 'scientific method,' and while being catholic in nature, it requires that the analysis be rigorous and systematic" (p. 8). His definition does not imply quantification. After some debate on the issue of the numerical quality of content analysis, Holsti (1969) settled on a definition that makes no reference to the quantification issue: "Content analysis is any technique for making inferences by objectively and systematically identifying specified characteristics of messages" (p. 14). This definition suits our purposes for the same reasons it suited his: it satisfies the three criteria of objectivity, systemization, and theoretical framework.

Two other observations are in order. First, in documents (unless commissioned by the inquirer), content is generally not specifically under the inquirer's control. He has to take what he can get and work from it. Second, as a result of this, the "specified characteristics" of the messages may need to emerge from the material itself rather than be imposed *a priori* by a theoretical construct. From our perspective, this is a most fortuitous circumstance, since it virtually guarantees that the categories will be grounded in the data and, hence, in the context.

There seem to be four major characteristics of content analysis on which most methodologists agree and a fifth that is in process of transformation. While different writers may state them slightly differently, the basic tenets of what constitutes solid and rigorous analysis are well known. First and most important, it is a rule-guided process. Each step is "carried out on the basis of explicitly formulated rules and procedures" (Holsti, 1969, p. 3). In order to satisfy the criterion of objectivity and to "minimize . . . the possibility that the findings reflect the analyst's subjective predispositions rather than the contents of the documents," rules must be derived, procedures delineated, and selection criteria defined. A subsequent analyst, using the same rules, procedures, and criteria for selection, ought to be able to arrive at the same inferences from the documents.

Second, content analysis is a systematic process. Holsti defined the systematic nature of the inquiry as conforming "to certain general canons of category construction [so] that the inclusion and exclusion of content or categories [are] done according to consistently applied rules" (p. 4). Once the rules have been clearly explicated, they are applied in the same way to each piece of content, whether the analyst regards it as relevant or not.

Third, content analysis is a process that aims for generality. The findings should, in the long run, display theoretical relevance, or, in the case of naturalistic inquiry (to extend the set of characteristics a bit further), they should further the development of insights with respect to context, which should serve in instances other than or beyond that of the single document in hand. In commenting about the issue of generality, or theoretical relevance, Holsti drives the point home forcefully: "Purely descriptive information about content, unrelated to other attributes of documents or to the characteristics of the sender or recipient of the message is of little value. . . . Such results take on meaning when we compare them with other attributes of the documents, with documents produced by other sources, with characteristics of the persons who produced the documents, or the times in which they lived, or the audience for which they were intended. Stated somewhat differently, a datum about communication content is meaningless until it is related to at least one other datum. . . . Thus all content analysis is concerned with comparison, the type of comparison being dictated by the investigator's theory" (p. 5).

Fourth, content analysis deals in manifest content. The investigator is of course often interested in drawing inferences from the documents that he is examining, but such inferences are a matter for later analysis. The content analysis itself is confined to the manifest (as opposed to latent) content of the documents, although content analysts themselves (Berelson, 1952; Holsti, 1969) have disputed the manifest-latent distinction. There is general agreement that in the *coding* stage of research, that is, "the stage at which specified words, themes, and the like are located in the text and placed into categories, one is limited to recording only those items which actually appear in the document" (Holsti, 1969, p. 12), while at the later *interpretative* stage, it is now generally agreed that it is permissible for the investigator to rely upon his insight, intuition, and imagination to draw inferences about latent content (decoding process), as well as to draw conclusions about the meaning of the manifest content (encoding process). This broader definition serves the needs of naturalistic inquirers well, since it is not only semantic symbols that are relevant to the research process but also the "issues" and "concerns" in the minds of the project staff and stakeholding audiences, contextual information (including description), and value systems operant in the context.

Fifth, content analysis has historically been defined as a quantitative technique. If it is used as a strictly quantitative method, content analysis allows the researcher a high degree of precision in the statement of conclusions, allows him to assign some degree of confidence to the generalization of results, and permits certain kinds of numerical manipulations to be performed on the data. But arguments against such a strictly quantitative interpretation of content can be made, including these: (1) the frequency of assertion is not necessarily related to the importance of that assertion (either to the sender or the recipient); (2) more meaningful inferences may occasionally be drawn from qualitative than from quantitative methods; and (3) emphasis on quantification of symbols and precision often comes at the cost of problem significance. Holsti (1969) cites a statistician on this point: "Far better an approximate answer to the *right* question, which is often vague, than an *exact* answer to the wrong question, which can always be made precise. Data analysis must progress by approximate answers, at best, since its knowledge of what the problem really is will at best be approximate" (p. 67). In any event, both quantitative and qualitative approaches are now deemed suitable, depending on the questions that need to be answered by the research.

Now that content analysis has been generally described, some comment about the coding process itself seems in order. The first problem beyond the acquisition of documents has almost always been what constituted good categories for coding. The decisions confronting the analyst fall under three general rubrics

(Holsti, 1969): "How is the research problem defined in terms of *categories*? What *unit* of content is to be classified? What system of *enumeration* will be used?" (p. 94). As Holsti notes, these are not separate decisions, but interrelated ones, and they are always made on the basis of the original formulation of the inquiry problem. In short, decisions with regard to these three crucial questions must be grounded in the problem to be investigated.

"Coding," according to Holsti, "is the process whereby raw data are systematically transformed and aggregated into units which permit precise description of relevant content characteristics" (p. 94). The coding process ought to be guided by two overriding principles. First, whatever method the inquirer may choose to code, that method (or set of categories or unit of analysis) has embedded in it assumptions pertaining to the nature of the data and whatever inferences may be drawn from them. Second, theory, hypotheses, and inquiry questions alone ought to guide the coding process and determine content categories. "In short, unless [the inquirer] can state explicitly *why* he is analyzing documents, he cannot intelligently work out a plan on *how* to do it" (Holsti, 1969, p. 94). The coding process, while it is essentially an intuitive one, informed by practice, theory, and careful reading, ultimately determines whether or not the resultant research is worthwhile, for without coding categories that fulfill canons of good taxonomic construction, the research will be incomplete or irrelevant or will possibly arrive at erroneous conclusions.

Canons of good category or taxonomic construction are five in number. Categories must first of all "reflect the *purposes* of the research"; the design must include conceptual definitions, which include both definitions of the variables with which the investigator is concerned and operational definitions. The latter specify the indicators that "determine whether a given content datum falls within" a given category (Holsti, 1969, pp. 94, 95). Second, categories must be *exhaustive*; that is, it must be possible to eventually place each datum in one category or another. Often this is accomplished by specifying the concepts (or variables) that define the study "as precisely as possible by characterizing its major properties; these would serve as rules by which coders would judge whether content units fall within its boundaries" (1969, p. 99). Third, categories should be *mutually exclusive*; that is, no single content datum should fit into more than one cell or category. Fourth, categories must be *independent*. The assignment of some piece of data should not in any way affect the classification of other pieces of data, although this rule is difficult, if not impossible, to satisfy when "content units are scaled along some dimension," or when "some form of ranking is used to assign values to content units" (1969, pp. 99, 100). Fifth, categories must be derived from a *single classification principle*. Levels of the analysis that are conceptually different must be kept separate (this refers chiefly to the manifest-latent problem discussed earlier).

Even with this set of rules, however, it is not clear how one goes about the creation of categories for unitizing and taxonomizing the symbols (or issues and concerns) identified; and, indeed, there are no simple answers to this question, although there are several "tacks" that one may take. The naturalistic inquirer would certainly want some or all of his categories to emerge from the data. In that way, the classification system finally derived would be a well-grounded one. At the present time, investigators seldom adopt the classification scheme of a predecessor; the emphasis on "unique" or "new" problems has tended to persuade inquirers that new classifications, new coding systems are called for. The classical emphasis upon theory testing, too, as opposed to the creation of grounded theory, has caused investigators to assume that new taxonomies are needed. But some consideration of the types of categories that have been used in the past would be useful and might serve as a starting point for the evaluator or inquirer who has not already utilized content analysis.

There are two broad typologies of categories: the "what is said" (or subject matter) dimension and the "how it is said" (or device) dimension. Within those two broad areas, some of the possibilities might include the following (adapted from Holsti, 1969):

"What is said" categories:
- Subject matter—what is the communication about?
- Direction—how is the subject matter treated (favorably, unfavorably, strongly, weakly, humorously, seriously)?
- Values—what values, goals, or needs are stated?
- Methods—what methods are utilized to achieve goals or intentions?

- Traits—what are the characteristics ascribed to the persons or contexts described?
- Actors—to whom is the performance of certain acts ascribed?
- Authority—at whose behest or in whose name are statements made?
- Origin—where, or from whom, does the communication originate? Unascribed documents will often come into the hands of an inquirer; that is, they will simply be listed as having come from a "project" or "program."
- Target—to whom is the document directed; that is, to what person or group or office?
- Location—where does the action take place or what site or event does the document describe?
- Conflict—what are the sources and levels of conflict?
- Endings—is there closure and, if so, are conflicts resolved happily, ambiguously, or tragically?
- Time—when does the action take place? If a series of documents exist, is there some implied chronological order to the sequence of events, or do all documents describe different perspectives and perceptions of the same event?

"How it is said" categories:

- Form or type of communication—what is the medium of communication (for example, a newspaper report, radio or television speech, editorial, project memorandum, quarterly progress report, personal letter, administrative log or journal, personal diary, or the like)?
- Form of statement—what is the grammatical or syntactical form of the communication?
- Device—what is the rhetorical or persuasive or propagandistic method used?

Since there are no standard norms of classification, the construction of categories is often a trial-and-error process, forcing the investigator to move between the data and either an *a priori* or a grounded theory. "Sorts" are performed on items of data; when these "sorts" do not account for all units of data, other tentative categories are generated. The process is completed by using either a combination of theory and data or a combination of theory building or context-construction and data. Categories are modified until the system is complete and each datum can be sensibly accounted for.

The designation of units of analysis is also a coding decision that may be made either prior to or during the actual analysis. The unit of analysis may be either a single word or symbol, a theme (which is defined as an assertion about some subject), the characters or actors about whom a communication is concerned, a grammatical unit, or the type of item (for example, film, book, or newspaper editorial). Again, as with the creation of a classification system, the selection of a unit or units of analysis depends upon three considerations: (1) which units best meet the needs of the researcher; (2) which units best fit the requirements of research, since the determination of the unit of analysis can mediate the results of the analysis; and (3) which units fulfill the criteria of "better data, more data, and least costly data."

If the analysis is to be carried out on a quantitative basis, systems of enumeration must also be devised, and these will form a portion of the body of rules that guide the analysis. Systems of enumeration identified thus far in a variety of content analyses include measures of time and space; actual appearance of the unit of analysis; measures of the frequency of the unit's appearance, and measures of its intensity. The last-named measure is of particular use when the analysis involves attitudes, beliefs, and values.

As with any method *qua* method in the social sciences, the determination of how one might go about obtaining a sample, as well as how reliability (or relevance) and validity (or fittingness) might be established, is unique to some extent to the method. The inquirer carrying out his first content analysis ought to make himself familiar with classical methodological works in content analysis and adapt the method to his particular needs. He should also note that this method is a rule-guided procedure. When its rules are clearly specified and its categories clearly defined, an independent researcher ought to be able to arrive at the same results using the same documents for analytic purposes. In other words, the research process itself—whether or not independent researchers would agree on the taxonomy—ought to be duplicable if the same rules and procedures are followed.

But the reader might wonder if document analysis is really like any other form of analysis. The answer is clearly yes. Bogdan and Taylor (1975), in their work on qualitative methods, place both personal documents and unstructured interviews into the same chapter. Moreover, the basic problem of formulating content analyses is identical with that of organizing and interpreting notes from unstructured interviews or from participant observations. In fact, lists of behavior types, or participant-nonparticipant observation "schedules" or protocols represent nothing less than *a priori* categorization, unitization, or taxonomic representations of what the observer might see. The creation of classification systems, the decision making with regard to units of analysis, and the formulation of taxonomic headings for subjects, concerns, issues, or behaviors under investigation—all utilize the methods of content analysis and abide by the same procedural canons. The methodologies in all three areas are virtually identical.

Methodology of Case-Survey Aggregation Analysis

As proposed by Lucas (1974b), the case-survey aggregation method is a means for aggregating "diverse case studies together under a common conceptual framework so that findings will be cumulative . . . to identify what it is we already 'know,' what it is we do not know, and what it is we suspect" (p. 1). The term *case survey* or *case study* is used in a somewhat broader definitional sense in this instance than is normally true in the social sciences. A case study here means any descriptive or evaluative analysis of a common social unit, a local program, or an agency. Included in this category might be "clinical studies of individuals, administrative studies of organizations, anthropological reports on primitive societies" (Lucas, 1974a, p. 8), evaluation reports, and activity reports on local programs. The strength of the method lies "in its capacity to integrate the findings of diverse studies about organizations and programs. It is more flexible in that many different types of studies using different measurement techniques can be brought together, and new concepts can be developed and considered that none of the original research ever addressed" (p. 12). Thus, the documentary case studies utilized for this type of research may be dramatically dissimilar in form or coverage from one another, as long as they are descriptive of some common social unit (for example, a series of mainstreaming in-service projects

at each of fifteen different locations, clinical studies of six para-
noid schizophrenics, each of whom believes he is Napoleon Bona-
parte, or evaluations of a dozen sites where National Science
Foundation curricula are being adopted).

The method has six basic characteristics:

1. A checklist—that is, a set of tightly defined questions and answers intended to ascertain information about certain outcomes of interest and the alternative determinants of those
   outcomes. Both the questions and possible answers to the questions emerge from the research problem and/or from a guiding
   theoretical paradigm or model.
2. A set of rules, which guides the search for, and the sampling of,
   case studies. Since the case-survey method is based upon the
   "universe" of all case studies that pertain to the common social
   unit under investigation, the search and sample rules are actually inclusion-exclusion rules that are formulated beforehand, so
   that bias in the selection of case studies does not occur.
3. A set of decision rules to be followed in dealing with the questions.
4. A group of reader-analysts who will apply the checklist to all
   the case studies.
5. A confidence scale on which each reader-analyst may record his
   subjective impression about the level of confidence he has in
   any judgment that he makes.
6. A means for checking reader-analyst reliability.

The Checklist. For illustration, we refer to a study (Lincoln,
1978) that was undertaken to explain why certain predictions
presented by competent sociologists of education (Sieber and
Lazarsfeld, 1966) in the mid 1960s about the future of bureaus
and institutes of research, development, and field service in
schools of education did not come to pass. After studying major
"bureaus" around the country, Sieber and Lazarsfeld arrived at
certain conclusions about their potential in the research and development arena. Had this potential been realized, it would indeed
have meant a bright and productive future for such units. For various reasons, however, some, if not all, of the hopeful predictions
about the future of these units failed to materialize. Thus, congres-

sional support for certain kinds of researcher training had not been forthcoming; certain assumptions about the nature of organizations made by Sieber and Lazarsfeld turned out to be invalid, as demonstrated by later research in organizational theory and behavior; and fiscal crises precipitated other forms of organizational action to support educational research and development. For many of the Sieber and Lazarsfeld propositions, it was possible to structure certain alternative hypotheses or "counterpropositions," based on recent documented history or research developments and discoveries. A sample set of propositions, with their counterpropositions, looked like this:

Proposition	*Counterproposition*
Research is a faculty priority; and when allowed to choose, faculty members overwhelmingly will choose research over teaching.	Teaching, not research, is a faculty priority in all institutions except private, doctoral-level, research-oriented institutions.
Team, especially interdisciplinary, research is better than research done by single individuals.	Team-type research is not necessarily better than research done by the lone researcher.
The reward systems of universities are, or will be, accommodating of multiple modes of research (for example, teamwork modes).	Reward systems of universities are, by and large, not multiply focused but singly focused, rewarding the lone researcher.
University-based research organizations grow out of the needs of researchers to increase their own opportunities for serious scholarship.	University-based research organizations—like most research subunits—grow out of administrative desire to create a unit to protect "precarious values" from erosion or attack.

The list of questions that reader-analysts were to respond to grew out of these propositional areas, which fell into five conceptual categories: (1) goals and missions of the bureau, (2) group processes and faculty reward systems, (3) activities and work roles of faculty, (4) unit integration (degree to which the bureau was integrated with the school of education as a whole), and (5) individual perceptions and motivations of the missions and processes. The list of propositions and counterpropositions gave rise to both the questions and the alternative determinants of outcome, which were listed in the form of possible answers to the questions. For the last proposition mentioned, for example, the checklist contained this item (among several addressed to the same conceptual category):

> What apparent motive was employed in justifying the creation of such a unit (that is, a bureau, institute, or center of educational research, development, and/or service)?
> 1. To create opportunities for extended or interdisciplinary scholarship.
> 2. To serve as a "holding company" for logistical or fiscal purposes.
> 3. To stimulate and model behavior for extra-bureau faculty.
> 4. To serve as a research resource and advisory facility.
> 5. Other (please describe).
> 6. Cannot tell from the case study [Lincoln, 1978, Appendix A].

Sixty-four questions and determinants of outcomes were thus generated to probe the five conceptual areas. Each of the question and answer sets was applied to each case study by each of three reader-analysts. (This was possible since the number of case studies was small; if the volume of case studies were large, each reader-analyst would only do a portion of the total analysis.)

Inclusion-Exclusion Rules (Searching and Sampling Procedures) for Case Studies. The first step in the process is the generation of a tight definition of the phenomenon under investigation. In this instance, only educational research, development, and service units housed in schools or colleges of education were considered. The possible universe of such units was determined by a search of files from the "Research of Institutions of Teacher Education" project (Clark and Guba, 1977) and a survey of deans of such units throughout the country. All such unit directors (or their deans) were solicited for documents pertaining to the bureaus—histories of the units, annual reports, staffing policies, five-year plans, and budgets, if available. All documents provided were included in the study except for highly redundant documents, documents that contained information on fewer than three outcomes of interest, and outdated documents.

Decision Rules for Questions. Concepts relevant to the inquiry—for example, reward systems for bureau members, budgetary arrangements for support of the unit, unit missions, and so on—were defined. Three preanalyzed case studies were provided to reader-analysts for guidance on how definitions were to be applied.

Reader-Analysts. Three reader-analysts were selected who had credentials in the area of educational research and development, as well as in organizational theory. One had directed a bureau of research and development. Each was trained in the definitions and concepts of the study, which were translated into the study's organizing rubrics, was "walked through" one case study with the investigator, and then was allowed to complete three case studies (discarded for historical bias from the final sample). This last step made it possible to establish reader reliability and interreader reliability coefficients.

Confidence Scales. Each item of the checklist was accompanied by three measures of confidence. First, the reader-analyst was given the option to signify that the case study did not contain any information relating to the item of interest. Second, the analyst was asked to provide, if he could, an actual page number in a specific document that supported the answer given or judgment made. Third, for each item the analyst indicated his confidence in the judgment on a five-point scale ranging from 1 (high confidence) to 5 (no confidence).

Interreader Reliability Measures. Reader-analysts were personally and individually trained by the investigator through use of preanalyzed cases. In addition, each reader-analyst was asked to complete three "trial" analyses that could then be intercorrelated. Reader-analysts who might not have shown a sufficiently high correspondence with ratings of peers and the investigator would have been eliminated (although, in fact, interreader reliability estimates were all .75 or better, both on trial cases and on the actual case studies).

Procedures. As in the case of content analysis, the generation of categories of interest is dictated by the research questions. Likewise, each step of the inquiry process is guided by rules that are developed to eliminate bias in the sampling and searching, to establish reliability and validity, and to ensure that definitions are rigorous to allow the study to be repeated by another set of analysts using the same rules and procedures.

Once all case studies have been analyzed with the checklist, results can be tabulated either by hand (if the number of case studies is relatively small) or by computer. In the particular case cited, all case studies were analyzed by each of the three reader-analysts. Because interreader reliabilities were not perfect, the investigator occasionally had to "adjudicate" responses herself—that is, return to the case study and determine the best possible answer. Frequencies were tabulated and conclusions drawn from the sixty-four items under the five broad organizing rubrics. The foregoing discussion should be sufficient to demonstrate that meta-analysis of data—especially of data that were intended for other purposes—is an extremely useful technique with certain kinds of documents.

Document analysis can therefore proceed in two different ways. First, it can involve content analysis of the documents themselves, along with their encoded and decoded messages. Second, documents may be analyzed as representatives of broader classes of theoretical rubrics for which they were not originally intended but for which, when subjected to certain aggregation techniques, they may yield certain new and broader forms of research data. However, analysis of records, a second technique for dealing with written accounts that are official, proceeds along a conceptually different track.

Analysis of Records

A record, as noted before, is a written residue that attests to an event or transaction or provides an accounting. Records can be categorized according to: (1) who holds them—federal, state, local, county, or municipal authorities, private corporations, credit corporations, health organizations, or banks, to name a few, or (2) to whom they are legally accessible—those accessible to the public, those inaccessible to the public, or at least to the public at large (they may be accessible to individuals—for instance, credit bureau ratings), and those that are not mentioned specifically by law. The types of records that are, for all intents and purposes, public, vary from state to state, although the amount of information available to reporters and the general public is increasing rapidly as a result of election campaign reforms and the push for political disclosure (Anderson and Benjaminson, 1976).

The first and most important injunction to anyone looking for official records is to presume that if an event happened, some record of it exists. But how does one determine what records he needs to look at in any given situation? How does the investigator find the trail he wants in the apparently untrackable wilderness of records he might consult?

Williams (1978) suggests a form of reconstructed logic for the investigative reporter: "The veteran has ingrained within himself a special style of reasoning. He knows how things normally work. If he observes a phenomenon, an effect, he wonders what caused it. He develops a hypothesis and begins checking it against observable facts. He works to back up the chain of facts, searching for information that will either support or negate his hypothesis. He tries different combinations of conflicting versions of a story until he finds the one in which salient points overlap" (p. 13). In a similar vein, Locklin (1976) comments: "I have a working theory that if I know something, if I know what the situation is, the date the money went, how much money went, who paid, who got, if I know that, I can usually prove it" (p. 7).

The central notion here is that of tracking. Guba (1978a) has identified "a common approach to the 'original research' which seems to be based on *tracking*. Actions of persons, whether legal or illegal, inevitably *leave tracks*: if one knows how things work, and if one suspects that a certain action has occurred, one can imagine *what tracks it must be leaving*; one then *looks for the tracks*, which have been 'warping and weaving' with the other circumstances of the matter, and one usually finds them, if they exist at all. Absence of tracks cannot be taken as an indication of innocence (the tracker may, after all, be inept), but their presence is proof positive—they constitute the 'smoking gun' " (p. 48).

While the image of a "smoking gun" may be a bit strong for the educational evaluator, there are many parallels between the in-

vestigative journalist's use of tracking and the evaluator's reconstruction of events and causal connections, although the educational evaluator will probably not encounter dishonesty, graft, cor-
ruption, or any of the various social ills that the investigative
reporter makes his daily fare. More often than not, the evaluator
will practice his craft in and around projects, programs, and
schools whose leaders are men and women of conscience, honestly
trying to get a job done. The sites will usually be public settings
(public schools or universities); the funds will usually be public
(state or federal); and the records that need to be perused will
probably be public, since recently enacted "sunshine" laws have
made such records accessible to anyone who needs or wants them
or at least to those who have a legitimate right to them.

How does the evaluator handle the records that he gets?
Guba (1978a) comments that for the investigative journalist "the
reconstruction of tracks and their verification is perhaps the most
distinguishing and characteristic feature. . . . It is by that process
that he keeps his task manageable, provides direction to his activity, and knows when he has reached a point at which he can com-
fortably stop looking further" (p. 49). The educational evaluator
would usually want to generate a series of working hypotheses
about what was happening on site. Starting from those hypotheses, he would seek the records (and documents) that allowed him
either to confirm or to disconfirm his hypotheses.

There is great similarity between the methods of investigative journalism with respect to records and Scriven's (1974a)
modus operandi (MO) method with respect to evaluation. Used to
verify cause-and-effect relationships, Scriven's MO strategy is one
that: (1) establishes all probable causes for an event or situation;
(2) checks to see which probable causes are in evidence; (3) checks
for the causal chain which is characteristic of each of the probable
causes which are present; and (4) labels as *the* most likely cause
that one whose characteristic causal chain is completed.

The tracking strategy of investigative journalism follows a
similar path. Most writers in the area imply that one must develop
a working hypothesis with respect to the subject of interest, determine which "tracks" or record trails would be left if the working
hypothesis were true, and then check the appropriate records to
confirm or disconfirm the hypothesis. For the educational eval-

uator, the notion of tracking falls somewhere between Scriven's method and that of the investigative journalist. While the journalist is looking for cause-and-effect relationships, the evaluator is searching for evidences of relatedness (Guba, 1978a). There are many methods that test for cause-and-effect relationships in a much more controlled fashion than does records analysis; and control, particularly of environments and contexts, is not what the naturalistic evaluator is seeking. The journalist (or detective) will probably want to search for preexistent records whose validity (because they are generally public and legal documents) is at least partially established. For the naturalistic evaluator, records may include not only what is already written but what can be "generated by additional procedures undertaken by the educational evaluator (a mode of operation [that] is not available to the investigative reporter in the large majority of cases)" (Guba, 1978a, p. 108).

Guba (1978a) cites examples of the work of the investigative reporter, the forensic pathologist (on whose work Scriven's method is built), and the educational evaluator. A typical problem for the investigative reporter might run thus:

> A municipal officer accepts a bribe to sway the administration on a certain issue favorably to the officer's "client." The client cannot pay the bribe directly since it is likely that the IRS would be attracted if the officer were suddenly to deposit a large, unaccounted-for sum. Instead, the client sells a desirable piece of property to the officer at bargain-basement rates; he in turn resells the property at its true value. The officer of course pays the tax on the capital gain, but the remaining money is "clean" (having been "laundered") and can be deposited without hesitation. But a trail has been left in the transfer of deeds, which the shrewd investigative reporter may uncover by an assiduous search of courthouse records. Of course, in real life this story is likely to have been complicated by the intervention of a dummy corporation to whom the client sold the property and which then resold it to the municipal officer. But those transactions also leave records; the tracking task is more difficult but the principle is the same [p. 106].

The forensic pathologist operates in much the same way, since "operative causes 'fulfill their [*modus operandi*] contracts,' that is, leave the full characteristic causal chain behind" (Guba, 1978a, p. 107). It is this causal chain for which the pathologist also searches. The example given is one that seems to routinely plague a favorite television show: "If, for example, a corpse were discovered which had both traces of poison and a gunshot wound in evidence, the killing cause is the one whose full causal chain can be traced. If, for example, the poison were of the type in which oxygen atoms in the blood were replaced by atoms of the poison, thereby effectively shutting off respiration, a chemical test of blood samples would show whether any appreciable number of red blood cells were affected; if not, one may conclude that it was the gunshot wound which did the trick. Conversely, if there were little or no bleeding around the gunshot wound, one could probably conclude that the effective agent was the poison. Checking on *both* characteristic causal chains would establish almost certainly whether gunshot or poison was the fatal agent" (Guba, 1978a, p. 107).

For an educational evaluator, application of the process would probably be slightly different, although the same principles would apply. Following is one example cited by Guba (1978a): "If it is asserted that a pupil's motivation to read is raised by a certain teaching approach, that assertion can be checked by looking at existing library withdrawal records, increases in sales for books of a certain kind at local bookstores, etc. . . . If it is asserted that a certain instructional outcome occurred because of the serendipitous introduction of certain originally unplanned teaching techniques, the existence of those techniques and their day-to-day impact on the classroom can be at least partially assessed by consulting log descriptions of classroom interactions. . . . If it is asserted that evaluation reports have systematically 'turned off' certain parent groups in the community, some insight might be gained into this problem by rereading local newspaper accounts of PTA meetings at which these reports were disseminated" (p. 108). Clearly, there are an infinite number of ways in which the tracking technique can be used. The practitioner of naturalistic evaluation will have, in retrospect, any number of recollections of how this technique might have been applied in his own work and will be able to generate a number of instances where it will be useful in the future.

There are three other inquiry techniques that are useful to the evaluator in analyzing records: triangulation, "circling and shuffling," and "filling."

Triangulation. Triangulation is not new in social research. It is, in fact, an old concept both in sociology and in anthropology, where it has come to mean the process of "comparing and contrasting information drawn from different sources, and/or determined by different methodologies (Guba, 1978a, p. 116). Triangulation is useful for verifying information on the same event from different actors or participants and also for producing more confidence in data generated by different methodologies. Webb and others (1966) contend that: "Once a proposition has been confirmed by two or more measurement processes, the uncertainty of its interpretation is greatly reduced. The most persuasive evidence comes through a triangulation of measurement processes. If a proposition can survive the onslaught of a series of imperfect measures, with all their relevant error, confidence should be placed in it" (p. 3).

But triangulation is important from another perspective for the naturalistic inquirer. Presumably one of the most important strengths of naturalistic inquiry is its ability to divorce itself from the unidimensional, value-consensual paradigm that has guided social action research and evaluation. The process of triangulation permits multiple value perspectives to emerge from the same context or event and allows for their explication and presentation alongside one another. In the course of checking "facts," the naturalistic inquirer causes differing perceptions and values to surface. That multiplicity of values then becomes warp and weft of the contextual fabric.

Circling and Shuffling. These terms are borrowed from the jargon of investigative journalism. They signify the steps taken to extend, complete, and bound an inquiry. "Circling," as defined by Williams (1978), is the process of taking data or information collected from a single source and "running it back around your circle of contacts for refutation or confirmation" (p. 80). This tactic involves talking with those who are presumed to be cooperative. "Shuffling" proceeds from the assumption that the contacts are noncooperative; they may be hostile or they may even be in league with the subject of the investigation, and the questioning may have to be done in a conflictual, rather than a cooperative, mode. The purpose of "shuffling" is not simply to verify or disconfirm, however. It is also to extend information. Not only will information from one source be checked against the stories of others (who are hostile sources), but some new information will also be sought.

Filling. "Filling" performs two functions: it sets the boundaries of the inquiry (which are also being set by availability of time, money, resources, records, and the like), and it completes the picture within those boundaries. The process of setting the boundaries, on the one hand, and filling in the spaces of the boundaries, on the other, is essentially that of achieving convergence and divergence in naturalistic inquiry (see Chapter Five).

These concepts appear to have utility for the naturalistic evaluator, just as they do for the investigative reporter or homicide detective. And, indeed, they need not be reserved for records analysis but can and should be used with all forms of data collection and extended to all the methodological techniques in the armament of the naturalistic evaluator.

Integrating and Using the Information Collected from Records

Unless one is a historian searching for a unique document or record, probably no single record will suit the purposes of the overall inquiry. Once again, the techniques of the patient detective or the investigative journalist prove useful. Files must be created that cross-index information and actors, and it is from these careful summaries and indexes that a coherent picture begins to emerge. There are basically seven steps for doing this:

First, a filing system is initiated by creating a folder for each person known to be involved in the inquiry. One may begin, in fact, with a single folder for a single person known to the investigator. Into this file should first go a detailed description of everything that is known about the person (a personal and/or professional history), along with copies of what others have written or reported about the person.

Second, as other persons become involved, or as the principals enter into transactions with one another, transaction folders are developed. Each "deal" or transaction has a folder of its own, and each transaction is cross-indexed with the original personnel folder(s).

Third, profiles are developed on each of the actors. Information relating to each individual's background and operating style are added to his folder during the inquiry as the original material is fleshed out and new information is received.

Fourth, chronologies are developed for the various transactions. When information becomes available (or is located), it may at first not appear to fit a pattern. But if dated chronologies are kept, events and transactions become easier to trace backward through time and also become easier to predict for the future. As a result we may find that on January 5, Mr. Smith had lunch with Mr. Jones; on January 5, Mr. Jones withdrew $5,000 from his bank account; on January 6, Mr. Smith deposited $2,500 in *his* account; on January 8, Mr. Jones was awarded an important contract over which Mr. Smith's office had jurisdiction; and on January 9, Mr. Smith deposited an additional $2,500 in his account.

Fifth, important items and events are cross-referenced as the files are developed. Thus, the transaction given as an example above might ultimately be noted both in the files of the two individuals and in their transactions files. Notations indicating cross-referencing would also be included in each file.

Sixth, files must be summarized on a systematic basis. In this way, the evaluator or investigator need not deal with original material each time he returns to the file, but rather has available to him a summary of what the file contains.

Lastly, entries in the files will give rise to hypotheses that must be checked or that point to information gaps that need to be closed. It is quite possible at this point that the original hypothesis that initiated the inquiry may have blossomed into several hypotheses or that the inquiry may have become extended in such a way as to include a web of events and transactions much larger than the investigator originally expected. The reader is reminded that the original Woodward and Bernstein inquiry into what became "Watergate" began as an interest in why a number of "third-rate burglars" would be interested in the files of a weak presidential candidate. Before the inquiry ended, it had toppled the "imperial presidency" of Richard Nixon. No such effort was ever originally intended; but the burglary, of course, led to a web of complex interactions and relationships that have not yet been fully sorted out or clarified.

This process of developing and keeping files, cross-indexing materials and references, and building chronologies appears to have many applications for the naturalistic inquirer. The utility of such a process, especially for larger inquiries and evaluations, where the management of an enormous flow of data in itself presents problems, is clear.

Is it safe, however, to trust the accuracy of records? The answer to that question is probably most of the time, yes, but sometimes, no. To trust records entirely is to be naive and to overlook the possibility of simple human error or forgetfulness or of deliberate lying on the part of those who furnish information. There are several important factors that bear upon the accuracy of records. For example, errors may be introduced by persons to whom the records pertain, either inadvertently (not being quite sure, for instance, of the value of the real estate one owns) or by intent. Errors may also be introduced by the data collectors who devise the records (for example, they may fail to count all the legitimate residents in a city block or may misinterpret information received). And, of course, errors may be introduced by recording or filing mistakes.

Moreover, certain changes in record-keeping systems can make some records noncomparable to others. If a local police department changes the way it defines "breaking and entering," for example, the statistics on the rate of that crime may change even though the true rate remains the same. In the same way, changes in the frequency or thoroughness with which some events are recorded may alter "true" statistics. One contemporary example would be the reporting of rape. It is not clear whether the incidence of rape across the United States is on the uprise, or whether the new feminist consciousness, coupled with more sensitive police handling of such crimes and their victims, has tended to make the reporting of rape more common. There are also errors due to temporal changes. Information recorded at one point in time may later become obsolete if it is not updated periodically.

Finally, errors may result from factors that enter into the

development of "official statistics." The reader is referred to the excellent dissertation by Johnson (1973) on "The Social Construction of Official Information." Johnson spent a year as a participant observer in a social welfare agency, and he documents in detail how "records" are generated in such agencies, in particular the required statistical reports that became the "official information" for the agency. To quote Johnson:

> To successfully complete such statistical reportings, in every instance the social workers were asked to "reduce" their knowledgeable understandings of their activities in the linguistic terms provided by a given report. As the members were held rationally accountable to so many different administrative structures and in so many different terms, it was only by making use of one's understanding of the situated official reporting context which allowed for the possibility of "making sense" of a given report, and to further impute the intentions of the reporting format. This means that the situational reporting context is not only partially independent of the organized features of the other official work contexts but, furthermore, this was commonly known by the social workers as one of their organizational facts-of-life. By making use of such an understanding, the social workers and/or administrative personnel in these welfare agencies used official documents and statistical reports in a continually ongoing and self-organizing attempt to change or stabilize the nature of their everyday practices' in accord with their individual motives, intentions, plans, dreams, fears, hopes, and so on [p. x].

Johnson is saying, then, that even official reports are responded to in terms of who gets the report, what its perceived purpose is, and what impact the respondent thinks it will have on him as a person and worker. Official data are, in short, doctored by respondents from a variety of perspectives.

For these reasons, and no doubt many others, it would be unsophisticated in the extreme to accept documents and records at face value. The wary inquirer will attempt a variety of means to certify or warrant that a record is accurate as represented, including checking other records that might triangulate the first and simply asking (at some point in the inquiry) the person about whom the document obtains.

Does the Use of Records Create Special Ethical Problems?

The answer is, of course, yes. This is especially true of records that are personal, private, or classified. Various state laws, as well as the federal Freedom of Information Act, make clear which documents will be available to private citizens and which will not. Among those documents not available are records that pertain to classified defense or foreign policy information or to personnel rules and practices of federal agencies, anything specifically exempted by federal statute, information that is privileged in civil litigation, bank records, and oil well data.

Investigative reporters give a number of reasons why they continue to seek (and occasionally try to obtain illegally) certain kinds of private records. They cite the public's right to know or the redress of criminal or civil wrongs. While these reasons are questionable even when invoked by journalists, they are most surely unethical for the evaluator. Nevertheless, there will be times when the acquisition of a document or record appears desirable, and it seems to be impossible to acquire it. The evaluator needs to carefully balance his sense of the public's right to know, the possible value of the record, and his willingness to engage in behavior that may be less than professional (for example, asking an "insider" to obtain the record from the files for him). The leak of the "Pentagon Papers" and the resultant break-in at the office of Daniel Ellsberg's psychiatrist are good examples of how records *may* be obtained, either from an inside source or through clearly illegal means. The naturalistic evaluator needs to ask whether he wants to be involved in either of those forms of record acquisition, especially if the records do not contribute to the public's right to know. The journalist's stance is that there are no documents and records that are inaccessible. Some just take more time or more devious means to procure than others. We think that that stance is simply not a tolerable one for the kind of inquiry that attends evaluative efforts. A method of gaining information that is clearly illegal is simply off limits to the naturalistic inquirer.

We have described some excellent techniques for making use of the variety of inexpensive and rich resources that may be found in documents and records. Both documentary analysis and record utilization are useful either on their own—that is, as a primary technique—or as supplementary techniques. With new fiscal constraints on the amounts that may be spent for research, both techniques need to be explored as weapons in the methodological arsenal of naturalistic evaluators. The strengths of the two techniques far outweigh the costs, and they can and do produce data that otherwise could be collected only by more costly means.

Unobtrusive Measures

> *"The waitress sings,*
> *'I can tell that you're a logger*
> *And not just a common bum*
> *Cause nobody but a logger*
> *Stirs his coffee with his thumb.' "*
>
> Webb and others, 1966, p. 141

Occasionally, an inquirer does not want to engage in an interaction with his respondent, or there is reason to believe that his "respondent" would refuse to engage in an inquiry effort. In such cases, the inquirer should, if possible, move toward "measures" that produce the least possible reactivity. In many instances, these may be unobtrusive measures. Unobtrusive measurement is the process of observing, recording, and analyzing human behavior or behavior patterns without the knowledge or awareness of those who are being observed. Sometimes the person being "observed" is not even present. What is measured are traces of his activity. Unobtrusive measures are signs that indicate a type of behavior or a behavior pattern but which are not meant to do so.

The most common reason for using unobtrusive measures, is as suggested above, that they reduce reactivity and therefore reduce the sensitivity of measurement. There are several types of sensitivity to which such measures address themselves: the "guinea pig" effect, or the sensitivity of persons who know they are being measured; the "role selection" effect, or the determination of the respondent of what role he should play in responding to the measurement; changes produced by the measurement itself, so that the respondent becomes sensitized by merely having been exposed to the measurement; "response sets" effects, that is, tendencies to respond in particular ways; interviewer effects resulting from the sex, age, race or other characteristics of the interviewer; or alterations in the measurement instrument itself through refinements or through changes in procedures.

Some examples of unobtrusive measures would include: hair style or clothing as indicators of the wearer's social class; eye-pupil size or nervous tics as indications of affective state; gestures and body language as indicators of openness; shortcuts across lawns as indicators of preferred traffic patterns; foreign language signs as indicators of the degree of integration of a neighborhood; worn, smudged condition of books as indicators of their use; library circulation records as indicators of the effectiveness of a course in literature appreciation; index numbers as indicators of the status of some area, for example, the Dow-Jones index as an indicator of market flows; diaries as records of personal thoughts; and many others. It ought to occur immediately to the reader that some of these indicators are very much like the documents and records used in document and record analysis and very much like nonverbal communication measures. But there are differences in how these various measures are used; and in the case of nonverbal communication measures and unobtrusive measures, there is also the difference that many unobtrusive measures may be made without a respondent being present, while nonverbal communication cues may only be gathered with a respondent present.

Webb and others (1966) have suggested a five-category typology for unobtrusive measures:

1. Physical traces, including both *accretion* and *erosion* measures
2. Archival records
3. Private records
4. Simple observations
5. Contrived observations

Each of these in turn may be broken down even further. For the first category of physical traces, an example of an erosion measure would be the wear and tear on floor tile in front of a museum display case as an indicator of the attractiveness of that display.

An example of an accretion measure would be the number of liquor bottles found in garbage cans as a measure of a community's drinking habits.

Webb and his colleagues suggest further that trace measures can also be classified as a function of the number and pattern of units of evidence, that is, remnants versus series (for an accumulative body of evidence); but the major categories seem to be the most useful, and they are the only ones regularly referred to in the literature.

Unobtrusive measures have great utility not only for reducing sensitivity to measures but also for carrying out triangulation. When an inquirer is triangulating for purposes of cross-validation, unobtrusive measures add to the repertoire of methods that may be used simultaneously with other more obtrusive or sensitive methods. Such measures are also useful whenever fairly straightforward qualitative measures are needed. (But it should also be noted that unobtrusive measures are often quantitative. The point is that such measures are sometimes qualitative and that a knowledge of their possibilities increases the qualitative inquirer's arsenal of techniques.)

Strengths and Weaknesses of Unobtrusive Measures

As with any inquiry effort, the methodological strengths of the tool have to be weighed against the weaknesses. Whenever possible, multiple measures ought to be employed so that the weaknesses of one method are counterbalanced by the strengths of another. The strengths of unobtrusive measures lie in eight areas. First, they tend to have at least face validity. Second, they are more often than not simple and direct. Third, they are inconspicuous and often noninterventional. Fourth, they are usually based on typical, natural behavior and hence are nonreactive. Fifth, they are easy to use in tandem, so that the strengths of one technique may be used to cover the weaknesses of another. They are therefore especially useful as supplementary, complementary, or cross-validating techniques. Sixth, they tend to be stable over time. Seventh, they exhibit a low "dross" rate; that is, the ratio of irrelevant to relevant information yielded by them is quite low. Finally, they are usually independent of language.

The weaknesses of these measures are probably four in number. First, unobtrusive measures are sometimes heavily inferential. For instance, do worn tiles really indicate the attractiveness of an exhibit or do they result from proximity to the washrooms? Second, unobtrusive measures often provide information in bits and pieces that may be hard to aggregate (quantitatively) or to interpret (qualitatively). Third, they cannot reach into all content areas as can, say, an interview, and in that sense they have limited applicability. Fourth, they cannot be easily controlled because they are natural forms of behavior, although only conventional inquirers are likely to label that characteristic a handicap.

Finding Useful Unobtrusive Measures. One of the chief weaknesses of the work of Webb and others (1966) seems to lie in their failure to provide strategies for locating unobtrusive measures that would be useful in given inquiries. Their book cites many unobtrusive measures that could be used in some situations, and it reviews the literature for instances in which such measures were in fact used very successfully. But it provides little guidance for the reader who says, "I have this particular situation to cope with, and it has such and such characteristics; what is a good unobtrusive measure *in this case*?"

The answer to that question seems to be twofold, and we would label the answers *accidental measures* and *systematic measures.* Accidental measures are those unobtrusive measures that one happens upon; that is, that occur in the context to someone whose powers of observation have been cultivated. For example, suppose an inquirer is doing a comparative study of efficiency in federal bureaucracies. In the course of a series of interviews, the inquirer has noticed that a number of persons have been chain-smoking. He wonders if this habit is pervasive and speaks to the stress that he has in other ways observed in members of the organization. On what appear to be casual trips through the agency, he first counts the number of persons who are smoking. He then counts the number of ashtrays that appear to be in use and the number that are heavily loaded with cigarette butts. Since most offices are cleaned at night, he can determine—over several days—what the average smoking rate might be for employees and managers in that agency. Without having been in the context, however, he might not have thought of the cigarette cue. Only when he found himself clouded in smoke did the unobtrusive measure occur to him.

Systematic measures, in contrast, are those that grow out of the logic of the inquiry itself. The technique that we find most useful here is to begin with an analysis of the questions that we want answered by the inquiry. Suppose, for example, we are given the task of discovering which of the museum displays to which schoolchildren are routinely exposed is most attractive to them. We would concentrate on an analysis of (1) the concept and (2) the situation. "Attractiveness" can be defined in many ways, depending on the audience: it can mean drawing power, beauty, acceptability, fascination, charm. The situation also has many elements: physical location of the exhibits, their accessibility, their proximity to other compelling exhibits, constraint of circulation patterns by ropes or aisles, time available for viewing, and the presence or absence of guides who pace and direct the viewing. If we want a measure, say, of drawing power in a particular situational configuration but also wish to avoid direct questioning of the viewers, what kinds of unobtrusive measures might be devised? We might look at wear patterns of floor tile, to be sure, but we might also look at fingerprints on the glass, the frequency with which taped descriptions of exhibits are played, the proportion of schoolchildren who are spontaneously drawn to one or another exhibit as a first choice on entering a room, the number of schoolchildren who return to an exhibit a second or third time, the number of questions that they ask about the exhibits, the number of souvenirs relating to an exhibit sold in the gift shop, the number of references made to the exhibit in subsequent weeks in reports written by the schoolchildren, and the like.

What we are suggesting is that an analysis of the questions that an inquirer wants to ask is likely to lead to some useful unobtrusive measures. Rarely does the existence of a particular unobtrusive measure lead an inquirer to use it without regard to the situation, and the strategy we describe here is not unlike the strategy of tracking records that we described earlier in this chapter.

One of the conceptual gaps that exists in the case of unobtrusive measures is that there are no dependable ways of creating them, that is, of devising them for any given situation. Much needed, as Lee Sechrest (1980) has suggested, is a taxonomy that will generate new unobtrusive measures. That taxonomy ought to cross the characteristics of things to be assessed with the characteristics of measures, that is, their frequency, magnitude, latency, proximity, and whether or not the behavior is group or individual. We do not, at this time, have any system that will allow for the genesis of new measures in a systematic manner.

Ethical Problems with Unobtrusive Measures. The very fact that unobtrusive measures are unobtrusive open them to ethical abuse. Webb and his colleagues (1966) recognize that fact but admit that they "have purposely avoided consideration of the ethical issues which [these measures] raise" (p. v). No doubt, they suggest, readers will find the techniques differentially acceptable and will vary in their "moral boiling points." It is up to social scientists, they aver, to develop criteria by which techniques can be judged for their ethical content. So far, satisfactory criteria do not exist, but "the multiple methods presented here may ... provide alternatives on which ethical criteria can be met without impinging on important interests of the research subjects" (p. vii). Indeed, Webb and others seem to feel that unobtrusive measures, based as they are on natural behaviors, may be among the more ethical of techniques: "If ethical considerations lead us to avoid participant observation, interviews, or eavesdropping in given circumstances, the novel methods described in this monograph may be of value not only in improving and supplementing our information but also in permitting ethically scrupulous social scientists to do their work effectively and to sleep better at night" (p. vii). In some ways, we find this view rather naive, since unobtrusive measures can lead to an increase in the use of deception. Even though it may be public and observable, there is no reason to believe that individuals wish to have their behavior systematically observed, recorded, and analyzed. There are questions of rights of privacy that obtain in the case of unobtrusive measures just as they obtain in other forms of inquiry, such as participant and nonparticipant observation.

Establishing Authenticity for Unobtrusive Measures. As we have noted, many unobtrusive measures have face validity, although many depend heavily on investigator inferences as well. In the latter case, the inquirer will have to come up with arguments to support the inference he is making—arguments preferably dependent on grounded information. Reliability is difficult to determine (for example, how does one establish the reliability of floor tile wear?), especially when the measure is of some physical element (for example, the amount of wear on the soles of children's shoes). For both of these purposes, triangulation and overlapped techniques can help to provide reliability. There is, however, rarely any doubt about the objectivity of these measures, detached as they are from human intervention in most cases.

Probably little training particular to this area is needed, save in the process of analysis of questions leading to identification of possible unobtrusive measures; *looking* and *listening* skills are more important. As the song of the waitress, given at the beginning of the section, points out, it is often the small things that count in unobtrusive measures. More people "stir their coffee with their thumbs" than might be realized.

Unobtrusive measures, like good participant observation, good interviewing, and good nonverbal communication, depend a great deal on who is doing the measuring. Many such measures are there for the taking, but most of us have become sufficiently inured to the environmental and behavioral patterns around us that we fail to see them. Other good unobtrusive measures go wanting because the logic and methodical analysis of questions that guide inquiry have not been taken far enough. But while it is true that we do not now have a complete taxonomy that would allow us to generate unobtrusive measures on a systematic basis, there are nonetheless many such observations that could be made without additional cost to any given inquiry effort. They should not be overlooked, as they provide additional information that is grounded in natural, "in context" behavior. And, as Lee Sechrest has commented, "It's fun to be furtive."

Chapter 9

Initiating and Organizing the Evaluation

This chapter deals with the steps involved in getting an evaluation under way. The evaluator has a client or sponsor for the evaluation with whom it is necessary to negotiate an evaluation contract or agreement. When such a contract has been agreed on, the next step is to put together a team of specialists who will carry out its terms. The team needs to gain entrée to the evaluation site, get established, and develop productive contacts. It must also sense out, and take account of, the various human and political factors that exist in the situation and that might affect the evaluation's progress. We shall consider each of these topics in turn.

Negotiating the Evaluation Contract

Evaluations are done for clients who commission the evaluation, provide for its legitimation, and pay for it. Since he who pays the piper calls the tune, the evaluator must have a firm understanding with the client about what the evaluation is to accomplish, for whom, and by what methods. The evaluator also needs to be protected against certain arbitrary and possibly harmful or unethical actions by the client, just as the client needs to be protected against an unscrupulous evaluator. The means for achieving these understandings and establishing these safeguards is the evaluation contract.

The contract may take the form of a simple letter of understanding or an elaborate legal document, but at a minimum it should deal with the following set of topics:

Identification of the Sponsor or Client. The sponsor or client commissioning the study should be identified, and his authority for commissioning it should be clearly established. Thus, it is inappropriate for an agency outside a school system—for example, a parent or community organization—to commission an evaluation of that school system without having obtained the consent of the school board. Of course, an agency that accepts funding from another agency accords to the funder *de facto* rights to commission an evaluation; nevertheless it is important that authority lines be clearly established and approvals obtained from all responsible authorities. No evaluation carried out at the mandate of an unidentified individual or agency can be considered legitimate.

Identification of the Entity To Be Evaluated. It is important that the evaluand be unambiguously identified and described. This entity may take many forms: a program, a project, a person or class of persons, a piece of instructional material, a curriculum, an organizational pattern, a proposal, an idea, and so on. There may be multiple descriptions of the evaluand in existence, in both written and perceived, or unwritten, form. For example, a new curriculum may be described in an original proposal, in a document written by its developers, in a marketing brochure, or in a letter to parents. It may be understood in a variety of different ways by stakeholding audiences (Farrar and others, 1979). The evaluation contract should call upon the client to furnish a description of the evaluand and to turn over to the evaluator all documents that might contain a relevant description. The client should also be aware of the evaluator's intent to solicit descriptions from all stakeholding audiences.

Purpose of the Evaluation. It might be assumed that the

purpose of the evaluation will be adequately stated in whatever charge the client gives to the evaluator. But there are several difficulties with this assumption.

First, the charge given to the evaluator may not be the charge that the client actually wants to accomplish. The real purpose of a given evaluation may be to whitewash a program's failure or to torpedo a program that, regardless of its merit, is in disfavor with someone in power. Thus, the evaluator is wise to keep in mind the possibility that he is being exploited by the client, even though such exploitation occurs only rarely.

Second, the charge given by the client may not be sophisticated enough. It may set certain goals for the evaluator that are inconsistent with good evaluation practice; for example, it may require the evaluator to seek what is essentially no more than management information and to forgo the responsibility of making judgments or recommendations. Or the charge may make an implicit definition of evaluation that the evaluator believes to be inappropriate in that situation.

Finally, the charge may not be sufficiently specific. We saw in Chapter Three that evaluation can take two forms: the determination of worth or the determination of merit. Moreover, evaluation can be undertaken for the sake of improvement or refinement (formative evaluation) or for the sake of assessing overall impact (summative evaluation). The combination of these two orthogonal dimensions generates four possibilities: formative merit evaluation, summative merit evaluation, formative evaluation of worth, and summative evaluation of worth. Each of these four possibilities has different intents, audiences, and standards.

The commissioner of an evaluation certainly has a right to specify the charge. If the evaluator has reason to believe that there is a hidden agenda, he may refuse the contract or at least may insist on bringing that hidden agenda to the surface. If the charge is not sufficiently sophisticated, the evaluator can negotiate a better statement. But the evaluator must be very sure that the charge is sufficiently specific in the terms set forth in Chapter Three. For surely, the evaluator who assesses merit when the client expects him to assess worth, or who believes the evaluation will aid in the refinement or improvement of an entity when the client expects to get impact data, is in trouble.

In all matters relating to purpose, negotiation is the key.

Misunderstandings about purpose are more likely than any other single reason to cause evaluations to misfire or to result in information that is of no use to anyone.

Sanction. Evaluations are commissioned by clients, but such commissioning does not constitute a sufficient sanction from all the relevant parties to ensure success. As Glass (1975) notes: "There are no techniques available to the contemporary evaluator that do not depend heavily for their validity on the cooperation of those persons being evaluated. . . . I know of no significant study which could not have been subverted by the deceit, passive resistance, or noncooperation of an unwilling group of subjects" (p. 11).

But even if Glass' points were not true, the evaluator would be well advised to seek sanction from each of the several audiences involved with or influenced by the entity being evaluated because it is immoral, and, in some cases, illegal not to do so. Subjects should not be deluded or exploited for the sake of gaining ostensibly more "valid" or "objective" data. Federal privacy laws virtually force evaluators to seek prior approval before records are invaded and personal information indiscriminately used.

It is unreasonable to expect the evaluator to have obtained sanction from every audience *before* the contract is negotiated. Indeed, it may not be possible to do so since the identification of relevant audiences is itself a task of some technical complexity, and all audiences may not be known until the evaluation has been under way for some time. But it is reasonable to expect the evaluator to recognize the importance of this task and to propose procedures in the contract for (1) identifying audiences and (2) securing their approval. Audiences should have the right to review proposed procedures and to reject them if they feel, on reasonable grounds, that they are inappropriate.

Audiences. The reader may feel that the term *audience* has been used thus far in this book in two quite different ways. At times, the term has referred to those groups of persons who had some *stake* in the entity being evaluated. Such groups may be expected to have concerns and issues about the entity being evaluated, and it is those concerns and issues that give focus to the evaluation. At other times, the term *audience* has meant those groups to whom an evaluation *report* is to be directed.

But this apparent confusion has been no accident, for we

mean to use the term in both its senses interchangeably. In other words, we believe that persons entitled to see reports must have a stake in the entity being evaluated. Different audiences, of course, will hold different stakes, and some will have larger stakes than others. But if one is a stakeholder at all, one is entitled to have one's concerns and issues plumbed, tested, and honored, as well as to receive reports relevant to them. It is a prime task of the evaluator to identify all stakeholding audiences, to take them into account in focusing the evaluation, and to report to them during and after the evaluation in forms and language suitable to their concerns and issues, on the one hand, and to their level of technical sophistication, on the other.

As we have already noted, it is unreasonable to expect the evaluator to identify all audiences before negotiating an evaluation contract, but the contract should specify both the evaluator's awareness of the need to carry out this task and the means he proposes to use for that purpose.

Methods of Inquiry. We have argued that a methodological orthodoxy pervades the field of educational evaluation (and, indeed, of social-behavioral inquiry in general). Rossi and Wright (1977) state the case perfectly: "There is almost universal agreement among evaluation researchers that the randomized controlled experiment is the ideal model for evaluating the effectiveness of a public policy. If there is a Bible for evaluation, the Scriptures have been written by Campbell and Stanley, . . . along with a revised version by Cook and Campbell. . . . The 'gospel' of these popular texts is that all research designs can be compared more or less unfavorably to randomized controlled experiments, departures from which are subject to varying combinations of threats to internal and external validity" (p. 13).

The "ideal" model thus includes designation of a particular design (preferably a randomized experimental design, but, failing that, some form of quasi-experimental design), definition of variables, a sampling plan, instrumentation, techniques to be used in analyzing data, and so on. At least, that is what most persons believe to be the case, if we can credit the quotation from Rossi and Wright. Unfortunately, the client all too often expects this kind of model. (Rossi and Wright do note that chances to conduct random controlled experiments in evaluation research are rare; most researchers use designs that are less than ideal.)

From the traditional point of view, it is imperative that the design be specified as carefully as possible, so that the client, among others, can judge its validity, reliability, and objectivity. From the emergent point of view espoused in this book, however, it is even more important that the methods of inquiry be clearly and unequivocally stated, so that not only is the client quite sure of what will not be done (that is, an experiment) but that he can be reassured about what *is* to be done and be given some basis for believing in the legitimacy of the proposed approach.

Most clients are not sophisticated about the technical aspects of evaluation methodology. They tend to believe assertions such as that of Rossi and Wright, and they are constantly reinforced in this belief by the constraints laid on them by others. For example, Title I directors as clients cannot escape the federal requirement that they use Model I, II, or III in their evaluations. Hence they will become very disturbed, and rightly so, if the evaluator is not "up front" about the approach he will take (if it is different from the orthodox approach). Candor is thus mandatory.

What should the evaluator do when asked to conduct an evaluation in which a particular approach—one to which the evaluator is not committed—is mandated by the funder? We would conduct the minimal evaluation possible to satisfy the mandates, while conserving as many resources as possible to produce additional (and presumably more useful) information by the preferred means. If numbers of such cases could be developed, it would soon become evident that the more traditional modes are overly constraining and steps would be taken to relax the requirements.

Emergent Design. Sponsors want evaluation designs to be specified in great detail in order to reassure themselves that the study will be cost efficient and rigorous. But the naturalistic evaluator finds it virtually impossible to be specific about such operational details as procedural steps, instrumentation, and sampling precisely because he intends each phase or stage of the evaluation to build upon all preceding steps.

We have noted that as often as not the major instrument that the naturalistic evaluator will use is the investigator himself—a human instrument that can utilize tacit cues to the best advantage and can deviate from structured formats when it seems appropriate to do so. For example, the direction of an interview may change sharply midway through, and this may redirect the entire inquiry. Sampling is almost never representative or random but purposive, intended to exploit competing views and fresh perspectives as fully as possible. Sampling stops when information becomes redundant rather than when subjects are representatively sampled.

The sponsor must be fully informed about the evaluator's intent to utilize an emergent (or rolling or cascading) design so that he will understand the reasons for this approach and its implications. The evaluator should understand that the sponsor is likely to be unusually anxious when asked to provide what might be construed as *carte blanche*; thus, he needs to set up mechanisms to inform the client of new developments as they occur. But the evaluator must beware of empowering the client to approve each new phase; extending that much authority to the client goes well beyond the need for reassurance and in effect takes the authority for making technical decisions out of the evaluator's hands. Negotiation about the emergent nature of the design should be confined to the initial contracting phase and should be directed at securing the client's approval; thereafter contacts between evaluator and client should be informational in character, intended to reassure the client rather than to seek sanction for the emergent steps.

Access to Records. The evaluation contract needs to deal explicitly with two kinds of records: those under the control of the sponsor or the staff of the entity being evaluated and those that the evaluator will keep.

We have seen that the appropriate use of existing records can add an important dimension to evaluation activity: it can both generate fresh insights and cross-check or triangulate information received in other ways. The evaluation contract should stipulate what records are to be made accessible and the processes to be followed in gaining access to them. The evaluator should be aware, however, that the granting of license by the sponsor or by senior administrative figures is no guarantee that access will in fact be granted by operational personnel, who may refuse to cooperate or may make the task so fiscally or logistically unfeasible that the evaluator is tempted to simply forgo use of the records. The contract should make provisions for direct appeal to sponsors or administrators for assistance should such contingencies arise.

As the evaluation proceeds, the evaluation team will in its

turn collect certain information and establish filing and processing methods for organizing it. Evaluation information enjoys no special legal privilege, so that, in case of challenge, the evaluator would probably be required by a court to open his files. For example, should anyone take offense at an evaluation report and legally challenge the evaluator to divulge the sources and the "raw" information on which the report is based, he would very likely have to do so.

This fact of life is especially crucial to the naturalistic evaluator, since so many of his methods fall into the category of "subjective" when viewed by the conventional criteria of the scientific paradigm. Field notes are likely to be a great deal more suspect than scores generated from a test based on national norms. The naturalistic evaluator should be especially careful, therefore, that field notes—of interviews, observations, unobtrusive indicators, nonverbal cues, and the like—be well kept and that his records show an adequate methodology for connecting the raw materials and any analyses or conclusions based upon them.

The evaluation contract should take explicit note of the problem of access to records. While the client may legally deny access to *his* records to the evaluator, the evaluator probably could not withstand demands for access to the records kept by him. The contract should authorize access for the evaluator to those records that he deems useful and should make provision for dealing with difficult situations. The contract should also make provision for orderly access to the evaluation records, including the important question of timing (for example, access should probably be reserved until after formal reports are made).

Confidentiality and Anonymity. It is common for evaluators to promise confidentiality and anonymity to informants. "No one will ever see individual data, and all reports will consist only of aggregated information in which individual identities are undetectable" is a common enough statement. Informants become reluctant to cooperate when they cannot be assured that their superiors or others with power over them will not have access to their responses and observations. Thus the client should agree in the contract not to press for such individual information.

But the evaluator should understand that the mere giving of reassurances of confidentiality and anonymity may not be enough.

Since evaluator files are not protected by any legal privilege, the evaluator ought to keep his files in a way that protects individual identities. The naturalistic evaluator in particular should note that, because he does not typically employ the large samples of individuals, schools, agencies, and so on that often appear in socio-behavioral studies, it is relatively easy to identify his sources of information. Quotation of a comment, for example, often divulges its source because there may be only one or two persons in a position to make that particular observation.

Certainly the contract should announce the evaluator's intention to extend promises of confidentiality and anonymity to informants and should require the sponsor's formal agreement to those terms. On his part, the evaluator needs to take steps to protect files against a too-easy individual interpretation and needs to exercise special caution in the reporting activity to protect informants from being easily identified. Promises of anonymity and confidentiality should be made with care and with full recognition of the factors that militate against keeping them. But once made, promises should be kept.

Evaluator Autonomy. The relationship of the evaluator to the sponsor is a delicate one. In many ways it parallels that between an attorney and his client or a physician and his patient. The attorney is required to be as candid with his client as possible, and the physician with his patient, so that a "fully informed decision" can be made about the advisability of a legal action or a surgical operation (Bok, 1978). But once having placed himself in the hands of the professional, the client or patient leaves it up to that professional to do what he deems best. There is no question of halting the attorney in the middle of a cross-examination or the surgeon in the act of removing the appendix in order to propose a different approach, reconsider the decision, or give explicit new directions.

Similarly, the sponsor of an evaluation is entitled to an explanation from the evaluator that will allow him to make a "fully informed decision." The evaluation contract may be viewed as a formal statement through which the basic conditions and requirements are laid out for the sponsor's inspection; the sponsor's signature on the contract attests to the fact that such information has been formally received and that he understands and agrees to the terms. But the evaluator should be careful to insert a statement guaranteeing that his autonomy will be respected in the making of professional decisions about the evaluation—a stipulation especially important to the naturalistic evaluator because of the emergent nature of his design. Since sponsors are human and may at times feel under sufficient pressure to disregard this stipulation, the contract should also contain provisions for appeal, negotiation, and resolution of grievances felt by either party.

Reporting. Reporting may be either formal or informal, and reports may be made to a variety of audiences. The contract should reserve to the evaluator the right to make reports in whatever forms and at whatever times are deemed appropriate. Moreover, the evaluator should have the option of reporting to all the audiences that are identified during the evaluation, in accordance with the provisions covering audience identification mentioned above.

If difficulties arise over reporting, they are likely to develop in relation to the final report. The contract should stipulate agreements for various aspects of that report. In general, the evaluator must insist that the responsibility for content is his alone. While the sponsor or any audience member is entitled to raise questions of factual accuracy, judgments and interpretations are the province of the evaluator. The evaluator should be wary of assigning the right to edit a report to any other party, since editing, even if ostensibly undertaken only for the sake of clarity or improvements in style, can also be used to change essential meanings. If the right to edit is assigned, the evaluator should reserve the right to change any editing if, in his judgment, essential meanings are changed thereby. In the same way, the evaluator should reserve the right to determine the form of the report—or the form should be stipulated in the contract *a priori.* The evaluator may also wish to utilize a different form for different audiences.

The timing of reports can be critical. Formative reports must be given when needed to ensure orderly development, refinement, or improvement. Decisions whose quality depends on the availability of evaluation data cannot wait until the evaluation results are fully and unequivocally "in." The contract should specify the schedule of reports that must be met.

Reports can be made through many different channels: they

can be formally presented at school board meetings, distributed through the mails, released to newspapers or television news staffs, or presented at "town meetings" called just for that purpose. Very often the appropriate channel depends on the particular audience to receive the report. The contract should reserve to the evaluator the right to select the appropriate channels or should specify the negotiation process through which clients and evaluators will reach a decision about them.

The contract should specify who has the authority to release a report. If the client feels that a report is inappropriate, badly timed, prejudicial, or whatever, can he elect not to release it? In practice, release authority is often balanced off against content control: the evaluator determines the content, and the client determines whether to release the report. If that arrangement is desired, it should be included in the contract. The order of release may become an issue as well; for example, a school board may prefer to have received a report *in camera* before reading about it in the local press.

Technical Specifications. It is wise to include within the formal contract a number of technical specifications, including at least the following:

a. *Agents.* Who will do the evaluation? What kind of training and experience have the evaluators had? What other similar evaluations have they done? Agencies that contract for evaluations often have standard "boiler plate" paragraphs that provide this kind of information and that can be routinely attached to any contract. Their inclusion provides the client some assurance of the quality of the personnel with whom he is contracting, and some idea of the scope and magnitude of the team with which he will have to contend.

b. *Schedule.* Beginning and ending dates of the evaluation should be included, as well as estimates of major events (for example, the schedule for a major round of interviews). The timing of reports and other products should be specified, insofar as it is possible to do so in advance.

c. *Budget.* The contract should also specify the full cost of the proposed evaluation, including both direct costs and necessary overhead. The budget should be broken down in sufficient detail so that its appropriateness can be judged. Most naturalistic evaluations are likely to be labor-intensive, so that the budget will reflect, in the main, personnel costs. There are several options in budgeting that the evaluator may wish to consider.

First, an evaluation may be projected that the evaluator is sure will yield certain information and lead to certain judgments; these outcomes are the minimum that can be expected. If everything goes well, however, it is possible that some additional benefits can be reaped. The naturalistic evaluator may feel that at a minimum he will be able to collect information responsive to a half-dozen top-priority issues, but that, depending on the degree of cooperativeness found in informants or the actual amount of time spent in interviewing, it may be possible to say something about *why* these particular concerns and issues emerged in the first place. Thus, at a maximum, it may be possible to say something about causes as well as about existing conditions. The evaluator may wish to provide the client the option of paying for the additional effort involved if it becomes apparent that additional gains are possible.

The evaluator may wish to provide several levels of budget— for example, conservative, nominal, and liberal budgets—that would differ in the amount and quality of service to be provided. The client may choose the level desired and be given the privilege of moving from level to level as the evaluation proceeds. In the latter case, however, the evaluator should be certain to guard against the possibility of client budgetary moves that militate against other rights reserved to the evaluator, for example, professional autonomy.

Some evaluators feel so confident of their ability to produce useful results that they are willing to stipulate contractually that the evaluation budget (or that portion of it that constitutes the evaluator's fee or honorarium) can be placed in escrow until it is shown that the evaluation has resulted in savings to the client at least equal to its costs. This stipulation, while not recommended, is at least useful to contemplate: it provides the evaluator a unique perspective from which to view his own presumed competence. Some portion of the budget may be placed in escrow (or otherwise withheld) to guarantee delivery of the final products.

d. *Products.* The contract should stipulate what the products of the evaluation are to be; usually this means stipulating the type and number of reports, but may also involve data displays and/or summaries, instrumentation, data-processing capabilities, trained personnel, or other by-products of the normal evaluation process. Such delivered products normally become the property of the sponsor or pass to his control; care must therefore be taken to be sure that they will be used with discretion.

Organizing the Evaluation Team

An evaluation team may already exist to carry out a particular evaluation, or it may have to be organized ad hoc. The first case might arise, for example, in a local school district, regional laboratory, or research and development center that has recurrent need for evaluation and elects to provide for this need through the establishment of a formal evaluation unit. The second case is typical of external, third-party evaluations, in which an evaluator contracts for a specific evaluation and organizes a team to carry out the contract. The ideas and approaches discussed below are applicable in either situation; the major differences are probably in the size or scope of the teams and the fact that, in the case of existing teams, provisions must be made for orderly movement of personnel from one project to another. Neither of these contingencies seriously affects the relevance or validity of the observations to be made; hence, the distinction between these two situations will not be systematically maintained in the following discussion. The reader will probably want to keep in mind the contingency for which he is planning, however, and to make whatever minor adjustments seem sensible in the particular case.

Why Use Teams? Even if an evaluation were so small that it might conceivably be carried out by a single professional, there would be some advantages to constructing a team anyway. Teams, first of all, provide for multiple roles. There are many different ways to conceptualize the mix of roles that is required to carry out an evaluation. Differentiations might be made, for example, on the basis of status—there may be a director, one or more senior staff members, one or more junior staff members, technicians, clerical personnel, and the like. Another way to think about the team roles is in terms of formal functions—services, reporting, data analysis, field relations, auditing, and others. Yet a third view may be had in terms of informal functions—for example, Douglas

(1976, pp. 211-212) describes a field research team as consisting of specialists such as the "sociability" or "entrée" specialist, the "quarterback" or team leader, the "bagman" or grantsperson, the observer, the specialist "good at finding people and organizations," and the "literary expert." Although this breakdown of a field research team is not an exact parallel to the evaluation team, it is useful to think of the evaluation team in analogous informal terms.

Which of these three perspectives should be followed in deciding upon the roles for an evaluation team? Probably all—thinking about status differentiations, functional specialization, and informal role taking probably would result in the most heuristic approach.

Second, teams provide multiple perspectives. Responsive evaluation takes seriously the pluralistic values likely to be held by the audiences it serves. We have noted that in evaluations addressed to questions of worth, it is essential to determine local contextual differences in values. It is unlikely that any single person could fully appreciate the many different value perspectives that might be projected by several audiences, but it is not unreasonable to suppose that an evaluation team could be so structured that its members might exhibit a certain complementarity to such different value positions. For example, team members might be chosen to represent teachers, parents, developers, and so on; different value positions are more likely to be honored if there are evaluation team members who, even if they do not share those values themselves, have some appreciation of them.

Another way of thinking about the question of perspectives is in terms of the disciplines represented on the team. Educationists, psychologists, sociologists, statisticians, and so on represent fundamentally different approaches to how evaluation should be conducted; indeed, it is a basic tenet of this book that the inquiry paradigm that has typically been used in evaluation, especially by psychologists and statisticians, may be inappropriate. We have also made the point, however, that compromises between, for example, quantitative and qualitative approaches, or rigor and relevance, are not only possible but desirable. Such compromises are best made when a variety of paradigmatic and discipline-oriented perspectives are represented on the evaluation team.

Third, teams make it possible to use multiple strategies. In responding to the concerns and issues raised by stakeholding audiences, an evaluation team may wish to pursue different strategies for different purposes. Some concerns and issues can be responded to on the assumption that subjects will be cooperative; in other cases a somewhat more investigative posture is required. In some cases an overt approach is needed, while in others a more covert study is called for. Some concerns and issues lend themselves to quantitative approaches, while in other cases qualitative methods would be preferred. Some concerns and issues can be attacked with preordinate designs; in other cases emergent or cascading designs are desirable. Each of these possibilities poses a dilemma; for example, an evaluator cannot be both cooperative *and* investigative, overt *and* covert, and so on. But in a team, different strategies can be allocated to different team members.

Fourth, teams provide rigor. In Chapters Four and Five we pointed out that naturalistic as well as scientific inquiries should meet criteria of rigor and suggested various means for achieving this, including split teams, audits, and triangulation. Each of these approaches to rigor can be carried out better by a team than by an individual. The split-team concept obviously requires a team. An audit requires an auditor who was not part of the original inquiry group. In triangulation, data coming from interviews, documents, observations, and other sources can be differentially generated by the team members who are the most skillful interviewers, analysts, observers, and so on.

Fifth, teams allow for both methodological and substantive representation. Scriven (1967) discussed the question of whether evaluation is best conducted by a professional evaluator, that is, one trained in evaluation technology, or by an amateur evaluator, that is, a substantive expert in the field encompassed by the evaluand. Scriven came down on the side of the professional evaluator largely on the grounds that evaluation called for an agent able and willing to make the value judgments required. It is clear, however, that one advantage of a team approach is that both technical and substantive expertise can be represented on it. With an evaluation team the question of professional versus amateur evaluation need not be an either-or proposition.

Sixth, teams provide mutual support. Evaluation can be a lonely game, especially when it is time to make judgments. We will see later that evaluations cannot be conducted in a vacuum; they are always influenced by human and political factors. But it is obviously much more difficult to pressure a team than an individual; when pressures are brought to bear, team members can provide one another with mutual support and understanding. That mutual support also serves to improve the ethical posture of the evaluation—in the context of a team, no single evaluator is likely to stray too far from the common norm. It is also much more difficult for the evaluator to enter into a conspiracy with the client for any illegitimate purpose. Both the psychic and ethical dimensions of an evaluation are thus well served by the presence of a team.

Finally, teams allow members to utilize special skills. Possibly the most important benefit of a team operation is that it makes possible the utilization of the special skills of each team member. No one person can be equally knowledgeable and adept at such diverse skills as interviewing, instrument development, statistical analysis, and developing key informants; indeed, training has become so specialized that emphasizing one subset of skill areas virtually precludes having knowledge about others. But teams can be developed to include persons representing the many different skill areas required; there is really no need for an observer also to be a computer programmer or an instrument developer also to be an interviewer.

Team Skills. Regardless of the composition of the team or the kinds of roles that are defined for it, it is essential that team members have, as a collectivity, certain broad classes of skills, namely, interface skills, data analysis skills, and data collection skills.

Interface skills relate to the various interactions between the team and its audiences and respondents. All audiences must be probed for concerns and issues, and that probing can only be accomplished in face-to-face, often one-on-one, encounters. These personal encounters require a great deal more of the evaluator than that he be merely a competent technician. All the human and political factors that inevitably are involved in an evaluation come to a focus in these interactions. The evaluation team must therefore include one or more persons competent to carry out such interactions with facility.

Data analysis skills include both qualitative and quantitative varieties. Team members with quantitative skills—statistics, computer programming, and so on—are needed not only because the team will inevitably become involved with quantitative approaches (since these may be called for by particular concerns and issues raised by audiences) but because much of the information obtained through qualitative strategies, for example, interviewing or document analysis, can be usefully transformed into quantitative statements. But it is the qualitative analysts who are most likely to complement a naturalistic approach and who are also most likely to be missing from the typical evaluation team. And we refer here not only to those persons who are doing full-time analysis—for example, those poring over documents and records—but also to those persons who are trying to make sense out of interview data, observations, and nonverbal cues as they go along. We may note that these skills are especially important in naturalistic research because of the feature of its emergent design. In most scientific approaches to evaluation, analysts are not really needed until the data have all been collected, but the typical naturalistic evaluation cannot proceed on a day-to-day basis without continuing data analysis.

Data collection skills include those needed to bring together the information required for responsiveness to audience concerns and issues. Again it is important that conventional skills be represented: survey researchers, persons skilled in experimental design and instrumentation, and the like. But naturalistic, responsive evaluation cannot take place without a liberal infusion of qualitative methods: interviewing, observing, analyzing documents and records, using unobtrusive and nonverbal indicators. These are the skills that we chose to emphasize in Chapters Seven and Eight; we did not intend by the omission of other, more traditional skills to slight their utility but simply to focus on those skills that have traditionally not been included in graduate-level training programs for evaluators. We believe that it is this congeries of skills that is the heart of naturalistic methodology; the evaluation team that does not contain persons with these skills is simply not competent, in our view, to operate in a naturalistic, responsive mode.

Team Size. How big should an evaluation team be? Obviously, the size of the team is dependent on the size of the evaluation task; a national evaluation of a new curriculum in fifty sites will clearly take a much larger team than an ad hoc evaluation of a program unit in a single classroom. But the size of the task is probably one of the least important determinants of team size; as we have already noted, an evaluation that could be accomplished by a single professional may be *better* accomplished by a team of moderate size.

There are two other factors that are heavily determinative of the ultimate size that a team can take: balance and budget. By "balance" is meant an appropriate distribution of the roles, skills, and perspectives that different team members bring to bear on the task. If the utility of a team is to be fully realized, there must be enough team members to fill various roles, provide various skills, and reflect the different value perspectives that inhere in the specific situation. Thus the person developing a team needs to do some preliminary investigation to determine what the appropriate mix might be. There is no formula for determining team size before the fact; each situation must be assessed on its own merits.

Budget is determinative of team size because it places a ceiling on the number of persons who can profitably be employed in an evaluation. Many budgets are so tiny (in proportion to the program or developmental budget) as to be absurd; evaluation, particularly of developing or emerging programs or projects, cannot be well accomplished for under 6 to 7 percent of the total budget of the entity being evaluated. Since evaluation tasks, particularly when a naturalistic strategy is being employed, are quite labor-intensive, some 70 to 80 percent of the available budget is expended on personnel; that is, in a properly funded evaluation, somewhere between 4.2 percent (.06 $\times$ 70) and 5.6 percent (.07 $\times$ 80) of the *program or project* budget will be expended on evaluation personnel. The ceiling on the number of team members feasible with a given budget may conveniently be estimated by determining the number of full-time equivalent personnel (FTE) that the given budget will buy, and dividing that FTE by .20, since it is not efficient for a team member to devote less than one day per week (20-percent time) to a team effort. So, for example, a budget estimated to provide for two FTEs might conceivably have as many as ten team members (2 $\div$ .20). That is probably an overestimate, however, since one of the team members—the director—will devote more time to the task than others. Nevertheless, the point is that while it would probably not be feasible to think of more than ten team members in this situation, it certainly would not be foolish to contemplate seven or eight. And seven or eight team members are probably sufficient to provide the balance required in the given situation. If they are not, the evaluation should probably not be undertaken.

Team Problems. While the use of teams for accomplishing evaluation tasks has certain benefits, it also has some deficits. Obviously, whenever two or more persons are required to work together toward some common end, the possibility exists that mutual incompatibilities will hamper productive work. Even such simple differences as the fact that some persons are "day people" while others are "night people" or that some persons prefer to have their work formally structured while others prefer to be allowed to "do their own thing" can produce crippling conflicts.

Moreover, when team members are involved in a naturalistic approach to inquiry, they need to communicate on a daily basis, sometimes under extremely taxing conditions. The possibility of miscommunication is therefore high, and such miscommunication may result in serious errors—for example, an inappropriate next step in an emergent design. As the team becomes larger, the possibility of miscommunication increases exponentially.

Reasonable persons, who are equally competent, may also differ when reaching interpretations or conclusions. Again, the probability that different interpretations will be made increases exponentially as the number of team members increases. But the naturalistic paradigm seems to have some advantage over the scientific in this case in that interpretations must be made almost on a daily basis to facilitate the cascading design; differences in interpretation thus come to light quickly and can be resolved before they become overly wide. In most cases, simple communication about the differences is sufficient to resolve them; however, since the team has presumably been developed in ways that reflect value differences, consensus will not always be possible. Of course, divergences may be reflected in the form of minority reports or alternative recommendations.

There is also a danger that, in an effort to provide balance and to include as many skills, roles, and perspectives as possible, leaders of the evaluation team will produce overspecialization. This is likely to happen in the case of a permanent unit, which services a large program—for example, the evaluation unit of a local school district or a state department of education. Overspecialization exacerbates the problems of miscommunication and differences in interpretation, and it adds another problem—the fact that each specialist will feel under some compulsion to introduce his own specialty into every situation. Kaplan (1964) speaks of the "law of the instrument," that is, give a child a hammer and it will find that everything needs to be pounded (p. 28). An overspecialized team is especially susceptible to this problem.

Furthermore, different team members may be committed to different inquiry paradigms. If, for example, our suggestion that evaluation teams should reflect a variety of perspectives is followed, it is likely that both the scientific and the naturalistic paradigms will be represented. We noted in Chapter Four that many ostensible differences between the paradigms can and should be negotiated. Nevertheless, there are some uncompromisable differences in assumptions between the paradigms. The team must strive for understanding, if not consensus, on these differences.

The final and most serious problem that arises when a team performs a naturalistic, responsive evaluation is that of coordinating team activities so that a design can emerge freely and efficiently and tests of rigor requiring split-team efforts can be carried out. As the several team members, individually or in groups, pursue their separate tasks, ways must be found to maintain communication so that day-to-day decisions about next steps can be made and all team members can be informed of them. In the naturalistic format, subsequent data collection builds on earlier experience, and the experience of all team members needs to be taken into account. If split teams have been formed for the sake of rigor tests, the teams must of course interact at regular and frequent intervals.

There are, then, some problems to be taken into account when forming a team, but they do not cancel out the benefits of using a team. They are matters that must not be overlooked by team leaders; if properly handled, however, they need not be destructive of good evaluation.

Getting Established at the Evaluation Site

The fact that an evaluation has been contracted with a legitimate client is of itself no assurance that the evaluator will be accepted by either the respondents or the audiences of the evaluation. Appropriate relations must be established with each group of subjects (that is, the persons from whom or through whom data will be gathered) and with each audience. We noted earlier Glass' (1975) observation that evaluation studies depend heavily for their success on the cooperation of the persons being evaluated and that unwilling subjects can, by deceit, passive resistance, or noncooperation, subvert any study. It is precisely for these reasons (although we believe that Glass somewhat overstates the case) that it is essential for the evaluator to become properly established at the evaluation site early in the game.

Each group of respondents and each audience are likely to have one or more gatekeepers, that is, persons who have the power to facilitate or to prevent access to the evaluator. Some of these gatekeepers will be in obvious positions of authority—for example, the school principal, the president of the PTA, or the director of the local Chamber of Commerce—but others will be less visible—for example, a veteran teacher, a student to whom other students defer, a local physician who has a history of speaking on behalf of other community members, and so on. Most of these informal gatekeepers will not be evident to the evaluator until he has spent some time on the site; thus, gaining their support is by no means an activity that is carried on simply at the beginning of an evaluation. Rather, the evaluator must make continuing efforts to identify such persons. It is unrealistic to expect, however, that all gatekeepers will lend their support. Strategies for dealing with uncooperative gatekeepers exist; the interested reader may wish to turn to such sources as Dexter (1970), Johnson (1975), and Douglas (1976) for guidance.

Each of the gatekeepers will require an explanation of what the evaluation is about, and each will keep his own counsel about whether the ostensible purposes of the evaluation and the information it is likely to produce are worth the inconvenience that it will cause or the political upheavals it is likely to engender. In providing explanations, the evaluator is well advised to be candid and to inform everyone as fully as possible to avoid later accusations of fraud or bad faith. At the same time the evaluator should avoid an overly technical or overly detailed explanation that is likely to confuse the respondents and to raise their anxiety unnecessarily. In general, explanations should be designed to satisfy questioners, while keeping the evaluator's options open and his status flexible.

Most gatekeepers will expect the evaluator to strike a bargain with them—that is, to enter into a tacit agreement on what the evaluation will involve. They need to know that neither they, as individuals, nor the organization in which they have a stake will be damaged or disrupted by the evaluator's activity. The evaluator may be required to make concessions about the way and the extent to which he will make evaluation data available, to provide assurance that he will protect his sources, to guarantee anonymity, and to terminate the evaluation activity (or some aspect of it) should it become too troublesome to the gatekeeper (or the gatekeeper may indicate a line beyond which he will not permit the evaluator to go without rescinding his support). The evaluator must consider carefully what commitments it is feasible to make; but, having made them, he must do his utmost to live up to them. Anything less would be unethical.

It may seem unrealistic to some readers that gatekeepers should be permitted to exercise much power when the evaluator in fact has sanction from a legitimate client and there is a valid reason for undertaking the evaluation. But it is simply naive to take such an attitude. Gatekeepers are gatekeepers precisely because they have power. And the evaluator should always remember that while he may be granted power by a gatekeeper, that gatekeeper can, by the same token, withdraw that power whenever it suits him to do so.

The power bases inherent in the local situation form one factor with which the evaluator must deal; another is the local language and culture. Each group of respondents and each audience is likely to have its own language, its own jargon, its own idiom, which the evaluator must learn, particularly if he proposes to work in the naturalistic mode. The several groups can be neither adequately understood nor adequately communicated with until reasonable mastery of their languages has been achieved. But *until* it has, the evaluator should avoid using the subjects' or the audiences' vocabulary and speech patterns; trying to pass himself off as "one of the boys" can result in spectacular failure. Further, the evaluator needs to become well acquainted with the cultural mores and value patterns of the groups with which he must deal. The evaluator who sees the world only through white, male, Anglo-Saxon eyes will miss most of what is really there in today's multi-ethnic, multivalued society (see Wax, 1971, for an instructive example).

The evaluator getting established at a site must also deal with the problem of developing and maintaining trust. To some extent trust is determinative of the degree of validity that one can accord to the information given by respondents. Whether or not the respondents are in a cooperative or noncooperative mode, their relationships to the evaluator will be positively influenced if they trust him, respect him, and believe in his integrity.

Trust, unfortunately, is not a state of mind that can be established once and for all. Trust must be established with each individual, over and over again—"Yes, I trusted you yesterday, but what have you done today to convince me that I should continue trusting you?" Johnson (1975) suggests that "the meanings of trust are individually and situationally specific" (p. 141). In reaching this conclusion, he contrasted his own experiences in field research with what he terms the "traditional" theories of developing trust, including: (1) the exchange theory of trust as developed by Wax (1971)—trust is developed by give-and-take between inquirer and subject; (2) the individual morality theory of trust as illustrated by John Dean—the inquirer must display certain "good guy" qualities that suggest his intentions are good; (3) the adoption of a membership morality—the inquirer commits himself to do anything within reasonable limits to protect and maintain the integrity of group membership; and (4) the psychological need theory—the inquirer must persuade the subjects that his inquiry will help satisfy some of their psychological needs.

Johnson concludes from his analysis that "the relationship of trust is a *developmental process* to some extent biographically *specific* in nature. . . . It no longer seems plausible to think in terms of developing trust as a specifiable set of procedural operations. Rather, two or more persons engaged in a common course of social action may develop a sense of trust between them. It is a reality necessarily fluid and changing, always subject to reinterpretation" (p. 94).

In dealing with problems of gatekeeper power, language and cultural differences, and development of trust, many fieldworkers have found it useful to turn to so-called key informants. Key informants are persons who participate in the local situation and are at the same time willing to act as members of the evaluation team, even if only informally. By virtue of their position within the local setting, they can provide the evaluation team with an "inside" view of the norms, attitudes, processes, and other important factors that characterize the local situation. Obviously such an inside perspective will be useful to the evaluator in any situation, but especially in those cases that involve conflict or require an investigative posture. In such cases key informants may be the only reliable source of information.

But of course key informants can also be misleading. In the first place, they have certain motives for becoming informants; these motives may cause them to present distorted or biased information or even misinformation. An informant whose motive is personal revenge or relief of an outraged sense of justice or virtue will not be entirely reliable. Further, it has been suggested that informants are often "marginal men" who might not be as well acquainted with actual group norms, attitudes, and other characteristics as they pretend to be (Scott, 1966). But it is probably equally true that such persons are marginal precisely because they have chosen to be nonconformists—and to be successful in a nonconforming role one must know norms and culture very well indeed. Thus nonconformists rapidly become, if they have not been from the first, astute observers of their own social group and its inner workings. But the evaluator who uses key informants should triangulate the information received from them in a variety of ways and rely on it only after some experience has shown that information received from a particular informant is dependable.

In his zeal to become well established at an evaluation site, the evaluator should not allow himself to become overinvolved with the local situation. (Anthropologists have come to refer to such over-identification as "going native.") First, by building too-close relationships with local persons, the evaluator sets up expectations for friendship, cooperation, and loyalty that cannot be violated later on even though the requirements of the evaluation may call for candor and openness. Second, the evaluator's judgment is severely blunted by overinvolvement; it is difficult to render balanced judgments about persons whom one perceives as "nice guys with families, who are very well intentioned about helping kids," and so on. Third, overinvolvement can lead to what Johnson (1975) has termed an "accommodative morality," the "principle of fitting in" (p. 213). While Johnson suggests that such accommodation is made in order to maintain the integrity of the persons and situations encountered, the need for accommodation must be balanced off against the requirement that the evaluator maintain his own autonomy; the latter cannot simply be surrendered in favor of the former. Fourth, it is possible that overinvolvement may cause the evaluator to shift his allegiance entirely, that is, to forget his responsibility to the sponsor of the evaluation and its several audiences and instead to feel a responsibility only toward the persons being evaluated. Finally, in extreme cases, the overinvolved evaluator stands in danger of being co-opted by local persons for *their* ends; that is, he may, consciously or unconsciously, be led to distort or even falsify the evaluation information. We have made the case in earlier chapters that the evaluator cannot maintain scientific objectivity; to imagine that one can do so is to pursue an unattainable Holy Grail. But the evaluator does have a responsibility to render as balanced a judgment as possible; the discharge of that responsibility can be aborted by overidentification with local persons and situations.

A final problem in getting established involves dealing with uncooperative respondents. Noncooperation is most likely to emerge when the evaluator is a third-party evaluator, commissioned by an outside client who has a legitimate interest or stake in the entity being evaluated. But in *all* evaluations there are factors that militate against openness and candor with the evaluator: everyone has made mistakes, everyone wants to put his best foot forward, and everyone has some facts that he would rather not share with an evaluator. Thus, the evaluator will from time to time find it necessary to adopt an investigative posture (see Guba, forthcoming) and to assume that information will not be volunteered or cheerfully made available by cooperative informants. Douglas (1976) suggests that under such circumstances, "rather than seeking entrée, we infiltrate the setting" (p. 167). Douglas provides some tactics for infiltration, as does Johnson (1975), who suggests that evaluators obtain information from an ally within the organization that can be used to devise a strategy for gaining admission; use a progressive strategy—ask for little things first and move on to the more important later; use persons lower in the hierarchy as allies in gaining approval from top levels; negotiate with each level or group in terms of its specific concerns and interests; and soften the focus of the inquiry so as to make it more acceptable (pp. 59-66).

Some of these tactics are ethically questionable and must be used with caution. If the ultimate challenge to the evaluator is to judge, he must, like Caesar's wife, be above suspicion.

Taking Account of Human and Political Factors

Until recently evaluation has been viewed primarily as a technical process very akin to research—indeed, the term *evaluation research* is commonly used. The fact that evaluation always involves human beings situated in a sociopolitical context has been systematically overlooked or, if recognized, deliberately excluded as beyond the pale of "objectivity." Yet human and political factors play crucial roles in every evaluation, and to ignore them or to act as if they did not exist is simply naive.

The Politics of Evaluation. One of the more compelling descriptions of how politics can affect evaluation is given by Brickell (1974) in a paper based upon his personal experience in doing evaluations. In preparing to write the paper, Brickell had gone to his shelf of completed evaluation reports in an effort to find an example of how politics had affected evaluation. As it happened, the very first report that fell to hand provided an excellent example, and so did the second, the third, the fourth, and so on. Indeed, every evaluation that he had ever conducted furnished illustrations, including these:

• An evaluation of the use of paraprofessionals, in which the ostensible purpose of using teacher aides to improve student learning had to give way to the political purpose of providing useful linkages between school and community and the subsidiary purpose of providing jobs for some community members. Brickell was warned that whatever his evaluation showed, his findings could not lead to the elimination of teacher aides, even if they were proved to be ineffective in improving student learning, because the political objectives were too important to school officials.

• An evaluation of a graduate teacher training program in which the client eventually took over data analysis and reporting himself to be sure that the program was portrayed in the most favorable possible light. The evaluator felt himself powerless to resist this move by the client.

• An evaluation in which a program was transferred from one funding agency to another. The second agency was anxious to show that the program was ineffective in order to justify closing it out and diverting the funds to other program efforts more clearly identifiable with the second agency. The evaluators found their role shifting from that of program critic to program advocate, using, as Brickell so very well put it, the "instinctive ability of every evaluator to bite the hand that feeds you while seeming only to be licking it" (1974, p. 5).

• An evaluation in which the client demanded that every negative finding be redrafted, reinforcing this demand with a threat not to renew the evaluation contract unless the evaluator complied.

• An evaluation in which the evaluated project was mounted in response to a request for proposals (RFP) that the evaluators themselves had written under earlier contract with the funding agency. After the contract had been awarded, the funder commissioned the authors of the request to become the project evaluators. That alone would have produced a conflict of interest, but this conflict was compounded by the fact that the evaluators had known from the beginning that the conditions and constraints written into the RFP could not possibly be met; they had constructed the RFP language to be responsive to the funder's biases. Thus the evaluators were in the position of evaluating a project that they knew could not be successfully carried out, while having to pretend all along that it could.

• An evaluation of a statewide system of computer-based information agencies in which all the important questions that anyone might wish to ask were finessed away by an advisory committee. The evaluative report thus touched only on peripheral, relatively meaningless issues.

After several facetious suggestions to the evaluator on means for escaping political influence ("be independently wealthy"), Brickell (1974, pp. 17-18) proposed the following more practical rules for dealing with a political context:

- Try to understand how the client thinks. Find out what he has to gain or lose from the evaluation.
- Reassure the client at the outset that you can interpret the findings so as to give helpful suggestions for program improvement, no matter what the findings of the study are.
- Find out what the powerful decision makers—the client and those who surround him—will actually use as criteria for judging the success of the project. You may, if you wish, also gather data on the official objectives of the project, or even on objectives that happen to interest you, but the important thing is to gather evidence addressed to the decision criteria.
- Try to get a supervisory mechanism set up for the evaluation contract that contains a cross section of all the powerful decision makers. Try to get it designed so that the members have to resolve the conflicts among themselves before giving you marching orders for the study or deciding whether to accept your final report.
- Write the report carefully, especially when describing shortcomings or placing blame, and do mention any extenuating circumstances. Review the final draft report before submitting it to the client for his review, making sure you can defend any claim you make.

If Brickell's paper represents an effort to describe the political climate of evaluation at a practical level Weiss (1973) takes on the question at a more conceptual level. She describes three reasons why political factors "intrude" upon evaluations.*

*The use of the term *intrude* betrays Weiss's predisposition, shared by many evaluators, to regard political factors as intrusions that hamper or constrain the evaluator in the pursuit of his "real" purpose rather than as contextual elements that are simply always there and that need to be taken into account.

First, the policies and programs with which evaluation deals are themselves the creatures of political decisions. They emerge from the rough-and-tumble of political bargaining, and attached to them are the reputations of legislative sponsors, the careers of administrators, the jobs of program staff, and the expectations of clients. The programs exist in a milieu concerned not only with program rationality but also with questions of long-term support. Hence, political fallout shapes the very definition of the evaluation study, and while the study is under way, political pressures may be at work to alter or to undermine it.

Second, because evaluation is undertaken in order to feed into decision making, its reports enter into the political arena, where evaluative evidence of program outcomes has to compete for attention with other factors that carry weight in the political process. The decision makers who may be affected by the evaluation are members of a policy-making system that has its own values and rules. Weiss (1973) notes: "Their decisions are rooted in all the complexities of the democratic decision-making process: the allocation of power and authority, the development of coalitions, and the trade-offs with interest groups, professional guilds, and salient publics" (p. 40). Evaluation is powerful because, among other things, it can clarify what the political trade-offs involve. Of course, Weiss suggests, evaluation is most likely to affect decisions when the evaluator accepts the values, assumptions, and objectives of the decision maker.

Third, evaluation itself has a political stance. By its very nature, it makes implicit political statements about such issues as the problematic nature of some programs and the unchallengeability of others, the legitimacy of program goals and program strategies, the utility of strategies of incremental reform, and even the appropriate role of the social scientist in policy and program formulation. An implicit political statement is involved in the decision to evaluate certain programs while passing over others. Finally, evaluations may themselves have political overtones: they are often commissioned from the outside, with findings being reported to outsiders, and the values of the evaluators, most often reformist and liberal, may clash with those of the subjects.

From the analyses by Brickell and Weiss, it seems safe to conclude that evaluation has strong political overtones and that evaluation is itself a source of political power. Thus, it is often asserted that information is power, and if a product of evaluation is information, the remainder of the equation is easily completed. There are many ways in which the political forces engendered can be brought to bear on evaluation. They can be brought to bear on the definition of evaluation employed (for example, power is more likely to be threatened when the evaluator uses a decision-oriented definition of evaluation); on questions of initial admission into evaluation (mediated by such factors as how the problem or question is posed and who is the client); on the criteria that are or are not to be used; on the variables (characteristics, problems, issues, concerns) that are or are not selected for study; on the design that is to be used; on the techniques of data collection that are permitted; on the sources of data that may or may not be tapped or that will be made accessible; and on the reports that are issued (including the uses that may be made of them).

Political factors are so pervasive in shaping evaluations that we can offer the following proposition:

> *Evaluation is always disruptive of the*
> *prevailing political balance.*

We feel it is incumbent on the evaluator, in every instance, to make an effort to determine the extent of political imbalance that will be induced by any proposed evaluation and to assess, as far as possible, whether the information likely to be derived from the evaluation is sufficiently weighty to warrant the resulting political upset. Unless the evaluator can answer yes to that question, he should not undertake the evaluation. In making this assessment, moreover, the evaluator should keep in mind that the force of the political imbalance that the evaluation will produce is likely to be focused on the evaluation itself; individuals whose power is enhanced by the findings will of course seek to support and defend those findings, but individuals whose power is reduced by the findings will attack and try to undermine the evaluation at every opportunity. The evaluator must be prepared to take the heat of such political infighting, or, in Harry Truman's immortal words, get out of the kitchen if he can't take the heat.

Human Factors in Evaluation. Glass (1975) suggests that there is a paradox about evaluation; he notes first that "the excellent state of affairs seems to emerge most surely when those on whom it depends feel that they are not being judged and evaluated, feel that their failures and shortcomings are understood and accepted, feel that their worth—as teachers, as administrators, as professionals—is unconditional, that is, not contingent on how they score on anyone else's scale of merit" (p. 9). But, Glass goes on to say, "it appears that people move truer and more certainly toward excellence to the extent that they clarify their purposes, measure the impact of their action, judge it, and move on—in a few words, evaluate their progress" (p. 9).

Most of us tend to believe both statements. Surely therapists and counselors are committed to the first, while personnel executives in organizations are committed to the second. Can both these assertions be right? Are they not inherently in conflict?

Evaluators, Glass charges, have tended to overlook this essential paradox and have overstressed the value of evaluation. In defense of their positions, Glass avers, evaluators make several "straw man" arguments. They speak, for example, of the "sanctity of science," apparently in the belief that evaluation and science are linked together and are justified by the same arguments. But, Glass responds, "if we choose to evaluate, it must be because we believe that in each instance the potential good outweighs the harm, not because evaluation is scientific and science is categorically worthwhile" (p. 11).

At other times, evaluators speak of the "public's right to know." But, Glass suggests, all rights are qualified; the question in each particular case must be whether the public's right to know exceeds other rights, for example, the individual subject's right to privacy. Evaluators also stress the "goodness of feedback." But data are not always an unmitigated good, Glass feels, and they frequently do damage. "Some feedback is bad; some feedback hurts more than it helps" (p. 11).

Glass discusses three possible reactions to this paradox. The first is to fail to take the paradox seriously, to treat it as a mere technical problem. But that is overly simplistic. A second reaction is to apply a "humanistic solution" to it: to use T-groups, organizational development, or some other form of "gentle self-evaluation." But Glass suggests that while this form of evaluation may not threaten people, it is not good evaluation either. "Clearly the paradox is not resolved by performing bad evaluations. Better to make no pretense at evaluation whatsoever than to substitute such a sham for the genuine article" (p. 12). Finally, Glass says, one may attempt to explain the paradox away logically. One might argue that it is only in a personal sense that a person does not benefit when evaluated and only in a social sense that a person cannot improve unless evaluated. But this argument, Glass believes, is valid only if the distinction between personal and social arenas is clear. Often this distinction is not clear, and it is in precisely these borderline areas that most evaluation occurs.

Glass's analysis leads us to offer a second proposition:

Evaluation is always dysfunctional to human performance.

At first the evaluator may be inclined to dismiss this proposition on such grounds as the immaturity of the person displaying the dysfunctional reaction or his lack of understanding of the "real" utility and meaning of evaluation. "If our subjects—or clients, or audiences, or whatever—were only more mature," we are wont to say, "or understood better the real utility of evaluation *for them,* these dysfunctional reactions would not occur." But these reactions should not surprise us, and they have little if anything to do with lack of maturity or understanding. All of us who are over forty are sufficiently mature to appreciate the importance of an annual physical examination. But which of us does not approach that ordeal with fear and trembling? For weeks before and for days afterward (until all the test results are finally in) we are beset by anxiety. In the same way, anxiety is a normal reaction to evaluation.

Again we stress the need for a decision on the part of the evaluator. Will the information that is likely to result from the evaluation provide a more than adequate trade-off for the dysfunctionality that it will produce? If the evaluator cannot answer yes to that question, we urge that the evaluation not be done.

Political and human factors are inevitably present in every evaluation situation and must be dealt with. They cannot be regarded as mere peripheral annoyances that distract the evaluator from his "real" task. The evaluator ought to be able to satisfy himself, at the beginning of each evaluation, that the information likely to result from the evaluation will be worth it in terms of the political imbalance and the human dysfunctionality that it will certainly induce. The evaluator who moves ahead without regard to these issues is not only incompetent but unethical as well.

Chapter 10

Identifying Key
Issues and Concerns

In this chapter we describe the second stage in conducting a naturalistic responsive evaluation: identifying the concerns and issues on the minds of stakeholding audiences, as well as the value frameworks within which those concerns and issues operate. We discuss the tasks of identifying audiences, selecting respondents to serve as information sources, collecting and analyzing information to yield the concerns and issues, inferring value frameworks, and testing the data for rigor.

Key Definitions

Naturalistic responsive evaluation uses as its organizer the concerns and issues raised by stakeholding audiences. It is useful at this point to recall the definitions of the key terms in this statement:

A stakeholding audience is a group of persons having some common characteristics (for example, administrators, teachers, parents, students, sponsors, clients, and the like) that has some stake in the performance (or outcome or impact) of the evaluand, that is, is somehow involved in or affected by the entity being evaluated. By virtue of holding a stake, an audience has a right to be consulted about its concerns and issues, to have those concerns and issues honored by the evaluator as he goes about his tasks, and to receive reports (or communication or feedback) from the evaluator that are responsive to those concerns and issues. The evaluator, in his turn, has the right to prioritize the audiences in terms of the level of stake each holds, and to respond to them in that priority order to the extent that his resources permit.

A *concern* is any matter of interest to one or more parties about which they feel threatened, that they think will lead to an undesirable consequence, or that they are anxious to substantiate (a claim requiring empirical verification). The importance of concerns may often be assessed by reference to the number of persons that express them, but a concern expressed by even one individual may, because of that individual's special perspective or degree of insight, be vital. The task of the evaluator is to develop information that confirms or disconfirms the concern or that illuminates or illustrates it in some way.

An *issue* is any statement, proposition, or focus that allows for different, often conflicting, points of view; any proposition about which reasonable persons may disagree; any point of contention. Whereas concerns may be advanced by single individuals, issues find expression only in the opinions of two or more persons. The task of the evaluator is to develop information that will aid in understanding two or more sides of an issue and perhaps help to resolve or reduce the conflict that will almost surely attend the different value positions represented by the sides of the issue.

Three additional elements will be defined here because of their relevance to identification of concerns and issues: descriptors, contextual factors, and values:

A *descriptor* is a statement of perception by one or more audience members about some element salient to the entity being evaluated. Often concerns and issues are rooted in faulty perceptions, and it is important to know how an individual perceives a situation in order to be able to interpret the concerns and issues that he may identify. For example, a parent's concern that a new math program does not teach children to balance a checkbook may be based on her perception that the instruction does not stress practical applications; it may be crucial to have the parent describe what she thinks is occurring in the classroom. Descriptors that appear to be important to the understanding of emerging concerns and issues can be checked by the evaluator for factual accuracy; those that are found to be inaccurate can be immediately reported back to the audiences. Thus, some concerns and issues will be eliminated from further consideration, while those that are found to be factually accurate form the basis for continuing investigation.

A *contextual factor* is any force or constraint that compels or inhibits some action and that is beyond the power of the persons dealing with the evaluand to control. Such factors may be concerns and issues that could be dealt with at some other level or in some other context but that are outside the scope of the context in which the evaluand is found. For example, a new curriculum may fail because teachers are not adequately trained to teach it, but the local school system may not have the power to require retraining because teacher competencies are set by the state certification authority, not by the local district. This situation might, of course, cause the emergence of a concern among the audiences of the certification authority and might result, if that authority were to be evaluated, in changes in certification guidelines. Within the scope of the curriculum evaluation, however, there is little that can be done.

A *value* is any principle or standard that leads to judgments of either relative or absolute utility, goodness, or importance or that guides choices among alternatives. Values range from the very intangible (for example, beauty, honesty, piety) to the very tangible (for example, economy, availability, repairability). Values may be held by individuals in quite idiosyncratic ways, but they are most often formed into systems of related values that characterize given social or cultural groups; it is in this sense that we can speak of "American" values, "Amish" values, "Southern" values, "teacher" values, and the like. Values are the fundamental bases for evaluative judgments. The naturalistic, responsive evaluator is careful to discern the nature of the values that exist in every context in which he works, to determine whether those values are consensual or pluralistic, and to take account of the existing values when he makes judgments or recommendations. It might be argued that one of the evaluator's salient responsibilities is to clarify the value structure surrounding each evaluation that he undertakes, making that structure apparent to each of the stakeholding audiences.

Identifying Stakeholders

The relevant audiences whose concerns and issues are to be the focus of the evaluation have been defined as those persons and groups that have some stake in the performance, outcome, or impact of the evaluand. A stake, of course, is a share or interest in an enterprise. Often the stake is fiscal in nature, but it can encompass a host of other possibilities, including reputation, career aspirations, political influence, time, energy, efficiency, and so on. The concept of *stake* is a very broad one, so that one can expect the range of relevant audiences also to be very broad. More peripheral audiences will be easy to overlook, as will audiences that, for one reason or another, elect to maintain low visibility (for example, minority audiences will sometimes wish to keep a low profile for fear that active or aggressive involvement will result in being even further disadvantaged).

The evaluator has a duty to identify all audiences, to do his best to determine what their concerns and issues are, and to honor and respond to those concerns and issues. Failure to do so may cause significant evaluation questions to be overlooked or to be diminished in importance. Justice and fairness require that everyone with a stake also have a voice. Evaluations always result in a restructuring of political power, so that the political posture of every audience needs to be taken into account. The mere act of investigation gives a special status both to the things that the evaluator chooses to investigate and to those that he chooses *not* to investigate. The act of evaluation provides a political legitimation difficult to achieve in other ways. Finally, evaluations are not usually soon repeated; the results of the initial evaluation are likely to dominate planning, resource allocation, and political balance for a long time to come.

What can an evaluator do to be certain that he has identified all the stakeholding audiences? There is no definitive answer to that question. Much depends on the skill of the evaluator and on his experience in similar situations. Nevertheless, there are some questions that an evaluator can systematically put to himself to facilitate this identification process. The first of these questions relates to the various agents involved in producing and using the evaluand.

1. Who developed (conceptualized, invented, planned, designed, built, produced) the evaluand? The developer may range from a lone teacher who devised certain methods for handling discipline problems in her class to a team that designed a master curriculum for possible national adoption.

2. Who provided the funds and other resources for the development? The funder may be a federal or state agency, a foundation, an ad hoc group (for example, the PTA of a school or a local chapter of Alcoholics Anonymous), or a local operating agency such as a school district, health services agency, or law enforcement agency.

3. Who identified the local need to which the evaluand is purportedly a response? In some cases the agent may have been the evaluator himself (from an earlier evaluation). The need may have been identified either through a formal process (an actual needs assessment or context evaluation) or through an informal process (a determination made by a teacher, administrator, or parent group on the basis of experience or intuition).

4. Who decided to apply the evaluand to the local need? The decision maker may be an individual teacher, a principal or superintendent, a school board, a judge (as in busing controversies), and so on.

5. Who provided the funds for the local application? Again, funds may be provided by a federal, state, or foundation program, an ad hoc group, or, most likely, a local operating agency.

6. Who provided the facilities, supplies, and materials that may be needed? Probably the groups identified in response to the preceding question will also have provided these items, but other groups may be involved, for example, a local church or a service club.

7. Who contracted for the evaluation? Who is the specific client with whom the evaluator negotiated? Most often the client

is a representative either of the local operating agency in which the evaluand is being used or of one of the funders referred to in questions 2 and 5 above.

Another set of questions refers to purported benefits:

1. Who are the presumed direct beneficiaries of the evaluand (for example, students whose learning will be improved because of a new curriculum or drug addicts who will be assisted to overcome their habit)?

2. Who are the indirect beneficiaries of the evaluand (for example, parents, children, spouses, employers or potential employers, or law enforcement officers) whose relationship with the direct beneficiaries is mediated, eased, or otherwise influenced by the purported benefits?

3. What groups might, as a result of the evaluation, be persuaded to adopt or adapt the evaluand in their own settings (for example, potential adopters in other school districts)?

A final set of questions relates to purported decrements:

1. What groups are systematically excluded from the benefits (for example, "normal" students excluded from programs designed for "the gifted," or normally advantaged youngsters excluded from programs designed for the disadvantaged)?

2. What groups perceive that there are negative side effects for them (for example, parents of children who live in the attendance district of a "good" school but who are bused to a "poor" school so that disadvantaged youngsters from the latter school may be bused to the former)?

3. Who suffers political disadvantage as a result of the use of the evaluand? Examples here would be professional educators who lose power when they are required, as a condition of funding, to establish "equity" groups that will have a major influence on decision processes, or suburban school administrators who lose power when they are forced to accept, by court order, children bused from contiguous metropolitan school districts.

4. Who suffers from lost opportunities, that is, opportunities that cannot be exploited because the resources needed to do so are being allocated to support the evaluand (for example, the allocation of resources to mount a tutorial program for the disadvantaged may preclude the simultaneous mounting of a school band program)?

Persons or groups identified in answering any of the above questions should automatically be included as audiences (although their concerns and issues need not be given equal weight). But it is possible that other audiences should also be involved, for example, labor unions in the case of a vocational-technical school or university admissions officers in the case of a college preparatory institution. The evaluator's knowledge of the particular situation should be exploited fully in an effort to identify these other audiences. But the evaluator may also wish to use a "ripple" technique, whereby he asks informants in already-identified audiences about other, possibly overlooked audiences. One way to accomplish this purpose is to ask informants questions like: "What groups exist that you know about that hold different opinions from your own group?" "What other groups do you know about that would benefit or lose as a result of the use of this evaluand?" "What groups do you know whose members have strong feelings, pro or con, about the entity being evaluated?" "If I wanted to get a real 'insider's' view of what's going on, to whom should I turn?" Any audiences so identified should be considered for possible inclusion, although not automatically since respondents may be misinformed or may wish for their own reasons to lead the evaluator astray.

Making Contact with Informants

The identification of an audience is the first step in eliciting from its members their concerns and issues. Particular members of that audience must be identified and solicited as informants—persons able and willing to provide information of interest to the evaluator.

Every audience will have one or more gatekeepers, as that term was used in Chapter Nine. Duly constituted groups, for example, the school district administration, the PTA, or the funding agency, are likely to have both formal gatekeepers, that is, persons who by virtue of their positions have the authority to approve or deny admission to the evaluator, and informal gatekeepers, that is, persons who can, through their influence, also approve or deny admission. The power to open or close an audience to an evaluator thus exists in persons who have the authority or the influence to do so or both. The evaluator cannot ignore either of these kinds of gatekeepers, since both can effectively bar him from fruitful involvement with audience members. Informal groups, for example, ad hoc groups of teachers, students, parents, potential adopters, and the like, will in all probability have only informal gatekeepers, but these persons may have just as much power as their formal counterparts.

The evaluator needs to deal with all gatekeepers along the lines suggested in Chapter Nine. It is to the gatekeepers that he will have to explain why he wants admission and what information he plans to seek; it is to them that he will have to make guarantees of anonymity, to strike bargains about what the *quid pro quo* will be, and so on. Only then will he be free to make direct contact with informants.

The selection of informants is a fairly complicated matter. The naturalistic evaluator is rarely interested in drawing some kind of random or representative sample of audience members; his concern is to optimize the information return he will receive from his investment of time, energy, money. His aim is to draw a purposive or theoretical sample from which he can optimize learning (Glaser and Strauss, 1967). How can such a sample be obtained?

It probably does not matter just where one starts. Indeed, since the evaluator's initial contact must, for political reasons, be with the gatekeeper, he may as well begin by soliciting nominations of useful respondents from that person. Of course, he must keep in mind that the gatekeeper is likely to nominate informants who will reflect his own point of view. This is not a problem, however, since the evaluator will want that point of view to be included anyway. What is important is that the evaluator solicit from each successive respondent nominations for other interviewees who represent perspectives as different as possible from that just given. The evaluator continues to seek out such nominees until only incremental gains in information are achieved from additional subjects. The criteria suggested in Chapter Five for determining when to stop collecting information—that is, exhaustion of sources, saturation, emergence of regularities, and overextension—are probably equally appropriate here.

Some of the informants that will be identified by this process may turn out to be useful "key informants," that is, persons who, in addition to being "insiders," are also willing to play roles on the evaluation team and to explain the norms, attitudes, processes, and other aspects of the local situation in depth and with candor. The evaluator should remain on the alert for such persons, remembering, however, that they may have reasons for playing such a role that will be detrimental to the purpose of the evaluation.

Eliciting Concerns and Issues

The task of identifying concerns and issues may be conceptualized as consisting of a number of stages or phases, including initial interviews, initial data analysis, member checks, dealing with misinformation, reiteration of interviews, and use of grounded questionnaires. We shall discuss each of these phases or stages, but the reader should not assume that we are setting down an inflexible chronological sequence. The phases may go on concurrently, and there may be recycling at other times than those formally designated. The analysis that follows should therefore be thought of as conceptual rather than as operational.

Initial Interviews. The evaluator will first interview each of the informants identified according to the procedure indicated in the preceding section. Of course most of the interview respondents cannot be designated in advance, since they will emerge only as the interviewing process unfolds. Thus one respondent may be identified only because he has been named by another respondent, and so on.

The interview is an indispensable tool for identifying concerns and issues. While other sources, for example, documents or records, will undoubtedly be useful for this purpose, it is only through the interview that the evaluator can fully explore an audience's perspective and the reasons for it.

Following the principles of interviewing as outlined in Chapter Seven (see also Dexter, 1970), the evaluator will move through several steps. Prior to the actual interview, the evaluator will contact each respondent and arrange for a time and place. In this initial contact the evaluator will need to explain to the respondent the reasons why he, the evaluator, wishes to interview the respondent, how the respondent came to be chosen as part of the interview sample, what guarantees of anonymity will govern the interview, and what will be done with the information that the interview will yield. The evaluator will probably provide the same rationale, although perhaps in truncated form, that he provided to the gatekeeper; explain to the respondent the particular importance of the information he can provide; indicate that the identity of the informant will be protected (if that is the case, or if not, what degree of public exposure the respondent may suffer as a result of granting the interview); and describe how the information obtained will be collated with or balanced off against that obtained from other informants. It is probably not necessary for the evaluator to indicate specifically that the interview is expected to contribute to a delineation of concerns and issues; that is a level of detail that it is probably not important for the respondent to comprehend, and its expression may generate too high a degree of anxiety and uncooperativeness.

In the actual interview, the evaluator will first try to make the respondent as comfortable as possible and put him in a cooperative frame of mind. Probably the best way to accomplish this is to ask the respondent to talk about himself, not necessarily in the context of the other information that the interview is expected to elicit. For example, the evaluator may ask, "How do you happen to be filling the role of _____ ?" or "Tell me what a typical day is like for you," or some other question that will permit the respondent to share with the interviewer information about himself in which he can take some pride or about which he can feel positive. This step gets the respondent into the set of speaking confidently and openly to the interviewer.

When some reasonable degree of comfort and rapport has been established, the evaluator will want to help the respondent order his mind with respect to the evaluand—the new curriculum, the treatment program for alcoholism, or whatever. The evaluator should not expect the respondent to be able to deal with this topic without first warming up to it. A productive approach is to ask the respondent to describe the evaluand, entity being evaluated, its context of use, and the actual conditions and operations involved in its application—all viewed, of course, from the respondent's perspective. The respondent will thereby begin to focus on the evaluand and recall details about it that might have been difficult to dredge up in response to specific questions. This description also serves the purpose of obtaining the respondent's perceptions of what is actually going on—perceptions that can later be tested against other sources for accuracy. These perceptual statements are also important in assisting the evaluator to identify the descriptors that he will subsequently use to develop adequate descriptions of the evaluand as seen by various audiences.

When the respondent has had a reasonable amount of time to structure his mind with respect to the evaluated entity, the evaluator should begin to question him about the concerns and issues that he perceives. The questioning should begin in a very open-ended way, focused on such general questions as: "Do you see any problems with this new program?" "What good is likely to come of it?" "What bad effect might it have?" "Do you agree with the claims made for it?" As the evaluator's knowledge of the situation grows, he may wish to add specific questions based upon what he has learned from other informants; these questions should be reserved for a time in the interview when the respondent has already volunteered whatever he can and will talk about and when he can be questioned on such specifics without biasing the voluntary report he gives.

As the interview draws to a close, the evaluator will wish to summarize what the respondent has told him and to ask the respondent for verification: "It seems to me that you have asserted these problems [lists them]. Is that in fact what you intended to tell me?" "Have I misunderstood you in any way?" "Are there other things that you would like to add?"

At the end of the interview, the evaluator should seek the respondent's recommendations for other audiences and other respondents to whom he might profitably talk: "To whom else should I speak to get some further information on these problems?" "Are there any other groups or individuals you can think of who would take a very different view than you have about what we have talked about?" "Are there persons who have some extended knowledge of these matters, either because of their special expertise, their particular role or status within the organization, or the people they come in contact with?" These questions will inevitably lead the evaluator to other productive sources, which should be tapped unless redundancy, emergence of regularities, exhaustion of sources, or overextension are encountered.

Initial Data Analysis. When the evaluator has interviewed

informants from each of the identified audiences and has determined that the utility of further data collection has diminished to marginal levels, he will want to turn to an analysis designed to produce lists of concerns and issues and to assess values. In fact, the evaluator will have begun this process with the very first interview and will have used the results of early responses to shape (in the spirit of emergent design) later data collection efforts. Thus, the data analysis task will have been largely completed at the same time that the "stop" decision is made, and only final refinements and embellishments will be needed.

The analysis will be carried out using the principles of content analysis described in Chapter Eight.

Unitizing the interviews (and other source materials). The evaluator first reads the available documents and interview protocols line by line. Any item of information that can possibly be construed as a descriptor, a concern, or an issue should be abstracted onto a separate three-by-five-inch card. The card should be cross-referenced to the interview or document so that the context of the item can later be reassessed should that prove useful or necessary. It will also be of interest later to observe whether certain classes of information tend to come from similar or different informants (for example, all teachers, or some teachers, some parents, some administrators, and so on). A preliminary categorization of "descriptor," "concern," or "issue" should be recorded on each card. No attempt should be made at this point to eliminate items; inclusiveness rather than exclusiveness should be sought. It is, after all, possible to eliminate items at any step in the process, but it is virtually impossible (or at least very difficult) to recapture an item after it has been dropped.

Categorizing—sorting the cards into look-alike piles. After all documents and field notes have been abstracted, the evaluator sorts the cards into look-alike piles. The first card automatically forms a category; the second card is then assessed to determine whether it is similar to or different from the first. If it is similar, it is placed onto the same pile, but if it is different, a new pile is formed. The process is repeated until all cards have been exhausted. In this initial sorting process some cards will appear not to fit into any of the existing piles, but at the same time will not have the "feel" of a new category. Such items should be placed into a provisional "miscellaneous" category but should *not* be discarded; that decision should be deferred to a later point in the process.

Characterizing (titling) the piles. The evaluator then reviews the piles he has created from several perspectives. First, he gives a title or name to each pile. This title or name should catch the "essence" of the pile—that feature or characteristic that intuitively led the evaluator to create such a pile in the first place. Second, the evaluator assesses the set of categories for relationships—he may find, for example, that several of the categories are quite similar and should be combined or, conversely, that some categories should be broken into separate elements. Or it may be that some categories should be subsumed under more generic ones. Finally, the evaluator assesses the items that were placed into the miscellaneous pile to ascertain whether they are captured by any of the refined headings, or whether some now appear to belong in a new category suggested by the derived set (a category that appears to be necessary to complete the logic of the derived set but that did not emerge in the initial analysis). Items that continue to be intractable should remain in the miscellaneous pile.

Assessing the category set. The evaluator next assesses the provisional set of categories that has emerged in terms of the criteria set forth in Chapter Five. The categories should be internally homogeneous, that is, should be unidimensional and as "look-alike" as possible, and externally heterogeneous, that is, as different as possible from category to category. If the evaluator experiences difficulty in assigning a large number of items to categories, the set probably fails on the criterion of heterogeneity. When a set appears to have internally homogeneous and externally heterogeneous categories, it satisfies the criterion of plausibility or integrability as discussed in Chapter Five. But the set should also be inclusive, that is, it should account for virtually all the information collected (the operational indicator of inclusiveness is a small or nonexistent miscellaneous category) and should be reproducible in the sense that a qualified auditor can verify both that the categories are logically related to the original documents or interviews and that the data items on the three-by-five-inch cards have been properly assigned to categories. The auditor should not have taken part in the original data collection and analysis and should preferably not be a member of the evaluation team.

Making preliminary adjustments. The evaluator can now adjust and refine his category set, noting particularly categories that seem to be called for by the logic of the set but that have not yet emerged and categories that appear to be incomplete. Further data collection should be made in subsequent iterations for such predicted or incomplete categories.

Member Checks. As noted in Chapter Five, the major criterion for a set of categories is its credibility to the audiences involved. When the preliminary set of categories has been developed by the processes described above, the evaluator should test it against the perceptions of audience members; that is, he should run "member checks."

It is probably most practical to carry out the check in two steps. First, the evaluator should draw a sample from among those informants included in the initial interviews—a sample selected in such a way that each of the stakeholding audiences is represented by several members (preferably members with different points of view). Since the data were derived through interviews with these persons, it is reasonable that the evaluator should check his interpretations with some of these same individuals. They should also be asked to point out any errors of fact that the evaluator may have made. As this sample of original respondents is reinterviewed, each should be asked to nominate a person who, in his opinion, feels the same as he does about the evaluand; by this process a roughly parallel sample of persons will be drawn who can evaluate the initial analysis from a pristine point of view. This new group should also be asked to comment on the factual accuracy and the credibility of interpretations made by the evaluator.

The "member-check" sample can serve a useful purpose in addition to that of commenting on data already collected: it can help the evaluator to confirm the existence of categories implied by the original data set but that had not yet emerged and to flesh out those incomplete categories of information already identified. The techniques of extending, bridging, and surfacing described in Chapter Five are useful here.

Dealing with Misinformation. The evaluator must be aware that his information, even if verified through member checks, may nevertheless be erroneous. Error may arise for the simple reason that people do make mistakes and, having made them, are incapable of detecting them in a later review (recall how often one makes the same addition error over and over in a fruitless effort to balance a checkbook). But there are other, more serious reasons, why misinformation is given and verified.

First, it should be noted that a particular respondent's knowledge and insight will not be inexhaustible. There are many things that a subject *cannot* tell the evaluator either because he does not know or because he lacks the necessary insight. Second, the subject's willingness to impart information to the evaluator will also vary, depending on the subject's perception of threat or vulnerability.

Douglas (1976) makes the point that there are two approaches to field studies. In the first, which he terms the cooperative mode, it is assumed that disorganization and conflict are deviant, extraordinary phenomena, that values are shared by all members of a group or society, and that cooperation is society's natural state (p. 43). But, Douglas asserts, these assumptions have had unfortunate consequences for field research, and he urges adoption of what he calls the conflict or investigative mode: "The investigative paradigm is based on the assumption that profound conflicts of interests, values, feelings, and actions pervade social life. It is taken for granted that many of the people one deals with, perhaps all people to some extent, have good reasons to hide from others what they are doing and even lie to them. Instead of trusting people and expecting trust in return, one suspects others and expects others to suspect him. Conflict is the reality of life; suspicion is the guiding principle" (p. 55).

While this statement appears a bit strong, it nevertheless has enormous implications for the evaluator. It is probably the rare case in which a subject intentionally deceives the evaluator, but there can be little doubt that the subject and the evaluator are often in a conflict of interest situation (Mirvis and Seashore, 1979). Many evaluations result in decisions to fund or not to fund a project; the reputations of program designers and implementors are on the line; jobs may be at stake. Under those conditions it is not surprising that subjects should wish to put a best foot forward, to hide even honest mistakes or to prevent the evaluator from reaching negative judgments.

Misinformation can be given intentionally or unintentionally and may relate to a variety of targets. It is analytically useful to think of those targets as falling into three categories: the self, others, and the institution (agency, program, project) in which the entity being evaluated is housed. The types of misinformation that may be encountered in an evaluation are summarized as follows:

Targets	Unintended	Intended
Self:	Self-deception	Lie
Others:	Misconception	Cover-up
Institution:	Myth	Front

Unintended misinformation about the self, which will be termed a *self-deception,* usually occurs because of a subject's lack of insight into his own dynamics or because of the need to maintain an integrated personality. Unintended misinformation about others, which will be termed a *misconception,* usually occurs because a subject is ignorant of or simply misinformed about what others think or do. Unintended misinformation about the institution or agency in which the evaluand is housed will be termed a *myth*; this usually arises because of a need to maintain institutional integrity and a sense of personal well-being.

Intended misinformation about the self will be termed a *lie.* Intended misinformation about others will be termed a *cover-up.* Intended misinformation about the institution or agency will be termed a *front.* This last is a kind of implicitly or explicitly agreed-upon story that hides certain undesirable aspects of the institution. So, for example, faculty members in a degree-mill institution may first suggest that their intent is to respond to the needs of persons who cannot leave their jobs in order to undertake full-time study. If that front is penetrated, they may admit that they are in business to respond to the need for quick credentialing. Finally, if pressed, they may admit that their interest is simply in collecting fees, with no concern for the quality of the degrees granted.

Intended misinformation is more difficult to detect than unintended, which frequently can be exposed through ordinary triangulation techniques. Thus, the evaluator may need to adopt adversarial investigative techniques in order to deal with intended misinformation. The interested reader may wish to consult Guba's (forthcoming) monograph of the relationship of methods of investigative journalism to educational evaluation for examples of relevant strategies.

Recycling. It would be an unusual case in which one iteration through the steps that have been described would be sufficient for the evaluator's purposes. The process needs to be recycled, perhaps more than once, before the evaluator can feel secure that he has isolated all relevant information. In the course of recycling, the evaluator will wish to establish beyond reasonable doubt that he has tapped all the audiences that have some stake in the entity being evaluated; to triangulate all information that is in any way suspect; to further refine his categories of descriptors, concerns, and issues; and to adopt an investigative mode if he feels that there are intentional efforts to deceive or mislead him.

Validating and Prioritizing. The number of informants that an evaluation team can tap for the identification of concerns and issues is limited. If the sample of informants has been properly selected with a view to optimizing information rather than being representative, the resulting information will undoubtedly be useful even if no other steps are taken to validate it. Nevertheless, some evaluators may feel more secure if the data have been exposed to a more representative group. Further, since for logical reasons not all issues and concerns can be dealt with, it is imperative that they be prioritized in some way. Both of these purposes can be satisfied by the use of a questionnaire sent to a larger sample of each audience.

While our posture throughout this book has been against the use of questionnaires, that objection is based on the fact that most questionnaires are ungrounded, that is, they spring from some *a priori* theoretical or conceptual formulation rather than from concrete data about real events. The questionnaire being proposed here is not subject to that criticism, since it is grounded on the analyzed responses of informants representing stakeholding audiences. The questionnaire need not have a complicated format; it would list the descriptors, issues, and concerns that had been identified and would request two responses:

1. A rating of descriptors, issues, and concerns for validity. The respondent would be asked to indicate, say on a three-point scale, whether each statement validly describes an element in the situation or phrases a concern or issue in realistic terms. The three-point response scale might consist of: 1—valid, 2—partly valid and partly invalid, and 3—invalid.

2. A prioritizing of concerns and issues (not descriptors). The respondent would be asked to indicate, say on a five-point scale, the absolute priority of the item; for example, 1—highest priority, to 5—lowest priority. Or the items might be prioritized by having the respondent apply a Q-sort.

Items that received a low rating on validity from each audience would be eliminated from further consideration. The evaluator should be alert to the possibility, however, that some audiences may deny the reality of a descriptor, concern, or issue because it is easier to do that than to face the implications of the real situation. Items about whose reality different audiences are in conflict, however, deserve further study.

Further, items that are not given high priority by any audience should be immediately discarded. But care should be taken not to determine the priority of any concern or issue simply on the basis of aggregation of ratings over all audiences. Audiences will probably differ on the priority that they accord to any given concern or issue, and those on which audiences differ appreciably are of special interest. These differences probably occur because of the different values held by different audiences.

A descriptor, concern, or issue should be taken seriously whenever: (1) all audiences agree about its reality and/or high priority; or (2) audiences disagree about its reality or priority. If all audiences agree that an item lacks validity or is of low priority, it can be safely disregarded (assuming only that there is no massive conspiracy on the part of all audiences to misdirect the evaluator— a remote but possible contingency).

Inferring Value Frameworks

The values of audiences are of interest to the evaluator because they are the basis for the judgments and recommendations that are the proper product of an evaluation. We have repeatedly stressed the need to identify values and have suggested that judgments of both merit and worth, but especially the latter, are inextricably tied to the values that different persons hold.

It would be helpful if there were some taxonomy that accounted for all existing values. But there is no such taxonomy, probably for the reason that values *are* relative; it is probably not possible, for example, for a person from a white, Anglo-Saxon, Protestant background to imagine the values that might be brought to bear in an aboriginal culture such as that of the Australian bushman or in a complex, sophisticated culture such as that of samurai Japan. The inference of values is thus not a simple matter of testing propositions against a checklist.

We suggest that for the evaluator's purpose, an audience's values can be reasonably well inferred from the issues and concerns that it identifies. A concern, we believe, implies a *value disjunction*; that is, the respondent perceives some situation or state of affairs that is inappropriate from the point of view of some value that he holds. Similarly, an issue implies two points of view resting on different values or on polar positions of the same value, that is, on *value trade-offs*. The evaluator thus must ask himself, when confronted with an identified concern, "*Why* is this a concern for this individual? What value might he hold that would produce this concern in this context?" Similarly, when confronted with an identified issue, the evaluator must ask himself, "What two values, or polar positions on what value, would produce this particular conflict?"

It requires only a little thought to realize that such judgments quickly come to involve infinite regresses. If, for example, a parent suggests that he is concerned because his child does not seem to be learning enough fundamentals in a math course to be able to carry out everyday tasks such as balancing a checkbook, we may well suggest that there is an underlying value, namely, that a child ought to have the skills necessary to cope with everyday tasks. But that answer seems only to raise yet another question: "Why would this parent hold *that* utilitarian value?" To which the answer might well be yet another value: "Because he believes that a person needs to be self-sufficient." And so on.

To avoid this problem of infinite regress, we suggest that evaluators attend only to *first-level values,* that is, the most plausible value statement by which a given concern or issue can be explained or understood. And while there is no definitive listing of values against which value inferences can be checked, we suggest that the evaluator might begin by considering the following set, while keeping in mind that any specific instance of a concern or issue might involve values not included here. In each instance we supply, first, a generic term, followed by a question that can be posed involving the value, and we end with one or more illustrative polar terms that characterize the extreme positions that can be taken on the value. A concern, we suggest, arises when a member sees a disjunction between one or more of these values and the evaluand, while an issue arises between contending parties who hold conflicting values or take positions at the polar opposites of a given value. The list follows:

1. Generic term: *Warrantability* or *relevance.*
   Question: Is the evaluand (the program, project, material, or whatever) justified or relevant?
   Polar terms: justified—unjustified (or capricious or arbitrary)
                   useful—nonuseful
                   affordable—nonaffordable
                   responsive to needs—not responsive to needs

2. Generic term: *Rationality.*
   Question: Is the evaluand rational?
   Polar terms: orderly—haphazard
                   systemic—disconnected
                   consistent—inconsistent
                   logical—illogical (on either theoretical or empirical bases)
                   continuous—discontinuous

3. Generic term: *Quality.*
   Question: Is the evaluand a valuable one?
   Polar terms: modern—archaic
                   artistic—prosaic
                   stylish—vulgar
                   innovative—mundane

4. Generic term: *Effectiveness.*
   Question: Is the evaluand effective?
   Polar terms: goal achievement—nonachievement

5. Generic term: *Efficiency.*
   Question: Is the evaluand efficient?
   Polar terms: economical—extravagant
                   conservative—wasteful

		prudent—careless
		reasonable load—overload
6.	Generic term:	*Ethicality.*
	Question:	Is the evaluand (or its application) ethical?
	Polar terms:	moral—immoral
		sensitive—insensitive
		equitable—nonequitable
		biased—unbiased
		just—unjust
		fair—unfair
		modest—immodest (vain)
7.	Generic term:	*Safety.*
	Question:	Is the evaluand safe?
	Polar terms:	safe—unsafe (physical safety)
		reinforcing—threatening (mental safety)
		orthodoxy—heterodoxy (social safety)
8.	Generic term:	*Human impact.*
	Question:	Is the evaluand humane?
	Polar terms:	happiness—unhappiness
		freedom—constraints
		autonomy—coercion
		socialization—individualization
		reconstruction—tradition
9.	Generic term:	*Political impact.*
	Question:	Is the evaluand politic?
	Polar terms:	expedient—impolitic
		aligned—challenging (or nonaligned)
		maintains power balance—upsets power balance
		liberal—conservative
		responsive to values—nonresponsive to values
		participative—nonparticipative
10.	Generic term:	*Accountability.*
	Question:	Is the evaluand (or are its proponents) accountable?
	Polar terms:	accountable—uncontrolled
		responsible—irresponsible

The process of assigning value bases to concerns and issues is a highly intuitive, inferential one. But naturalistic inquirers have traditionally welcomed such tasks as a challenge to their ingenuity and insight. Nor is it the case that the evaluator cannot check on the validity of his inferences; there are at least three such checks possible:

First, the process of prioritization by means of the questionnaire technique outlined above is likely to result in somewhat different assignments of priority to different concerns and issues. These differences ought to be explainable, at least in part, in terms of the value patterns determined for each audience by inference from the concerns and issues they have identified. Some audiences might typically be concerned with, for example, rationality, effectiveness, and efficiency, while others might be more concerned with ethicality, human impact, political impact, and accountability. We might expect the former audience to place systemic concerns higher and the latter to place them lower; if that were not the case, the value assignments would surely be suspect.

Second, different audiences will tend to generate different concerns and take different positions on issues, depending on their value patterns. If the issues were, for example, a curriculum decision between "back to basics" and electives, we might expect the systemically oriented audience posited above to support the former and the humanely oriented audience to support the latter. If that were not the case, value assignments would again be suspect.

Third, the strategy of testing interpretations with audience members is always available to the evaluator. While audiences are not always aware of their underlying values, in general one would expect them to recognize their predispositions once they were pointed out. The evaluator who could not get fairly general agreement from an audience about the characterization he made of their value patterns would be well advised to return to the drawing board.

In summary, the evaluator has several distinct tasks with respect to the delineation of values. First, it is incumbent upon him to discern the nature of the value patterns that exist in every context, using the inferential approach outlined above. He should determine whether the values in a given instance are consensual or pluralistic (the latter will probably be by far the more frequent case). Next, the values must be taken into account in making whatever judgments and recommendations are called for. The probability is good that different, perhaps even conflicting, judgments may be made, depending on which audience's values are brought to bear. Finally, it is the evaluator's responsibility to make clear to every audience the values that it holds, as well as the values held by other audiences, and to delineate the differences in judgments that are brought about by the application of the different value sets. Indeed, it can be argued that one of the major contributions that an evaluator makes in any given situation, beyond the act of evaluation itself, is this clarification of value differences —a clarification that should lead ultimately to greater understanding by each audience of all the others.

Testing the Rigor of the Identification Process

In Chapter Five it was suggested that the products of naturalistic inquiry, like those of any inquiry paradigm, ought to meet certain criteria of rigor, namely, *truth value* (internal validity), *applicability* (external validity or generalizability), *consistency* (reliability), and *neutrality* (objectivity). How can one demonstrate, for any given evaluation, that the concerns and issues that are identified can meet the tests associated with these criteria?

Truth Value. A number of suggestions were made in Chapter Five about how to improve the probability that the data of an inquiry would have high truth value and how to test the truth values of whatever data did emerge. We suggested that the inquirer monitor subject responses closely and spend enough time on site to offset distortions arising from the inquirer's presence. The inquirer was cautioned to develop suitable levels of rapport with subjects but to avoid "going native." It was pointed out that distortions might arise from bias introduced either by the inquirer or by the subjects and that the inquirer needed to be sensitive to this possibility and guard against it. Finally, it was suggested that further distortions could be introduced into the data because of the specific data-processing techniques employed, and the inquirer was cautioned to employ monitoring techniques to reduce these distortions as much as possible. These are tactics that the evaluator can and should employ, for they provide the evaluator with an *a priori* argument for the truth value of his findings.

We suggested further that structural corroboration of the

data be established. The data need to "hang together" in the same way that the plot details of a good detective story do. This requirement can probably be fulfilled by following the suggestions made earlier in this chapter for testing and refining the set of concern and issue categories. Such testing and refining should produce a necessary and sufficient set that is logically consistent and is sufficient to account for all (or virtually all) the observations made by respondents. Data that are questionable can be tested through triangulation and cross-examination, until corroboration does occur or the falsity of subsets of the evidence can be demonstrated.

Finally, the evaluator can devote sufficient time and energy to fulfill the requirement of persistent (repeated and continuous) observation that will permit him to differentiate typical from atypical situations and to identify the enduring and pervasive qualities that characterize the situation. It is also possible to prepare special referential materials—for example, an audio recording of interviews or a video recording of a classroom situation—that can be used as touchstones for testing later categorizations and interpretations.

With respect to testing credibility with audiences, the usual tactic of member checks is open to the naturalistic evaluator. Items of information, categories generated to classify them, and interpretations made from them can all be taken back to audiences for their reaction. Of course, some of the audiences may, for reasons of their own, choose not to validate the evaluator's interpretations even when they are correct. To avoid this contingency, it was suggested in Chapter Five that the inquirer should engage in continuous checking, should rely on indirect methods, should be prepared to adopt an investigative posture, should exploit audience differences by asking each to comment on the positions apparently taken by the others, and should utilize multistage communication, going to surrogate or representative audiences for preliminary validations before turning to the audience as a whole. These tactics are all available to the naturalistic evaluator; indeed, the recycling step recommended above in the process of eliciting concerns and issues lends itself well to their application.

Applicability. We have suggested that there are two classes of evaluation: merit and worth. In the former, generalizability is an automatic feature, since what is being evaluated is an intrinsic characteristic of the evaluand that accompanies it into every context. But the determination of worth is a very different matter: the fact that worth is context bound renders the concept of generalizability more or less meaningless. What does become a salient question is the conditions under which what is believed to be true in one context may also be true in a second. To determine that requires an assessment of the degree of "fittingness" between one context and another. It was suggested in Chapter Five that fittingness could be best assessed through the use of "thick descriptions" of each of the contexts involved; comparison of these thick descriptions would make it possible to determine the degree of fittingness.

We suggest that the required thick descriptions are automatically generated by the processes discussed earlier in this chapter for eliciting descriptors and for inferring audience values. The collectivity of descriptors and inferred values provides the best basis for making a judgment about the similarity between two settings. The obligation of an evaluator is thus not to establish the external validity or generalizability of his findings and interpretations but rather to provide the descriptive and value data base that will make it possible for someone else in another setting to make the judgment by collecting comparable data there. More will be said of this in Chapter Eleven.

Consistency. We pointed out in Chapter Six that consistency is frequently not an issue for the naturalistic evaluator, who may be more interested in differences than in similarities and who, because he believes that reality is multilayered, may think that a failure to demonstrate consistency results less from faulty methodology than from different observers viewing different realities. But insofar as it is important to be able to deal with questions of consistency, three strategies were suggested: overlap methods, stepwise replication, and the audit.

Overlap methods are available because of the likelihood that different sources of information will exist in any evaluation and can be exploited to identify concerns and issues. Obviously the primary method is the interview, but data resulting from the interview can be played off against available documents (for example, project proposals), observational data (for example, teachers may say one thing but their classroom behavior may suggest another), and even unobtrusive techniques (parents may claim to be exercised about something but may not attend meetings and hearings directed at ameliorating the problem). The evaluator should employ alternative strategies for producing or testing the concerns and issues that emerge. The use of overlap methods is primarily a test of validity, of course, but if the same concerns and issues can be identified from several methods used in tandem, the reliability of the findings is also improved.

Stepwise replication is possible if a team of more than one person is involved—a likely contingency if the advice of Chapter Nine is followed. The team should be divided into two halves and assigned to independent subsets of data sources. Provision should be made for communication between the teams at crucial times, probably on a daily basis to satisfy the requirements of the emergent design and to permit each team to cross-check the insights developed by the other.

Finally, an independent auditor should be employed, resources and time permitting, to review the entire process and to attest to its likely reliability. Adequate documentation of the entire evaluation process must be maintained to facilitate the work of such an auditor.

Neutrality. It was suggested in Chapter Five that the issue of neutrality, often called objectivity, was a false one and that it was generated by a peculiarity in definition that stressed the quantitative rather than the qualitative aspects of that concept. We proposed that in order to give the concept adequate meaning within the naturalistic paradigm, it is necessary to shift from a stress on the objectivity of the inquirer to the confirmability of the data. Data confirmability is a more cogent test of neutrality than certifiability of the investigator, it was asserted. The naturalistic evaluator who has followed the advice given to this point will in fact be in a prime position to document confirmability. He will have cross-checked and triangulated all his data and will have elicited confirmation of both data and interpretation from the several audiences through member checks. It will be clear to the evaluator that different interpretations are functions of different value positions, which will have been explicitly documented. The likelihood that biases will go undetected under these circumstances is slim indeed.

On balance, then, the naturalistic evaluator should have no difficulty in establishing the rigor of his data and interpretations. Techniques for doing so are available and can be incorporated into the ongoing procedures with at least as much ease as rigor tests can ever be incorporated into inquiries, whatever the paradigm may be. The case was made in Chapter Five, moreover, that naturalistic methods are, on balance, at least as rigorous as those that characterize the scientific approach, and in some instances may be even more rigorous. The naturalistic evaluator should not shrink from the task of testing for rigor; the means are available, feasible, and will probably result in judgments of adequate rigor if the naturalistic evaluator has followed, even minimally well, the advice that we have offered.

An Example

The example that follows is meant to give the reader a "feel" for what descriptors, concerns, and issues might look like, how they might be classified into categories, and how values might be inferred from them. The example is not meant to be typical; it is simply an anecdote to illustrate how concerns and issues might be used to produce some specific foci for an evaluation inquiry.

The Situation. The focus for this particular evaluation was the governance structure of a local school system; specifically, the evaluation set out to study the formal structures, mechanisms, and processes used to develop and determine school policy. Of special interest was the extent to which these governance structures were open to inputs from various stakeholding audiences, which were to be identified as part of the evaluation process.

The evaluation was carried out using teams that attended meetings of the school board and PTA, read documents (for example, board minutes and local newspaper editorials), and interviewed a number of persons drawn from the identified stakeholding audiences, including members of the school board, members of the central administrative staff, principals, teachers, students, parents, members of the city's mayoral staff, and influential persons in the community itself, including ministers, Chamber of Commerce executives, and officials of taxpayer groups. Most of the interviews were formal in nature—arranged in advance and carried out by appointment—but others were conducted informally—door-to-door in the community or in a local bar or laundromat. In all cases the focus for the data collection activity was the governance structure of the school and the degree to which the respondent thought that he had input into that process.

Analytic Process. Interview protocols and other source materials were subjected to the detailed, line-by-line analysis suggested earlier in this chapter. Concerns and issues relating to the governance process were abstracted onto three-by-five-inch cards, as were descriptors. The cards were then categorized. Certain of the concerns and issues were seen to transcend local control and so were classified as contextual factors. The categories established for the carded items were able to account for about 90 percent of the abstracted information—a reasonable level of inclusion.

Listed below are examples of concerns, issues, descriptors, and contextual factors. It is not possible to illustrate the fact that the categories accounted for most of the items or that they met the requirements for a necessary and sufficient set—logistical considerations preclude doing so. What *is* illustrated is the first cut that was made in this particular study; other categories were suggested by those that had emerged and were followed up in subsequent iterations.

Descriptors. Seven categories of descriptors emerged that were judged to be relevant to the inquiry at hand. These were labeled: citizen input process, teacher input process, lobbying group inputs, level of citizen support, nontax fiscal support sources, school board accountability, and community demography. Examples of each as recorded on three-by-five-inch cards follow:

Citizen Input Process

• Citizens have formal input into governance processes through advance notice of school board agendas. The local newspaper publishes the minutes of each board meeting verbatim.
• Parents have informal input into governance through twice-yearly meetings with the superintendent and his staff.
• Input on the location of a proposed new building will be provided by an ad hoc parent advisory group appointed by the PTA.

Teacher Input Process

- Teachers are involved in governance through the personnel policy advisory committee.
- Teachers are regularly consulted by members of the superintendent's staff whenever curriculum changes are contemplated.

Lobbying Group Inputs

- The League of Women Voters publishes a systemwide newsletter to inform people about educational matters, with the support of the school system's administration.
- The People's Alliance is funded by a local foundation as a voice for welfare recipients and other disadvantaged groups.
- The nominating assembly, said to be representative of the "elite of the uptown community," has had mixed success in proposing board candidates. The alternative is an independent taxpayer's association, which aims to protect the "small man's" interest.

Level of Citizen Support

- People support the schools. If there is an issue, it is settled quickly. "People grumble for a while, but the community heals its wounds quickly."
- The community is supportive of education but at the same time poses high expectations for the schools.

Nontax Fiscal Support Sources

- There is a local school foundation that provides small sums (up to $20,000 annually) to help schools acquire or renovate priority items.
- The local Chamber of Commerce, in conjunction with small business establishments in the community, raised $100,000 to provide for a new greenhouse for the agribusiness program.

School Board Accountability

- The people let the board handle governance once elections are over; in that sense the governance process is closed.
- The school board is held strictly accountable by the people for every action and decision it takes.

Community Demography

- The east side is characterized as the "bad end" of town in which the "poor folks" reside.

- The town is "small enough so that you can make two phone calls and get something done, but big enough to be fun to play with."

The reader may have noticed several omissions from the above list; for example, there is no set of descriptors dealing with student input into the governance process. Such evident omissions became the basis for follow-up activity during successive iterations.

Contextual Factors. Three categories of contextual factors—forces or constraints that compel or inhibit some action but that are beyond the power of persons in the local situation to control—were identified. These were labeled: state-level fiscal constraints, local foundation constraints (the foundation being one maintained by a national industry headquartered locally), and teacher certification.

State-Level Fiscal Constraints

- The property tax plan imposed by the state legislature usurps taxing authority from local governmental units. Local levies are frozen so that the revenue production capabilities of local municipalities are severely limited.
- There have been budget problems since the local school budget was reduced by $700,000 to come into conformity with a state law that emphasized equal spending per student throughout the state.

Local Foundation Constraints

- The foundation exerts a disproportionate influence on the schools—for example, in determining where they are to be built.
- The chairman of the board of the industry supporting the foundation became involved with local schools when he decided that his children were not being properly educated; since then the foundation has exerted influence to have the schools mount those programs that the industry's executives believe constitute good education (mainly college preparatory programs).

Teacher Certification

- State law mandating the master's degree as a condition for permanent tenure has so watered down master's programs in the state universities that having the degree does not increase a teacher's worth by very much.

- Mandated course requirements for teacher certification do not provide the kind of training needed by the teachers in this community.

Concerns. Six categories of concerns relating to governance were uncovered; these were labeled: citizen lockout in decision making; arrogation of power by superintendent, staff, and school board; school board quality; policy or decision inequities; nonrepresentativeness of boards and forums; and lack of cooperation with city government. Examples follow:

Citizen Lockout in Decision Making

- The school board cut out elementary art despite parental opposition.
- The board sometimes holds illegal private meetings to avoid having to deal with the public.
- The superintendent is said to be autocratic and unwilling to share decision making with the public.

Arrogation of Power by Superintendent, Staff, and School Board

- The board is said to make decisions on the whim of the superintendent.
- School staff have little to say in school affairs—the superintendent and his cabinet are in charge.
- School decisions involve dialogues among the superintendent, the board, the cabinet, and building principals—decision-making is closed to other influences.

School Board Quality

- School board members are greatly influenced by the regions of the community they represent; for example, those from rural areas try to keep out new influences.
- To be elected, a board member must have an old family tie, or he will not be trusted by the voters.

Policy or Decision Inequities

- The principal of the east end high school (the "poor" section of town) receives more central office supervision than any other principal.

- A new high school intended to serve several attendance districts was placed in the center of an upper-middle-class precinct, requiring children from the other, poorer precincts to be bused to the building.

Nonrepresentativeness of Boards and Forums
- Urban citizens dominate the school board; no one speaks for the rural population.
- Ninety percent of the members of forums appointed for the sake of providing input on important school decisions are professionals.

Lack of Cooperation with City Government
- There is no formal relationship between the school corporation and the city government.
- School personnel have been invited to participate on a committee considering land development for residential use, but none have attended.

Again, gaps in the categories can quickly be noted; for example, there seems to be very little expressed concern with the relationship of governance to fiscal policy. Obviously such matters can be followed up. The reader should also note that concerns are not accepted *de facto* by the evaluator; rather they are the basis for planning subsequent data collection activity that will generate data related to those issues retained after prioritization.

Issues. Issues, it will be recalled, are propositions about which reasonable persons may hold different views. Three issues germane to governance arose in the study; these were labeled: centralization versus decentralization, professional versus lay policy determination, and elected versus appointed boards. It should be noted that issues are not normally stated as such by a respondent; typically any given respondent will discuss only his own perception or point of view. Issues are identified by juxtaposing such perceptions from two or more persons who hold differing views. Of course, in many cases the opposing perspective is implied by the statement that any given respondent makes. Some examples:

Centralization Versus Decentralization
- The respondent advocates a "linear, bureaucratic, administrative

hierarchy" in which teachers and citizens have little to do with district-wide policy formulation.
- The respondent indicates that teachers should influence curriculum decisions in their own classrooms or departments but that the central administration should be in charge at broader levels.

Professional Versus Lay Policy Formulation
- Board members are not professional educators and so should not become involved in curriculum policy formulation.
- Most citizens do not wish to be involved in school matters and that's the way it should be: citizens should let the professionals decide.

Elected Versus Appointed Boards
- Appointed boards are to be preferred to elected ones because there is greater potential for selecting qualified persons interested in quality education, but appointments can be politically motivated.
- Elected boards are better than appointed ones because they represent the interests of the people who elected them.

Again it should be noted that evaluators use issues as points of departure for collecting information responsive to them; they do not accept them at face value.

Inferring Values. What will be exemplified here is how values may be inferred, on a provisional basis, by consideration of concerns and issues one at a time. It should be stressed that this process is only the first step in a real situation; values ascribed to any audience on the basis of one issue or concern would have to be verified from examination of all other issues and concerns, and a sensible overall posture would have to be described. Nevertheless, the process begins with consideration of single concerns and issues; that is the key step on which all others are based. For simplicity's sake we shall use as examples the first items listed in the six "concern" and three "issue" areas considered above.

1. Concern area: Citizen lockout in decision making.
   Expressed concern: The school board cut out elementary art despite parental opposition.

Likely values: Quality (since art is often thought of as adding quality to a curriculum)

Ethicality (fairness)

Human Impact (happiness)

2. Concern area: Arrogation of power by superintendent, staff, and school board.

Expressed concern: The board is said to make decisions on the whim of the superintendent.

Likely values: Warrantability (justified, responsive to needs)

Rationality (systemic, logical)

Ethicality (sensitive, equitable)

Political Impact (expedient, nonparticipative)

3. Concern area: School board quality.

Expressed concern: School board members are greatly influenced by the regions of the community they represent; for example, those from rural areas try to keep out new influences.

Likely values: Warrantability (justified)

Rationality (logical)

Safety (orthodoxy)

Political impact (aligned, maintains power balance)

Accountability (irresponsible)

4. Concern area: Policy or decision inequities.

Expressed concern: The principal of the east end high school (the "poor" section of town) receives more central office supervision than any other principal.

Likely values: Ethicality (equitable, biased)

Safety (orthodoxy)

Political impact (aligned, maintains power balance)

Accountability (controlled, responsible)

5. Concern area: Nonrepresentativeness of boards and forums.

Expressed concern: Urban citizens dominate the school board; no one speaks for the rural population.

Likely values: Ethicality (equitable)
Political impact (maintains power balance, nonparticipative)

6. Concern area: Lack of cooperation with city government.

Expressed concern: There is no formal relationship between the school corporation and the city government.

Likely values: Rationality (justified, useful)
Effectiveness (goal achievement)
Efficiency (prudent)
Political impact (participative)

1. Issue area: Centralization versus decentralization.

Expressed issue: The respondent advocates a "linear, bureaucratic, administrative hierarchy" in which teachers and citizens have little to do with district-wide policy formulation.

Likely values: Rationality versus ethicality and political impact.

2. Issue area: Professional versus lay policy formulation.

Expressed issue: Board members are not professional educators and so should not become involved in curriculum policy formulation.

Likely values: Warrantability and rationality versus safety, political impact, and accountability.

3. Issue area: Elected versus appointed boards.

Expressed issue: Appointed boards are to be preferred to elected ones because there is greater potential for selecting qualified persons interested in quality education,

| | but appointments can be politically motivated. |
| Likely values: | Quality and effectiveness versus ethicality and political impact. |

Many of the judgments made above are debatable, and it is likely that the analysis is incomplete. Nevertheless, the reader will be able to infer something about the nature of the process and to visualize the results that occur.

Chapter 11

Gathering Useful Information

===============================

In this chapter we move beyond identification of concerns and issues to a consideration of what kinds of information must be collected by the evaluator and how that information might best be obtained. We shall discuss the kinds of information required, the sources of that information, and certain other considerations.

Kinds of Information Required

The responsive evaluator working within the naturalistic paradigm must generate five kinds of information: descriptive information, information responsive to concerns, information responsive to issues, information about values, and information about standards relevant to worth and merit assessments.

Descriptive Information. Information is needed about the *entity being evaluated*, the *setting* in which it is used, and the *conditions* under which both use and evaluation take place. These descriptions need to be made at several points in time: prior to implementation of the evaluand, at the time of initial implementation, and at later times during the evaluation period. Information about each of the three objects (entity, setting, and conditions) at these several points in time will serve as the "thick description" that has been called for at various places in this book. This thick description in turn can serve as the basis for extrapolating findings to other settings should anyone wish to do so.

The *entity being evaluated* is of course the program, project, material, or other focus of the evaluation. While every evaluand will require certain unique descriptors to capture its essence, an adequate description will speak to several categories in particular:

First, the objectives, purposes, intents, or goals of the entity should be described. Such descriptors may range from the very specific behavioral objectives set for targets to the more general objectives intended by an outside sponsor or funder—for example, achieving greater equity for certain target groups. The more specific objectives may be easier to establish than the broader intention, which may not be stated at all to avoid political or other complications.

Next, the targets of the evaluated entity should be specified in such terms as grade level, ability level, ethnic or sex group, and so on. The target groups will be those that have been previously identified (see Chapter Ten) as the beneficiaries of the entity. It is also useful to describe any groups that may be disadvantaged if the entity is implemented.

The substantive focus or thrust of the evaluand should be described. So, for example, the evaluand may be a curriculum in fifth-grade social studies, a program intended to acquaint alcoholics with the physiological concomitants of excessive drinking, and so on.

The materials and facilities required to implement activities should be specified. These may include textbooks, workbooks, shops, tools, halfway houses, juvenile detention centers, and whatever other physical support elements are needed.

The agents required to implement the entity in question should be described. The number of agents (teachers, corrections officers, social workers, and so on), their level of general training (for example, certificated elementary teacher, trained social worker with master's degree), and their specific level of training with respect to the evaluand (for example, completion of a two-week training workshop mounted by the developers) should be specified. Any special characteristics of the agents (for example, membership in a minority group) should be mentioned.

The schedule of the several activities called for to implement the evaluand should be outlined.

The relation of the evaluand to other programs and activities should be set forth. It is likely that the entity will be part of an institutional structure of some complexity, being either a replacement for or complement to a number of other ongoing programs or activities. The evaluand must "connect" with these other elements, either in the sense that these other programs or activities provide inputs to the evaluand (students trained to some prerequisite level of competence, for example), or in the sense that certain outputs or products of the evaluand provide inputs to other elements. Such points of integration or articulation should be carefully specified.

Special constraints or characteristics should be noted. The evaluand may have been designed with special conditions in mind: to serve a particular cultural subgroup, to serve as a point of transition between two previously existing program elements that had not heretofore been adequately articulated, to reduce the costs of providing certain services, and so on. Such special conditions or constraints should be carefully delineated.

Costs of implementing the evaluand should be estimated. An assessment of costs should include not only fiscal investments but also time, energy, and lost opportunity costs. The latter include diversion of personnel from other possible activities and the inability to pursue other programs once the decision to implement the evaluand is made. Care should be taken, however, to distinguish normal operating costs from the unusual costs that accompany development as well as from those associated with initial implementation. The latter two are once-only costs, often defrayed from special contingency funds or outside grants, while operating costs are continuous and ongoing and thus represent the most valid estimate of what it will cost the school district, social service agency, or court to implement the entity.

The *setting* for the evaluand also includes a number of elements: the larger setting—organization, group, community, culture—within which the evaluand is being implemented and that must be described in a demographic sense; the value characteristics of the groups within that setting; and perhaps most importantly, some needs assessment or context evaluation that set the stage for the evaluand to be introduced in the first place.

The larger setting is described in terms of demographic variables. One important source for such information is census data for the community at large; these data will provide primarily ethnic and socioeconomic indicators. In addition, the characteristics of the particular organizational setting should be described—the social welfare agency and its catchment area, the school system and the particular schools in which the entity is to be used, the juvenile court system, and so on.

The value characteristics of the stakeholding audiences and other reference groups should be described. Much of this information will come from the analyses of concerns and issues outlined in Chapter Ten. In addition, any special value characteristics of the community at large should be included. Is it a southern Baptist town? Is the area dominated by Amish culture? Are there particular ethnic characteristics—a Scandinavian or an Oriental community? And so on.

A needs assessment or context evaluation is essential because the evaluand has presumably been introduced in response to some designated need or because a context assessment uncovered a special problem or opportunity. What is the evidence that some new program is desirable, that some organizational changes should occur, that some personnel additions should be made, that some retraining should take place, and so on? In many instances formal needs assessments or context evaluations will already exist, perhaps carried out earlier by the same evaluation team now involved in assessing the evaluand. In other cases actions will have begun because of some intuited need: teachers realizing from their experience that their pupils are not grasping the essentials of first-grade reading instruction, or juvenile officers becoming aware that the recidivism rate is too high. The evaluator must assess whatever evidence of this sort is available and collect additional, or more formal evidence, when that seems to be indicated.

The *conditions* surrounding the use of the evaluand must also be described. These include what Stake (1967) has termed the antecedents and transactions involved. Antecedents comprise all the prior conditions assumed to have been met before the evaluand was operationalized. These include the entry behavior of the targets (for example, that students shall be at least two grade levels behind as measured by a standardized reading test or that juvenile court offenders shall have appeared in court on at least three separate occasions); the qualifications of the persons on whom the implementation will depend, the nature of the facility and the materials that will be used; the schedule of activities that will occur; and so on.

Transactions include all the actual interactions between agents and targets—the nature of the classroom instruction that will occur and of the homework assignments that will be given, the counseling interviews that will be held between corrections officers and juvenile offenders, and the like.

If we move now to consideration of timing, we note that there are three different temporal descriptions that may be made of entities, settings, and conditions. There are, first of all, intended evaluands, settings, and conditions. These are the elements that were in the minds of developers and planners prior to the actual implementation activities. The evaluand was expected to have certain targets, substantive foci, agents, and so on; the setting was anticipated as being in a certain community with certain characteristics; the antecedent conditions and transactions were projected to reflect the overall logic of the evaluand's use. These intended elements may be determined from a variety of sources: original proposals and planning documents, working papers and "think" pieces, needs assessments, records of negotiations between contending groups, and many others. Recollections of original intentions may also be provided by key actors through interviews. Intensive document analysis and open-ended interviews are thus called for to accomplish the task of specifying intended evaluands, settings, and conditions.

But, of course, unforeseen circumstances may arise that prevent the intentions from being carried out. Teachers may have less training than they need to implement the program effectively. Constraints imposed by funding agencies for special projects may require expansion or truncation of the target audiences. Moreover, the intentions spelled out on paper may be made deliberately grandiose for funding or public relations purposes, while other intentions may not be mentioned at all in the official documents. The evaluator who assumes that an implemented evaluand will be substantially similar to the intended entity is either naive or incompetent. Thus, field observations of the evaluand in use, of the setting as it actually exists, and of the conditions that actually obtain are absolutely essential.

These first two kinds of descriptions—intended and implemented—require documentation by the evaluator. Not only must perceptions be developed from documents, interviews, and observations, but their accuracy must be validated. The third type of description—variations—requires, in addition to documentation, ongoing and continuous monitoring. Variations in the entity, setting, and conditions can occur for a variety of reasons. In some cases the reluctance or resistance of the actors in the situation produces unwanted changes. Adaptations to fit the evaluand to the local situation may have to be made. The simple passage of time allows the action of various historical factors to make their contribution to change. Most of all, the continuing activity of the evaluator himself, if it is taken seriously by the actors and if it produces meaningful information, will contribute to a continuously changing set of circumstances. Only field observation under naturalistic conditions will suffice to maintain adequate monitoring. It may be noted in passing that these variations that inevitably occur are anathema to the conventional evaluator, especially one dependent on pre-post experimental designs, because they introduce new sources of variance not controlled in the experiment. For the naturalistic evaluator, however, they become an important and interesting source of information that needs to be documented and related to other changing circumstances.

When the evaluation has been accomplished, the information that has been collected and aggregated will provide the kind of "thick description" that we have urged throughout this volume. Rather than doing an evaluation under "typical" or "representative" circumstances that then become the basis for a hoped-for generalizability, the naturalistic evaluator provides information that interested persons in other contexts can use to determine the probability of "fit" between the findings of his evaluation and their own contexts. If the situation in context A is adequately described, someone in context B, assuming he has comparable data available for *that* context, can reach a reasonable assessment about whether the entity would produce the same kinds of impacts there. If a needs assessment or context evaluation demonstrates a similar need, problem, or opportunity, and if the setting and conditions are similar, then there is probable cause for asserting that the entity is also worth trying in context B. It should be noted, however, pursuant to the argument we made in Chapter Three, that adoptive formative and summative evaluations are still required in B.

Concerns-Oriented Information. If the evaluator has followed the steps outlined in Chapter Ten, he will have identified and prioritized a number of concerns. Each will pose its own information requirements, and the evaluator should collect relevant information about each retained concern and issue (after prioritization) to the extent that his resources permit.

What kind of information should he look for? The analysis of bounding conditions that we made in Chapter Five provides guidance. First, information that *documents* the concern is needed. Concerns rest on perceptions, and those perceptions may or may not be isomorphic with the facts of the case. Thus the evaluator should look for data that either confirm or refute the concern as stated. For example, consider the following concerns (we have selected these from the examples given in Chapter Ten) and some possible kinds of information that bear upon them:

"School board members are greatly influenced by the regions of the community they represent; for example, those from rural areas try to keep out new influences." Can that concern be substantiated? The composition of the board is known, and the areas of the community from which they are elected can also be ascertained. Moreover, records of votes are kept, so that it is a simple matter to determine whether members from rural areas have tended to vote for or against propositions that might be interpreted as representing "new" influences.

"There is no formal relationship between the school corporation and the city government." Formal relationships are matters of record. Is there a municipal committee that has representation from the school corporation? Do interviews with city government officials confirm that the school administration has been invited to participate in certain actions but refused? Or does nominal participation occur, but with attendance of school officials at official meetings being poor (as indicated by the minutes)?

"The board sometimes holds illegal private meetings to avoid having to deal with the public." Even private meetings must be called by someone, and secretaries may recall correspondence or telephone calls to set them up. Meetings must also occur somewhere; motel clerks may recall having arranged private dinners or having provided meeting rooms on such occasions. Or, the person who originally voiced this concern may be able to provide details of a specific instance that could be checked for accuracy.

Or we may take other examples that bear more directly on program evaluation:

"My son is enrolled in the new math course but he is not learning such simple things as how to balance his checkbook or to estimate the costs of making a personal loan at the bank." The syllabus of the program might be examined to determine whether such practical applications are provided for. Students and teachers might be interviewed to discover their perceptions about whether such applications are taught. Indeed, a simple test could be devised to discover whether, at the end of the course, the students enrolled in it could carry out such applications.

"I do not have the time to learn what I would need to know to teach in the new program; I am busy enough as it is with my present duties." Program developers and decision makers might be interviewed to discover what intentions they have about making retraining opportunities available; for example, providing substitute teachers so that regular teachers could be released for retraining, or providing stipends to reimburse teachers for the extra time they might need for retraining.

"The program is intended to provide extra tutoring for disadvantaged youngsters who have fallen behind in grade-level performance, but I doubt whether the children are sufficiently motivated to profit from it." Tutors might be interviewed to discover whether, in their experience, low levels of motivation characterize the enrolled youngsters. Observations could be made of the tutoring sessions to assess the degree of involvement the students display. Students could themselves be interviewed to determine their affective reaction to the experience.

Obviously, each concern could be tested for reality. Those concerns that are found to be based on faulty perceptions can be dismissed from further consideration (although a report is due the stakeholders about why their perceptions were found to be faulty). Those that are found to have some basis in reality may then be pursued in additional ways.

Second, information that assesses the *causes* for the concerns that are found to be realistic is needed. In many instances the collection of such causal information will be beyond the scope of the evaluation. Some concerns are so complex that major social inquiries would be required to deal with them, and many could not be dealt with at all given the present state-of-the-art of inquiry methodology. But many other instances are well within the competence and resources of the typical evaluator. The school board member who always votes the convictions of his constituency may simply be responsive to a political fact of life. The school administration and the city government officials may fail to establish formal relationships simply because they represent different political parties. The school board may hold illegal private meetings because a particularly vindictive local newspaper editor seizes on every public discussion to pillory its members. The new math program may not provide for practical applications because theory is taught this semester and applications the next. The teacher may believe her concern about retraining is based on available time when in fact it is based on anxiety about her own competence to learn something new "at her age." Students may not be motivated because the materials used in the tutoring experience are culturally inappropriate. Most causes of this kind can be identified by a local evaluator without very much difficulty if he is able and willing to spend some time in inquiry directed at them.

Third, information that assesses the *consequences* of a concern is needed. Most concerns imply the consequences that are feared—school boards that hold illegal meetings will be self-serving in their dealings; children exposed to new math will not be able to display mathematical competence in their everyday lives, and so on. The evaluator will not always be in a position to assess consequences because not enough time will have elapsed for them to be felt. In such cases he may be able to identify similar situations in which certain consequences did become apparent. While generalization is not something we recommend, there is surely no reason not to profit from experience elsewhere if, on the grounds of fittingness, that experience appears to be germane. Or the evaluator may be able to draw upon expert opinion and judgment to predict what is likely to happen. In those instances in which consequences *can* be checked, the evaluator should do so. Actions of a school board, whether decided upon in legal or illegal meetings, do have public consequences; is it the case, for example, that this board, which conducts private meetings, makes decisions, however arrived at, that are detrimental to the community? And conversely, despite the fact, say, that the record of this board is otherwise impeccable, is it the case that the public has lost confidence in it because of uncertainty about what really goes on at those illegal meetings?

Fourth, information that assesses possible *contraventions* is needed. If a concern is real, something ought to be done about it. But what? The evaluator is sometimes in a position to deal with this question. Once a concern is documented, and its possible causes and consequences are at least partially known, solutions can be proposed. The evaluator may make the obvious suggestion; for example, he may urge that "sunshine" laws be more rigorously enforced or that the math course be restructured to permit at least some practical applications. In other instances the task may be more difficult; if students in a tutorial program are unmotivated to participate, what can be done to provide a reward system that will motivate them? To answer that question may require the concentrated attention of an experienced learning psychologist. But the evaluator can at least pinpoint such resources and may be able to provide a channel for tapping them.

Issues-Oriented Information. The procedures outlined in Chapter Ten result in the identification not only of concerns but also of issues about which reasonable persons may disagree. The responsive evaluator is faced with the question of what kind of information he should collect that would be most useful in dealing with issues—clarifying and, if possible, resolving them.

The phrase *reasonable persons* is somewhat misleading, for it suggests that only those issues that are evidently based on some form of rational argument rather than on a political or emotional one are admissible for the evaluator's consideration. But to take such a posture would be very naive indeed. Virtually every issue, however it may be characterized by outside observers, is thought to be rational by both its proponents and its opponents; to suggest otherwise not only does nothing to resolve the issue but may in fact prevent its resolution. Furthermore, it matters little whether someone's position on an issue is based on rational, emotional, or political considerations; the position has been taken and the issue drawn. What can the evaluator do about issues, whatever their bases may be? We believe that he can clarify the reasons for a position, test the validity of those reasons, and determine the advantages and disadvantages of each so that trade-offs can be assessed and understood.

Clarifying the reasons for holding some opinion on an issue involves making the values underlying the position as explicit as possible. For example, in the value analysis of Chapter Ten, it was asserted that those persons opting for centralization of school governance were probably doing so because they tended to value rationality (logical, systematic, orderly approaches), while those persons opting for decentralization were probably doing so because they valued ethicality (sensitive, equitable, unbiased approaches) and took political impact seriously (liberal, challenging, value-responsive, participative modes). If those analyses are correct, they can form the basis for clarification. The evaluator can work with those stakeholding audiences (or subgroups of those audiences) to determine the precise nuances that those value positions carry in this particular context. And once each side knows the basis for the other's judgments, understanding, if not agreement, will certainly be enhanced.

The analysis in Chapter Ten indicated that those favoring elected over appointed school boards were likely to do so on grounds of ethicality and political impact, while those favoring appointment believed that higher quality and effectiveness would result. Again, the evaluator can probe these presumed positions to clarify their meaning for each audience and so enhance understanding.

Or, taking an example from another arena: in so-called

back-to-basics movements, educational conservatives are often pitted against progressives who want schools to fulfill a variety of functions other than teaching basic reading, writing, and arithmetic. In a value analysis using the taxonomy of Chapter Ten, it is likely that the "back-to-basics" group would be found to stress warrantability (are the "frills" justified and affordable?), effectiveness (how much can the schools do at one time?), and accountability (how long can the schools continue to engage in such irresponsible behavior?). In contrast, the proponents of a progressive curriculum are likely to stress such matters as quality (a modern, innovative program), ethicality (an equitable and sensitive program), and human impact (freedom and expression). Simply exposing and clarifying these value positions constitute a major achievement for the evaluator.

Validating the reasons underlying choices among issue alternatives (once these are clarified and understood) is important. Unless the reasons can be shown to have validity, the issue disappears; conversely, if the reasons do have validity, the issue is surely one that must be dealt with. To demonstrate validity, the evaluator can collect evidence of two kinds: conceptual and empirical. Thus, in the centralization-decentralization case noted above, the evaluator can turn to situations in which centralization or decentralization has been chosen. Is it true that centralization has led to rationality and decentralization to equity and participation? Further, are there any ways of conceptually interpreting centralization so that it becomes something other than authoritarian and mechanical? And does decentralization always imply a humane and liberal philosophy? In short, the evaluator can do a great deal to illuminate an issue by bringing experiential and analytic evidence to bear. Of course, those data are more persuasive if they have been collected in the local situation and are based on local experience and local analysis. But if local data are not available, the evaluator should turn to whatever sources he can find—even the research literature may have a contribution to make!

In the issue of elected versus appointed boards, the evaluator can search for evidence bearing on the two contentions. In situations in which boards are appointed, is there any evidence to show that they operate more effectively or that the appointees are of higher quality than those who are elected? Or is there any evidence to show that elected boards are less ethical or more open to political persuasion than appointed ones? Would not careful analysis show that appointees are as likely to be responsive to those who appoint them as are elected members to those who vote for them? And is it not just as possible to subvert an appointee as an elected member?

In the conservative-progressive curriculum case, the evaluator can gather data on what constitutes a progressive curriculum (is everything beyond "basics" a "frill?"), on whether progressively oriented schools are irresponsible and nonaccountable, or on whether modernity in and of itself always means improvement.

Assessing the trade-offs between the alternative options defining an issue is a relatively simple matter once the clarification and validating steps have been completed. Those issues that still remain, that is, whose reasons have been validated, can be resolved only by making a choice from among the available options, and the trade-offs involved in those choices can now be sensibly assessed.

Imagine, for instance, that the data in the centralization-decentralization issue show that centralized governance systems are likely to be more efficient but that decentralized governance systems are likely to result in "better" decisions because they are made closer to the point of action. The decision makers in this situation can now know precisely what will be gained or lost if the decision is made one way or the other.

Again, imagine that the data in the elected-appointed board issue show that elected boards are more likely to be responsive to their constituencies while appointed boards are more likely to be sensitive to professional considerations. The gains or losses from either choice are once more apparent.

Finally, imagine that the data in the conservative-progressive curriculum issue show that conservative curriculums are likely to produce higher levels of basic skills in children but that progressive curriculums are likely to produce children better able to adjust to rapid social and cultural changes. Again, the trade-offs involved in making either decision are clear.

These examples illustrate what the evaluator should do in dealing with issues, but they also tend to cover up the inherent difficulty of the task. In developing these examples, we made glib assumptions in order to move from each level to the next (clarifying to validating to assessing trade-offs). In most actual situations, definitive information that would allow the issue to be dealt with easily and straightforwardly does not exist. Issues tend to be too complicated for such an easy solution. Moreover, the typical evaluator is not likely to have either the time or the resources to probe the issues (even those at the top of his priority list) as deeply and as meaningfully as he would like. Nevertheless, there are useful steps that *can* be taken, and it must be clear that whatever the evaluator can do to enlarge his audiences' perspectives and increase their understandings is worthwhile and constitutes a defensible investment of scarce resources.

Information About Values. Values will have been inferred by analysis of expressed concerns and issues, as indicated in Chapter Ten. But there are at least three things that the evaluator should do with these inferred values:

First, he should clarify the values. The values that have been identified depend on the inferences of the evaluator and on the provisional taxonomy proposed in Chapter Ten. The inferences could be in error, or the taxonomy could be inadequate to capture the nuances of the particular local context. Moreover, the nature of a value in a particular context may be rather different from the same value in another context; so, for example, rationality as understood by the faculty of a philosophy department is likely to be rather different from rationality as understood by the workers in a school cafeteria. The evaluator should thus take his inferred values into the context to clarify, refine, and expand their meanings in local terms.

Second, the evaluator should seek to determine the source or basis for the values that have been identified. Reasoned values have a different quality from merely intuited ones. Why is a particular stakeholder group so concerned about, say, political impact? Has there been some earlier experience that has demonstrated the importance of this value to them? Or do they hold this value simply because it was inculcated as part of their socialization into the community culture? Some concerns and issues may disappear if the audiences come to realize that they hold values for no good reason; conversely, one expects a high degree of commitment to a value that has been established because of an intense earlier experience or because of logical derivation from some fundamental principle.

Third, the evaluator should seek to determine the degree of conviction with which various values are held. Some values are weaker than others. But if there are no counterpressures, even weak values will be determinative at decision points. At the same time, only the strongest values will hold up in the face of determined opposition or counterargument. The evaluator should know how each of his stakeholding groups regards the values they hold in order to gain some sense of the ease with which concerns can be dealt with or issues resolved.

Information About Standards. Evaluation must end in judgments, and judgments, as we have repeatedly noted, cannot be rendered in the absence of standards. In Chapter Three we suggested that the appropriate sources of standards depended upon the kind of evaluation that was being done: formative or summative merit evaluations or formative or summative worth evaluations.

For both formative and summative *merit* evaluations, we proposed, the appropriate source of standards was a panel of substantive experts. Merit, it will be recalled, is concerned with intrinsic aspects of the entity—those more or less generalizable qualities that accompany the entity into whatever context it might go and that are essentially independent of that context. Thus the appropriate source of merit standards is a group of persons especially knowledgeable about that class of entities of which the evaluand is an instance, for example, professional colleagues in the case of a professor and substantive experts—physicists, linguists, and so on— in the case of a curriculum.

It is incumbent upon the evaluator conducting merit evaluations to assemble such a panel of experts for the purpose of stipulating the standards that will be used. Fortunately, however, the term *assemble* need not be interpreted to mean a literal, physical assemblage. Often there are shortcuts that can be taken. For example, it seems likely that in the case of a curriculum innovation in the social studies, literature exists from which appropriate standards can be inferred. (There may in fact be literature available that specifies standards rather thoroughly.) Or, a panel might be queried by mail or telephone, and some consensus-building technique such as the Delphi might be employed to allow the panel to converge on some set of standards. The possibility always exists, however, that experts will not be able to agree, so that there may be multiple standards for the evaluator to consider, depending on which group of experts he may invoke.

In the case of formative *worth* evaluations, we suggested in Chapter Three, the appropriate source of standards is an assessment of the local context and values. These sources will already have been tapped by the evaluator in developing descriptive information and identifying values; it remains for the evaluator to apply those materials to the entity to reach a judgment. For example, it would be clear that a curriculum that was based largely on patterns of upper-middle-class life would probably not be appropriate in a blue-collar community. Similarly, a curriculum that was essentially humanistic would probably not be acceptable in a community that held to values of, say, rationality and safety.

It is the case of *summative* worth evaluation that poses the most difficult problems for the evaluator. We suggested in Chapter Three that the appropriate standards for such an evaluation are to be found in a local needs assessment. An evaluand is locally (or contextually) worthy to the extent that it eliminates or ameliorates problems found in the local setting.

But what is a need? And how are needs determined? These questions have not been well addressed by the profession, and we do not pretend to provide a definitive answer here. But it may be worth examining some of the issues involved.

Writing during the heyday of a curriculum movement based on responses to "felt" needs, Bode (1938) took serious exception to that approach on grounds that continue to have great relevance for the concept of needs assessment in evaluation. Bode pointed out that there are a number of problems with the concept of need —for example, the difficulty in distinguishing an authentic need from a "felt" need or from a desire; the fact that needs are probably infinite in number and cannot all be identified; the fact that needs are often in conflict so that responding to one may undermine another; or the fact that needs may not be apprehended by the person having them but may nevertheless be very real.

Reasoning from such bases, Bode decided that single needs do not mean much in and of themselves; what is necessary to interpret needs adequately is some kind of pattern or set of values. In short, we need to understand a setting or context before a pattern of needs makes much sense. And so we seem to have come full circle, for we have just decided that worth estimates must be based on patterns of detected needs. How can we move outside this circle?

The answer seems to be, "Not very well," or "With great difficulty." Some methods for carrying out needs assessments make no effort to do so. Most published instruments for assessing needs are very general and do not account for local context at all. A good case in point is found in the Center for the Study of Evaluation's *Elementary School Evaluation Kit: Needs Assessment* (1972). Needs are defined as shortfalls on various goals that have been "compiled from reviews of elementary school curriculum guides, textbooks, and related sources, which encompass the full range of student performance"—knowledge, psychomotor skills, attitudes, and interests (p. 5). These goals can be presented to various audiences such as parents, teachers, school board members, and students by means of either a Q-sort or a Likert scale response mechanism. On the basis of the audiences' responses the highest scoring "needs" can be selected and prioritized. But of course this approach suffers from a number of very serious deficiencies; it is ungrounded in the actual situations that it is intended to assess, and it fails to take explicit account of the values reflected in the goals themselves or that might be held by different groups. And of course no need can emerge that was not built into the instrument in the first place.

Several prominent evaluation theorists have recently turned their attention to the needs assessment problem; while their suggestions still fall short of being definitive, they have some value.

Scriven and Roth (1977) suggest that "needs assessments have been for some time the most ludicrous spectacle in evaluation. The usual 'models' are farcical and decisions based on them are built on soluble sand" (p. 25). They propose a new definition of need as follows:

> Z needs $X = Z$ would (or does) significantly benefit from X, and Z is now (or would be without X) in an unsatisfactory condition [p. 25].

The first condition, that of significant benefit, eliminates the possibility of needs being equated with wants or preferences. For example, children may need a cavity filled, but they certainly don't want it done; people may think that they need laetrile, but it certainly doesn't follow that they do. The second condition, that of being (or potentially being) in an unsatisfactory state, avoids the problem that someone calls something a need simply because he will benefit from it; thus one would surely benefit from possessing a million dollars, but one doesn't need it because without it one would not necessarily be in an unsatisfactory state. Of course, this new definition does not escape reliance on values; the terms *significantly* (as in "significantly benefit") and *unsatisfactory* (as in "an unsatisfactory condition") obviously require specification within some value framework, and they may be defined differently in different contexts (as Scriven and Roth no doubt would agree).

Scriven and Roth (1977) also point out that there are different levels of analysis for a need. Thus one can speak of a performance deficit (which is the classic way of defining a need—the difference between a performance and a standard), a treatment deficit, or a resource deficit. Thus, the students in a particular school may be deficient in mastery of reading skills as shown by test scores, and such a deficiency is clearly a performance deficit. But further analysis may indicate that students read poorly because their teachers lack the skills to teach reading effectively—a treatment deficit—and the remedy would be to retrain teachers. But to retrain teachers requires mounting an in-service program, and thus a resource deficit is also involved.

Commenting on the Scriven-Roth proposals, Waterman (1977) suggests that their analysis misses one important parameter of a need, and that is that every need is conditional. Thus, one needs food only if one wishes to sustain life. One needs to get a car fixed only if one intends to use it. Needs always imply certain conditions, usually those built into the educational system by our society's system of values. Waterman suggests that every need should be examined from several perspectives to be sure that it does not rest upon some idiosyncratic value. Otherwise, he warns, we might find that many of our "treatment needs" are simply assumed because we are locked into a social system that for example, calls for school years of 180 days, instruction for five hours daily, and so on. Or, to put it another way, we should be careful of what values we hold; they may trap us into identifying needs that might be better left unfilled.

Roth (1977), in a further discussion of needs, returns to the classical definition of a need, but makes some useful emendations to it and contrasts it with the definition proposed by Scriven and Roth (1977). She suggests that needs have traditionally been defined in the literature in terms of *discrepancies,* namely, that $X - A = N$, where N is the need, X is the "target" state, and A is the actual state. But, she suggests, there are at least five ways in which "target state" can be conceptualized. Depending on which conceptualization is used, five different kinds of needs can emerge:

N_1 = goal discrepancy = an *ideal* — an actual state.
N_2 = social discrepancy = a *norm* — an actual state.
N_3 = essential discrepancy = a *minimum* — an actual state.
N_4 = desired discrepancy = a *desire* (want) — an actual state.
N_5 = expectancy discrepancy = an *expectation* — an actual state.

It is clear from this analysis that what is defined as a need depends on the definition of the target state. And that definition is not a random matter; it is heavily dependent on the value structure and interests of the definer.

Roth (1977) goes on to contrast this discrepancy definition with Scriven and Roth's (1977) definition cited above. She points out that the Scriven-Roth definition has some advantages: it is clear about who it is that needs what (and that's practical and concrete), it indicates a dependency relationship between Z (the person having the need) and X (the thing needed), and it notes that X must be both beneficial and necessary. But, she notes, there is also a disadvantage to this approach: one must know what Z needs before the tests implied by the definition can be applied. Nevertheless, it is an advantage of the discrepancy definition that it points precisely to the difference between some current state and a target state (any one of five). But it fails to express a dependency relationship, which is the essence of a need. Thus, Roth concludes, the two definitions are complementary and both ought to be used, first to discover a discrepancy (some X that Z *might* need) and then to apply the tests so that one can with assurance say that the discrepancy represents a real need.

What can be concluded from the above discussion? Surely we are far from being able to describe needs assessment as an exact science. Further, if we accept Roth's conclusion that the best approach is to use both the discrepancy definition and the tests definition, we must be struck by the overwhelming roles that values play in determining needs. The discrepancy definition suggests five kinds of needs that depend on such concepts as *ideal, norm, minimum, desire, expectation,* all of which are clearly value formulations (even the apparently objective term *norm* represents a value choice, for to define an average as a target state may involve a large number of value judgments). The tests definition, moreover, also implies value judgments, for it requires the evaluator to determine significance of benefits and the degree of satisfactoriness of a condition.

Needs, then, cannot be objectively assessed. And if needs assessments are to be used as the standards for summative evaluations of worth, then those evaluations cannot be objective either; at least, they cannot be value free. But that should come as no surprise; our entire contention about worth, as outlined in Chapter Three, is that it is heavily dependent on local contextual assessments, including values.

What is to be avoided is the implication that evaluators can do objective needs assessments with generalizable instruments that can be applied in all situations in some standardized way. On the contrary, the evaluator must make every effort to be certain that any instrument that he does use is carefully grounded in local conditions. The evaluator who bases his worth evaluations on standardized needs assessment instruments produces evaluative information of little local utility. Indeed, this posture is virtually identical to that of using a nationally standardized instrument to judge a local curriculum without first ascertaining whether the items of that test have validity for the curriculum in question. They may or may not, but one cannot know without looking at both the test and the local curriculum. Similarly, one cannot tell whether a nationally standardized instrument to assess needs has contextual validity unless one looks both at the instrument and at the context in which it is to be used. More often than not the evaluator will find that the context and the instrument do not really match well.

The difficulties with conventional needs assessment being

pointed to here involve more than abstract questions of validity or rigor or generalizability. Needs assessment have an enormous impact, especially when they are cloaked as scientific and objective assessments that "tell the truth" about the local situation whether local stakeholding groups realize it or are willing to own up to it or not. In the first place, needs assessments provide political legitimation. Moreover, if an evaluator takes a needs assessment seriously as the source of standards for worth evaluations, that assessment will to a large extent determine what he looks at, what he sees, and what conclusions he will come to. Finally, needs assessments, once completed, tend to be used (and revered) for some time; other options or perspectives are ruled out. Thus, needs assessments have great political implications. Their misuse can be disastrous.

How, then, should the ethical evaluator go about generating needs assessments that can be used as the source of standards for evaluations of worth? First, he must be very cautious, knowing that the concept of "need" is slippery and that the profession has not, to date, developed a sound way of dealing with it. Second, he can eschew the use of nationally standardized instruments and focus upon developing an instrument that is grounded in local values. Third, in developing his approach, he can acquaint local stakeholding groups with their options: the kinds of target states they may specify to determine what discrepancies exist, and the definitions they may offer for testing the discrepancies that are uncovered. Fourth, remembering the emphasis that responsive evaluators place on pluralistic values, he can point out to audiences that judgments of worth may differ sharply, depending on which definitions are used. And finally, he should recall how these needs assessments were in fact obtained, lest he make of them an orthodoxy that admits of no deviations or exceptions. Needs assessments, he must realize, are not absolute; they are the result of imperfect efforts to deal with as yet poorly understood concepts. Unfortunately, we cannot do without them, but we need not allow ourselves to be overwhelmed by them either.

Sources of Information

We turn now to the question of the sources of the information described in the preceding section. Many of these sources have already been implied, but it is useful to make them explicit.

As far as required *descriptive* information is concerned, the evaluator should turn to multiple sources. For information about intended evaluand and conditions, he should consult original proposals and other planning documents, working papers and "think" pieces, needs assessments, and other available documentary sources. Persons involved in the original planning should be interviewed to discover their recollections. For intended setting information, the evaluator should consult sources of demographic data, for example, census reports, needs assessments, and the results of his own studies about community (stakeholder) values. For descriptive information on implementation of, and time variations for evaluand, conditions, and setting, he should mount a program of monitoring and observation. Over time some systematic instrumentation may be developed for this purpose, but it should not be developed *a priori* because then it may not be grounded in the realities of the situation.

For information responsive to *concerns and issues,* the evaluator needs to turn to whatever sources are implied by the high-priority concerns and issues with which he intends to deal. These concerns and issues may demand very conventional treatment, and in such cases the responsive naturalistic evaluator should not hesitate to use conventional means. For example, parents or teachers may be concerned that a given reading program does not produce a year's growth in reading ability for a year's instruction; the most efficient way to assess this concern is to employ a standardized reading test (being sure of its curricular validity) in a pre-post design. The reader should also note that it is *not* possible to specify information sources for concerns and issues in advance of identifying and tapping stakeholding audiences; the sources can be determined only *after* the concerns and issues have been identified and prioritized. This insight lends additional meaning to the concept of an "emergent" design.

For information dealing with *values,* the evaluator begins by analyzing emergent concerns and issues as described in Chapter Ten. Once he has made a tentative diagnosis, he returns to the audiences to clarify the values and to flesh them out in terms of their nuances in the particular setting. Interviews with representatives of the stakeholding audiences should suffice for this purpose. In addition, the evaluator seeks to elicit from his interview respondents the sources of the values they hold (did they learn them from their parents, in an ethics course in college, as the result of an earlier experience with the schools in the community, as the result of an incident in a neighboring school system that attracted a great deal of notoriety, and so on), and he also endeavors to estimate the degree of conviction with which the values are held.

For information dealing with *standards,* the evaluator turns to various sources, depending on the kind of evaluation involved. For formative or summative merit evaluations, the evaluator solicits the opinions of expert panels, which he may physically convene at the local site or utilize "at a distance" by mail or telephone, probably with some consensus-building technique such as the Delphi. The evaluator may also find appropriate listings of criteria in the professional literature. For formative worth evaluations, the evaluator turns to his earlier analysis of local values and the local setting to deduce appropriate criteria. For summative worth evaluations, the evaluator carries out local needs assessments.

In order to carry out the data collection activities outlined above, the responsive evaluator must be well versed in virtually every known tactic and strategy of data collection and analysis. While the emphasis in this book has been on the naturalistic paradigm buttressed by qualitative methodologies, the responsive evaluator cannot assume that all concerns and issues will be amenable to such approaches. It will be recalled from Chapter Four that the evaluator is mandated to assess every phenomenon that he proposed to investigate in terms of paradigm assumptions and to choose that paradigm whose assumptions best fit. It certainly cannot be assumed that such assessment will lead in every case to the choice of the naturalistic paradigm—that depends on what concerns and issues are raised. Moreover, as also noted in Chapter Four, the postures that have traditionally developed around each paradigm probably have no more intrinsic validity than did the cutting off of four inches from the shank end of the ham have validity as "the way you cook ham." The properly trained evaluator, even though his predisposition may be toward naturalistic, qualitative approaches, will be willing and able to apply other paradigms and techniques when they are called for.

Thus the responsive naturalistic evaluator may at times (1) find himself involved with both traditional and emergent designs, with instrumentation, and with analytic methods; (2) need to devise a "best mix" of strategies that will deal with the information requirements of the concerns and issues that are identified and assigned high priority; or (3) need to utilize a variety of conventional and emergent analytic techniques to converge on the needed information. Only a very broadly trained evaluator who is secure with the approaches and techniques of all paradigms can carry out such an assignment well.

Chapter 12

Reporting Results Effectively and Making Recommendations

In this final chapter we consider the last stage in the evaluation process: reporting. In the initial section of the chapter we deal with some general considerations: to whom one reports, about what, when, and with what criteria in mind to guide report development. We move then to a brief discussion of the forms of reports, with major emphasis on the case study as the most appropriate form for reporting the results of naturalistic, responsive evaluations. In the third section, we discuss the methodology of case studies in some detail. Finally we take up the question of what kinds of judgments and recommendations may be appropriate in a report, and whose role it is to make those judgments and recommendations.

Turning to the first question, to whom does the evaluator report? Traditionally, evaluation reports have been made to the evaluator's client—the person or group that commissioned the evaluation and paid for it. But the responsive evaluator has obligations to go well beyond this traditional practice. We noted in Chapter Ten that each audience has a *right* to be consulted about its concerns and issues, to have those concerns and issues honored by the evaluator as he goes about his tasks, and to receive reports that are responsive to those concerns and issues. We stress again that audiences have a *right* to receive reports and that evaluators have a duty to provide them.

It does not follow, however, that every audience should receive the same report; both the form and the substance of a report may differ from audience to audience, depending on such considerations as an audience's visibility, its previous knowledge of, or experience with, the evaluand, and its sophistication. With respect to form, some audiences may profit most from a technical report, while others may not be able to deal with anything other than an informal, oral report that relies heavily on visual aids. With respect to content, reports ought to vary as a function of the particular concerns and issues in which that audience is most interested.

Whatever the form may be, there are certain items of information that the report should communicate to each audience. Thus, descriptive information of the type described in Chapter Eleven should be made available. This "thick description" provides each audience with a kind of "vicarious experience" of the entity being evaluated (Stake, 1975).

Information that is responsive to the concerns and issues raised by this audience and, if pertinent, by other audiences must also be provided. At the very least, each audience should receive whatever information has been collected about their high-priority concerns and issues. Such information, it will be recalled from Chapter Eleven, might include, in the case of concerns, documentary evidence and information that assesses causes, consequences, or contraventions; and, in the case of issues, information that clarifies the issues and tests the validity of the reasons audiences cite for holding certain views on those issues. Each audience ought to know, too, in what priority their concerns and issues are held in contrast to the concerns and issues raised by other audiences. Each audience should receive reports on concerns and issues raised by other audiences that, in the judgment of the evaluator, are important to that audience, if only for the sake of understanding and appreciating the value positions of those other audiences (who are part of the larger context).

Each audience must be given information about values—its own as well as those of other audiences—so that values will be clarified for everyone, will be grounded in some source or base, and will be assessable in terms of the degree of conviction with which each is held by the several audiences. Value conflicts should be highlighted. In addition, information about the standards that have been applied to the information in order to reach judgments and recommendations must be made available. The source of the standards should be clear, and adequate qualifications should be included so that the audience is disabused of the notion that these standards are in fact absolute or inviolable.

It will be argued below that the reaching of judgments and recommendations is a matter for interaction between the evaluator and the several audiences; the report should, however, highlight the judgments and recommendations that need to be made and provide the basic information from which they can jointly be fashioned by the evaluator and the audience.

Two other points might be made about report contents. First, the report ought to be clear about the purpose of the evaluation. What is included in a report will certainly depend on whether the evaluation is a formative or summative evaluation of *merit* or a formative or summative evaluation of *worth*. And, second, the report should be made in the natural language of the audience receiving it.

As for the timing of reports, the contract with the client may well call for certain reports to be delivered on some specified schedule. But the evaluator should not conclude that these formally specified events constitute all the reporting that will be done. Reporting is more usefully construed as a continuous activity. That fact is most obvious in the case of formative evaluations, which are likely to involve both formal and informal interactions between the evaluator and (at least) the developers on a frequent, if not a daily, basis. But it should be evident that "reporting" will occur in every interaction between the evaluator and another person. An exchange of information will occur in every observation and in every interview (certainly one cannot keep the subject from drawing inferences by noting what is observed, what questions are asked, when notes are taken, and so on). Further, the naturalistic evaluator will probably carry out several iterations of data collection, building subsequent iterations at least in part on information collected in earlier ones. As questions become more focused and specific, audience members involved in interviews can make more concrete inferences about what the evaluator takes to be important and why. The evaluator will also be interested in carrying out "member checks" for a variety of purposes—for example, to make certain, during each interview or observation, that he has understood correctly and to establish credibility for his overall conclusions and recommendations. Thus, it cannot be assumed that reporting occurs only on those occasions when formal reports are delivered.

A variety of criteria for judging evaluation reports have been published; the responsive naturalistic evaluator should take account of these, insofar as they apply to his situation (he would be less concerned, for example, about scientific criteria of rigor than would some other evaluation theorists and practitioners). But there are other considerations that are also germane to his situation.

First, the "natural language" of each audience is likely to have its own idioms, its own rhythm, its own labels, its own hallmarks. The evaluator must have learned this language in order to communicate with and understand the audience in the first place; these insights should now be used in report preparation. The fact that such use is counseled does *not* imply that the natural language of the audience itself ought to be used—we would not suggest, for example, that a report directed at an audience of students should use the idiom of the high school corridor or that a report directed at teachers should use the professional jargon of educators. Nothing is more quickly detected, and labeled as artificial and "phony," than efforts to appear to be one of the "good old boys" —an insider—by using language forms that the audience will understand as "its own." But we are suggesting that the natural language of the audience must be understood and taken into account if reports are to communicate well. One reason traditional evaluation reports are so little used is that they take account of the natural language of other evaluators rather than of the several audiences that they are intended to inform.

Second, responsive evaluation represents a departure from the assumption common to earlier models of evaluation that value consensus is possible and likely. Different audiences do have different values, and we have suggested that it is a major responsibility of the evaluator to detect these value differences. The responsive evaluation report that did not reflect value differences and assess their impact on the overall situation (beginning with a description of context and ending with their meaning for final judgments and recommendations) would simply not conform to this basic requirement.

Third, most audiences will have but a limited view of the nature of the entity being evaluated. Even those persons most involved with an educational program—the teachers and students—will nevertheless "know" it in but a limited way. Other more peripheral audiences, for example, parents or community members, may have a seriously distorted view; many of the concerns and issues that these peripheral audiences might raise can be eliminated simply by making appropriate information available. The evaluation report ought to communicate what the evaluand is like when seen from or experienced within the perspective of other audiences. The descriptive information routinely gathered by the evaluator will be useful to serve this purpose, but written or tabular description should be supported by other materials that give this vicarious experience in more meaningful ways: "parent" days at school, films or videotapes, audio recordings, "testimony" given by central participants, or exposure to artifacts—skits, papers, art objects, or whatever is appropriate. It is probably just as important for central audiences to know about the perceptions (and misperceptions) of peripheral audiences as vice versa—teachers, for example, ought to know the concerns that parents have, even if those concerns are based on wrong or incomplete information.

Fourth, very little is known about the factors that influence audiences to accept or reject reports. But the possibilities inherent in some studies of audience tendencies are exemplified in several recent papers (Braskamp, Brown, and Newman, 1978; Brown, Braskamp, and Newman, 1978; Newman, Brown, and Littman, 1978). The first of these studies found, for example, that ratings of the objectivity of the evaluator depended on his official title; an evaluator identified as a researcher was rated higher than one identified as an evaluator, who was in turn rated higher than one identified as an art educator. The study by Brown, Braskamp, and Newman found that the use of jargon did not reflect adversely on the perceived proficiency of the evaluator but that the presence or absence of data on which recommendations were based made little difference either! The paper by Newman, Brown, and Littman, which is in fact a summary of three other studies, found, among other things, that a female evaluator was rated as higher in proficiency and credibility than was a male evaluator, provided the evaluator was in the same professional group as the reader (either in education or business in these studies), but that if the evaluator and reader came from different professional groups, the male evaluator was rated higher. These findings are certainly not definitive, but they are indicative of criteria that need to be studied further and brought to bear on reports, especially responsive reports that place so much stock on credibility.

Fifth, evaluation is most useful when it increases the understanding that persons have of the entity being evaluated. Robert Stake and Joel Weiss have indicated in public comments that they believe that the ultimate test of the validity of an evaluation is the increase in audience understanding that it produces. The evaluator who applies that test of validity to his reports cannot go far wrong.

Sixth, human and political factors surround every evaluation. Hence, the evaluator needs to assess the trade-offs between the human dysfunctionality and political imbalance that an evaluation inevitably produces and the meaningfulness and utility of the information that the evaluation can be expected to produce. The evaluator should be aware that it is the evaluation report, more than any other element in the evaluation process, that induces the human dysfunctionality and produces the political imbalances. The report epitomizes the evaluation and brings, into a single place, all the elements that cause anxiety or power dislocations. Everyone reading the report will be assessing how its findings and recommendations affect him personally. Reports will always be interpreted within the existing political milieu. The report will necessarily (because information *is* power) remove power from some and extend it to others. The evaluation report that is sensitive to these issues, and handles them appropriately, will fare a great deal better than one blind to them.

Forms of Reports

It is all too easy to think of the evaluation report as a thick technical document full of tables, statistical formulas, and unreadable appendices. But of course there are many different kinds of reports, as the reader already knows. Reports differ along a variety of dimensions, such as:

- Formative-summative. The purpose of the report may be to help improve or refine an entity or to render an overall judgment of its impact.
- Formal-informal. Reports may be formal, orthodox, conventional, rigorous, and technical or informal, unusual, unconventional, "soft," and nontechnical.
- Written-nonwritten. Reports may take the form of extensive written documents, or they may be made orally, through films, tapes, or skits, or in a variety of other nonwritten forms.

These and other dimensions describe possible distinctions in reporting forms or styles. But a more important distinction has to do with whether the form of the report fits the basic inquiry style that characterized the methodology of the evaluation. Formal, written reports, similar to reports of research that are found in scientific journals, seem to fit the "style" of the scientific paradigm, while other forms seem more appropriate to the "style" of the naturalistic paradigm.

Denny (1978, p. 2), basing his treatment upon an earlier analysis by Wolcott (1976), distinguishes several types or levels of inquiry reports:

- The *ethnology* is a "theoretical statement about relationships and meanings within a group or among a number of societies," and represents the most encompassing form of report that can be written within the naturalistic paradigm.

- The *ethnography* is "a basic descriptive work on which ethnology is based. Further, an ethnography is a *complete* account of some culture-sharing group." Less extensive in scope than the ethnology, the ethnography is nevertheless the basic conceptual block on which ethnologies are based.
- The *case study* is "an intensive or complete examination of a facet, an issue, or perhaps the events of a geographic setting over time."
- The *story* "documents a given milieu in an attempt to communicate the general spirit of things. The story need not test theory; need not be complete; and it need not be robust in either time or depth." The story is a kind of "journalistic documentation," a "first cut at understanding enough to see if a case study is worth doing." Denny describes himself as a storyteller and sees his contribution to the Stake and Easley (1978) National Science Foundation case studies on science teaching as that kind of effort.

If we may take this taxonomy as descriptive of the kinds of reports that might be generated in naturalistic studies, it is useful to ask at which level a naturalistic evaluation report might best be pitched. Both the ethnologic and the ethnographic levels seem too large in scope. Certainly evaluations will not in general be ethnologies—"theoretical statement[s] about relationships and meanings" —nor are they likely to be complete accounts of some culture-sharing group—ethnographies. At the other extreme, storytelling as a kind of "journalistic documentation" that need not be "complete" or "robust" seems to be less than what is needed. If evaluations are not merely descriptions but also involve judgments, some degree of completeness and robustness is certainly desirable. By elimination, then, we come to the case study as the best among the available types.

The Case Study

Denny (1978) defines the case study as "an intensive or complete examination of a facet, an issue, or perhaps the events of a geographic setting over time." Stake (1978b, p. 2) suggests that "the case need not be a person or enterprise. It can be whatever 'bounded system' (to use Louis Smith's term) is of interest. An institution, a program, a responsibility, a collection, or a population can be the case" (p. 5). MacDonald and Walker (1977) suggest that a case study is an "examination of an instance in action" (p. 181). Other, not very rigorous definitions that have been offered of the case study include "a snapshot of reality," "a slice of life," "a microcosm," "an episode," "an action unit," "a depth examination of an instance," and "the intensive examination of a unit."

Many different forms of writing have been labeled "case studies," as the following list suggests: individuals (developmental histories, etiologies of psychopathologies); agencies or organizations (social work agencies, banks, university departments); societies (nude beaches, community influentials); cultures (Trobriand Islanders, Potlatch Indians); movements (yippies, Zen Buddhists); events (freshman orientations, presidential inaugurations); incidents (strikes, nuclear accidents); methodologies (an instance of use of critical path analysis, an application of geocode analysis); programs (Comprehensive Employment Training Act, Head Start); projects (development of a new curriculum, a national study of schools, colleges, and departments of education). The range of information that has been included within a case study has varied from a few test scores for an individual to volumes of demographic, social, industrial, and cultural information for an entire society.

The content of a case study is determined chiefly by its purpose, which typically is to reveal the properties of the class to which the instance being studied belongs. But this general statement takes on quite different meanings as one becomes more specific about purpose. We have found it convenient to think in terms of four classes of purpose that seem to capture most of the purposes stated in actual case studies: (1) to chronicle, that is, to develop a register of facts or events in the order (more or less) in which they happened; (2) to render, that is, to depict or characterize; (3) to teach, that is, to provide with knowledge, or to instruct; and (4) to test, that is, to "prove" or to try. Of course, any given case study may have multiple purposes, although a case may become overly complex if it endeavors to deal with a large number of purposes simultaneously.

It may help to understand these four purposes by providing some examples of each:

To *chronicle:*   to record the salient steps taken in the development of an automobile fuel injection system; to give a history of the events leading to the decision on the part of coal miners to strike; to assess the evidence leading to a verdict of conviction in a criminal court case.

To *render:*   to describe the operations of the tellers' windows in a large commercial bank; to make clear the interactions between teachers and students during the course of a fifth-grade mathematics lesson; to provide a sense of what it is like to be in a class of retarded students.

To *teach:*   to acquaint students with the basic role expectations held for some vocational role, such as accounting; to develop an understanding of the decision-making process as it occurs in executive suites of major industries; to develop contrasts between different forms of government—for example, democratic and communistic—in order to highlight the distinctions in the two approaches.

To *test:*   to describe relationships between assembly line workers and their supervisors so as to provide a test for the hypothesis that reinforcement of "right" behavior leads to greater productivity; to describe the events and circumstances (individual productivity experiments) that lead to the formation of theories of staff morale (the so-called Hawthorne effect); to weight the various factors reinforcing or constraining the implementation of a new curriculum so as to lead to appropriate judgments of program effectiveness.

The reader may have noticed that the three examples given with respect to each purpose differ along a systematic dimension. The first example is always factually oriented; the second has an element of interpretation in it, while the third has some judgmental qualities. If these three elements—fact, interpretation, evaluation—are crossed with the four purposes already defined, a typology of case studies of twelve cells emerges. This typology is shown in Table 9. Each cell is, moreover, divided into two aspects: action and product. The verb describes what the case study analyst *does* in preparing that kind of case study, while the noun indicates the *nature* of the resulting case study.

For example, given the purpose "to chronicle," the appropriate action at the factual level is to *record,* and the products of this recording are *registers.* At the interpretative level, the appropriate chronicling action is to *construe,* and the products of such construction are *histories.* At the evaluative level, the appropriate action is to *deliberate,* and the products of such deliberations are items of *evidence.*

Given the purpose "to render," the appropriate action at the factual level is to *construct,* and the products are *profiles.* At the interpretative level, the appropriate action is to *synthesize,* and the products of this synthesis are *meanings.* At the evaluative level, the appropriate action is to *epitomize,* and the appropriate products of this rendering at the evaluative level are *portrayals.*

Given the purpose "to teach," the appropriate action at the factual level is to *present,* and the products of presentations are *cognitions.* At the interpretative level, the appropriate action is to *clarify,* and the products of clarification are *understandings.* At the evaluative level, the appropriate action is to *contrast,* and the products of such comparisons are *discriminations.*

Finally, given the purpose "to test," the appropriate action at the factual level is to *examine,* and the products of such examination are *facts.* At the interpretative level, the appropriate action is to *relate,* and the products of such relating are *theories* (or explanations). Finally, at the evaluative level, the appropriate action is to *weigh,* and the products of this weighing are *judgments.*

The reader will have noted the arbitrary quality of the labels placed on each of the cells. One can wonder, for example, whether at the factual level of chronicling, the action term *document* and the product term *accounts* might not be better choices than the terms *record* and *registers.* But there seems to be little point in belaboring what must remain essentially an arbitrary matter. What is important is that the reader sense and appreciate the meanings

Table 9. Case-Study Types

Purpose of the Case Study	Levels of the Case Study					
	Factual		Interpretive		Evaluative	
	Action	Product	Action	Product	Action	Product
Chronicle	Record	Register	Construe	History	Deliberate	Evidence
Render	Construct	Profile	Synthesize	Meanings	Epitomize	Portrayal
Teach	Present	Cognitions	Clarify	Understandings	Contrast	Discriminations
Test	Examine	Facts	Relate	Theory	Weigh	Judgments

Note: The table describes case studies that were carried out for general inquiry purposes (research) as well as for evaluation. Most research case studies would be classified in one or more of the cells indicated in the "factual" or "interpretive" columns, while most evaluations would be classified in the "evaluative" column. Research activity cycles through the "chronicle," "render," and "test" purposes, while evaluative activity tends to focus on "test." "Teach" is a purpose not commonly found in either research or evaluation activity.

Source: The authors are indebted to the participants in an evaluation-training workshop for personnel of the University of Virginia and Virginia Polytechnic Institute and State University conducted at Charlottesville in November 1979, and to members of one of the author's classes in qualitative methods, who criticized earlier versions of this table and made useful suggestions for its improvement.

of the cells as implied by the crossing of row and column headings; the particular names used in each cell are of little moment in and of themselves.

By definition, if one is engaged in writing an evaluative case study, one ought to focus on the terms in the evaluative column of Table 9. At the same time, one should not lose sight of the fact that a major purpose of most evaluations, whether formative or summative, is to test something, and testing, as we see from Table 9, can occur at factual, interpretative, and evaluative levels. The evaluator should therefore concentrate, in writing a case study, on the *test* row and the *evaluative* column of Table 9. All the elements of this row and this column are important to include in the case study, but most important of all is the lower right-hand cell— the weighing of information to produce judgments. Judging is the final and ultimate act of evaluation.

But while it is relatively easy to describe the areas of content that should be included in an evaluative case study, it is not nearly so easy to describe the methods for actually writing it. What seems to be involved is, at heart, a literary, perhaps even an artistic, process. Freud is said to have remarked that he was astonished and chagrined because his own case studies so closely resembled short stories rather than the more scientific reports that he sought to emulate. Nevertheless, Freud's case studies turned out to be enormously useful in redirecting the entire field of psychopathology into new avenues. Whether regrettable or not, the writing of case studies cannot be reduced to a series of rules such as those that guide the writing of a report of a biological or chemical experiment. Probably not much more can be said than that the usual principles of good composition—the writing of understandable prose—apply.

We can return to the question of why a case study rather than, say, the more conventional technical report might be selected as the vehicle for a naturalistic evaluation report. There is, after all, nothing intrinsic to responsive naturalistic evaluation that compels the use of any particular reporting form. Why then elect the case-study?

First, the case study provides the "thick description" so important to the naturalistic evaluation. Moreover, the provision of this information makes it possible for persons in other settings interested in the possible worth of the entity being evaluated in *their* contexts to make a rapid determination about fittingness.

Second, the case study is grounded; it provides an experiential perspective. In contrast to many other approaches to evaluation that depend on *a priori* instrumentation, design, or hypotheses, the case study is ideal for the presentation of the grounded data that emerges from the context itself.

Third, the case study is holistic and lifelike. It presents a picture credible to the actual participants in a setting, and it can easily be cast into the "natural language" of the involved audiences. That Freud's cases read more like short stories than like scientific reports will be recognized as a virtue if the criteria of adequate communication and increased understanding are applied.

Fourth, the case study simplifies the range of data that one is asked to consider—it can be streamlined so as to best serve the purposes that the evaluator has in mind. Rather than being confronted with endless technical tables, the reader is provided the essential information in a focused, conversationlike format.

Fifth, the case study focuses the reader's attention and illuminates meanings. Rather than being asked himself to integrate a wide variety of information supplied in disparate forms, the reader is presented with a well-integrated statement that points out the essentials (and their relationships) and discards the remainder.

Finally, and perhaps most importantly, the case study can communicate more than can be said in propositional language. The case study builds on the "tacit knowledge" of its readers. It is a reporting vehicle appropriate to the understanding and language of audiences. It leads, as Stake (1978b) has suggested, to "naturalistic generalization" in contrast to "scientific generalization," that is, to generalization arrived at "by recognizing the similarities of objects and issues in and out of context and by sensing the natural covariations of happenings" (p. 6). Stake suggests that when "explanation, propositional knowledge, and laws are the aims of an inquiry, the case study will often be at a disadvantage. When the aims are understanding, extension of experience, and increase in conviction in that which is known, the disadvantage disappears" (p. 6). And, of course, most evaluations that have pretensions to being responsive in form aim for the latter goals. The case study provides the reader with the kind of information that permits him to bring to bear *all* his knowledge, not merely that which he can state in spoken language. To put it in the common parlance of the day, the case study emits "vibes" that give the reader a sense of the actual substance of the case. Placed in the actual situation, the reader of a case study would sense many things that he could not scientifically document but in which he would have a great deal of confidence; the case study provides him with a vicarious setting in which the same kinds of inferences can be made. We all know more than we can say; the case study provides a vehicle for the transference of that kind of wordless knowledge.

But of course case studies have their disadvantages too. The use of any technique of data collection, analysis, or reporting must always be considered in a context of trade-offs. Thus, case studies can oversimplify or exaggerate a situation, leading the reader to erroneous conclusions about the actual state of affairs. Case studies also depend heavily on the interpretations of the writer and on his selection of the information to be presented. If the technical report leans too heavily in the direction of presenting "raw" information that must be processed by the reader, the case study too often presents processed information that the reader must take on faith. Writer biases or errors in judgment cannot easily be detected.

It is also objected that case studies are not sufficiently scientific. Presumably this criticism means that case studies are not sufficiently objective or neutral, and, no doubt, the reader who seeks a pool of data from which to draw his own conclusions will be disappointed by the typical case study. A related criticism is that case studies are opportunistic or serendipitous rather than representative. This argument is based on the notion that case studies are, in effect, one of a kind, and hence do not allow for scientific generalization.

Again, case studies are at best only partial accounts but give the impression of being the whole; that is, they tend to masquerade as a whole when in fact they are but a part—a slice of life. Of course, no study carried out by whatever paradigm can ever represent the whole; even the *Encyclopedia Brittanica* cannot satisfy that criterion.

It is undeniable that case studies are even more politically

sensitive than typical evaluation reports. Because they are focused
on particular units, because they provide a basis for tacit inferences, and because they can often be identified with the actual
elements (subjects, settings, programs, and so on) being evaluated,
so that it is difficult to maintain anonymity, case studies are more
likely than other kinds of reports to upset political balances. While
this criticism is probably true, it simply indicates one reason why
case-study evaluations are more likely to be attended to than are
typical evaluation reports.

Three other aspects of the case study as a reporting technique might be noted. First, the question is often raised about
how the adequacy (rigor) of case studies can be determined. How
can one know whether a case study is valid, reliable, and so on?
But of course the same question can be raised about almost any
technique—how can one know whether an experiment, for example, is adequate? The answer is that the adequacy of any inquiry is
largely dependent on the adequacy of its components. It is difficult to talk about the validity or reliability of an experiment as a
whole, but one *can* talk about the validity and reliability of the
instrumentation, the appropriateness of the data analysis techniques, the degree of relationship between the conclusions drawn
and the data upon which they presumably rest, and so on. In just
this way one can discuss the processes and procedures that undergird the case study—were the interviews reliably and validly conducted; was the content of the documents properly analyzed; do
the conclusions of the case study rest upon data? The case study
is, in regard to demonstrating rigor, not a whit different from any
other technique.

Second, case studies seem to involve unusual problems of
ethics. An unethical case writer could so select from among available data that virtually anything he wished could be illustrated.
Such a selection might occur for an improper reason (for example,
the evaluator allows himself to be used to whitewash a problem)
or for reasons of ignorance or naiveté on the evaluator's part. The
evaluator may also indulge in rationalizations: he does not want to
harm innocent people, he does not want to allow some negative
results to swamp the positive ones, and so on. While any inquiry
can be "shaped" by the evaluator, the case study is especially susceptible to such manipulation. Readers of case studies need, there-

fore, to be especially concerned with the reputation and integrity of the case-study writer; the writers themselves need to be aware of the possibility of such bias and to guard against it (for example, by utilizing an outside auditor to check every step they take in developing the case).

In the name of protecting anonymity or for the sake of "sharpening" the issues, the case-study writer may also decide to combine elements from several real cases into a more "typical" picture. Teacher performance in implementing a particular curriculum innovation, for instance, may be discussed by drawing upon interview and observation data from many teachers in the belief that such a composite is "better" than a discussion of a large number of actual cases with all their idiosyncratic deviations. Such case studies can be misleading unless the reader knows that the situation or person represented is not real and may in fact be a statistical or representational artifact. A case study that suggests that a "composite" person is comfortable because he has his head in the oven and his feet in the icebox is obviously very misleading.

Another ethical problem is that it is often possible for persons with some acquaintance with the situation to identify the site of the case study and even the persons referred to in it. Promises of anonymity are extremely difficult to keep. It is probably wise to act on the principle that each subject "owns" the data that relate to him, so that those data cannot be used without his explicit consent after he has been fully informed about their expected use and the potential dangers to him.

Third, it must be noted that the means for being instructed in the "art" of case-study writing are not easily at hand. It is virtually impossible to find adequate guides in the literature for the development of case studies. The skills needed to do an adequate job of case-study construction are, unfortunately, not generally taught in university research or evaluation courses, although they may be found in writing courses taught in departments of English. MacDonald and Walker (1977) point out, in relation to learning how to do case studies, that "apprenticeship is the usual means of induction into its techniques" (p. 183). Perhaps the best advice that one can give the novice is to read a large number of case studies to see how they are put together, to associate with good case-study writers to get a feel for "how it goes," and to practice writing case studies, soliciting critiques from knowledgeable connoisseurs and responding to them.

Making Judgments and Recommendations

The complete act of evaluation, virtually all experts now agree, involves *both* description and judgment. There seems to be little difficulty in assigning the task of describing to the evaluator, but there is a real question whether the evaluator can or should carry out the task of judging. Scriven (1967) makes the point that willy-nilly, the evaluator must accept this task, if for no other reason than that there is no one more qualified or unbiased than he. Nevertheless there are some good reasons why the evaluator might take pause.

A personal recollection by one of the present authors clearly illustrates the dilemma. In the mid 1960s he was at work, with others, in developing the Context-Input-Process-Product (CIPP) model. A presentation was made by Stufflebeam and Guba to faculty members of Ohio State University. The point was made, in presenting the definition of evaluation then adhered to by CIPP theorists, that evaluation was a process of "delineating, obtaining, and providing" information for decision making. But the question was raised by some of the faculty members whether, in fact, CIPP evaluators would permit themselves to be used to generate whatever information decision makers seemed to want, with no concern whether the desired information was appropriate. Just as Scriven had suggested that evaluators had a duty to evaluate objectives, rather than merely to collect information about discrepancies between objectives and performance, so these faculty members seemed to be insisting that CIPP evaluators had a duty to determine whether the decisions to be made, and the processes by which they were made, were appropriate and, yes, even ethical.

At that time, the response by Stufflebeam and Guba was to assert that evaluators did not in fact have that responsibility—they could not undertake to sit in judgment on the decision maker's rationality or ethicality. But, the response came, if that were the case, was not the evaluator simply making it possible for the decision maker to use the evaluator as a dupe? Yes, that was possible, Stufflebeam and Guba replied, but if the evaluator arranged the data in such a way that the decision maker had only one option, then the evaluator was in fact co-opting the right of the decision maker to decide; a computer could as easily determine what to do if the evaluator's data showed the most rational decision to be X. And there the matter rested; the choices seemed to be that the evaluator would not get involved in the decision-making process, in which case he could easily become a dupe, or that he would become involved in the decision-making process, in which case he would co-opt the decision-maker's choices.

This dilemma cannot be resolved so long as the evaluator and his client (whether decision maker, as in the CIPP formulation, or in some other role) maintain independent roles. If either one of them reaches the judgments and recommendations on his own, the study may well be impaled on one or the other horns of the dilemma. But if the evaluator and the client *interact* in producing judgments and recommendations, that is, if the judgments and recommendations are produced through a process of negotiation, then each can make a proper contribution from a posture of integrity.

Here, as in other instances, responsive, naturalistic evaluation seems to have a marked advantage over its competitors. The approach requires constant interaction between evaluator and relevant stakeholding audiences. The evaluation process moves through several iterations; it makes credibility checks possible at each stage and invites negotiation on points of difference. As the process moves into later stages and sufficient data begin to be available, judgments and recommendations can be included in this checking and negotiating process. By the time a final report is ready, the judgments and recommendations that should appear in it are well known to all, will surprise no one, and will, moreover, have the sanction of the stakeholding audiences involved.

Of course, it is likely that different stakeholders, because of their differing perceptions and values, will wish to make different judgments and recommendations, which might not only be inconsistent but might actually be in conflict. Under such circumstances the evaluator has no choice but to present all these points of view, but he can also undergird them with information about the values involved. The conflicts may then be resolved by some other approach—for example, that proposed by Rippey (1973) under the heading of transactional evaluation.

References

Adams, R. "On the Effective Use of Anthropology in Public Health Programs." *Human Organization,* 1955, *13,* 15-51.

Adams, S. J. *Interviewing Procedures: A Manual for Survey Interviewers.* Chapel Hill: University of North Carolina Press, 1958.

Akeret, R. V. *Photoanalysis.* New York: Pocket Books, 1975.

Alkin, M. C., and Fitz-Gibbon, C. T. "Methods and Theories of Evaluating Programs." *Journal of Research and Development in Education,* 1975, *8,* 2-15.

Allport, G. W. *The Use of Personal Documents in Psychological Science.* Bulletin 49. New York: Social Science Research Council, 1942.

Almy, M., and Geneshi, C. *Ways of Studying Children.* (rev. ed.) New York: Columbia University Press, 1979.

383

Altick, R. D. "Hunting for Manuscripts." In R. D. Altick (Ed.), *The Scholar Adventurers*. New York: Macmillan, 1950.

American Educational Research Association. *Four Evaluation Examples: Anthropological, Economic, Narrative, and Portrayal.* Monograph Series on Curriculum Evaluation, No. 7. Washington, D.C.: American Educational Research Association, 1974.

Anderson, D., and Benjaminson, P. *Investigative Reporting.* Bloomington: Indiana University Press, 1976.

Anderson, S. B., Ball, S., Murphy, R. T., and Associates. *Encyclopedia of Educational Evaluation: Concepts and Techniques for Evaluating Education and Training Programs.* San Francisco: Jossey-Bass, 1975.

Andreski, S. *Social Science as Sorcery.* New York: St. Martin's Press, 1972.

Argyle, M. *Bodily Communication.* New York: International Universities Press, 1975.

Argyris, C. "Dangers in Applying Results from Experimental Social Psychology." *American Psychologist,* 1975, *30,* 469-485.

Ashcraft, N., and Scheflen, A. E. *People Space: The Making and Breaking of Human Boundaries.* New York: Doubleday, 1976.

Atkin, M. J. "Practice-Oriented Inquiry: A Third Approach to Research in Education." *Educational Researcher,* 1973, *2,* 3-4.

Attneave, F. "How Do You Know?" *American Psychologist,* 1974, *29,* 493-499.

Babchuk, N. "The Role of the Researcher as Participant Observer and Participant-as-Observer in the Field Situation." *Human Organization,* 1962, *21,* 225-228.

Back, K. W. "The Well-Informed Informant." *Human Organization,* 1956, *14* (4), 30-33.

Balinsky, B., and Burger, R. *The Executive Interview: A Bridge to People.* New York: Harper & Row, 1959.

Banaka, W. H. *Training in Depth Interviewing.* New York: Harper & Row, 1971.

Barcus, F. E. "Communications Content: Analysis of the Research, 1900-1958." Unpublished doctoral dissertation, University of Illinois, Urbana, 1959.

Barker, R. G. "Explorations in Ecological Psychology." *American Psychologist,* 1965, *20,* 1-14.

Barker, R. G. *Ecological Psychology.* Stanford, Calif.: Stanford University Press, 1968.

Barker, R. G., and Associates. *Habitats, Environments, and Human Behavior: Studies in Ecological Psychology and Eco-Behavioral Science.* San Francisco: Jossey-Bass, 1978.

Barker, R. G., and Wright, H. F. *Midwest and Its Children: The Psychological Ecology of an American Town.* New York: Harper & Row, 1955.

Barzun, J., and Graff, H. F. *The Modern Researcher.* New York: Harcourt Brace Jovanovich, 1970.

Becker, A. De V. "Alternative Methodologies for Instructional Media Research." *Audio-Visual Communication Review,* 1977, *25,* 191-194.

Becker, H. S. "Problems of Inference and Proof in Participant Observation." *American Sociological Review,* 1968, *58,* 652-660.

Becker, H. S. *Sociological Work.* Chicago: Aldine, 1970.

Becker, H. S., and Geer, B. "Participant Observation and Interviewing: A Comparison." *Human Organization,* 1957, *16,* 28-32.

Becker, H. S., and Geer, B. "Participant Observation: The Analysis of Qualitative Field Data." In R. N. Adams and J. J. Preiss (Eds.), *Human Organization Research.* Homewood, Ill.: Dorsey Press, 1960.

Becker, T. M., and Meyers, P. R. "Empathy and Bravado: Interviewing Reluctant Bureaucrats." *Public Opinion Quarterly,* 1974-1975, *38,* 605-613.

Bellman, B., and Jules-Rossette, B. *A Paradigm for Looking: Cross-Cultural Research with Visual Media.* Trenton, N.J.: Ablex Publishing, 1977.

Benjamin, A. *The Helping Interview.* New York: Houghton Mifflin, 1969.

Bennett, J. W., and Thaiss, G. "Survey Research and Sociocultural Anthropology." In C. Glock (Ed.), *Survey Research in the Social Sciences.* New York: Russell Sage Foundation, 1967.

Benson, T. W. *An Orientation to Non-Verbal Communication.* Chicago: Science Research Associates, 1976.

Bentley, A. F. *Inquiry into Inquiries: Essays in Social Theory.* Boston: Beacon Press, 1954.

Berelson, B. *Content Analysis in Communication Research.* New York: Free Press, 1952.

Berreman, G. D. *Behind Many Masks: Ethnography and Impression Management in a Himalayan Village.* Ithaca, N.Y.: Society for Applied Anthropology, 1962.

Berreman, G. D. "Behind Many Masks: Ethnography and Impression Management in a Himalayan Village." In D. P. Warwick and S. Osherson (Eds.), *Comparative Research Methods.* Englewood Cliffs, N.J.: Prentice-Hall, 1973.

Bingham, W. V., and Moore, B. V. *How to Interview.* (4th ed.) New York: Harper & Row, 1959.

Birdwhistell, R. L. "Body Motions Research and Interviewing." *Human Organization,* 1952, *11,* 37.

Birdwhistell, R. L. *Kinesics and Context: Essays on Body-Motion Communication.* Philadelphia: University of Pennsylvania Press, 1970.

Blaisdell, E. A., Jr., and Gordon, D. "Selection of Occupational Therapy Students." *American Journal of Occupational Therapy,* 1979, *33,* 223-229.

Bloch, M. *The Historian's Craft.* New York: Vintage Books, 1964.

Bochner, S. "An Unobtrusive Approach to the Study of Housing Discrimination Against Aborigines." *Australian Journal of Psychology,* 1972, *24,* 335-337.

Bode, B. "The Concept of Needs." In B. H. Bode, *Progressive Education at the Crossroads.* New York: Newsom, 1938.

Boehm, A. E., and Weinberg, R. A. *The Classroom Observer: A Guide for Developing Observation Skills.* New York: Columbia University Press, 1977.

Bogdan, R. *Participant Observation in Organization Settings.* New York: Syracuse University Press, 1972.

Bogdan, R., and Taylor, S. J. *Introduction to Qualitative Research Methods.* New York: Wiley, 1975.

Bok, S. *Lying: Moral Choice in Public and Private Life.* New York: Random House, 1978.

Bolch, J., and Miller, K. *Investigative and In-Depth Reporting.* New York: Hastings House, 1978.

Bollens, J. C., and Marshall, D. R. *A Guide to Participation.* Englewood Cliffs, N.J.: Prentice-Hall, 1973.

Boruch, R. F., and Reis, J. "The Student, Evaluative Data, and Secondary Analysis," in press.

Bowen, E. S. *Return to Laughter.* New York: Doubleday, 1964.

Brady, J. *The Craft of Interviewing.* Cincinnati: Writer's Digest, 1976.

Brandt, R. *Studying Behavior in Natural Settings.* New York: Holt, Rinehart and Winston, 1972.

Braskamp, L. A., and Brown, R. D. (Eds.). *New Directions for Program Evaluation: Utilization of Evaluative Information,* no. 5. San Francisco: Jossey-Bass, 1980.

Braskamp, L. A., Brown, R. D., and Newman, D. L. "The Credibility of a Local Educational Program Evaluation Report: Author Source and Audience Characteristics." *American Educational Research Journal,* 1978, *15,* 441-450.

Braybrooke, D., and Lindblom, C. E. *A Strategy of Decision.* New York: Free Press, 1963.

Brian, D. *Murderers and Other Friendly People.* New York: McGraw-Hill, 1973.

Brickell, H. M. "The Influence of External Political Factors on the Role and Methodology of Evaluation." Paper presented at annual meeting of American Educational Research Association, 1974. (*Research Evaluation Development Paper Series,* no. 7. Northwest Regional Educational Laboratory, Portland, Oreg., 1975; and in T. D. Cook and others, *Evaluation Studies Review Annual.* Vol. 3. Beverly Hills, Calif.: Sage Publications, 1978.)

Brickell, H. M. "Needed: Instruments as Good as Our Eyes." Occasional Paper Series 17. Kalamazoo: Evaluation Center, Western Michigan University, July 1976.

Bronfenbrenner, U. "The Experimental Ecology of Education." *Educational Researcher,* 1976, *5,* 51-115.

Bronfenbrenner, U. "Toward an Experimental Ecology of Human Development." *American Psychologist,* 1977, *32,* 513-531.

Brown, R. D., Braskamp, L. A., and Newman, D. L. "Evaluator Credibility as a Function of Report Style: Do Jargon and Data Make a Difference?" *Evaluation Quarterly,* 1978, *2,* 331-342.

Brunswik, E. "Representative Design and Probabilistic Theory in a Functional Psychology." *Psychological Review,* 1955, *62,* 193-217.

Bruyn, S. T. *The Human Perspective in Sociology: The Methodology of Participant Observation.* Englewood Cliffs, N.J.: Prentice-Hall, 1966.

Budd, R. W., and others. *Content Analysis of Communications.* New York: Macmillan, 1967.

Burnett, J. "Event Description and Analysis in Microethnography of Urban Classrooms." In F. A. Ianni and E. Storey (Eds.), *Cultural Relevance and Educational Issues: Readings in Anthropology and Education.* Boston: Little, Brown, 1973.

Buron, T. L., and Cherry, G. E. *Social Research Techniques for Planners.* London: Allen & Unwin, 1975.

Burstein, L. "Secondary Analysis: An Important Resource for Educational Research and Evaluation." *Educational Researcher,* 1978, *7,* 9-12.

Cambre, M. "The Development of Formative Evaluation Procedures for Instructional Film and Television: The First Fifty Years." Unpublished doctoral dissertation, Indiana University, 1978.

Campbell, D. T. "Degrees of Freedom and the Case Study." *Comparative Political Studies,* 1975, *8,* 175-193.

Campbell, D. T. "Qualitative Knowing in Action Research." Kurt Lewin Award Address, Society for the Psychological Study of Social Issues, September 1974.

Campbell, D. T., and Stanley, J. C. "Experimental and Quasi-Experimental Designs for Research on Teaching." In N. L. Gage (Ed.), *Handbook of Research on Teaching.* Chicago: Rand McNally, 1963.

Cannell, C. F., and Kahn, R. L. "Interviewing." In G. Lindzey and E. Aronson (Eds.), *The Handbook of Social Psychology.* (2nd ed.) Vol. 2. Reading, Mass.: Addison-Wesley, 1968.

Caplow, T. "Dynamics of Information Interviewing." *American Journal of Sociology,* 1956-1957, *62,* 165-171.

Carroll, J. M. *The Third Listener: Personal Electronic Espionage.* New York: Dutton, 1969.

Cartwright, D. P. "Analysis of Qualitative Material." In L. Festinger and D. Katz (Eds.), *Research Methods in the Behavioral Sciences.* New York: Holt, Rinehart and Winston, 1953.

Carver, R. P. "The Case Against Statistical Significance Testing." *Harvard Educational Review,* 1978, *48*(3), 378-399.

Center for the Study of Evaluation, UCLA. *Elementary School Evaluation Kit: Needs Assessment.* Boston: Allyn & Bacon, 1972.

Christensen, H. T. "Cultural Relativism and Premarital Sex Norms." *American Sociological Review,* 1960, *25,* 31-39.

Cicourel, A. V. *Method and Measurement in Sociology.* New York: Free Press, 1964.

Cicourel, A. V. *Cognitive Sociology.* New York: Free Press, 1974.

Clark, D. L. and Guba, E. G. *A Study of Teacher Education Institutions as Innovators, Knowledge Producers, and Change Agents: Final Report.* National Institute of Education, NIE Project No. 4-0752, Indiana University, April 30, 1977.

Clark, G. K. *The Critical Historian.* London: Heinemann Educational Books, 1967.

Coles, R. "Confessions of a Premier Child Specialist." *Learning,* 1979, *7,* 40-42.

Collier, J., Jr. *Visual Anthropology: Photography as a Research Method.* New York: Holt, Rinehart and Winston, 1967.

Converse, J. M., and Schuman, H. *Conversations at Random: Survey Research as Interviewers See It.* New York: Wiley, 1974.

Cook, T. D. "The Potential and Limitations of Secondary Evaluation." In M. S. Apple, M. S. Subkoviak, and J. R. Luffler (Eds.), *Educational Evaluation: Analysis and Responsibility.* Berkeley, Calif.: McCutchan, 1974.

Cook, T. D., and Reichardt, C. I. (Eds.). *Qualitative and Quantitative Methods in Evaluation Research.* Beverly Hills, Calif.: Sage, 1979.

Council of Social Science Data Archives. *Social Science Data Archives in the United States.* New York: Council of Social Science Data Archives, 1967.

Cronbach, L. J. "Course Improvement Through Evaluation." *Teachers College Record,* 1963, *64,* 672-683.

Cronbach, L. J. "Beyond the Two Disciplines of Scientific Psychology." *American Psychologist,* 1975, *30,* 116-127.

Cross, H. *The People's Right to Know: Legal Access to Public Records and Proceedings.* New York: Columbia University Press, 1953.

Curt, C. J. *Non-Verbal Communication in Puerto Rico.* New York: National Assessment and Dissemination Center, 1978.

Dalton, M. *Men Who Manage.* New York: Wiley, 1959.

Davin, F. *Inside Intuition: What We Know About Non-Verbal Communication.* New York: McGraw-Hill, 1973.

Deich, R. F., and Hodges, P. M. *Language Without Speech.* New York: Brunner/Mazel, 1977.

Denny, T. "Storytelling and Educational Understanding." Address delivered at national meeting of International Reading Association, Houston, Texas, May 1978.

Denzin, N. K. *Sociological Methods: A Sourcebook.* Chicago: Aldine, 1970.

Denzin, N. K. *The Research Art: A Theoretical Introduction to Sociological Methods.* Chicago: Aldine, 1970.

Denzin, N. K. "The Logic of Naturalistic Inquiry." *Social Forces,* 1971, *50,* 166-182.

Denzin, N. K. *Sociological Methods.* New York: McGraw-Hill, 1978.

Derickson, F. "Some Approaches to Inquiry in School-Community Ethnography." *Anthropology and Education,* 1977, *8,* 58-69.

Dexter, L. A. *Elite and Specialized Interviewing.* Evanston, Ill.: Northwestern University Press, 1970.

Diener, E., and Crandall, R. *Ethics in Social and Behavioral Research.* Chicago: University of Chicago Press, 1978.

Dipboye, R. L., and Flanagan, M. L. "Research Settings in Industrial and Organizational Psychology." *American Psychologist,* 1979, *34,* 141-149.

Dittman, A. T., and Wynne, L. C. "Linguistic Techniques and the Analysis of Emotionality in Interviews." *Journal of Abnormal and Social Psychology,* 1961, *63,* 201-204.

Dodge, M., and Bogdan, R. "Participant Observation: A Promising Approach for Educational Technology." *Phi Delta Kappan,* 1974, *56,* 67-69.

Dohrenwend, B., Klein, D., and Richardson, S. *Interviewing: Its Forms and Functions.* New York: Basic Books, 1965.

Dollard, J. *Criteria for the Life History, with Analyses of Six Notable Documents.* New York: Peter Smith, 1935.

Douglas, J. D. *Investigative Social Research.* Beverly Hills, Calif.: Sage, 1976.

Duverger, M. *An Introduction to the Social Sciences.* New York: Praeger, 1961.

Egan, G. *The Skilled Helper: A Model for Systematic Helping and Interpersonal Relating.* Monterey, Calif.: Brooks/Cole, 1975.

Eisner, E. W. "Instructional and Expressive Objectives: Their Formulation and Use in Curriculum." *AERA Monograph Series in Curriculum Evaluation,* No. 3. Chicago: Rand McNally, 1969.

Eisner, E. W. "The Perceptive Eye: Toward the Reformation of Educational Evaluation." Stanford, Calif.: Stanford Evaluation Consortium, December 1975.

Eisner, E. W. *The Educational Imagination.* New York: Macmillan, 1979.

Ekman, P. "Body Position, Facial Expression, and Verbal Behavior During Interviews." *Journal of Abnormal and Social Psychology,* 1964, *68,* 295-301.

Ekman, P., and Friesen, W. V. *Unmasking the Face: A Guide to Recognizing Emotions from Facial Clues.* Englewood Cliffs, N.J.: Prentice-Hall, 1975.

Ellsworth, P. C. "From Abstract Ideas to Concrete Instances: Some Guidelines for Choosing Natural Research Settings." *American Psychologist,* 1977, *32,* 604-615.

Farrar, E., and others. *Views from Below: Implementation Research in Education.* Cambridge, Mass.: Huron Institute, 1979.

Fast, J. *Body Language.* New York: M. Evans, 1978.

Festinger, E., and Katz, D. *Research Methods in the Behavioral Sciences.* New York: Dryden Press, 1953.

Fiedler, J. *Field Research: A Manual for Logistics and Management of Scientific Studies in Natural Settings.* San Francisco: Jossey-Bass, 1978.

Fienberg, S. E. "The Collection and Analysis of Ethnographic Data in Educational Research." *Anthropology and Education,* 1977, *8,* 50-57.

Filstead, W. J. *Qualitative Methodology.* Chicago: Rand McNally, 1970.

Filstead, W. J. (Ed.). *Qualitative Methodology: Firsthand Involvement with the Social World.* Chicago: Markham, 1978.

Flaherty, E. W., Barry, E., and Swift, M. "Use of an Unobtrusive Measure for the Evaluation of Interagency Coordination." *Evaluation Quarterly,* 1978, *2,* 261-273.

Forcese, D. P., and Richer, S. *Social Research Methods.* Englewood Cliffs, N.J.: Prentice-Hall, 1973.

Forsdale, L. *Non-Verbal Communication.* New York: Harcourt Brace Jovanovich, 1974.

Fox, D. *Fundamentals of Research in Nursing.* New York: Appleton-Century-Crofts, 1966.

Frazier, M. E. "Case-Study Approach to Educational Research." In R. H. Jones (Ed.), *Methods and Techniques of Educational Research.* Danville, Ill.: Interstate Printers and Publishers, 1973.

Frick, T., and Semmel, M. I. "Observer Agreement and Reliabilities of Classroom Observational Measures." *Review of Educational Research,* 1978, *48,* 157-184.

Friday, N. *My Mother, My Self.* New York: Dell, 1978.

Garrett, A. *Interviewing: Its Principles and Methods.* New York: Family Service Association of America, 1959.

Gatz, F., and Hoagland, G. "A Guide to Interviewing in Qualitative Research." Unpublished paper, Indiana University, 1978.

Geertz, C. "Thick Description: Toward an Interpretive Theory of Culture." In C. Geertz, *The Interpretation of Cultures.* New York: Basic Books, 1973.

Geertz, C. "On the Nature of Anthropological Understanding." *American Scientist,* 1975, *63,* 47-53.

Gerbner, C., and Holsti, O. (Eds.). *The Analysis of Communication Content.* New York: Wiley, 1969.

Gibbs, J. C. "The Meaning of Ecologically Oriented Inquiry in Contemporary Psychology." *American Psychologist,* 1979, *34,* 127-140.

Glaser, B. G., and Strauss, A. L. *The Discovery of Grounded Theory.* Chicago: Aldine, 1967.

Glass, G. V. "A Paradox About Excellence of Schools and the People in Them." *Educational Researcher,* 1975, *4,* 9-13.

Glass, G. V. (Ed.). *Evaluation Studies Review Annual.* Vol. 1. Beverly Hills, Calif.: Sage, 1976a.

Glass, G. V. "Primary, Secondary, and Meta-Analysis of Research." *Educational Researcher,* 1976b, *5,* 3-8.

Goffman, E. *Presentation of Self in Everyday Life.* New York: Doubleday, 1959.

Goffman, E. *Asylums.* New York: Doubleday, 1961.

Goffman, E. "On Face Work." In E. Goffman, *Interaction Ritual: Essays on Face-to-Face Behavior.* New York: Doubleday, 1967.

Goffman, E. *Frame Analysis*. New York: Harper & Row, 1974.

Gold, R. "Roles in Sociological Field Observations." *Social Forces*, 1958, *36*, 217-223.

Goldman, E. (Ed.). *Research Methods and the Counselor*. New York: Wiley, 1978.

Good, C. V. *Introduction to Educational Research*. (2nd ed.) New York: Appleton-Century-Crofts, 1963.

Goode, W. J., and Hatt, P. K. *Methods in Social Research*. New York: McGraw-Hill, 1952.

Goodlad, J., and others. *Behind the Classroom Door*. Worthington, Ohio: Jones, 1970.

Gorden, R. L. "Dimensions of the Depth Interview." *American Journal of Sociology*, 1956, *6*, 158-164.

Gorden, R. L. *Interviewing: Strategy, Techniques, and Tactics*. (rev. ed.) Homewood, Ill.: Dorsey Press, 1975.

Gottschalk, L., Kluckhohn, C., and Angell, R. *The Use of Personal Documents in History, Anthropology, and Sociology*. New York: Social Science Research Council, 1947.

Gray, W., and others. *Historian's Handbook*. (2nd ed.) Boston: Houghton Mifflin, 1964.

Gross, N., Gisquieta, J., and Berstein, M. *Implementing Organizational Innovations: A Sociological Analysis of Planned Educational Change*. New York: Basic Books, 1971.

Guba, E. G. "The Failure of Educational Evaluation." *Educational Technology*, 1969, *9*, 29-38.

Guba, E. G. "Problems in Utilizing the Results of Evaluation." *Journal of Research and Development in Education*, 1975, *8*, 42-54.

Guba, E. G. *Metaphor Adaptation Report: Investigative Journalism*. Research on Evaluation Project Monograph. Portland, Oreg.: Northwest Regional Educational Laboratory, 1978a.

Guba, E. G. "The Methodological Rigor of Qualitative Methods." Paper presented at University Council for Educational Administration workshop on Qualitative Methods in Administrative Research, Bloomington, Ind., November 1978b.

Guba, E. G. *Toward a Methodology of Naturalistic Inquiry in Educational Evaluation*. Monograph Series, No. 8. Los Angeles: Center for the Study of Evaluation, University of California, 1978c.

Guba, E. G. "Investigative Journalism." In N. L. Smith (Ed.), *Metaphors for Evaluation: Sources of New Methods.* Beverly Hills, Calif.: Sage, forthcoming.

Gusfield, J. R. "Fieldwork Reciprocities in Studying a Social Movement." *Human Organization,* 1955, *14,* 29-33.

Hage, G. S., and others. *New Strategies for Public Affairs Reporting: Investigation, Interpretation, and Research.* Englewood Cliffs, N.J.: Prentice-Hall, 1976.

Hall, E. T. *The Silent Language.* New York: Doubleday, 1959.

Hall, E. T. *The Hidden Dimension.* New York: Doubleday, 1966.

Hall, E. T. *Beyond Culture.* New York: Doubleday, 1976.

Hamilton, D. "Making Sense of Curriculum Evaluation: Continuities and Discontinuities in an Educational Idea." In L. S. Shulman (Ed.), *Review of Research in Education.* Itasca, Ill.: Peacock Publishers, 1977.

Hamilton, D., and others. *Beyond the Numbers Game.* Berkeley, Calif.: McCutchan, 1977.

Hammond, P. E. (Ed.). *Sociologists at Work.* New York: Basic Books, 1964.

Hammond, R. L. "Evaluation at the Local Level." In B. R. Worthen and J. R. Sanders, *Educational Evaluation: Theory and Practice.* Worthington, Ohio: Jones, 1973.

Harper, R. G., Wiens, A. N., and Matarazzo, J. *Non-Verbal Communication: The State of the Art.* New York: Wiley, 1978.

Harral, S. *Keys to Successful Interviewing.* Norman: University of Oklahoma Press, 1954.

Harrison, R. P. *Beyond Words: An Introduction to Non-Verbal Communication.* Englewood Cliffs, N.J.: Prentice-Hall, 1974.

Heapley, J. "The Problem of Theory and Case Research." In J. A. Culbertson and S. P. Hencley (Eds.), *Educational Research: New Perspectives.* Danville, Ill.: Interstate Printers and Publishers, 1963.

Hecht, K. A. "The Development of a Chronology of Critical Events for Evaluation and Policy Research." Paper presented at annual meeting of the American Educational Research Association, New York, 1976.

Henley, N. M. *Body Politics.* Englewood Cliffs, N.J.: Prentice-Hall, 1977.

Hennig, M., and Jardim, A. *The Managerial Woman.* New York: Doubleday, 1976.

Henry, J. "My Life with the Families of Psychotic Children." In G. Handel (Ed.), *Psychosocial Interior of the Family.* Chicago: AVC, 1967.

Herriott, R. E. "Ethnographic Case Studies in Federally Funded Multi-Disciplinary Policy Research: Some Design and Implementation Issues." *Anthropology and Education,* 1977, *8,* 106-114.

Hersen, M., and Barlow, D. H. *Single Case Experimental Design.* Elmsford, N.Y.: Pergamon Press, 1976.

Hildreth, G. H. *A Bibliography of Mental Tests and Rating Scales.* (suppl. to 2nd ed.) New York: Psychological Corp., 1945.

Hockett, H. C. *The Critical Method in Historical Research and Writing.* New York: Macmillan, 1955.

Hoffer, E. *The True Believer.* New York: Harper & Row, 1951.

Holsti, O. R. *Content Analysis for the Social Sciences and Humanities.* Reading, Mass.: Addison-Wesley, 1969.

Homans, G. C. *The Nature of Social Science.* New York: Harcourt Brace Jovanovich, 1967.

House, E. R. (Ed.). *School Evaluation: The Politics and Process.* Berkeley, Calif.: McCutchan, 1973.

House, E. R. "Justice in Evaluation." In G. V. Glass (Ed.), *Evaluation Studies Review Annual.* Vol. 1. Beverly Hills, Calif.: Sage, 1976.

House, E. R. "Naturalistic Observation: Formal and Informal Difficulties." *Child Study Journal,* 1978a, *8,* 17-28.

House, E. R. *The Logic of Evaluative Argument.* Los Angeles: Center for the Study of Evaluation, University of California, 1978b.

Hughes, J. A. *Sociological Analysis: Methods of Discovery.* London: Nelson, 1976.

Hyman, H. H., and others. *Interviewing in Social Research.* Chicago: University of Chicago Press, 1954.

Iannaccone, L. "The Field Study in Educational Policy Research." *Education and Urban Society,* 1975, 7, 220-245.

Institute for Social Research. *Interviewer's Manual.* Ann Arbor: Institute for Social Research, University of Michigan, 1976.

Jackson, P. W. *Life in Classrooms.* New York: Holt, Rinehart and Winston, 1968.

Jacobs, G. (Ed.). *The Participant Observer.* New York: Braziller, 1977.

Jahoda, M., Deutsch, M., and Cook, S. W. *Research Methods in Social Relations.* Vol. 1: *Basic Processes.* New York: Dryden Press, 1951a.

Jahoda, M., Deutsch, M., and Cook, S. W. *Research Methods in Social Relations.* Vol. 2: *Selected Techniques.* New York: Dryden Press, 1951b.

Jahoda, M., and others. *Research Methods in Social Relations: Revised One-Volume Edition.* New York: Holt, Rinehart and Winston, 1966.

Jick, T. D. "Mixing Qualitative and Quantitative Methods: Triangulation in Action." *Administrative Science Quarterly,* 1979, *24,* 602-611.

Johnson, J. M. "The Social Construction of Official Information." Unpublished doctoral dissertation, University of California, San Diego, 1973.

Johnson, J. M. *Doing Field Research.* New York: Free Press, 1975.

Johnson, R. F. Q. "Pitfalls in Research: The Interview as an Illustrative Model." *Psychological Reports,* 1976, *38,* 3-17.

Joint Committee on Standards for Educational Evaluation. *Standards for Educational Evaluation.* Chicago: Rand McNally, 1980.

Jones, B. (Ed.). *Kinesics and Context: Essays on Body Motion Communication.* Philadelphia: University of Pennsylvania Press, 1970.

Jones, J. E. "The Sensing Interview." In J. Jones and J. W. Pfeiffer (Eds.), *Annual Handbook for Group Facilitators.* La Jolla, Calif.: University Associates, 1973.

Kahle, L. R. (Ed.). *New Directions for Methodology of Behavioral Science: Methods for Studying Person-Situation Interactions,* no. 2. San Francisco: Jossey-Bass, 1979.

Kahn, R. L., and Cannell, C. F. *The Dynamics of Interviewing.* New York: Wiley, 1966.

Kaplan, A. *The Conduct of Inquiry.* San Francisco: Chandler, 1964.

Kinsey, A. C., Pomeroy, W. B., and Marton, C. E. *Sexual Behavior in the Human Male.* Philadelphia: Saunders, 1948.

Knapp, M. L. *Non-Verbal Communication in Human Interaction.* New York: Holt, Rinehart and Winston, 1978.

Koppelman, K. L. "The Explication Model: An Anthropological

Approach to Program Evaluation." *Journal of Educational Evaluation and Policy Analysis,* 1979, *1,* 59-64.

Krames, L., Pliner, P., and Alloway, T. *Non-Verbal Communication.* New York: Plenum Press, 1974.

Krathwohl, D. R. "The Myth of Value-Free Evaluation." *Educational Evaluation and Policy Analysis,* 1980, *2,* 37-46.

Kuhn, T. S. *The Structure of Scientific Revolutions.* International Encyclopedia of Unified Science. Vol. 2, No. 2. (2nd ed.) Chicago: University of Chicago Press, 1970.

Kuhn, T. S. *The Essential Tension: Selected Studies in Scientific Tradition and Change.* Chicago: University of Chicago Press, 1977.

Labovitz, S., and Hagedorn, R. *Introduction to Social Research.* New York: McGraw-Hill, 1971.

Lazarsfeld, P. F., and Rosenberg, M. (Eds.). *The Language of Social Research.* New York: Free Press, 1955.

Lazarsfeld, P., and Sieber, S. D. *Organizing Educational Research.* Englewood Cliffs, N.J.: Prentice-Hall, 1964.

Leenders, M. R., and Erskine, J. A. *Case Research: The Case Writing Process.* School of Business Administration, University of Western Ontario, 1973.

Liebow, E. *Tally's Corner.* Boston: Little, Brown, 1967.

Lincoln, Y. S. "An Organizational Assessment of the Potential of Bureaus as Agencies for Knowledge Production and Utilization." Unpublished doctoral dissertation, Indiana University, 1978.

Lincoln, Y. S., and Guba, E. G. "The Distinction Between Merit and Worth in Evaluation." *Educational Evaluation and Policy Analysis,* 1980, *2,* 61-72.

Lindzey, G., and Aronson, E. (Eds.). *The Handbook of Social Psychology.* (2nd ed.) Reading, Mass.: Addison-Wesley, 1968.

Lipset, S. M., and Hofstadter, R. (Eds.). *Sociology and History: Methods.* New York: Basic Books, 1968.

Locklin, B. J. "Transcript of Discussion by Bruce J. Locklin." Urban Policy Research Institute, Investigative Reporting Seminar. Beverly Hills, Calif.: Urban Policy Research Institute, 1976.

Lofland, J. *Analyzing Social Settings: A Guide to Qualitative Observation and Analysis.* Belmont, Calif.: Wadsworth, 1971.

Longstreet, W. S. *Aspects of Ethnicity.* New York: Columbia University Press, 1978.

Lortie, D. C. *Schoolteacher: A Sociological Study.* Chicago: University of Chicago Press, 1975.

Lucas, W. *The Case Survey and Alternative Methods for Research Aggregation.* Santa Monica, Calif.: Rand Corporation, 1974a.

Lucas, W. "The Case-Survey Method: Aggregating Case Experience." Santa Monica, Calif.: Rand Corporation, 1974b.

Lutz, F. W., and Ramsey, M. A. "The Use of Anthropological Field Methods in Education." *Educational Researcher,* 1974, *3,* 5-9.

McCall, G. J. "Data Quality Control in Participant Observation." In G. J. McCall and J. L. Simmons (Eds.), *Issues in Participant Observation: A Text and Reader.* Reading, Mass.: Addison-Wesley, 1969.

McCall, G. J., and Simmons, J. L. (Eds.). *Issues in Participant Observation: A Text and Reader.* Reading, Mass.: Addison-Wesley, 1969.

McDaniel, C. O. *Research Methodology: Some Issues in Social Science Research.* Dubuque, Iowa: Kendall, Hunt, 1974.

MacDonald, B., and Walker, R. "Case Study and the Social Philosophy of Educational Research." In D. Hamilton and others (Eds.), *Beyond the Numbers Game.* Berkeley, Calif.: McCutchan, 1977.

Madge, J. *The Tools of Social Science.* London: Longman, 1953.

Magoon, A. J. "Constructivist Research." *Review of Educational Research,* 1977, *47,* 651-693.

Maier, N. *The Appraisal Interview.* New York: Wiley, 1958.

Manheim, H. L. *Sociological Research: Philosophy and Methods.* Homewood, Ill.: Dorsey Press, 1977.

Manning, P. K. "Problems in Interpreting Interview Data." *Sociology and Social Research,* 1967, *51,* 302-316.

Marceil, J. C. "Implicit Dimensions of Idiography and Nomothesis: A Reformulation." *American Psychologist,* 1977, *32,* 1046-1055.

Mead, M. *Blackberry Winter: My Earlier Years.* New York: Morrow, 1972.

Mehrabian, A. *Nonverbal Communication.* Chicago: Aldine-Atherton, 1972.

Meisells, S. J. (Ed.). *Special Education and Development.* Baltimore: University Park Press, 1979.

Melbin, M. "Field Methods and Techniques: An Interaction Recording Device for Participant Observation." *Human Organization,* 1954, *13,* 29-33.

Merton, R. K. "The Focused Interview." *American Journal of Sociology,* 1946, *51,* 541.

Merton, R. K., Fiske, M., and Kendall, P. L. *The Focused Interview.* New York: Free Press, 1956.

Merwin, J. C. "Historical Review of Changing Concepts of Evaluation." In R. W. Tyler (Ed.), *Educational Evaluation: New Roles, New Means.* Chicago: University of Chicago Press, 1969.

Merwin, J. C., and Womer, F. B. "Evaluation in Assessing the Progress of Education to Provide Bases of Public Understanding and Public Policy." In R. W. Tyler (Ed.), *Educational Evaluation: New Roles, New Means.* Chicago: University of Chicago Press, 1969.

Metfessel, N. S., and Michael, W. B. "A Paradigm Involving Multiple-Criterion Measures for the Evaluation of the Effectiveness of School Programs." *Educational and Psychological Measurement,* 1967, *27,* 931-943.

Miles, M. B. "Qualitative Data as an Attractive Nuisance: The Problem of Analysis." *Administrative Science Quarterly,* 1978, *24*(4), 590-601.

Mill, J. S. *A System of Logic.* London: Longman, 1906. (Originally published 1843.)

Miller, D. B. "Roles of Naturalistic Observation in Comparative Psychology." *American Psychologist,* 1977, *32,* 211-219.

Miller, D. C. *Handbook of Research Design and Social Measurement.* Pt. 2. (3rd ed.) New York: McKay, 1977.

Miller, S. M. "The Participant Observer and 'Over-Rapport.'" *American Sociological Review,* 1953, *18,* 97-99.

Mirvis, P. H., and Seashore, S. E. "Being Ethical in Organizational Research." *American Psychologist,* 1979, *34,* 766-781.

Mitchell, W. D. "Finding Out What Happens in the Field: The Use of Field Logs." *Evaluation Quarterly,* 1979, *3*(3), 427-445.

Mitroff, I. I., and Kilmann, R. H. *Methodological Approaches to Social Science: Integrating Divergent Concepts and Theories.* San Francisco: Jossey-Bass, 1978.

Moore, R. L., and others (Eds.). *Gathering and Writing News: Selected Readings*. Washington, D.C.: College and University Press, 1975.

Morris, D. *Manwatching: A Field Guide to Human Behavior*. New York: Abrams, 1977.

Murphy, H. J. *Where's What: Sources of Information for Federal Investigators*. New York: New York Times, 1976.

Murphy, J. T. *Getting the Facts: A Fieldwork Guide for Evaluators and Policy Analysts*. Santa Monica, Calif.: Goodyear Publishing, 1980.

Nachmias, D., and Nachmias, C. *Research Methods in the Social Sciences*. New York: St. Martin's Press, 1976.

Neier, A. *Dossier: The Secret Files They Keep on You*. New York: Stein and Day, 1975.

Newman, D. L., Brown, R. D., and Littman, M. I. "Sex Bias in Program Evaluation: A Function of Reader and Report Characteristics." Paper presented at annual meeting of American Educational Research Association, Toronto, March 1978.

Nottingham, E. "From Both Sides of the Lens: Street Photojournalism and Personal Space." Unpublished doctoral dissertation, Indiana University, 1978.

Noyes, D. "Raising Hell: A Citizen's Guide to the Fine Art of Investigation." San Francisco: Mother Jones Magazine, n.d.

O'Keefe, K. G. "Methodology for Education Field Studies." Unpublished doctoral dissertation, Ohio State University, 1968.

Okun, B. F. *Effective Helping: Interviewing and Counseling Techniques*. North Scituate, Mass.: Duxbury Press, 1976.

Olesen, V. L., and Whittaker, E. W. "Role-Making in Participant Observation: Processes in the Researcher-Actor Relationship." *Human Organization*, 1967, *26*, 273-281.

Oppenheim, A. N. *Questionnaire Design and Attitude Measurement*. New York: Basic Books, 1966.

Orenstein, A., and Phillips, W. R. F. *Understanding Social Research: An Introduction*. Boston: Allyn & Bacon, 1978.

Paisley, W. J. "Studying 'Style' as a Deviation from Encoding Norms." In G. Gerbner and others (Eds.), *The Analysis of Communication Content Development in Scientific Theories and Computer Techniques*. New York: Wiley, forthcoming.

Parlett, M., and Dearden, G. (Eds.). *Introduction to Illuminative*

Evaluation: Studies in Higher Education. Beverly Hills, Calif.: Sage, 1978.

Parlett, M., and Hamilton, D. "Evaluation as Illumination: A New Approach to the Study of Innovatory Programs." Occasional Paper, No. 9. Edinburgh: Center for Research in the Educational Sciences, University of Edinburgh, 1972.

Patton, M. Q. "Alternative Evaluation Research Paradigm." Grand Forks: North Dakota Study Group on Evaluation, 1975.

Patton, M. Q. *Utilization-Focused Evaluation.* Beverly Hills, Calif.: Sage, 1978.

Patton, M. Q. *Qualitative Evaluation Methods.* Beverly Hills, Calif.: Sage, 1980.

Paul, B. D. "Interviewing Techniques and Field Relationships." In A. L. Kroeber and others (Eds.), *Anthropology Today: An Encyclopedia Inventory.* Chicago: University of Chicago Press, 1953.

Payne, S. J. *The Art of Asking Questions.* Princeton, N.J.: Princeton University Press, 1951.

Perloff, R. (Ed.). *Evaluator Interventions: Pros and Cons.* Beverly Hills, Calif.: Sage, 1979.

Peterson, W. *Population.* New York: Macmillan, 1969.

Phillips, B. S. *Social Research: Strategy and Tactics.* New York: Macmillan, 1976.

Pizer, V. *You Don't Say.* New York: Putnam's, 1978.

Pliner, P., Krames, L., and Alloway, T. *Nonverbal Communication.* New York: Plenum Press, 1975.

Polanyi, M. *The Tacit Dimension.* New York: Doubleday, 1966.

Pool, I. de S. (Ed.). *Trends in Content Analysis.* Urbana: University of Illinois Press, 1959.

Popham, W. J. (Ed.). *Evaluation in Education.* Berkeley, Calif.: McCutchan, 1974.

Popham, W. J. *Educational Evaluation.* Englewood Cliffs, N.J.: Prentice-Hall, 1975.

Powdermaker, H. *Stranger and Friend: The Way of the Anthropologist.* New York: Norton, 1966.

Presson, H. *The Student Journalist and Interviewing.* New York: Rosen Press, 1967.

Proshansky, H. M. "Environmental Psychology and the Real World." *American Psychologist,* 1976, *31,* 303-310.

Provus, M. "Evaluation of Ongoing Programs in the Public School System." In R. W. Tyler (Ed.), *Educational Evaluation: New Roles, New Means.* Chicago: University of Chicago Press, 1969.

Provus, M. *Discrepancy Evaluation.* Berkeley, Calif.: McCutchan, 1971.

Ravetz, J. R. *Scientific Knowledge and Its Social Problems.* Oxford, England: Clarendon Press, 1972.

Rayder, N., and others. "On Aggregation, Generalization, and Utility in Educational Evaluation." *Journal of Educational Evaluation and Policy Analysis,* 1979, *1*(4), 31-40.

Reece, M. M., and Whitman, R. N. "Expressive Movements, Warmth, and Verbal Reinforcements." *Journal of Abnormal and Social Psychology,* 1962, *64,* 234-236.

Reik, T. *Listening with the Third Ear: The Inner Experience of a Psychoanalyst.* New York: Farrar, Straus & Giroux, 1949.

Reinhard, D. L. "Methodology for Input Evaluation Utilizing Advocate and Design Teams." Unpublished doctoral dissertation, Ohio State University, 1973.

Reinharz, S. *On Becoming a Social Scientist: From Survey Research and Participant Observation to Experiential Analysis.* San Francisco: Jossey-Bass, 1979.

Rich, J. *Interviewing Children and Adolescents.* New York: St. Martin's Press, 1968.

Richardson, S. A., Dohrenwend, B. S., and Klein, D. *Interviewing: Its Forms and Functions.* New York: Basic Books, 1965.

Rippey, R. M. (Ed.). *Studies in Transactional Evaluation.* Berkeley, Calif.: McCutchan, 1973.

Rist, R. C. "Ethnographic Techniques and the Study of an Urban School." *Urban Education,* 1975, *10,* 86-108.

Rist, R. C. "On the Relations Among Educational Research Paradigms: From Disdain to Detente." *Anthropology and Education,* 1977, *8,* 42-49.

Roberts, J. I., and Akinsanya, S. K. *Schooling in the Cultural Context.* New York: McKay, 1976.

Rokkan, S. (Ed.). *Data Archives for the Social Sciences.* The Hague, Netherlands: Mouton, 1966.

Rose, A. M. "A Research Note on Interviewing." *American Journal of Sociology,* 1945, *51,* 143-144.

Rosenfeld, L. B., and Civiky, J. M. *With Words Unspoken: The Nonverbal Experience.* New York: Holt, Rinehart and Winston, 1976.

Rosenshine, B., and Furst, N. "The Use of Direct Observation of Study Teaching." In R. M. W. Travers (Ed.), *Second Handbook of Research on Teaching.* Chicago: Rand McNally, 1973.

Rossi, P. H., and Wright, S. R. "Evaluation Research: an Assessment of Theory, Practice, and Politics." *Evaluation Quarterly,* 1977, *1,* 5-52.

Roth, J. "Needs and the Needs Assessment Process." *Evaluation News,* 1977, *5,* 15-17.

Salasin, S. "Exploring Goal-Free Evaluation: An Interview With Michael Scriven." *Evaluation,* 1974, *2,* 9-16.

Sanders, W. B. *The Sociologist as Detective: An Introduction to Research Methods.* (2nd ed.) New York: Praeger, 1976.

Schatzman, L., and Strauss, A. L. *Field Research: Strategies for a Natural Sociology.* Englewood Cliffs, N.J.: Prentice-Hall, 1973.

Scheflen, A. E. *Body Language and Social Order: Communication as Behavioral Control.* Englewood Cliffs, N.J.: Prentice-Hall, 1972.

Scheflen, A. E. *Human Territories: How We Behave in Space-Time.* Englewood Cliffs, N.J.: Prentice-Hall, 1978.

Schlesinger, J. S. "Nonverbal Communication: Information and Application for Counselors." *Personnel and Guidance Journal,* 1978, *4,* 183-87.

Schwartz, H., and Jacobs, J. *Qualitative Sociology: A Method to the Madness.* New York: Free Press, 1979.

Scott, M. "Some Parameters of Teacher Effectiveness as Assessed by an Ecological Approach." *Journal of Educational Psychology,* 1977, *69*(3), 217-226.

Scott, W. R. "Field Methods on the Study of Organizations." In J. G. March (Ed.), *Handbook of Organizations.* Chicago: Rand McNally, 1966.

Scriven, M. "The Methodology of Evaluation." *AERA Monograph Series in Curriculum Evaluation,* No. 1. Chicago: Rand McNally, 1967.

Scriven, M. "Objectivity and Subjectivity in Educational Research." In L. G. Thomas (Ed.), *Philosophical Redirection of*

Educational Research. Chicago: University of Chicago Press, 1972.

Scriven, M. "Goal-Free Evaluation." In E. R. House (Ed.), *School Evaluation: The Politics and Process.* Berkeley, Calif.: McCutchan, 1973.

Scriven, M. "Maximizing the Power of Causal Investigations: The *Modus Operandi* Method." In W. J. Popham (Ed.), *Evaluation in Education.* Berkeley, Calif.: McCutchan, 1974a.

Scriven, M. "Prose and Cons About Goal-Free Evaluation." *Evaluation Comment,* 1974b, *3,* 1-4.

Scriven, M. "Merit vs. Value." *Evaluation News,* 1978, *8,* 20-29.

Scriven, M., and Roth, J. "Special Feature: Needs Assessment." *Evaluation News,* 1977, *2,* 25-28.

Sechrest, L. "Use of Innocuous and Noninterventional Measures in Evaluation." In B. R. Worthen and J. R. Sanders, *Educational Evaluation: Theory and Practice.* Worthington, Ohio: Jones, 1973.

Sechrest, L. (Ed.). *New Directions for Methodology of Behavioral Science: Unobtrusive Measurement Today,* no. 1. San Francisco: Jossey-Bass, 1979.

Sechrest, L. "Unobtrusive Measures and Naturalistic Evaluation." Paper presented at annual meeting of the American Educational Research Association, Boston, April 1980.

Secretary's Advisory Committee on Automated Personal Data Systems, U.S. Department of Health, Education, and Welfare. *Records, Computers, and the Rights of Citizens.* Cambridge, Mass.: M.I.T. Press, 1973.

Selltiz, C., Wrightsman, L. S., and Cook, S. W. *Research Methods in Social Relations.* New York: Holt, Rinehart and Winston, 1976.

Selltiz, C., and others. *Research Methods in Social Relations.* (Rev. ed.) New York: Holt, Rinehart and Winston, 1959.

Semmel, M. I., and Thiagarajan, S. "Observation Systems and the Special Education Teacher." *Focus on Exceptional Children,* 1973, *5,* 1-12.

Sergiovanni, T. "Reforming Teacher Evaluation: Naturalistic Alternatives." *Educational Leadership,* 1977, *34,* 602-607.

Sevigny, N. J. "Triangulated Inquiry: An Alternative Methodology for the Study of Classroom Life." *Review of Research in Visual Arts Education,* 1978, *8,* 1-16.

Sherwood, H. *The Journalistic Interview.* New York: Harper & Row, 1969.

Shipman, M. D. *The Limitations of Social Research.* London: Longman, 1972.

Shrock, S. A. "The Ecological Perspective in Educational Research: Its Rationale and Implementation." Paper presented at annual meeting of Association for Educational Communications and Technology, Miami, Fla, April 1977.

Sieber, S. D. "The Integration of Fieldwork and Survey Methods." *American Journal of Sociology,* 1973, *78*(6), 1335-1359.

Sieber, S. D., and Lazarsfeld, P. *The Organization of Educational Research in the United States.* New York: Bureau of Applied Social Research, Columbia University, 1966.

Simon, J. L. *Basic Research Methods in Social Science: The Art of Empirical Investigation.* New York: Random House, 1969.

Sjoberg, G. "The Interviewer as a Marginal Man." *The Southwest Social Science Quarterly,* 1957, *38*, 125-132.

Sjoberg, G., and Nett, R. *A Methodology for Social Research.* New York: Harper & Row, 1968.

Slocum, W. L., Empey, L. T., and Swanson, H. S. "Increasing Response to Questionnaires and Structured Interviews." *American Sociological Review,* 1956, *21*, 221-225.

Smith, E., and Tyler, R. W. *Appraising and Recording Student Progress.* New York: Harper & Row, 1942.

Smith, H. W. *Strategies of Social Research: The Methodological Imagination.* Englewood Cliffs, N.J.: Prentice-Hall, 1975.

Smith, L. "An Evolving Logic of Participant Observation, Educational Ethnography, and Other Case Studies." *Review of Research in Education,* 1978, *6*, 316-377.

Smith, L., and Keith, P. *Anatomy of Educational Innovation: An Organizational Analysis of Elementary School.* New York: Wiley, 1971.

Smith, N. L. *Truth, Complementarity, Utility, and Certainty.* Research on Evaluation Project Monograph. Portland, Oreg.: Northwest Regional Educational Laboratory, 1978.

Solzhenitsyn, A. *One Day in the Life of Ivan Denisovich.* New York: Praeger, 1963.

Speizman, W. *The Purposes of Exploratory Fieldwork.* Unpublished document, n.d.

Spradley, J. P. *The Ethnographic Interview.* New York: Holt, Rinehart and Winston, 1979.

Spradley, J. P. *Participant Observation.* New York: Holt, Rinehart and Winston, 1980.

Stacey, M. *Methods of Social Research.* Elmsford, N.Y.: Pergamon Press, 1969.

Stake, R. E. "The Countenance of Educational Evaluation." *Teachers College Record,* 1967, *68,* 523-540.

Stake, R. E. "Objectives, Priorities, and Other Judgment Data." *Review of Educational Research,* 1970, *40,* 181-212.

Stake, R. E. (Ed.). *Evaluating the Arts in Education: A Responsive Approach.* Columbus, Ohio: Merrill, 1975.

Stake, R. E. "Should Educational Evaluation Be More Objective or More Subjective? More Subjective!" Paper presented at annual meeting of American Educational Research Association, Toronto, April 1978a.

Stake, R. E. "The Case-Study Method in Social Inquiry." *Educational Researcher,* 1978b, *7,* 5-8.

Stake, R. E. "Validating Representations: The Evaluator's Responsibility." In R. Perloff (Ed.), *Evaluator Interventions: Pros and Cons.* Beverly Hills, Calif.: Sage, 1979.

Stake, R. E., and Easley, J. A., Jr. (Eds.). *Case Studies in Science Education.* Urbana: Center for Instructional Research and Curriculum Evaluation, University of Illinois, 1978.

Stake, R. E., and Gjerde, C. "An Evaluation of T-CITY, The Twin City Institute for Talented Youth." *AERA Monograph Series in Curriculum Evaluation,* No. 7. Chicago: Rand McNally, 1974.

Starch, D., and Elliott, E. C. "Reliability of Grading Work in Mathematics." *School Review,* 1912, *21,* 254-259.

Steiner, E. *Logical and Conceptual Analytic Techniques for Educational Researchers.* Bloomington: Indiana University Monograph, 1978.

Stone, P. J., and others. *The General Inquirer.* Cambridge, Mass.: M.I.T. Press, 1966.

Stratton, R. G. "Ethical Issues in Evaluating Educational Programs." *Studies in Educational Evaluation,* 1977, *3,* 57-66.

Strauss, A., and Schatzman, L. "Field Methods and Techniques: Cross-Class Interviewing." *Human Organization,* 1955, *14*(2), 28-31.

Stufflebeam, D. L. "An Introduction to the PDK Book, *Educational Evaluation and Decision-Making.*" Paper presented at 11th annual Phi Delta Kappa Symposium on Educational Research, Ohio State University, June 1970.

Stufflebeam, D. L., and others. *Educational Evaluation and Decision-Making.* Itasca, Ill.: Peacock Publishing, 1971.

Stufflebeam, D. L. "Administrative Checklist for Reviewing Evaluation Plans." Kalamazoo: Evaluation Center, Western Michigan University, 1974a.

Stufflebeam, D. L. "Evaluation According to Michael Scriven." In W. J. Popham (Ed.), *Evaluation in Education.* Berkeley, Calif.: McCutchan, 1974b.

Sullivan, H. S. *The Psychiatric Interview.* New York: Norton, 1970.

Terkel, S. *Working.* New York: Avon Books, 1975.

Theory into Practice, 1977, *16* (entire issue).

Thomas, W. I., and Znaniecki, F. *The Polish Peasant in Europe and America.* Chicago: University of Chicago Press, 1918.

Thompson, J. J. *Beyond Words: Nonverbal Communication in the Classroom.* New York: Citation Press, 1973.

Tikunoff, W., Berliner, D. C., and Rist, R. C. *An Ethnographic Study of the Forty Classrooms of the Beginning Teachers Evaluation Study: A Known Sample.* Technical Report No. 75-10-10-5. San Francisco: Far West Laboratory for Educational Research and Development, 1975.

Todd, A. *Finding Facts Fast.* New York: William Morrow, 1972.

Trow, M. "Comment on Participant Observation and Interviewing: A Comparison." *Human Organization,* 1957, *16,* 33-35.

Tubbs, S. L., and Carter, R. M. *Shared Experiences in Human Communication.* Rochelle Park, N.J.: Hayden, 1978.

Turner, R. (Ed.). *Ethnomethodology.* Middlesex, England: Penguin Books, 1974.

Tyler, R. W. *Constructing Achievement Tests.* Columbus: Ohio State University Press, 1934.

Tyler, R. W. *Basic Principles of Curriculum and Instruction.* Chicago: University of Chicago Press, 1950. © 1950 by the University of Chicago.

Tyler, R. W. (Ed.). *Educational Evaluation: New Roles, New Means.* Chicago: University of Chicago Press, 1969.

Tymitz, B., and Wolf, R. L. *An Introduction to Judicial Evaluation and Natural Inquiry.* Washington, D.C.: Nero and Associates, 1977.

Udy, S. H. "Cross-Cultural Analysis: A Case Study." In P. E. Hammond (Ed.), *Sociologists at Work: Essays on the Craft of Social Research.* New York: Basic Books, 1964.

Vidich, A. "Participant Observation and the Collection and Interpretation of Data." *American Journal of Sociology,* 1955, *60,* 356-358.

Vidich, A., and Bensman, J. "The Validity of Field Data." *Human Organization,* 1954, *13*(1), 20-27.

Warwick, D. P. "Survey Research and Participant Observation: A Benefit-Cost Analysis." In D. P. Warwick and S. Osherson (Eds.), *Comparative Research Methods.* Englewood Cliffs, N.J.: Prentice-Hall, 1973.

Warwick, D. P., and Osherson, S. (Eds.). *Comparative Research Methods.* Englewood Cliffs, N.J.: Prentice-Hall, 1973.

Waterman, S. "Comments on Needs Assessment Article in *EN* #2." *Evaluation News,* 1977, *3,* 21-22.

Wax, R. *Doing Fieldwork: Warnings and Advice.* Chicago: University of Chicago Press, 1971.

Webb, E. J. "Physical Traces: Erosion and Accretion." In B. J. Franklin and H. W. Osborne (Eds.), *Research Methods: Issues and Insights.* Belmont: Wadsworth, 1971.

Webb, E. J., and others. *Unobtrusive Measures.* Chicago: Rand McNally, 1966.

Weinberg, R., and Wood, F. H. (Eds.). *Observation of Pupils and Teachers in Mainstream and Special Education Settings: Alternative Strategies.* Minneapolis: Leadership Training Institute, University of Minnesota, 1975.

Weinstein, A. S. "Evaluation Through Medical Records and Related Information Systems." In M. Guttentag and E. Struening (Eds.), *Handbook of Evaluation Research.* Beverly Hills, Calif.: Sage, 1975.

Weisberg, H. F., and Bowen, B. D. *An Introduction to Survey Research and Analysis.* San Francisco: W. H. Freeman, 1977.

Weiss, C. "Where Politics and Evaluation Research Meet." *Evaluation,* 1973, *1,* 37-45.

Weitz, S. (Ed.). *Nonverbal Communication: Readings with Commentary.* Oxford, England: Clarendon Press, 1974.

West, S. G., and Gunn, S. P. "Some Issues of Ethics and Social Psychology." *American Psychologist,* 1978, *31,* 30-38.

Wheeler, S. (Ed.). *On Record: Files and Dossiers in American Life.* New York: Russell Sage Foundation, 1969.

Whyte, W. F. *Street Corner Society.* Chicago: University of Chicago Press, 1943.

Wicke, R. J., and Josephs, E. H. *Techniques in Interviewing for Law Enforcement and Corrections Personnel.* Springfield, Ill.: Thomas, 1972.

Wicker, A. W. "Ecological Psychology: Some Recent and Prospective Developments." *American Psychologist,* 1979, *34,* 755-765.

Willems, E. P., and Raush, H. L. *Naturalistic Viewpoints in Psychological Research.* New York: Holt, Rinehart and Winston, 1969.

Williams, P. N. *Investigative Reporting and Editing.* Englewood Cliffs, N.J.: Prentice-Hall, 1978.

Williamson, J. B., Karp, D. A., and Dalphin, J. R. *The Research Craft: An Introduction to Social Science Methods.* Boston: Little, Brown, 1977.

Willis, G. (Ed.). *Qualitative Evaluation.* Berkeley, Calif.: McCutchan, 1978.

Wilson, S. "Explorations of the Usefulness of Case-Study Evaluations." *Evaluation Quarterly,* 1979, *3,* 446-459.

Wolcott, H. "Criteria for an Ethnographic Approach to Research in Schools." In J. T. Roberts and S. K. Akinsaya (Eds.), *Schooling in the Cultural Context.* New York: McKay, 1976.

Wolf, R. L. "The Application of Select Legal Concepts to Educational Evaluation." Unpublished doctoral dissertation, University of Illinois, 1974.

Wolf, R. L. "An Overview of Conceptual and Methodological Issues in Naturalistic Evaluation." Paper presented at annual meeting of the American Educational Research Association, San Francisco, April 1979a.

Wolf, R. L. *Strategies for Conducting Naturalistic Evaluation in Socio-Educational Settings: The Naturalistic Interview.* Occasional Paper Series. Kalamazoo: Evaluation Center, Western Michigan University, 1979b.

Wolf, R. L. "The Use of Judicial Evaluation Methods in the For- mulation of Educational Policy." *Educational Evaluation and Policy Analysis,* 1979c, *1,* 19-28.

Wolf, R. L., and Tymitz, B. "Ethnography and Reading: Matching Inquiry Mode to Process." *Reading Research Quarterly,* 1976-1977, *12,* 5-11.

Wolf, R. L., and Tymitz, B. "Toward More Natural Inquiry in Education." *CEDR Quarterly,* 1977, *10,* 7-9.

Wolfgang, A. "The Silent Language in the Multicultural Class- room." *Theory Into Practice,* 1977, *16*(3), 145-152.

Worthen, B. R. "Characteristics of Good Evaluation Studies." *Journal of Research and Development in Education,* 1977, *10,* 3-20.

Worthen, B. R., and Sanders, J. R. *Educational Evaluation: The- ory and Practice.* Worthington, Ohio: Charles A. Jones, 1973.

Wundt, W. *The Language of Gestures.* The Hague, The Nether- lands: Mouton, 1973.

Young, P. V. *Interviewing in Social Work.* New York: McGraw- Hill, 1935.

Zelditch, M., Jr. "Some Methodological Problems of Field Studies." In G. J. McCall and J. L. Simmons (Eds.), *Issues in Participant Observation: A Text and Reader.* Reading, Mass.: Addison-Wesley, 1969.

Zigarmi, D., and Zigarmi, P. "The Psychological Stresses of Ethno- graphic Research." Paper presented at annual meeting of Ameri- can Educational Research Association, Toronto, March 1978.

Name Index

411

Subject Index

Adaptability, of evaluator, 131-132
American Educational Research Association, 24, 91, 384
Analytic units, in paradigms, 65, 75
Anonymity: and case studies, 379; and contract negotiation, 277-278
Antecedents: in countenance model, 12; in naturalistic inquiry, 79-80
Applicability: for concerns and issues, 326-327; and rigor, 103-104, 115-120. *See also* Validity
Applying, in context-input-process-product model, 15
Assessment. *See* Needs assessment

Audiences: concerns and issues of, and convergence, 92-97; contract negotiation on, 273-274; for reports, 364-369. *See also* Stakeholding audience
Audit: for concerns and issues, 328; and consistency, 122-123; of interview data, 186. *See also* Consistency

Boundaries: establishing, 88-91; problems of, 86-87
Bridging, as divergence strategy, 98, 99
Budget: in contract specifications, 280-281; and team size, 287-288

417